ENERGY AND INTERNATIONAL WAR
FROM BABYLON TO BAGHDAD AND BEYOND

World Scientific Series on Energy and Resource Economics
(ISSN: 1793-4184)

Published

Vol. 1   Quantitative and Empirical Analysis of Energy Markets
         by Apostolos Serletis

Vol. 2   The Political Economy of World Energy: An Introductory Textbook
         by Ferdinand E Banks

Vol. 3   Bridges Over Water: Understanding Transboundary Water Conflict,
         Negotiation and Cooperation
         by Ariel Dinar, Shlomi Dinar, Stephen McCaffrey & Daene McKinney

Vol. 4   Energy, Resources, and the Long-Term Future
         by John Scales Avery

Vol. 5   Natural Gas Networks Performance after Partial Deregulation:
         Five Quantitative Studies
         by Paul MacAvoy, Vadim Marmer, Nickolay Moshkin & Dmitry Shapiro

Vol. 6   Energy and International War: From Babylon to Baghdad and Beyond
         by Clifford E. Singer

World Scientific Series on Energy and Resource Economics – Vol. 6

ENERGY AND INTERNATIONAL WAR

FROM BABYLON TO BAGHDAD AND BEYOND

Clifford E Singer

University of Illinois at Urbana–Champaign, USA

World Scientific

NEW JERSEY · LONDON · SINGAPORE · BEIJING · SHANGHAI · HONG KONG · TAIPEI · CHENNAI

Published by

World Scientific Publishing Co. Pte. Ltd.

5 Toh Tuck Link, Singapore 596224

USA office: 27 Warren Street, Suite 401-402, Hackensack, NJ 07601

UK office: 57 Shelton Street, Covent Garden, London WC2H 9HE

British Library Cataloguing-in-Publication Data
A catalogue record for this book is available from the British Library.

World Scientific Series on Energy and Resource Economics — Vol. 6
ENERGY AND INTERNATIONAL WAR
From Babylon to Baghdad and Beyond

ISBN-13 978-981-279-158-0
ISBN-10 981-279-158-2

Typeset by Stallion Press
Email: enquiries@stallionpress.com

Printed in Singapore by B & JO Enterprise

Contents

List of Figures   vii

List of Tables   ix

Acknowledgments   xiii

Preface   xv

PART ONE: FROM HAMMURABI TO NAPOLEON   1

  1. Just a Commodity   3

  2. Slaves, Gold, and Silver   15

  3. Sources of Conflict Until the Concert of Europe   29

PART TWO: COAL AND NON-ENERGY MINERALS   47

  4. Steamer Coal in the Colonial Era   49

  5. Franco-Prussian War Sets the Stage   59

  6. Coal and Iron in the Great War   65

  7. Coal in Asia before WWII   77

  8. Coal, Steel, Customs, and the EU   83

  9. Conflict over other Solid Mineral Resources   89

 10. An End to Cross-border Warfare over Solid Minerals?   113

PART THREE: OIL   117

 11. Oil and Commerce   119

12. Oil from WWI to WWII   129

13. Oil and World War II   139

14. Before the Iran–Iraq War   153

15. Iran and Iraq   161

16. Gulf War I   167

17. Sanctions and Inspections   179

18. Iraq after 9/11/01   191

19. Oil and War   219

**PART FOUR: URANIUM, NATURAL GAS,   225
                AND RENEWABLES**

20. France and Uranium   227

21. French Neocolonialism in Africa   241

22. Natural Gas Resources and Transport   249

23. Liquefied Natural Gas and Security Developments   269

24. Hydropower   283

25. Other Renewable Resources   297

26. It's about Oil   309

PART FIVE: THE FUTURE   313

27. Troubled Producers   315

28. Uncoordinated Consumers   327

29. Spoilers   355

30. Transition to Sustainability   371

Bibliography   383

Index   421

List of Figures

3.1.   Recurring instability of peace before fertility transition   35

3.2.   Factors influencing stability of peace after industrialization   39

3.3.   European Union's stable ship of state   39

3.4.   Swedish fertility and mortality rates   41

6.1.   Western front in WWI   71

8.1.   From the 1957 ECSC to the 2004 EU   86

9.1.   Areas awarded to Chile at various times, and area awarded to Peru in 1929   91

9.2.   Western Sahara and its former and current claimants, Mauritania and Morocco   93

11.1.   Mergers directly related to the history of standard oil   126

12.1.   Region included in the Red Line Agreement   135

13.1.   Former Italian claims in Africa   140

13.2.   Stumbling blocks on Germany's drive toward Baku   146

15.1.   Oil fields in Kuwait and near the Iran–Iraq border   165

21.1.   African countries where France intervened militarily from 1960–1964   243

22.1.   Proposed extension of natural gas pipeline from   263
         Turkmenistan through Afghanistan and Pakistan
         to India

29.1.   Israeli security barrier 2002 plan   360

30.1.   Biennially averaged energy use rates (points) and fits   375
         with periodic variations (curves with multiple maxima)
         and background trends (other curves)

30.2.   Extrapolated annual use trend for fluid fossil fuels   376
         (oil and natural gas)

30.3.   Extrapolated nuclear energy use rates for the   379
         United States, other temperate region countries
         except for Japan, and for the entire world. Energy
         use rates plotted are the thermal energy released
         in nuclear power plants before conversion to
         electricity

30.4.   Extrapolated nuclear energy use rates for Japan,   379
         the Republic of Korea (ROK), countries in the
         Association of Southeast Asian Nations (ASEAN),
         and other countries lying wholly between 40°
         north and south latitude (Trop). Energy use rates
         plotted are the thermal energy released in nuclear
         power plants before conversion to electricity

List of Tables

1.1.	Oil price	6
4.1.	Welsh coal uses	55
4.2.	Freight rate from Cardiff	56
6.1.	US pig iron and steel	67
6.2.	Coal and steel production in 1914	72
9.1.	US Government "strategic" mineral stockpiles	96
9.2.	Net US import reliance for selected nonfuel minerals	100
9.3.	Kimberley process participants	103
9.4.	Global platinum group metals production and reserves	109
11.1.	Crude oil production up to 1910	122
12.1.	Casualties in World War I	133
12.2.	Crude oil production from 1910 to 1950	136
13.1.	Percentage of world oil production in 1940	143
14.1.	Saudi Arabian light crude oil prices	159
16.1.	Turn of the century crude oil prices	169
18.1.	Iraq occupation progress metrics	211
18.2.	US troop levels in Iraq	213

18.3.   Casualties and attacks in Iraq from May 2006   214

20.1.   US and French installed nuclear capacity   232

20.2.   Annual reactor-related uranium requirements   234

22.1.   Energy content equivalents   253

22.2.   South American natural gas reserves   265

23.1.   World LNG imports by origin in 1993   271

23.2.   World LNG exports and imports in 2006   272

23.3.   US price of Canadian natural gas   274

23.4.   Annual natural gas consumption by region   275

27.1.   Top 15 exporters' total petroleum production   316
        and exports

27.2.   Next 15 exporters' total petroleum production   318
        and exports

27.3.   Economic indicators for some petroleum exporters   319

27.4.   Economic and political indicators for some   321
        petroleum exporters

27.5.   Instability index   324

28.1.   Petroleum imports   328

28.2.   Petroleum importer percentages   330

28.3.   Membership of OECD, IEA, EU, and NATO   334
        in 2007

28.4.   US biofuels targets in 2007 energy bill   339

28.5.   OECD petroleum stocks   341

28.6.   Various non-OECD petroleum stocks and possible   343
        storage capacity

28.7.   Fuel prices for 2004, in $US2008   345

28.8.   Petroleum product prices and taxes and prices as   346
        of January 7, 2008

28.9.   China's fuel efficiency standards   349

29.1.   Partial list of US aid to Israel   364

30.1.   Anglo-American roles in Middle East conflicts   373

Acknowledgments

Nicholas Pederson did research for the material on France and uranium, and T. S. Gopi Rethinaraj provided data on population, economic output, and energy use. Matthew Rosenstein, Becky Osgood, and Samantha Singer helped with editing and formatting, and Sheila Roberts and Merrily Shaw provided valuable administrative support. Jessica Moyer provided many useful references. Support from the John D. and Catherine T. MacArthur Foundation through International Programs and Studies under the leadership of Earl Kellogg at the University of Illinois at Urbana-Champaign and through the Center for Science, Technology, and Security Policy under the leadership of Norman Neureiter at the American Association for the Advancement of Science were essential for providing the research environment where many of the ideas in this book were developed; but the choice of content of the book is solely the responsibility of the author and not of any institution or other individual. The able support of Ms. Sandhya, Ms. Pauline Chan and Ms. Yvonne Tan Hui Ling at World Scientific Publishing is especially appreciated.

The book is dedicated to my wife Brigitte for her infinite patience with its preparation and to Samantha and Dyson in the hope they may live to see a world without major international wars.

Preface

Wars have been fought over control of resources since the dawn of civilization. Control of valuable minerals and energy has been a focal point of conflicts from before the Conquistadors sacked the Americas through to the present day. The industrial revolution put energy resources on center stage. The questions about energy and security addressed in this book thus remain of central importance to the military strategy and economies of industrialized countries. This book deals with wars in general, but the emphasis is on major international wars of a scale that involve the transport of 50,000 or more troops for the purpose of invading another country. The reason for this emphasis is that maintaining the capability to conduct this scale of operation requires a major national commitment. This level of military preparedness has more profound political impact than domestic border control or occasional contributions to smaller-scale multilateral peace-keeping operations.

The interplay between control of resources and war has evolved dramatically since the Babylonians and others in the Ancient World fought for land and slaves. After a first chapter that takes a quick look at the means and motivation of warfare before the industrial revolution, this book provides a more detailed examination of the role of coal and other solid mineral resources in warfare. It then examines oil, natural gas, uranium, and renewable energy resources to see how their roles in conflict have been evolving over time.

Industrialization did not just transform the economies of nations and the importance of energy resources. It also transformed the kind of wars nations fought. For millennia, clans and city-states and nations had fought for slaves and other spoils of war and for the control of agricultural land and trade. Before the 19th century, men mostly walked and rowed and sailed to wars over these things. By the 20th century, the mineral resources that powered industrial states had become a primary focus of the battles between them. During World War I, an entire generation of fighting age men was committed to a struggle over control of coal and iron resources in Europe. The genesis of the European Union after World War II signaled a determination that nations would never again fight over coal and iron. But this was not the end of the story of energy and security.

For it was oil that was the critical natural resource that shaped the course and outcome of World War II. A confrontation over oil-rich Iran in 1946 also signaled the onset of the cold war. Even after the cold war, who would have control over oil resources was a central bone of contention during the wars with Iraq that started in 1990 and 2003. However, there is a finite amount of oil that is worth getting out of the ground. Thus, it will not endlessly be seen worthwhile to fight over who has control over oil. So when and how will conflicts over oil end? This is the central question addressed in this book.

If there is eventually to be an end to wars over who controls coal and oil, what then about other solid minerals? Gold, silver, nitrates, phosphates, copper, and the newly valuable element tantalum were at times objects of conflict. After these conflicts abated, there remained the problem of conflict over diamonds — but this directly affected only a few impoverished African countries.

During and after World War II, nuclear weapons and nuclear power made uranium suddenly important. After WWII, France championed the Common Market in the hope of ending wars in Western Europe. All the same, France also decided to stop relying on German coalfields for production of electrical energy. France also wanted to make sure it would never again need to rely on tardy western allies to thwart invasion from the east. For these purposes France turned to uranium for electricity and nuclear weapons. Until the 1990s about half of this uranium came from France's sphere of influence in Africa. Then France ratified the Comprehensive

Nuclear Test Ban Treaty and became comfortable with relying on the open international market for uranium. By 2005, only India had concerns about accessing the international market to assure it would have supplies of uranium for an ambitious civilian nuclear program. Then serious discussion began on giving India access to the international uranium market was reached between the Indian prime minister and the US president. Although the ensuing negotiations were convoluted, one way or another India was likely to gain access to the international uranium market as it became an ever larger potential customer.

At the beginning of the 21st century, natural gas was poised to gradually overtake oil as the world's leading energy source. There were occasional political strains over contract terms for international natural gas shipments. However, both the broader geographical distribution of resources and the greater dominance of pipelines for regional transport of natural gas made it less likely to be an object of international war than oil was. Thus, it seemed that if nations could find peaceful means for allocating control over oil, then they might well be able to do the same for natural gas.

The remarkable conclusion drawn here is that major international wars, centered on who has control over energy and other mineral resources, are poised to come to an end. Moreover, a global transition to lower human fertility rates and saturation of population growth are marginalizing war over agricultural land and water and relegating fighting over them primarily to internal conflicts. No longer will the quest for *Lebensraum,* to find a place for burgeoning populations, be used to justify wars between industrial states. With the World Trade Organization expanding its scope and free trade pacts proliferating, the type of wars fought between the European powers over control of trade in the 17th and 18th century and the colonial wars of the 19th and early 20th centuries also appear to be a thing of the past.

Wars are not just fought over economic issues, but every war does have an economic dimension. If energy is really the last great economic resource that nations find it worth fighting over, then what will be the future of major international wars? Will leaders nevertheless succeed in whipping up war fever for political purposes at odds with national economic interests? Or will major international wars follow officially approved slavery into the dustbin of history? The answer lies too far into the future for this book to predict. What will be found here is an examination of new economic circumstances, unique in all of human history, that make this a question that the next generation of citizens and leaders must take seriously.

Part One

FROM HAMMURABI TO NAPOLEON

Chapter 1

Just a Commodity

Oil, is it a strategic commodity? Or is it just one of many useful materials whose prices fluctuate?.[1] Those who view oil as having unique strategic significance also see the oil-rich Middle East as strategically critical.

Both of these views were once well founded. Up to Indian independence in 1947, the Suez Canal was a strategically important connection between Britain and its empire. Indeed, a maritime connection between the Mediterranean and the Red Sea had military significance even before AD 770 when the Caliph who founded Baghdad closed an ancient canal "to prevent supplies from reaching his enemies in Arabia".[2] However, the British and French gave up on direct control of the Suez Canal after the Suez War in 1956. When the canal was closed for eight years after the 1967 Arab–Israeli War, enough transport alternatives were developed that traffic through the canal actually declined in the 1980s.[3]

From the conversion of the British navy to oil starting just before World War I (WWI) to the final defeat of the Axis powers in 1945, oil gained central strategic importance in war between industrialized countries. Britain relied on oil from Persia during WWI. Germany's North Africa campaign in World War II (WWII) was part of a three-pronged thrust aimed at gaining control of oil-producing regions. Japan's fateful attack on Pearl Harbor was aimed at removing a threat to takeover of oil production in Southeast Asia. All of the Axis onslaughts in WWII were fatally crippled by shortages of liquid fuels.

Particularly in the United States, gasoline rationing after the 1973 Yom Kippur War reinforced the idea that oil also has critical economic importance. Thereafter, it was widely believed that $50–100/barrel

3

oil would have unacceptable economic impact.[4] US foreign policy and military planning assumed that covert or overt action might be necessary to influence control over strategically important Mid-east oil.

These conclusions are a textbook example of generational lag. Generational lag is evident when policy decisions are made with a mindset applicable only when current leaders were young. This book repeatedly deals with the connection between generational lag, international war, and energy. Generational lag will be evident in blunders made from the Franco-Prussian War through WWI, WWII, the Suez War, and the subsequent Arab–Israeli and Persian Gulf wars. However, the catastrophic consequences of the two world wars prompted Western Europe to escape from shackles of generational lag after WWII. This escape will also happen for oil in the present century. Nevertheless, the lessons of the past will be only slowly learned, for the reasons to be described.

Oil and the US Military

First, it is important to explain why oil is not in fact a strategic commodity for industrialized countries in this century, either from a military or economic perspective. A 2006 study by the JASON group points out why imported oil is not militarily strategic for the US government, which commissioned the study. As reported in this study, the US Department of Defense (DOD) accounted only for 1.8 percent of United States oil consumption, out of a total 1.9 percent by the government as a whole.[5] Fossil fuels accounted for less than 3 percent of the US national defense budget; and the JASON study pointed out a number of energy efficiency improvements that could keep this percentage at about the same level in the face of higher oil prices and also increase operational flexibility. Two US Gulf of Mexico oil platforms would be sufficient to produce the amount of oil used by DOD, at production costs of under $30/barrel.

The JASON report also addressed the question of whether control of foreign refining capacity was necessary to maintain US military operational flexibility. The primary potential concern is that the US Air Force accounts for the majority of DOD oil consumption, and military jet fuel is a special blend that is not widely available. However, the additives needed for converting widely available commercial fuel to Air Force requirements were said to be produced for about five cents per gallon of jet fuel. This is such a small fraction of the fuel cost and volume that both the expense and logistic problem of delivering military jet fuel are manageable without relying on refining capacities located only in the Middle East.

Economic Impact of Changing Oil Prices

A more substantive question is whether one who has control of Mideast oil production is of enough central economic strategic importance to require decisive intervention in Mid-east conflicts. Table 1.1 provides useful insight.[6,a] This table lists inflation-adjusted international prices, and the price limits on US domestic oil production. The international price patterns after 1973 and 1998 are similar, but the price controls on part of the United States production helped make the domestic market response different. President Nixon, familiar with relatively smooth operation of gasoline rationing during WWII, presided over domestic price controls that aggravated shortages. Price controls were applied starting in 1971 for other reasons, but they continued to apply to about 60–70 percent of US domestic production before being abolished by Ronald Reagan in January of 1981.[7]

Oil price control had already been imbedded in a broader set of wage and price controls that preceded the Arab embargo of oil shipments to the United States following the 1973 Yom Kippur war. Oil price controls had already contributed to heating oil shortages in the beginning of 1973. Then there were particularly inconvenient long queues for motorists buying gasoline, and a response of even–odd day rationing during the oil embargo. By suppressing the US production, price controls continued to put upward pressure on global oil prices, by an estimated 13 percent, after enactment of the 1975 Energy Policy and Conservation Act.[8] These events created a widespread

---

[a] The global oil prices listed in Table 1.1 are for the beginning of each year, which is why the effect of the 1973 Yom Kippur War first shows up in the entry for 1974.

Table 1.1.   Oil price ($US2008/barrel)

Year	Global	U.S.	War
1972	10		
1973	10		Yom Kippur
1974	43	25	
1975	42	25	
1976	43	25	
1977	43	25	
1978	42	25	
1979	40	32	
1980	69		Iran–Iraq
1981	76		
1982	75		
1983	72		
1984	59		
1985	57		
1986	53		
1987	30		
1988	31		
1989	22		
1990	30		Kuwait
1991	37		
1992	24		
1993	24		
1994	18		
1995	23		
1996	24		
1997	30		
1998	20		
1999	13		
2000	30		
2001	24		
2002	21		
2003	31		Iraq
2004	29		
2005	36		
2006	58		
2007	57		
2008	91		

Source: USEIA (2003a, 2006, 2008); USBLS (2008); Williams (2007).

impression that reductions in available oil imports caused serious disruption of everyday economic activity. This disruption was aggravated by price controls that interfered with the more recently experienced kind of market response to price spikes. This lesson has been learned the United States, and the price control response has not repeated in there.

Some think that international oil price spikes cause global recessions. This has not been true recently. When measured in terms of what currencies actually buy locally, this was also not true during the 1973–1986 period of high global oil prices. The local "purchasing power parity" of all of the world's gross domestic products (GDPs) together increased during every year from 1973 to 1986, growing at an average annual rate of 2.9 percent. Global per capita GDP also increased during this time, at an average annual rate of 1.5 percent.[9]

The "petrodollars" paid to oil producers do not simply disappear from the global economy. To be of any use to oil exporters, their revenues must either be invested for the future or spent on imports. By near the end of 2007, for example, oil-rich nations had foreign investments totaling four trillion dollars. Of this the majority was invested in the United States and much of the rest in Europe, totaling something under three trillion dollars in these places overall.[10]

While the world as a whole avoided declining years of purchasing power from 1973 to 1986, oil price shocks of 1973 and 1979 were followed by 2–3 year periods of combined US recession and inflation. Based on quantitative modeling, economists Robert Barsky and Lutz Killian attributed these periods of "stagflation" primarily to preceding money supply over-expansions.[11] William Poole, president of the Federal Reserve Bank of St. Louis, recently reviewed the question of links between oil prices and inflation.

> The 1973 and 1979 episodes did not feature inflationary spirals triggered by the oil shocks. Instead, they are characterized by preexisting, general inflationary pressures that an alternative monetary policy could have avoided. The first oil shock in 1973 occurred against a background of clear economic overheating in the United States.

U.S. monetary policy was very expansionary in 1971 and 1972, leading to excessive growth of aggregate demand that, even in the presence of price controls, spilled over into rising inflation in 1973. By
October 1973 — that is, the month of the first oil shock, but largely
before its impact could be felt in the CPI — inflation had reached
8.1 percent on a 12-month basis, a sharp rise from the 3.2 percent
rate over the 12 months ending in October 1972. Annual CPI inflation subsequently rose to 11.8 percent in October 1974 and peaked
at 12.2 percent in November 1974.[12]

By early 2008, the US economy used half as much energy for each
trillion dollars of inflation-adjusted GDP as in 1973, while the proportions of energy supplied by oil were about the same. If Barsky,
Killian, and Poole were right about the situations in 1973 and 1979,
then there was even less reason to suspect high oil prices as the primary cause of any significant disruption of the US economy in 2008
and the following few years. It is true that oil prices exceeding
$100/barrel apparently had psychological effect on stock market
prices more generally.[13] However, while there were real concerns in
the United States in 2008 about a recession, the primary cause for
concern appeared to be fallout from a reduction in liquidity in connection with foreclosures of mortgages made to customers without
prime credit ratings.

Another lesson, from Table 1.1, is that decisive US interventions
in Middle East conflicts from 1973 on have been *counterproductive*
from the point of view of the impact on international oil prices. The
US intervention in 1973 was to airlift military equipment that helped
Israel gain the edge in the Yom Kippur War needed to retain control
of all of the territory it had occupied in 1967. During the 1980–1986
period of elevated oil prices of the Iran–Iraq war, the United States
provided Iraq intelligence support[14] and military protection for oil
shipments needed to finance staving off a determined counterattack
by Iran. In 1990, there was a brief oil price spike as Kuwaiti oil production was disrupted during the US-led counterattack on Iraq. In
2003, a previous policy of "smart sanctions" that could have
expanded Iraqi oil production was overturned in favor of an invasion

and occupation of Iraq. By 2008 that country's oil production had still not returned to 2002 levels, much less than those achieved before the 1990 war. This book will review the complex of motivations for each of these interventions and their likely future consequences. For now it suffices to simply repeat the observation, made by well-known economist Milton Friedman at the time of the preparations for the 1990 war against Iraq, that reducing oil prices is not in itself a very sensible reason for such interventions.[15]

Energy and War

Oil is a finite resource. So it is *inevitable* that it will become of ever decreasing economic importance. At some point along the way, it will sink in that oil is just another industrially useful commodity, not such a strategic commodity that it is worth shedding blood over who controls it. A central theme of this book is gaining insight into when and how this transition will occur.

During the first half of the 20th century, coal and iron were considered strategic commodities. In WWI, millions died trying to shift trench lines dug along fronts designed to protect access to sources of coal and iron. After WWI, trade policies aimed at protecting what were viewed as strategic heavy industries contributed to global economic depression and set the stage for WWII. In the run-up to WWII, one of the motivations for Japanese expansionism was control of these resources in northern China. Signaled by the formation of the European Coal and Steel Community in 1952, disputes over these commodities came to be dealt with through trade negotiations rather than warfare. There will be similarities and differences in how oil makes this transition. The next part of this book examines the history of coal, iron, and war to get some insight into these similarities and differences.

In the shift away from oil as the world's dominant industrial energy source, natural gas and uranium will play significant roles. This raises the question of whether new conflicts will break out over control of these resources. Natural gas is more conveniently shipped by pipeline between nearby countries than over the high seas in tankers.

Natural gas resources are also more broadly geographically distributed than for oil. So far, these differences have made disputes over access to natural gas resources easier to settle through trade negotiations than for oil. Uranium that can be extracted at costs that have little effect on the price of nuclear energy is even more broadly geographically distributed. Nevertheless, France's effort to retain preferential access to uranium resources in Africa in the 20th century left an enduring legacy. The role of uranium in France's interventions in Africa will thus be examined here as well.

The primary focus of this book is on energy and *international* war. There are two reasons for this. One is simply to make the scope of the work more manageable. The other is that countries and alliances that have the industrial capacity to launch foreign military interventions, notably NATO, also have the greatest potential for fielding the alternative energy production and efficiency measures that will be adopted during the shift away from oil as a dominant industrial energy source. Well after they make this shift, control of revenues from residual production in oil exporting countries may continue as a stimulus for violent internal conflict. The scope of such internal conflicts is a very complex topic. It will be avoided here except insofar as the effects of internal conflicts spill over into neighboring countries. Such is the case, for example, for the connections between conflicts involving Southern Sudan, Darfur, and Chad.

Resource Wars

Other mineral resources have also long been the focus of domestic and international conflict. This has led to the view that conflicts over energy resources are only part of a series of seemingly endless violent conflicts over control of limited natural resources. These have included metals, virgin timber, nitrates, and phosphates. In each case, international conflicts over control of these resources have come and gone. The reasons for this are examined in this book for each of these other resources.

There have also been conflicts connected to diamonds and water. Diamonds are of continuing concern both because they put so much value in easily transported small packages. In some places they can be mined without the economic stability needed to open up the vastly expensive mining operations needed to be economically competitive for resources like copper. The Kimberley process aimed at reducing the motivation for the so-called blood diamond conflicts is a particularly interesting international initiative and is reviewed in this book. Thomas Homer–Dixon[16] and others have examined the relationship between water and that conflict in detail. A survey of the literature suggests that international conflicts over water resources are more likely to be resolved by negotiation than warfare, for the reasons described below.

The Broader Context

The main jumping-off point on energy and international war in this book is the Franco-Prussian War of 1870–1871. During that war, the German high command received information on a geological survey of the mineral resources in occupied France. In deciding what portions of France to annex after the war, the boundary was carefully drawn to include the surface outcroppings of high-grade iron resources in Lorraine. Since access to high-grade iron ores reduces the amount of energy needed to process them into steel, this in effect amounted to a seizure of a valuable energy resource. This was the beginning of the end of the dearly bought Concert of Europe that had largely kept the peace between the major European powers since the disaster of the Napoleonic Wars.

Despite the important roles of energy-relevant resources in the settlement of the Franco-Prussian War and the conduct of the world wars that followed, control over energy resources was in no case the immediate precipitant of these wars. Instead, France and then Germany blundered into initiating catastrophic wars due to concerns over other matters. France initiated the Franco-Prussian war following a dispute over its historical concern about influencing which monarch was placed on the throne of neighboring countries, something that would soon become irrelevant. The Austrian and German emperors blundered into starting WWI with overlapping views of the importance of imperial prestige that led the Austrian emperor to over-react to events of marginal importance in the Balkans. The ironic result was the elimination of monarchy in both empires. Germany and Japan launched WWII under the mistaken impression that their populations needed more living space. What had not sunk in was that by the late 1930s falling birth rates and industrial transformation had already made this irrelevant. In each case historical context and generational lag set the stage for what was to follow.

Each war that is fought has its historical roots in wars that preceded it, back to the dawn of civilization. Each country that has managed to escape from what seemed an endless cycle of wars has done so by emerging from past conflicts with a determination not to repeat previous mistakes. This history is too complicated for a thorough review here, but a brief survey will bring out some important themes.

Going back to antiquity, the role of slavery connects in interesting ways to the more recent history of war and natural resources. As slavery gave way to other methods of tying agricultural workers to specific plots of land, territorial conquest held out the promise of a more durable source of income than the plunder campaigns that scourged the Eastern Hemisphere before the Middle Ages. The industrial revolution precipitated campaigns to end both slavery and serfdom, setting the stage for the conflicts of primary interest here.

Another important theme is the interplay between war and trade. The quest for control of trade in gold and slaves from Western Africa played an important role in warfare even before the age of global Western exploration dawned in the 15th century. With the age of discovery and the consequent decimation of the indigenous population of the New World, precious metals and slaves became important parts of a broader struggle over control of access to markets. This struggle spawned many wars. The drama played out during the mercantilist, colonial, and revolutionary periods of the 18th, 19th, and 20th centuries.

The new millennium presents the world with a situation unprecedented in human history. For the first time, the earth's population is more than half way to a projected stable level. Global food production potential is likely to remain large enough to feed everyone through domestic production and international trade, without hordes of warriors and migrants being driven to campaigns of conquest for lack of any other alternative.

A global system has been developed for negotiating trade disputes without resort to violence. Energy resources remain unusual in lying outside the scope of this system, however, which keeps the study of energy and war particularly interesting.

This broader context provides the background for an important question posed toward the end of this book. When oil comes to be seen as just a commodity, not a strategic commodity, will its place as a strategic commodity be taken by other resources? If not, how will industrialized countries not directly involved in substantial territorial disputes react to such an unprecedented situation? Will domestic politics in larger industrial countries allow the kind of less militarized posture that has evolved in lower population countries like Sweden and Canada? In short, what will be the future of international war overall? Answering these questions is beyond the scope of this book. What this book will establish is that these are becoming interesting questions to ask.

Endnotes

[1] Learsy (2005).
[2] Classic Encyclopedia (2008).
[3] Columbia Encyclopedia (2004).
[4] Mouawad (2005); Grynbaum (2007).
[5] Dimotakis *et al.* (2006).
[6] USEIA (2003a, 2006a,b,c, 2008a,b,c); USBLS (2008); Williams (2007).
[7] Taylor and Van Doren (2006).
[8] Smith (1981).
[9] Maddison (2001).
[10] Weisman (2007).
[11] Barsky and Killian (2001).
[12] Poole (2007).
[13] Krauss (2008).
[14] Tyler (2002).
[15] Conry (1994).
[16] Homer–Dixon (1999).

Chapter 2

Slaves, Gold, and Silver

Slavery provides an interesting background for the study of energy and war for three reasons. First, human beings are the most energy efficient natural converters of calories to mechanical energy useful to other humans. Slaves were thus an important component of the energy economy of societies that relied heavily upon them for labor. Second, like warfare, slavery was once widely believed to be an institution endemic to the human condition. The torturous path by which such a deeply held belief evolved from conventional wisdom to heresy provides an object lesson. This example may give us some insight into how international war might to come to be seen as just as dysfunctional in the current century as widespread slavery did in the 19th century. Third, the British campaign against slavery after the Napoleonic wars provided the initial impetus for the use of steamer coal on warships. More fundamentally, Britain's harnessing of coal to the steam engine provided it an economic advantage in a mercantilist global system over competitors whose empires had been more dependent on slave labor. This provided a viable economic environment for the abolition movement to achieve its long-thwarted goal of suppressing the slave trade.

It was the search for easily exploitable riches that brought conquistadors to the mainland of the Western Hemisphere. This meant gold and silver. Gold had long played an important role in the history of war. Gold bullion and coinage played an essential role in the economy of the ancient world in the West, particularly for paying soldiers.[1] The capital of the Byzantine empire repeatedly fended off military threats with payments in precious metals, until its treasuries were emptied of gold and silver by sacking crusaders in 1204.

15

The Moroccon thrust southward in West Africa was aimed at controlling trade routes through which gold from West Africa traveled.[2] Gold continued to play a significant role in warfare through to the Great Boer War of 1899–1902.[3] However, it was the quest for precious metals in the New World that was to precipitate the most profound transformation of a continent's human population in recorded history. Primarily but by no means exclusively as a result of the introduction of new diseases, the Pre-columbian population of the New World probably decreased by well over half as a result of contact with Europeans.[4]

Slaves, Serfs, and Peasants

Control of slaves, serfs, and peasants provided most of the energy needed to service the predominant economic activity up to the industrial revolution, namely agricultural production. Many traditional laws on slavery were written down in the Babylonian code of Hammurabi around 2250 B.C.[5,a] These laws attest to how ancient an institution forced human labor is. It was not until after 1815 that Britain intimidated and cajoled Europe into abandoning the slave trade. Well into the 19th century, control of human labor acquired through war helped supply the muscle power needed for agricultural production. Serfdom, Chinese autocracy, the South Asian caste system, the New World haciendas, and empressing sailors and drafting soldiers eventually proved to be a more efficient system than slavery for harnessing human labor and the armies needed to conquer and defend control of it.

While the human being is the most energy-efficient natural organic producer of useful labor, draft animals require a great deal of land to feed and can be viewed as something of a luxury. D. Gale Johnson notes this about US agriculture: "In the 1920s, the output of one out of four cropland acres was required to feed draft animals…".[6] In previously depopulated North America, large amounts of available land per farmer allowed this luxury on a wide scale, and in some cases turning tough prairie sods may have even required it.

---

[a] Here B.C. means before the common era.

In more saturated population conditions common in much of the Old World, the energy put into agricultural production was dominated by human stoop labor. This labor was sometimes supplemented with animals where a powerful energy source had to be applied to a special task.

Nor were wind or fossil fuels much used as a source of energy even for inland transport in the early stages of the industrial revolution (nominally from 1750 through the end of the Napoleonic Wars). Eckel[7] said this about transport and communication:

> The world of 1750 was more limited in this regard than we are apt to realize, and it would be difficult for an exploring expedition today to find a place as badly off for transportation as were France and England then. Despite popular romances as to the duration of old Roman roads, they did not as a matter of fact exist in seventeenth or eighteenth century Europe. There were sailing vessels on the seas and along the coasts; there were practically no canals or good roads; the inland transport was effected by pack animals or carts; and the horses used were of a grade which could not be sold for beef to-day.
>
> What this meant in the way of transporting food or other commodities is hard to comprehend. We may assume, I think, that in Europe of 1750 the average cost of transporting a ton of anything to market, roads and cattle considered, must have been well over fifty cents a mile in our present currency... If I am right in my cost estimates, it is clear that a manufacturer ten miles away from his main market in 1750 would have been as badly located as if he were five hundred to a thousand miles away from it today. Under such conditions there was obviously no inducement for a great industry to build up around a supply of raw materials, unless that supply happened to lie very near a good market. There was in fact no inducement to build up great units anywhere. The natural course for industry to follow then was to have a large number of small units, each located near a good market. The only exceptions to this rule would come from groupings around a water power, in rare instances where power would be cheap enough to compensate for long distance to market; or the more important concentrations along the

lower reaches of a navigable river, where the question of transportation to market became simpler. Other than these — very small groups of workers, or better yet, household manufacture.

Although the time for the beginning of the industrial revolution is often set at about 1750, Eckel notes that changes in the transportation and the energy used to power it up to 1815 came slowly.

> The first improvements in transportation came, indeed, before the new industrialism had found its new source of power; and they took the lines of real roads and canals, both in England and in France. During the decades from 1750 to 1780 there were fast improvements made in both directions and in both countries...
>
> After the steam engine had once been put into practical shape by Watt, attempts to utilize it for water transport were almost immediate. Even before any mill was run by steam the problem of steamboat operation was well on its way to solution, as is shown by the earlier American and English projects around 1785. But it took thirty years to produce a commercial success in this line, and Fulton's *Clermont* was the first vessel to make a real voyage under steam...

In much of Asia even draft animals were often too expensive to be used for transport of materials. So transport was largely on the backs of men, women, and children into the 19th century and beyond. Two important exceptions to the dominance of human labor for transportation had profound military consequences in the millennium just past. One of these was nomadic life on the central Asian steppes, where domesticated animals rather than grain cultivation sometimes dominated the agricultural economy. Skill on horseback that developed there formed part of the basis of the 13th century Mongol conquests as far west as Austria and south to Burma.[8] These conquests helped open up parts of the world to devastating epidemics, including Europe's infamous Black Death plagues.

The other exception was the application of wind power to transoceanic voyages by ships carrying heavily armored troops and cannon by the 15th and 16th centuries. These ships signaled the end of the era of slave galleys when six European sail-driven galeases helped decisively defeat Turkish galleys at the battle of Lepanto in 1571.[9] The harnessing of sail power for trans-oceanic voyages also enabled the devastation of the indigenous populations of the new world. According to Maddison:

> The pattern of mortality, migration, and population growth in the Americas and Australia was changed drastically by the encounter with Western Europe. The relatively densely populated agrarian civilizations of Mexico and Peru were quickly destroyed by the sixteenth century Spanish conquest mainly because of the inadvertent introduction of European diseases (smallpox, measles, influenza, and typhus). Shortly thereafter the traffic in slaves introduced yellow fever and malaria. The consequences were devastating for the indigenous population. At least threequarters of them perished... In Latin America as a whole, mortality was about twice as big proportionately as Europe's loss from the Black Death.[10]

Organization of Human Energy

Slavery has only occasionally been the dominant source of human labor. Adult male slaves were probably too difficult and dangerous to keep usefully enslaved in large numbers in hunter-gatherer encampments and early small agricultural settlements. When Mesopotamian and Egyptian kingdoms extended their control over food sources in wide enough areas to prevent escaped slaves from becoming self-sufficient, it became possible for larger slave populations to be controlled. By the time the Babylonians had captured Jerusalem in 697 B.C. and sent an estimated 3000 Hebrews into slavery in Mesopotamia this system was well established.[11]

Not all slaves were acquired through combat. Amongst the Hebrews, for example, men would sell their children or even themselves into slavery as a result of debt or just to avoid starvation.[12] In ancient Greece, slavery became in effect part of a caste system. There, some slaves had minimal rights and could even acquire property and occasionally buy their freedom. Originally, the household slaves who acquired these rights were a luxury in ancient Greece, but with economic development came a greater demand for the organization of labor than individual households with the occasional slave could provide.

The trend toward an increasing fraction of slave labor in ancient Europe reached its apex in the imperial Roman period. In particular, the Italian peninsula in classical times used captured slaves on a large scale for agricultural labor. This led to a vicious and ultimately unsustainable cycle of conquest to provide labor for slave-dependent landholders. Slaves themselves had no interest in defending the empire, and in the case of the 135–71 B.C. Servile Wars they provided antiquity's largest scale and temporarily successful slave revolts.[13]

The harvesting of slaves through conquest was not a significant source of primary energy. The reason for this is that half-of-sustenance calorie intake allows even the previously best-fed of people to work for only about a hundredth of the time it takes to breed them, not to mention the calories used up during their transport. It is true that slaves taken to the New World were often worked to death over several years. But this represented a brutal depreciation of the human body viewed as an energy conversion machine, not the harvesting of people as an energy source.

Imported slavery was very widespread and persistent in the New World. Surviving indigenous population in places like Spanish North America initially had the alternative of disappearing into the background population rather than being bound to unpaid labor. African slaves completely removed from their native environment had no such option.

When organized social systems covered a wide enough area, it became workable to tie more cooperative agricultural labor to the land rather than pay for overhead of supervising reluctant slave labor. Examples are serfdom, the South Asian caste system, and the Chinese Confucian social system — all methods of tying peasant labor to the land at subsistence levels with no hope of advancement. Early on having a slave population of perhaps 5 percent, China did not need to evolve into a slave society.[14] With emphasis on the education of a large complement of literate scribes who could run an efficient system of peasant taxation, China did not need massive reliance on slavery. Likewise, the caste system in India helped provide the economically functional equivalent of serfdom.

One often thinks of serfdom in Europe as a medieval phenomenon except in Russia. However, as Eckel points out:

> The first half of the eighteenth century, with wars and bad harvests, had shown in every direction of trade and industry a falling off from the better conditions that had marked an earlier period, and these conditions naturally reacted most painfully upon the agricultural laborer and on the workman in the few mines and mills then operated. It may be recalled, for example, that even in Scotland the coal miners were serfs, attached to the mine and transferable with it, until around the time of the American Revolution.[15]

Similarly, inescapable indebtedness to the company store or the hacienda in the New World persisted into the 20th century. Indebtedness in the Latin American hacienda system was even inherited from one generation to the next. Inherited indebtedness persisted in Nepal even near the end of the 20th century, when Maoist insurgents sought popular approval by overturning this system in areas under their influence.

Precious Metals and the Money Supply

Tying the money supply to the vagaries of metal deposit discoveries in distant locations was repeatedly associated with economic disruptions until the final abandonment of the gold standard by the United States during the Great Depression. In light of this history, it is easy to overlook how important precious metals sometimes were in allowing the existence of any kind of reasonably stable currency in earlier turbulent times. Nor did the abandonment of the gold standard by any means completely solve the problem of monetary stability. The collapse of unsustainable currency exchange rates sometimes had global consequences, notably during the so-called Asian flu economic disruption precipitated by the collapse of the Thai currency in 1997.

Even in countries with floating currencies, problems that complicate understanding of the economic role of oil have recurred. Inadequate regulation of savings and loan activities in the United States in the 1980s was one example, mirrored again by the impact of lax standards for US mortgage loans that led to a global credit crunch in 2007. The conquistador period is interesting both because of its historical connection to these modern-day problems and it affected mind-sets concerning the connection between natural resources and war for generations to follow.

Silver, Trade, and War

In the Western and Eastern Roman Empires, silver was not widely used as a base for coinage. Gold was in too short supply for use in everyday transactions, leaving these to barter or a mishmash of copper-based coinages.[16] During the Middle Ages, silver increasingly became a medium of financial exchange in the West, but silver supplies were limited. The development of a globally useful currency awaited the opening of new silver mines in Peru and in New Spain (Mexico). From 1540 to 1640, "Spanish America produced more silver, on a more regular basis and for a longer time, than any other region of the world".[17] Moreover, standards were developed and widely applied to counter the tendency to devalue financially useful silver by mixing it with undue amounts of baser metals. Paper money useful only within China and other monetary instruments of more limited use could now be exchanged on a global basis for a standard of reliable value, both by high volume traders and ordinary merchants. The greater quantity and regularity of this new source of silver allowed for a steady and predictable growth of the money supply and a corresponding expansion of global trade.

Not surprisingly, this important new natural resource played a significant role in the nature of war, as it so strongly influenced the European, New World, and global economies. At the center of this storm was Spain, ruled by Hapsburg monarchs from 1516–1700. The Spanish incursion into the New World mainland started with the world's last major military campaign where plunder was the primary objective. Leveraging disaffection with the brutal rule of indigenous American empires, small Spanish forces managed to collapse the Inca and Atzec empires and run off with large amounts of their accumulated treasures. Plunder campaigns disrupt the production of wealth, however, so the Spanish turned to direct control of mining operations in the Americas. The island of Hispaniola had produced the first modest amounts of gold that had whetted the Spanish appetite for New World conquest, but the real early source of wealth from the Americas lay in its silver deposits.

The influx of silver from the Americas had a very different effect on Spain and maritime nations to its north. Being the direct recipient of the bulk of the silver shipments, Spain was able to tap them to support consumption without developing a more durable foundation for its own economy. England and the Low Countries provided much of the goods that Spain imported, the production of which stimulated their early industrial development. Coming somewhat later to the game in the 16th century, France under Louis XV joined into the mercantilist enterprise. Spain's rivals were successful in protecting their own domestic markets and trading positions while forcing less economically developed Spain into trading concessions that Spain's powerful merchant importers found favorable to their own interests.[18]

By virtue of careful attention to marriage arrangements, the Hapsburg monarchs presided over a tangled web of domains that were much more geographically dispersed than the more compact kingdoms of France and England. Nowhere was this more problematic for them in the 17th century than with their prolonged and ill-fated attempt to hold onto provinces in the Low Countries during the 1568–1648 Eighty Year's War. Payments for soldiers and their supplies were dependent upon and only possible for such a long time because of the continuing influx of silver to Spain from the New World. This unproductive use of a boon from a new natural resource has been compared to the "curse of oil," a term coined to describe the tendency toward corruptions and despotism that often accompanied new oil wealth after the 1973 price rises.[19]

Dutch Wind and Water

The temptation that led to Spain's long and debilitating attempt to hold on to its Dutch provinces is understandable, given the vibrancy of the Dutch economy at the time. More than in anywhere else in Western Europe before what is normally thought of as the industrial revolution, the Netherlands forged an economy with an important use of energy resources other than human labor. This put it in the forefront of European economic development.

Maddison (2001) describes the remarkable nature of the Dutch economy in this era and its implications into the 19th century.[20] "From 1400 to 1700, Dutch per capita income growth was the fastest in Europe, and from 1600 to the 1820s its level was the highest." An important part of the role of non-human energy sources in the Dutch economy was by sails for ships. "Hanseatic trade from the Baltic had relied to a large extent on the short land route from Lübeck to Hamburg. The Dutch pioneered the sea route through the Danish sound, which though longer, was cheaper. In 1437–1441 the Hanseatic League engaged in hostilities to try to drive Dutch ships from the Baltic, but, with support from Danzig, the Dutch kept the right to trade." Passing through the narrow sound between Denmark's largest island and Sweden only required navigating coastal waters. Fishing drew the Dutch into the open ocean. "Dutch shipyards developed a new type of factory ship (a herring 'buss'), with nets, rigging and processing facilities which permitted crews of 18 to 30 men to gut, clean, salt, and barrel the herring while at sea. Vessels of this type could make three trips a year of five to eight weeks during the open season from June to December. By the 1560s there were 400 Dutch vessels of this type operating from the province of Holland, with ownership concentrated on urban investors. At this time, the Dutch were exporting herring to the Baltic rather than importing (see de Vries and van der Woude).[21,b]

---

[b] In the 19th century, limitations on global supplies of lamp oil from whales would eventually help launch the petroleum industry, but this was as yet a long way off.

In the 17th century, Dutch ships embarked on whale fishing off Spitzbergen in the Artic."

Wind was also used on land in the Netherlands, with the classic four-panel windmill becoming a symbol through to the 20th century for Holland. "Windmills were used as a source of power for pumps which controlled water flow in canals. As de Vries[22] noted: 'Much of fourteenth century Holland was, in effect, a new country. Only in east-Elbian Germany can one find reclamation being carried out in so systematic a manner and over such large tracts.'" The importance of Dutch wind power on land persisted into the 17th century and beyond. Referring to a work published in 1690, Maddison notes: "The Dutch economy was highly specialized, importing a large part of its food, hiring mercenaries to fight in its wars, and concentrating its labor force in high productivity sectors. Its flat terrain permitted substantial use of wind power. High density urban settlement, good ports and internal waterways reduced transport and infrastructure costs, cheapened government services, and reduced the need for inventories."

Surface layers of organic fuels were also exploited by the Dutch on a substantial scale. "In the large areas of the Northern Netherlands there were layers of peat several metres deep which were a potential source of cheap energy for many purposes. After 1600, about 275,000 hectares of these peat-bogs were stripped. Engineering skills in land reclamation, drainage, and pumping were easily transferable to peat extraction. In the Groningen area, urban investors set up companies to exploit this resource on a large scale on confiscated monastic lands."

With this level of prosperity and a high value of labor in a period where population growth had not caught up with economic growth, the Dutch were prompted to use draft animals for transport. "Transport of peat, hay, wheat, cattle, timber, building materials and other heavy freight became a good deal cheaper in the middle of the 17th century, because of the creation of a network of canals equipped with tow-paths. Drawn by horses, canal barges carried freight, mail and passengers on regular schedules, at seven kilometers an hour, day and night, at frequent intervals between all areas of the country."

Given the dependency of monarchies of the time on control of land and trade for income, Spain's persistence in trying to hold on to the Netherlands during the Eighty Years' War is not surprising. Dutch harnessing of energy resources played an important role in making the Netherlands so valuable. The Dutch energy economy was based primarily on wind and water flows as renewable resources. Still, it is notable that the depletion of peat much faster than nature makes it is an early example of coveted economic growth based on a non-renewable resource in the context of international conflict. (The involvement of England and France made the Eighty Years' War an international conflict, not just an internal secession struggle against Spain.) Particularly interesting here is use of confiscated monastic lands for peat extraction for urban investors, at least some of whom where presumably Protestant. This is an early example of a conflict with religious overtones affecting the transfer of an economically significant non-renewable energy resource.

The Anglophone history of the industrial revolution dates and locates itself beginning in the middle of the 17th century in England. Our modern vision of the industrial revolution is of teaming valleys of factories with coal-driven steam engines powering textile mills and large-scale steel foundries. In fact, per capita iron production in Britain was only three to five pounds (about 2 kg) in 1800, compared to about 500 pounds (230 kg) in 1870.[23] During the Napoleonic Wars, ships were powered by sail, soldiers walked or road horses to war, and the grain they ate was sometimes still ground in water-powered mills. Iron was used for very limited purposes such as nails, horseshoes, and cannon. The remarkable advancements in textile and other industries that were made in the 18th century owed much to the Dutch precedent and very little as yet to the digging of coal as an energy source on a large scale.

However, due to the growth of English and French naval power and the mercantilist policies of the era, Dutch access to global markets became impeded. According to Maddison: "From 1651 onwards Dutch shipping and Dutch exports had restricted access to the ports of the United Kingdom and were barred from trade with English and French colonies. When these countries waged war with the Netherlands they did so with the concentrated energy of modern nation states — very different from the way Spain dissipated its energy." Largely because Dutch independence provided a useful buffer for Britain against continental powers, the Netherlands mostly retained its sovereignty up to the present day. However, by the 19th century the Dutch had irreversibly lost their chance for the kind of global dominance that would allow them to write the standard history of the industrial revolution. As Maddison writes of the Dutch:

> There was a decline in production of exports of textiles (particularly the Leiden woolen industry), fisheries and shipbuilding. The volume of foreign trade dropped 20 percent from 1720 to 1820. During this period UK exports rose more than sevenfold in volume, and French by more than two and threequarters.[24]

As it turned out, Britain would play a much larger role than the Netherlands in the utilization of a new energy resource on a rapidly increasing scale in the 19th century: coal.

Endnotes

[1] Spufford (1989).
[2] Davidson, 1998).
[3] Kohn (1999, p. 60).
[4] Maddison (2001, p. 37); Diamond (1997).
[5] Harper (1904).
[6] Johnson (2002).
[7] Eckel (1920, p. 206).
[8] Kohn (199, pp. 307–310).
[9] Parker (1995, p. 122).
[10] Maddison (2001, p. 37).
[11] Meltzer (1971, p. 22); de Vries and van der Woude (1997, pp. 242–254).
[12] Meltzer (1971, p. 31).
[13] Kohn (1999, p. 438).
[14] Carey-Webb (2002).
[15] Eckel (1920, p. 245).

[16] Spufford (1989).
[17] Marichal (2006, p. 27).
[18] Stein and Stein (2000).
[19] Pipes (1982).
[20] see Maddison (2001, pp. 75–88) for the following seven quotes.
[21] de Vries and van der Woude (1997).
[22] de Vries (1974, p. 27).
[23] Eckel (1920, Chapter 2).
[24] Maddison (2001, p. 82).

Chapter 3

Sources of Conflict Until the Concert of Europe

Before proceeding directly to energy and war during the industrial era, it is worth taking a look at the nature and causes of wars that led up to this period. This brief survey will start with the end of the Thirty Years War in 1648 and end with the Napoleonic Wars in 1815.

Wars over Territory and Trade in Europe and Asia

The middle of the 17th century saw the Manchu conquest of China through 1650, the Mogul victory over Persia in 1650, and the resolution of Reformation conflicts with the Peace of Westphalia in 1648. The Peace of Westphalia concluded the 1618–1648 Thirty Years' War and left the Holy Roman Empire only with titular control of German principalities. Sweden gained territory on the Baltic. "France received Alsace and most of Lorraine and a border at the Rhine; Switzerland and the United Provinces (northern states of the Netherlands) gained their independence; and the Holy Roman Empire granted equality to Catholic and Protestant States".[1] Westphalia largely settled the question of European states' rights to determine their own religious practices, but it by no means put an end to wars between European nations.

From Westphalia until the French revolution in 1789, one primary source of income for continental European monarchies was rents earned off agricultural lands. The other was tariffs, providing perhaps half as much income overall as rents. (Here "rents" is used in the narrow sense of income connected to land holdings, and thus does not include tariffs charged on trade.) Mercantilist tension over control of

29

global trade played an important role in a number of wars. The immediate precipitant of the 1701–1714 War of the Spanish Succession,
known as Queen Anne's War in North America, was an attempt by
French merchant interests to leverage more favorable trade terms
through succession of a Bourbon French monarch to the Spanish
throne.[2] Control of trade was also a central issue in the 1756–1763
Seven Years War, known to Americans as the French and Indian War
that ceded Canada to Britain.[3] In Europe this war was a successor to
the 1740–1748 War of the Austrian Succession. During that war a
desire for control over larger land holdings led Prussia's Fredrick "the
Great" to annex Silesia (now in Poland) and repeatedly attempt to gain
Bohemia, which is roughly the modern Czech Republic.[4]

Gaining control of trade routes was one of the major motivations
behind the remarkable expansion of the Russian Empire starting with
Mocsovy independence from the Mongols in 1480. Under Peter the
Great, Russia battled Sweden to gain control of Livonia and Estonia
on the Baltic. Under Catherine II, bitterly fought wars from 1774 to
1792 gained Russian the Crimea on the Black Sea.[5]

In South Asia, following its victory over Persia in 1650, the Mughal
empire continued to expand its control over agriculturally productive
lands, reaching its greatest extent under Aurangzeb (1656–1707).
This brought it into conflict in the south with the expanding Maratha
Confederacy. In China, the major military challenge facing the Ching
dynasty from 1644 to the end of the 18th century was suppression
of internal rebellions. In Southeast Asia, the situation was more complicated. The spice trade had early on attracted the interest of Europeans.
This included the Spanish in the Philippines, the Portuguese and
Dutch in the East Indies, and then the French on the mainland.
A series of wars between Burma, Siam, and Vietnam pitted them against
each other for control of the agriculturally productive areas along rivers
that drain into Southeast Asia from the north.[6]

Plunder, Trade, and Territory in Pre-colonial Africa

West Africa is of particular interest when it comes to natural resources
and conflict.[7] This region played an important role in the history of

gold and slavery. Later its uranium and oil resources became important. In West Africa, by the end of the 16th century the Muslim Songhay empire stretched along the Sahel, south of the Sahara desert from above the Bight of Benin almost to the west coast. This empire sat astride the trade route from the Gold Coast to the Mediterranean, from which it derived significant wealth. In 1590, fresh from a decisive defeat of Portugal, Morocco attacked from the north and took the important cities of Timbuktu and Gao on the northernmost bend of the Niger River. The Songhay empire collapsed under pressure from subsequent internal revolts. Until the much later onset of French colonalism, independence from external rule was then obtained by non-muslim rulers of the Mossi states between the upper tributaries of the Volta River, including much of modern-day Burkina Faso. Tension between peoples of the Sahel and south and nearer the West African coast continued to be a recurring theme in West African politics to the present day.

Morocco gained substantial revenues from control of trade in gold and other goods, but this came at too high a cost in military terms. From 1680 to 1770 Saharan Taureg raiders occupied towns along the Niger River that the Moroccans had previously taken. They tried to rejuvinate the gold-based trade through the Sahara, but were weakened by continuing warfare and had limited success. A succession of smaller states to the west consolidated control over farming economies but did not expand into larger empires.

To the east in the Sahel, the Kanem-Bornu states, including much of modern-day Niger, had managed to fend off the Songhay through the 16th century. Farther east, in the region around Lake Chad, the Hausa states had advanced territorial control and government organization in the context of a series of wars and defensive arrangements aimed at plunder and protecting farmers from raiding. The various Hausa states, including Katsina and Kano, failed to unite into a larger empire and instead remained locked in a series of wars over control of caravan trade. In Southern West Africa, control of farming and trade to the coast were the primary sources of contention involving the Nupe and Jukun along the middle Niger and Benue rivers. Nearer the coast were the Yoruba Oyo empire, the Edo in Benin, and the city-states of the Niger delta.

In the 18th century, an Islamic reform movement promulgated originally by Fulani cattle herders affected the approach to governance taken in several West African states. The Fulani states did not form a unified empire, but together they reopened West Africa to international travel for traders and Muslim scholars. In the process, they also facilitated an expansion of the capture and trade of slaves in West Africa.

The geography of the numerous islands in the Niger river delta region favored the development of small city states. In trade by sea from the 16th through 18th centuries, the peoples in this region prospered at the expense of slaves from the north. In the early 21st century the tables would be turned, with forces farther north in Nigeria profiting from delta region oil in a way that people in the delta region sometimes used violent methods to resist or try to gain a share of the cash flow.

Conflict in East Africa, all of the way down to South Africa, was heavily influenced by early expansions from West and North Africa. In the interior the primary economic issues were control of farming and herding territory. Along the coast, trade was important. The slave trade connected slave raiding in the interior to slave trading both locally and increasing with time to the East African coast.[8]

Napoleon Bonaparte

The Westphalian settlement at the end of the Thirty Years War is usually cited as the foundation of the modern system of nation states and diplomatic interchange. After Westphalia, European monarchs determined that the world should be divided into a set of countries with well-defined borders and rulers. Monarchs and emissaries would be immune from capture, ransom, or execution. Monarchs usually no longer led their own troops into battle but instead relied on generals and officers to do so. Losing monarchs who ceded part of their territory to settle a war could remain on their thrones. The risk of life and limb in battle generally fell on recruited or empressed soldiers and sailors and junior officers rather than their leaders. As population pressure grew in the 18th century, the loss of thousands of able-bodied men, poor or powerless enough to be recruited or dragooned into military service, was considered no great matter by some of the aristocracy. Kept within reasonable limits, wars between European States could continue on more or less indefinitely without threatening the overarching structures of power in Europe.

The Napoleonic Wars were a radical departure from the previous wars involving European powers since 1648. Napoleon was an upstart corporal from an obscure island, catapulted to the head of an expansionist empire following a popular revolt in France. His marauding armies, swollen in numbers by unprecedented massive conscription, lived off the land of the regions they conquered and sowed devastation in their wake. By the time Napoleon was finally defeated, this new brand of warfare had shaken Europe to its core. The re-established monarchies of continental Europe determined that this experience should not be repeated. They set about to form a Concert of Europe, which succeeded in largely keeping the peace between major European powers for a century. Two exceptions were the Crimean War of 1853–1856 and the Seven Weeks War between Austria and Prussia in 1866. Another more portentous interruption of the Concert of Europe was the Franco-Prussian War of 1869–1870, which is discussed in Chapter 5. After these wars the combatants eventually aligned with each other. Germany and Austria–Hungary formed an alliance in 1879. Britain and France allied with their erstwhile Russian opponents starting in 1894.

Why Wars Were Fought

It is clear that economic factors played an important role in the history of repeated warfare. Plunder, including the capture of precious metals and slaves, was an economic incentive from ancient times through the end of the African slave trade. Control of agriculturally productive land and trade provided stronger motivations in the somewhat more stable political environments that evolved outside of Africa after recovery from the continent-sweeping conquests of the Mongols and Spanish conquistadors.

For the individual soldier who lays down his life in battle rather than flee, pure self-centered economic interest is not a sufficient motivation. Forced recruits could sometimes be put in a position of facing marching into a line of fine or being cut down by the sabers or pistols of their own officers if they refused. However, the officers, and in many cases the enlisted men, had to be motivated to sign up voluntarily for facing such a fate. In some cases this resulted simply from economic desperation, either for them or their immediate families. More broadly effective was getting soldiers and the general populace to buy into some sort of motivation that went beyond the physical needs of themselves or their immediate families. Real or exaggerated claims about grievances or existential external threats were often invoked. Fighting unit élan, clan or ethnic identity, and patriotism were also enlisted in the cause.[a] Often these were combined with claims of moral superiority and the prospect of religious salvation to try to motivate participation in war. Here all of this is lumped together under the banner of what will be called ideology, broadly understood.

By no means did all conflicts of economic interest lead to war, even where this was an operationally feasible option. Whether to opt for war or not in a given situation depended on the preferences of individual leaders, and of the people whose cooperation they needed in order to launch a war. Some were more risk averse than others. Some sought glory, others stability. Some had moral qualms about the depredations of war, others not.

One way of visualizing the competing influences of economics, ideology, and psychology on security problems is as an inverted triangle. This triangle has psychology on the bottom point and economics and ideology at the other two corners (see Fig. 3.1). If economics carries the greater weight, it may pull ideology toward it. This can promote the national ascendancy of new religious ideas (like Protestantism), nationalist or ethnically oriented interpretations of history, or even influential new political economic ideologies like

---

[a] A sweeping historical view of the interaction of combat and culture is given in Lynn (2003).

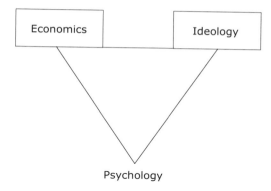

Fig. 3.1.   Recurring instability of peace before fertility transition.

Marxist–Leninism. On the other hand, a religious, ethnic, nationalist, or political ideology can take on a life of its own. This can drag countries and their leaders down to ruin in a manner transparently at odds with their own economic interests. All of this pivots on the psychology of individual national leaders and others with enough influence to guide their decisions. The inability of Napoleon Bonaparte and Aldolf Hitler to understand the limitations of the military power they controlled are but two particularly spectacular examples of how the psychology of individual leaders has influenced the course of history.

   Since this book is about energy and international war, it is natural here to begin an examination of the motivations for war by looking first at its economic ramifications. However, even when ideologies are mobilized in support of economic interests, they can interact in complex ways with those interests. The influence of ideology can persist even if the originally accompanying economic motivation is substantially altered. Moreover, it should become clear from cases that will be examined later in this book that the psychological profiles of individual leaders can make a critical difference, with different leaders prone to make different decisions even when faced with similar economic and ideological contexts.

   In a different type of work, it could be equally useful to start by looking at the ideological context in which economic considerations play out. After all, the economic positions of different religious, linguistic, or ethnic communities have often evolved to where they are in part just because of these underlying distinctions between different groups of people. From this point of view, ideological considerations can be considered to be the foundations of conflict. Economic factors still play a role, at least because it takes resources to fund the operations of participants in a conflict.

Yet another kind of work could take a particular interest in the type of people who become leaders charismatic or influential enough to lead a people into war. Such a study would then concentrate on how such leaders mobilize the ideological support and financial resources needed to execute their plans.

For any study of what precipitates wars, it is not the particular launching off point that is critically important. What is essential is that each of the three points of the triangle in Fig. 3.1 be visited to the extent that it is an important piece of the puzzle. To use a more contemporary example, comparing three different explanations of principle security threats to the United States points out the potential pitfalls of a more blinkered approach. Two of these came from two candidates for the Republican presidential nomination in a televised debate two days before the 2008 New Hampshire primary. The third was put forth by several high officials of the US administration in the lead-up to the 2003 invasion of Iraq.

According to Congressman Ron Paul, threats to the United States from al Qaeda derive from the history of US interventions in the Middle East (including interventions and troop deployments in oil producing countries, Saudi Arabia being one explicitly mentioned). From this point of view, previous and ongoing US actions connected to concern over who has control of the production of oil are central to the reasons behind attacks on US citizens and personnel.[9]

According to former Arkansas governor Mike Huckabee, the essential problem is the existence of an ideologically motivated group of Islamic jihadists, referred to as "Islamofacists." A transcript of Huckabee's comments includes "...when there is a serious threat to this country, it is not a threat because we happen to be peace-loving people; it's a threat because in the heart of the radical Islamic faith — not all Islam, and that's what's very important. This isn't an Islamic problem; this is a jihadist problem. This is an Islamofascism problem. And if you read the writings of those who most influenced — and Governor Romney mentioned Said Qutub, executed in Egypt in 1966. He is one of the major philosophers behind this. And the fact is, there is nothing about our attacking them that prompts this. They are prompted by the fact they believe that they must establish a world-wide caliphate that has nothing to do with us other than we live and breathe, and their intention is to destroy us".[10] From this point of view, an explanation based solely on a purported ideological fixation is sufficient, directly rejecting Paul's suggestion to consider what might have contributed to its evolution.

Before the 2003 invasion of Iraq, its leader Saddam Hussein was portrayed as having a monomaniacal fixation of making use of every possible pathway to obtaining weapons of mass destruction and in league with the perpetrators of the 2001 high-jacked airplane attacks in the United States. He was purported to have all of Iraq locked in his despotic thrall, with all Sunnis and Shia alike ready to rise up and greet incoming forces as liberators once he and his henchman were swept from power. From this point of view, understanding the psychological profile and potential capabilities of a dictatorial leader is the essence of what is needed to make a decision about initiating war.

To be fair, each of these synopses is taken from what are essentially short "sound bites" and may well not represent the underlying breadth of understanding of the people to whom they are attributed. Taken as they stand here, however, they leave open obvious questions connected to the limitations of uni-dimensional views of sources of conflict. Paul's comments leave open the question of what people sympathetic to al Qaeda would do if the United States did indeed withdraw its supposedly offending military forces and stop giving financial aid to repressive governments. Huckabee's comments sweep aside the complexities of the economic and cultural framework in which ideology evolves. The above portrayal of Suddam Hussein proved not only to be contra-factual in its portrayal of Iraqi weapons research and development and support for al Qaeda. It also avoided any analysis of just what were the Iraqi leadership's likely motivations for its various actions leading up to the invasion of Iraq in 2003.

Things Change with Time

The precariously balanced triangle in Fig. 3.1 gives a reasonable impression of the situation with warfare in Europe during many times before 1648 and up through 1815. It does not do justice to the situation within Europe subsequently during much of the 19th century. It certainly does not adequately represent the current likelihood of war between member states of the European Union. The reason for this is that the degree to which decisions between war and peace hang on the decisions of individual leaders depends on the economic and institutional context in which they operate. During the Concert of Europe from 1815 to 1914, economic rivalries were largely transferred overseas. Moreover, friction over access to trade, inherent in the mercantilist framework, was gradually replaced by a negotiated colonial division of overseas lands susceptible to European rule.

The European situation during time of the Concert can be represented visually as in Fig. 3.2. The peace was still fragile, but prudence and the memory of the chaos during the Napoleonic wars usually kept the balance. The three major exceptions already noted point out the importance of psychological and economic factors determining whether or not the balance was maintained. From the perspective of Otto von Bismark, the famous "Iron Chancellor" of an eventually united Germany, the Austro-Prussian and Franco-Prussian wars were limited actions aimed at promoting the German states' economic and political interests. From a French perspective, its "emperor" Louis Napoleon, Bonaparte's nephew, took actions that helped set up the 1853–1856 Crimean War and formally started the 1870–1871 Franco-Prussian War. In both cases he blundered France into wars that ultimately had unsatisfactory outcomes for his monarchy. Underlying the Crimean War were more serious problems with the balance of power and the temptations presented by the gradually eclipse of the formerly formidable Ottoman Empire, as described in Chapter 6.

As economic and political evolution proceeded in Western Europe and some other regions after WWII, it became possible to visualize the marginally stable equilibrium, illustrated in Fig. 3.2, could transition from temporary to permanently stability, as in Fig. 3.3.

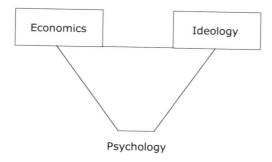

Fig. 3.2.   Factors influencing stability of peace after industrialization.

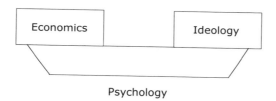

Fig. 3.3.   European Union's stable ship of state.

The type of stable situation illustrated in Fig. 3.3 is now most dramatically apparent within the European Union. The combination of economic and ideological factors that previously led to war amongst the future EU members has been transformed by a new institutional framework. This framework appears so stable that even the most erratic psychology of national leaders and elites is unlikely to tip the balance toward internecine warfare. There are certainly contrasts between the personal styles and predilections of flamboyant leaders like Italy's and France's Nicolas Sarkozy and Italy's Prime Minister Bernado Bertolucci and the more staid approaches of Germany's Angelina Merkel and Britain's George Brown. Nevertheless, all have been firmly cemented to work within an institutional and economic framework that makes revisiting previous centuries' wars between their countries out of the question. This is a state of affairs virtually unthinkable in 15th and 16th century Europe.

After its disastrous 1957–1960 "Great Leap" and the 1966–1976 Cultural Revolution, a united mainland China also appeared to have recovered from earlier periods of competing warlords, world war, and revolution to reach the kind of internal stability illustrated in Fig. 3.3. When it comes to international war, the Association of Southeast Asian Nations may have now reached a stable equilibrium of the type illustrated in Fig. 3.3, even as internal political turmoil continues to reappear in some of its member states. This might also apply to Latin America.

Historical Importance of the Demographic Transition

Without going into enormous detail, from an economic perspective it is easy to understand why the precariously balanced triangle shown in Fig. 3.1 repeatedly toppled toward war before the industrial revolution. For rarely then, except for limited periods of time, did the growth of food supply keep up with the potential growth of population in the absence of devastating epidemics or violent conflict. In the special case of generally isolated Japan from the 7th to the mid-19th century, disease and war were mostly kept at bay. There, "over the long run, the major check to Japanese population expansion came from famines and hunger crises. Disease and war were much less important than in China (and Europe)…".[11]

From Neolithic times on, almost every group eventually had the choice of banding together in violence against a group seen as outsiders, or facing debilitating hunger or even starvation. Small elites politically organized on a sufficiently large scale might concentrate enough resources to avoid a slide toward personal deprivation. Still, even the most powerful kings and emperors had ever to look over their shoulders at the specter of mass violence from without or within. Only after population started to be limited by the demographic revolution of lower fertility rather than high mortality could these cycles begin to be broken.

The best-documented historical example of the demographic revolution comes from a long series of statistics on Sweden. The birth–date rates in Sweden were 1.12 percent from 1861 to 1870, and 1.13 percent from 1891 to 1900. By 1921–1930 the birth rate

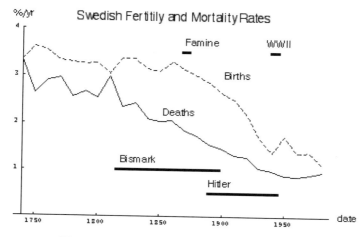

Fig. 3.4. Swedish fertility and mortality rates.

had fallen rapidly to approach the lower death rate, and the annual population growth rate was down to 0.44 percent.[12,b] Before the decline in fertility, shown in Fig. 3.4, caught up with the decline in mortality, there was a famine in Sweden in 1867–1868. At that time emigration to America provided some relief. In the 20th century, vast tracks of American agricultural land would no longer be available for the resettlement of Swedes and other Europeans. However, by the 1920s, the fertility rate had declined to the point where population growth in Sweden no longer had to be kept in check by famine, disease, emigration, or war as in earlier centuries. Sweden's last engagement in war was its coalition with Russia and Austria to repel Napoleon Bonaparte's invasion of Russia in 1812. Around then was the last time that high levels of fertility and mortality rates were about equal in Sweden. After that, Sweden opted for armed neutrality and never had to suffer the ravages of another major war.

---

[b] The differences in birth–death rates in Sweden were 3.14–2.02 = 1.12 percent from 1861–1870, and 2.71–1.64 = 1.13 percent from 1891–1900. By 1921–1930 the birth rate had fallen even faster that the death rate, and the annual population growth rate was down to 1.75–1.21 = 0.44 percent.

The beginning of the industrial revolution roughly coincided with the start of the demographic revolution, in France. During the Concert of Europe period from 1815 to 1913, there was a noticeable effect from the demographic revolution diffusing to countries like Sweden and Germany. However, European birth rates were still substantially higher than the death rates during this period. During this period a precarious balance was mostly obtained between the competing economic and ideological interests in Europe. Early 19th century European leaders grew up in the shadow of all-out war in Europe. Even Germany's Chancellor Otto von Bismark promoted the use of military force only for the sharply limited goal of achieving German unification. However, by 1914 a set of monarchs was in charge who harked back to old visions of imperial glory and had seemingly forgotten the terrible cost of war raging all over Europe.

The mindset of Adolf Hitler's generation was cast at a time when fertility rates still greatly exceeded death rates. By the 1930s fertility and mortality rate in much of Europe would be nearly in balance, but the die was cast on a coming war before the implications of this new development had sunk in. The consequences of this are spelled out in Chapters 5–13.

Theories of Conflict

The illustrations in Figs. 3.1–3.3 point out some of the factors that influence decisions between war and peace. Taken together, they also highlight the importance of considering how these interactions evolve over time. What they do not do is provide a useful theory of how this occurs. There is an enormous literature on this topic, which would be hard to do justice here. A brief summary of four different approaches, taken from Legro and Moravscik will have to suffice here.[13,c]

---

[c] Not particularly disguised in their work, titled "Is anyone still a realist?" is that it is a critique of one of the approaches the supporters of which might respond that the summary they provide is oversimplified. Nevertheless, for the present purposes the summary by these authors provides a useful starting point for thinking about theories of conflict.

The point of view taken here is that different theoretical approaches are useful when applied to different situations. For the period 1648–1812 in Europe, the ruling monarchs can be viewed as making the final decisions on competing over limited resources in the absence of a useful institutional framework for limiting warfare. This corresponds roughly to the point of view taken by *realist* schools of international relations. From 1815–1914 in Europe there were no formal institutions preventing international conflict, but after the Napoleonic wars there was greater appreciation of the dysfunction of internecine European warfare and the benefit of cooperation on an internally peaceful division of access to trading partners outside of Europe. This viewpoint is consistent with what is sometimes called a *liberal* view of international relations. After WWII, the evolution of the European Union led to one of the most dramatic examples of formal institutional arrangements aimed at making warfare between the cooperating nations obsolete. The *institutionalist* view of international relations stresses the importance of such arrangements.

Looking at the internal dynamics of how nations make decisions about war and peace leads to another set of controversies that complicate simpler pictures that view nations as unitary actors interacting in one or another framework. Running somewhat at odds with three types of theories just described is an approach that Legro and Moravscik called *epistemic*. This set of viewpoints contains "theories and explanations about the role of collective beliefs and ideas on which states rely in calculating how to realize their underlying goals".[14] One example is the concept of "exceptionalism," the idea that a particular country has a unique role in history to bring a better sense of order to the world. Examples include the French idea of *mission civilatrice* discussed in Chapter 21, and the British concept of the "white man's burden." In hindsight these concepts look like transparent whitewash for imperialism based on other economic and political motives. This did not keep these constructs from being taken seriously by legions of civil servants and missionaries sent around the world under their cover at the time. A more recent example of the idea of exceptionalism is the evolution from Ronald Reagan's image of the United States as a beacon of civilization like "city on a hill" to

Paul Wolfowitz's vision of a benevolent global *pax Americana*. The comments by Huckabee quoted above are another example of an exceptionalist theory, in this case attributed to a group of people that he identifies as Islamic jihadists.

Occasionally this book will touch on the individual and collective psychological origins of exceptionalist visions, particularly in interesting cases where the underlying psychology has led to decisions on war that turned out to be catastrophic. For one of the main themes of this book is that nations need not be viewed as doomed to an endless replay of conflicts where only the actors and the bones of contention change from time to time. Rather, this book stresses the important albeit imperfect process of learning from past mistakes.[15] A recurring theme here starts with the observation made above that current leaders were schooled in the mindsets of a previous generation. Leaders thus often fail to realize that the economic goals they seek through violent means have already become obsolete by the time they launch wars aimed at realizing these goals. The consequences of this generational lag will become increasingly apparent as this book works through the industrial revolution to the recent past and present, where technological innovation accelerates to the point where the lag in generational mindset leads to repeated miscalculation.

The goal in this book is not to hold up each theory of war and peace to the mirror of history to see which one works best for all time. Instead, it draws upon ideas from each theory as their concepts seem most appropriate to the era and topic at hand. The point is to illuminate how the role of natural resources and particularly of energy resources has interacted with individual psychology and collective ideology to influence the way that nations have made and will make decisions about war and peace. Useful theoretical constructs are referenced here as a means to that end, not sought as the goal itself. Illuminating the evolving role of energy and other natural resources in international conflicts is meant to show that the question of whether major international wars will continue is an interesting one, not to answer the question of how and when such wars will come to an end.

As noted above, economic factors are only one facet of the motivations for warfare. This is clear even in the 1648–1789 European political context. For this period the autocratic mode of governance temps us to simplify nations' decisions about war as being made by "unitary rational actors".[16] During this period, the lack of transnational institutions that arose much later in Europe allows us to look at the decisions of these actors as using military force where necessary to maximize power or security in a situation of international anarchy. Attempts to maximize royal income and security were closely connected, since the ability to raise armies depended on the availability of that income. However, there was also an important role for ideology (here again taken to include religious, ethnic, and nationalistic factors as well as political ideology). For example, there were clearly competing economic interests between emerging non-aristocratic Protestant-oriented capital and Catholic-oriented landed aristocracy in the early 17th century. Nevertheless, commitment to religious ideology must also have helped propel the 1618–1648 Thirty Years War between European Protestants and Catholics into the disastrous conflicts that the Peace of Westphalia finally had some success in resolving.

Moreover, decisions about agreeing or refusing to go to war are ultimately made by individuals. It is individuals' psychology that determines the response to competing economic and ideological pressures. For example, Louis Napoleon was living in the shadow of his illustrious uncle Bonaparte as Louis' wife pressed France to initiate the fateful Franco-Prussian War in 1870. Austrian Emperor Franz-Joseph had a long history of domestic struggle with a domineering mother who put a high value on imperial pomp. This was part of the psychological backdrop when he allowed concern with imperial prestige to entangle him in Bosnia in a way that eventually led Europe to disaster in WWII.

Endnotes

[1] Kohn (1999, p. 493).
[2] Stein and Stein (2000).
[3] Kohn (1999).
[4] Browning (1993).
[5] Barraclough (1978).
[6] Barraclough (1978).

7 Davidon (1998).
8 Shillington (1995).
9 ABC News (2008).
10 ABC News (2008).
11 Maddison (2001, p. 38).
12 de Vylder (1996).
13 Legro and Moravscik (1999).
14 Legro and Moravcsik (1999, p. 11).
15 c.f. Schroeder (1994a, 1994b); Krüger and Schroeder (2004).
16 Legro and Moravcsik (1999).

Part Two

COAL
AND NON-ENERGY
MINERALS

Chapter 4

Steamer Coal in the Colonial Era

Sail, horse, and foot soldier were the sources of energy that moved navies and armies through the Napoleonic campaigns, but a radical transformation was about to start. Coal would become the dominant source of energy for industrial economies and their military forces in the 19th century. Along with this came an enormous growth in the use of steel in industry, for rail transport in both peace and war, and in merchant marines and naval forces. Smelting of iron ore to make steel used coal as an energy source. The better the grade of iron ore, the less energy needed to smelt it. Thus, access to high-grade iron ores became important along with access to the output of coal mines.

By WWI, coal and steel production had become so important that over eight million men would die, most of them in three years of vain attempts to move battle lines enough to shift the preponderance of this production from one side to another. After WWII, struggles over production of coal and steel were permanently moved from the battlefield to the negotiating table. Following how these transformations, from the Napoleonic to WWI to post-WWII eras, occurred is both fascinating and instructive. This story starts here with the role of the steamship.

Coal, Naval Power, and 19th Century Colonialism

Steamships played an important part in the suppression of the slave trade after the Napoleonic wars, and they eventually made a convenient source of quality steam coal a major national asset. So ideal and close to port was Welsh steam coal that it was shipped half way around the world even though vast amounts of other coal deposits existed in China and many colonial possessions. The result was that the commercial and military naval power behind European colonialism came to be dependent on coal, but did not rely on coal deposits in colonies themselves.

Coal-powered steamships started to have an important impact on inland waterways as early as the 1820s. Paul Johnson notes that the British had a particular interest in application of this new technology to its commitment to abolish the slave trade.[1] This observation has an interesting connection to the questions treated in this chapter and the previous one. These concern the causes of international conflict, and how energy relates to the future of conflict. Slavery is of interest here because some modern-day analysts point to slavery as a possible analogue of war between developed nations: an institution once thought to be intrinsic to the human condition, but later determined to be dysfunctional and eventually abolished throughout most of the world. As it turned out, the invention of steamships played an important role in the abolition of slavery.

The first really useful steamboat was developed by Robert Fulton, by one account, the 246th most important person of the second millennium.[2] Here is a brief summary. (The numbers in parentheses in the following quote refer to similar rankings of Napoleon and Talleyrand.)

Others produced prototype steamboats, but Fulton made the dream work. He tested his first steam-boat in the Seine, then offered the ship to the French. But Napoleon (16), who had rejected Fulton's newfangled submarine as dishonorable warfare, said *non* again. "A charming man and brilliant conversationalist," said French minister Talleyrand (419) about Fulton, "but I'm afraid the poor fellow's cracked." When the British turned him down too, a frustrated Fulton returned to America. With partner Robert Livingston, he launched a steamboat run on the Hudson River between New York and Albany in 1807. The 150 foot steamship, with huge paddlewheels on each side, was named the *Clermont*, but the jeering public called it "Fulton's Folley." Nobody laughed long: the boat cut the trip from four days to thirty-two hours...

In the Napoleonic period the French and the British were preoccupied with land armies and with the high seas, where steam-powered warships did not yet look practical. Britain's particular concern with major inland waterways around the world followed the final peace treaty of the Napoleonic Wars in 1815. In this treaty, France agreed to abolish her extensive slave trade. By 1818, in return for loan waivers and £700,000 in the currency of the time, Britain had convinced Portugal and Spain to condemn the slave trade. Britain also convinced Spain to join the Netherlands and Portugal in mutual rights of search to help put down the trade after 1820. There were some setbacks with lax US enforcement of a 1825 law making international slaving a capital offense. Also, several large South American countries did not join Chile in eliminating slavery internally until the 1830s through 1850s. Indeed, the final formal abolition had to wait until Brazil abolished slavery in 1888.[3] Nevertheless, Britain was committed by 1815 to try to end slavery exports from the West Coast of Africa. This commitment required steamships to push up into the inland rivers. Johnson refers to correspondence about this from a former slave named Bathurst, who bought his freedom and then prospered as a merchant as one about 6000 former slaves who went from the United States to its settlement in Liberia.

To reinforce its high seas patrols, the British government was driven to what became known as "gunboat diplomacy." The first mention of it came in a letter from Bathurst to one of the West Coast governors, Charles Turner, 19 December 1825. When native chiefs prove recalcitrant in cooperating with antislavery measures, he wrote, "A Gun Boat, or vessel of a similar description containing 40 or 50 men, who should be chosen from those most inured to the climate, would … serve as a rallying-point for such of the Neighbouring Tribes as may be disposed to cooperate heartily in suppressing the Slave Trade: and would materially relieve the Cruizers employed on this coast." The first steamboat arrived on the cost in 1827; steam was important because it enabled authority to push right up the rivers, where sail was baffled.[4]

According to Johnson, the anti-slavery campaign was pursued by Britain not only in the Atlantic, but also around the Indian Ocean from Madagascar to Oman to India.[5] In what amounted to an alliance with Britain, Omani ruler Seyyid bin Sultan Ali Bu Saidi agreed to abolish a lucrative slave trade. By 1826, through cooperation with the British he had "built up 'a more efficient naval force than all the native princes combined, from the Cape of Good Hope to Japan,' and by its means established a maritime empire from Aden to the head of the Persian Gulf." This cemented a long-standing British presence in the Persian Gulf. This presence would last until Britain's failure (with France and Israel) in the Suez War of 1956 as the United States opposed their efforts. Britain's military presence in the Persian Gulf would resurface again with the United Kingdom providing the largest contingents of forces to aid the United States in its actions against Iraq after the cold war.

The French naval defeat at Trafalgar in 1805 set the stage for over a century of almost uncontested British domination of the high seas by Britain's Royal Navy and private East India Company. Johnson describes the situation in the two decades following the final defeat of Napoleon in 1815.

> For all practical purposes, the South Atlantic, the South and Central Pacific, and the South Seas generally were controlled solely by Britain. From 1815 and for many decades, the Indian Ocean was a British lake. There, the power of the Royal Navy was reinforced by the East India Company, which had its own army and navy. The French strategist Baron Charles Dupin, in an address to the Institute de France, enviously remarked: "From the banks of the Indus to the frontiers of China, from the mouths of the Ganges to the mountains of Tibet — all acknowledge the sway of a mercantile company, shut up in the narrow streets of London." The big East Indiamen, insured for £250,000 or more, weighed up to 1,200 tones. They operated a monopoly of the Britain–India trade until 1813 and were preponderant in it until the 1840s, and they retained the monopoly of China trade until 1833.[6]

By the 1820s, coal was becoming an important driver for naval power. A global network of coaling stations thus became a central cog in the machinery of British power projection.

> The navy, in turn, depended on bases, which became increasingly important as coal-fired steamboats began to joint the fleet in the 1820s. Ships using wind power could be provisioned at sea, careen themselves on any deserted tidal beach, and at a pinch could stay out of harbor for years. But steam warships, though vital to the Navy's increasing security role because of their ability to follow slavers, pirates, and other antisocial elements upriver, needed coaling stations.[7]

Steam warships were not always available where needed in the 1820s. Piracy was a continuing threat in that decade to British trade in and out of the port of Singapore, which was taken over by the British in 1819 and fortified at the instigation of Thomas Stanford Raffles. Malay and Philippine pirate prows were a particular problem, as noted by Johnson.

> What the navy preferred to do was to sink the praus by gunfire, no easy matter. The alternative was to mount search-and-destroy operations on the pirate coasts and islands. The ideal craft for these operations were the new flat-bottom steam warships, mounting big guns. But neither the [East India] company nor the navy was yet ready to supply them for Southeast Asia, so such missions often had to be conducted in rowing boats, launched from warships and commanded by young lieutenants or midshipmen, in peril of their lives. For most of the 1820s, a brig and a schooner, sometimes backed by a sloop from the East Indies Squadron, constituted the only patrol on the Singapore Straits. Things improved in 1830 when Rear Admiral Sir Edward Owen arrived to take charge and began a systematic study of the patterns and economies of piracy, as a prelude to devising countermeasures. Some naval experts thought piracy could never be wiped out in these waters, just as today's police are skeptical about eliminating burglary in New York or London or

eradicating the Mafia in Italy. Owen was not so pessimistic, but he concluded that naval forces, however strong, could not succeed alone: the structure and way of life of local societies had to be changed. The only way to do that, as the next generation discovered, was by direct rule — colonialism — just the solution Raffles believed was unnecessary.[8]

Evidently the quest for energy resources themselves was not what originally propelled Britain to set up coaling stations around the world. Britain had adequate coal resources right at home to fuel the industrial revolution to the end of the 19th century and beyond.

The antislavery campaign can be viewed as either the source or the excuse for a spectacular expansion of British naval power and trading. However it is viewed, the British anti-slavery campaign was a pivotal point in a long chain of economic developments leading from the code of Hammurabi and the Babylonian captivity of the Jews to the Anglo-American-led invasion that placed US troops in Baghdad in 2003. The next key links in this chain were the conversion of the globally dominant British navy first to coal and then to oil. The availability of large quantities of high quality steamer coal near the coast in Wales supported the first of these conversions.

The Rise and Decline of South Wales Coal Exports

The global impact of the shipping of British coal in the 19th century was remarkable. Of particular importance was the location of large resources of high-qualify steamer coal very near the Bristol Channel coast in South Wales. Research by Michael Asteris helps explain this.[9]

From its initial rapid expansion of use in the first half of the 19th century, Welsh coal was the most important power source for naval shipping through to WWI. This started with the construction of coal docks at the Welsh port city of Cardiff from 1839–1841. UK coal exports rose rapidly from 1850 to 1890. This can be seen from the top half of Table 4.1. South Wales' resources were sufficient to increase coal exports all the way to 1913. This can be seen from the bottom half of Table 4.1.

Table 4.1. Welsh coal uses (millions of tons per year).

Year	Bristol Channel ports exports	
1850	0.4	
1860	1.7	
1870	3.5	
1880	6.9	
1890	12.5	

	South Wales exports	Domestic use of S. Wales coal
1895	14.7	18.3
1900	18.5	20.8
1905	20.0	23.2
1910	25.2	23.5
1913	29.9	26.9

Source: The rise and decline of South Wales coal exports (Asteris, 1986), Tables 1 and 4.

From 1863 to 1872, remarkable advances in engine technology helped stretch out Welsh steamer coal resources as demand grew rapidly. Indeed, in this interval "the fuel consumption of new marine engines was reduced by one half".[10] This kept up demand that allowed gross output from South Wales to increase through 1913. However, labor productivity peaked at 314 tons/year per man in 1883 and declined to 228 tons in 1911. Given that domestic use of Welsh coal also increased continuously from 1895 to 1913, this required a substantial increase in coal-mining manpower. This trend turned out not to be a serious problem for the British navy, because in 1911 it made a fateful decision to convert to oil.

There are three reasons that Welsh steamer coal was so important for naval shipping. It was located close to port; it was particularly suitable for powering military as well as civilian vessels; and technological improvements arose to allow more efficient use of a large but limited resource.

The advantage to Britain of having good coal resources located close to port was remarkable. Overland coal transport costs to port

Table 4.2.   Freight rate from Cardiff ($US2008 per ton of coal).

Year	Lisbon	Port Said	Bombay
1864	161	177	199
1874	106	119	157
1884	74	85	117
1894	45	40	60
1904	48	39	62
1909	40	39	54
1913	57	40	84

Source: The rise and decline of South Wales coal exports (Asteris, 1986) Table 7.

were nearly half again as large from the western German Ruhr Valley region as in Wales. In 1913 the respective rates per ton were two shillings and ten pence vs. one shilling and eleven pence. Converted to $US at 2008 prices, this corresponds to $19/ton for Germany compared to $13/ton for Wales.[a] The $19/ton shipping costs from the Ruhr to port were nearly a quarter to a half of the cost of shipping coal from Cardiff to sites as far as Bombay or Egypt's Port Said in 1913 (Table 4.2). Within-country rail shipping costs were typically comparable to that for shipping by sea for three thousand miles, or nearly 5000 km.[11]

The British navy's experience with trying to use other English coal sources gives an indication of how especially well suited Welsh coal was for warships.[12] Not surprisingly, other UK mining regions put pressure on the government to get a share of lucrative military contracts. However, other coals did not stoke as well and produced smoke that interfered with visibility. Mixing different coals compensated for these difficulties but proved to be too complicated. Along with the difficulty of getting Asian-origin coal to port under 19th century conditions, this may help explain why the British were willing to rely on "tried and true" Welsh coal, even if they sometimes had to ship it nearly half way around the world.

---

[a] House of Commons Library (1999); Historical Foreign Exchange (2003); USBLS (2008).

The British Parliament passed a bill in June 1914 on conversion of British navy to oil.[13] This bill was passed in ignorance of how imminent was the oncoming 1914 war. It simply acknowledged the superiority of oil as a warship fuel. However, this bill also heralded the replacement more generally of coal by oil for transport just as the more readily extractable Welsh steamer coal resources were becoming seriously depleted. Indeed, coal demand was nearly static from 1913 to 1928.[14] Globally, oil-driven shipping expanded rapidly from 1914 to 1939, by which time "less than half of all merchant vessels were coal-fired, while warships had converted almost completely to oil".[15]

Endnotes

[1] Johnson (1991).
[2] Gottlieb *et al.* (1998).
[3] Consulate General of Brazil (2003).
[4] Johnson (1991, p. 332).
[5] Johnson (1991, p. 335).
[6] Johnson (1991, p. 338).
[7] Johnson (1991, p. 339).
[8] Johnson (1991, p. 354).
[9] Asteris (1986, pp. 25–40).
[10] Asteris (1986, p. 30).
[11] Asteris (1986, p. 33).
[12] Asteris (1986, pp. 28–29).
[13] Asteris (1991).
[14] Asteris (1986, p. 41).
[15] Asteris (1986, p. 42).

Chapter 5

Franco-Prussian War Sets the Stage

Started over other issues in 1870, the Franco-Prussian War transferred Lorraine iron fields in northwestern France to newly unified Germany. The invention of a new industrial process for using these phosphate-laded ores would soon make them valuable. This contributed to Germany's iron production greatly outstripping France's by the time of WWI. Thus, the settlement ending the Franco-Prussian War marks the beginning of a political contention of control of resources that would reverberate all of the way past the end of WWII.

The Franco-Prussian War did not of course arise out of thin air. The run-up to the Franco-Prussian War included the 1853–1856 Crimean War and the 1866 Seven Week's Austro-Prussian War.

Preludes to the Franco-Prussian War

In 1850, reportedly seeking distraction from troubles in France and piqued at the Russian Czar's refusal to address him as befitting an emperor, Louis reasserted old and dormant rights for Roman rather than Orthodox Catholic monks to oversee holy places in Jerusalem. That city was at the time part of the Turkish Ottoman Empire, whose government was referred to as the Porte. "In February 1850 the Turks sent a diplomatic note to the French, giving two keys to the great door of the Church of the Nativity to the representatives of the Catholic Church. At the same time, the Porte sent a firman [decree] giving secret assurances to the Orthodox Church that the French keys would not fit the lock".[1] In 1852 France took control of the holy places anyway, challenging both Russian prestige and piquing

59

Russia's concern that the Ottomon Empire might be leaning toward French influence.

The more direct precipitant of the Crimean War was the 1853 Russian invasion of Ottoman Moldova and Wallachia (in southern modern-day Romania). Following a conference on the issue in Vienna, Russia withdrew, but the Ottomon Sultan declared war anyway. The Turks were thus the ones that actually started the Crimean War, but Louis Napoleon had aggravated the face-off with Russia over an issue that was insignificant compared to the ramifications of war between the major European powers. This time his monarchy survived, since Britain stood with France against Russia. In the Franco-Prussian War he would stand alone, and as a consequence lose his throne as the French monarchy was finally abolished once and for all.

During the Crimean War, Austria disappointed the Russian Czar's expectation that it would side with him instead of remaining neutral. As a result, Austria was left to face Prussia alone when Prussia started its campaign to unify the German states with its 1866 Seven Week's War against Austria. The Austrian Parliament had earlier refused to make the appropriation needed to equip its army with modern rifles. As a result, a soldier's rate of fire on the Prussian side was three times faster, contributing to a quick Prussian victory. The resulting incorporation of Schleswig-Holstein, Hanover, Hesse, Nassau, Frankfurt, and Prussia's old German Federation into a new Prussian-dominated North German Federation completed the first part of Chancellor Otto von Bismark's goal of uniting the German states.

Portentously, the humiliation of Austrian Emperor Franz-Josef in this war made him determined to hold on to possessions in the Balkans. This fixation would ultimately bring down the whole house of cards of peace amongst major powers in Europe that lasted from 1871–1914.

Germany

The immediate starting point for the Franco-Prussian War was that "a Prussian effort was made to put a Hollenzollern prince, related to the Prussian royal house, on the Spanish throne in 1870…"[2] Kohn says that Bismark deliberately provoked the war. Other accounts claim that Louis Napoleon stumbled into the war upon the prodding of his wife, even after the German nominee withdrew his candidacy for the Spanish throne. Without going into such detail, Eckel agrees that the war was a result of French miscalculation.[3]

The detailed sequence of events started with a 1870 "communication between King William of Prussia (later German Emperor William I) and his premier, Otto von Bismarck."

> In June, 1870, the throne of Spain was offered to Prince Leopold of Hohenzollern-Sigmaringen, a relative of King William. Leopold at first accepted the candidacy, but withdrew it in July after the French government had protested. During these transactions William and Bismarck were taking the waters at Ems, Germany. There the French ambassador Comte Benedetti, in an interview with the king, requested William's guarantee that the candidacy of Leopold to the Spanish throne would never be renewed. William rejected the request. Bismarck, intent on provoking war with France, made the king's report of the conversation public (July 13) in his celebrated Ems dispatch, which he edited in a manner certain to provoke the French. France declared war on July 19, and the War began.[4]

Evidently, the French ambassador led Louis Napoleon into a trap by not letting sleeping dogs lie concerning the immediate question of the Spanish succession. Then the French ruler foolishly tripped the spring on the trap himself, making France the aggressor in the war. Bismark's primary aim was likely to bring the southern German states into the German confederation without France getting in the way. The war accomplished this aim, but had the French had the foresight to let this happen without stumbling into a disastrous military defeat then they might have been better off in the short run and everybody better off in the long run.

Alsace–Lorraine

A German desire for French iron and coalfields is not what precipitated the Franco-Prussian War. Evidently the German high command was not even consciously aware of the fields until a relevant report reached them part way through the war. According to Eckel, even immediately after the war, in 1871, "we find little trace of any recognition that anything serious had happened to the world".[5] The Germans did deliberately draw the new boundary around the surface exposures of the Lorraine iron fields. They included new coal resources as well, in addition to sitting on other French territory until a large indemnity was paid. However, there is no indication that obtaining more coal and iron was their primary aim at the outset. In other words, it is quite possible that Bismark's plan succeeded beyond his primary goals. It also succeeded all too well, given the terrible trouble that the question of the possession of the border lands between Germany and France would eventually cause.

Thomas-Gilchrist and Steel

Eckel explains why the Thomas-Gilchrist refinement of the basic Bessemer steel-making process in 1879 made the Lorraine iron fields industrially useful and thus militarily important.[6] This process involves lining a Bessemer converter with basic minerals. This allows use of acidic phosphorus ores like the Lorraine ones, and produces fertilizer as a valuable byproduct besides. The original Bessemer process invented in 1855 and commercialized in 1860, works as follows:

> Bessemer process [for Sir Henry Bessemer], industrial process for the manufacture of steel from molten pig iron. The principle involved is that of oxidation of the impurities in the iron by the oxygen of air that is blown through the molten iron; the heat of oxidation raises the temperature of the mass and keeps it molten during operation. The process is carried on in a large container called the Bessemer converter, which is made of steel and has a lining of silica and clay or of dolomite... As the air passes upward through the

molten pig iron, impurities such as silicon, manganese, and carbon unite with the oxygen in the air to form oxides; the carbon monoxide burns off with a blue flame and the other impurities form slag. Dolomite is used as the converter lining when the phosphorus content is high; the process is then called basic Bessemer. The silica and clay lining is used in the acid Bessemer, in which phosphorus is not removed...[7]

French vs German Production

The basic Bessemer process also opened up new opportunities for French steel production. According to Eckel, the geologists who advised Germany on the Lorraine iron fields mistakenly thought they did not continue underground into the portion left in France.[8] In fact, these deposits did continue in an exploitable way well away into France from the territory annexed by Germany in 1871.[9] Nevertheless, German iron and steel production rapidly outstripped that of France and remained way ahead throughout the stalemate on the Western Front during WWI, which until WWII was known as the "Great War."

Endnotes

[1]   Bloy (2002).
[2]   Kohn (1999, p. 175).
[3]   Eckel (1920).
[4]   Columbia Encyclopedia (2001b).
[5]   Eckel (1920, p. 55).
[6]   Eckel (1920, p. 59).
[7]   Columbia Encyclopedia (2001a).
[8]   Eckel (1920).
[9]   Roester (1921); Bichelonne and Angot (1939).

Chapter 6

Coal and Iron in the Great War

The events of WWI seared into the minds of its survivors a conviction that each nation's industrial base had to be protected from foreign competition as a critical matter of national security. The struggle over coal and steel production in the first three years of WWI contributed heavily to this conviction.

France had entered WWI apparently not fully aware of what a critical role the control of coal and iron production in Belgium and its French borderlands would play. In the end, France would lose over a million men and suffer six million total casualties trying to recover allied superiority in coal and iron production. The entry of the United States finally tipped the balance both in coal and iron production and also in the course of the war. The interchange of industrial technology between Europe and the United States set the stage for this.

Industrial Revolution in Britain

The development of an energy-efficient steam engine played a critical role in the industrial revolution. In 1698 Thomas Savery patented a steam engine and in 1711 Thomas Newcomen built one, but these were very inefficient designs because most of the energy was lost in steam exhaust on each engine stroke. Then, James Watt built a steam engine, patented in 1769, which reclaimed the heat required to turn water into steam by condensing the steam back to water rather than expelling it. His engine was used for mine draining, and it transformed operations in cotton and woolen mills.[1] This invention would prove to be a landmark event in the evolution of the relationship between energy and security.

Britain took the lead in explosive growth of energy use around 1825, after recovery from ten years of depression following the Napoleonic wars. With the peace allowed in Europe by the results of the Congress of Vienna, Britain turned her attention full force to the rest of the world. Britain promoted free trade in Latin America and acquiesced to US demands for an open-door policy in the Far East. Elsewhere, Britain started with a mercantilist policy, using force where necessary to squeeze competitors like the Dutch out of overseas markets. Later, Britain turned to a policy of direct colonial administration to maintain control of trade, most notably in South Asia. Steamships and steam-driven railroad engines moved materials to and from the factories and markets of industrial Britain through to the point of its maximum global dominance around 1870. Railroads, pioneered by George Stephenson and his son Robert, played a key role:

> Stephenson was a semiliterate coalyard maintenance man with a North England accent thicker than a vein of anthracite. His eloquence was in his hands. He was a whiz at improving and designing the steam-driven machines coming into vogue in the early nineteenth century, and in 1825 he built the twenty-five-mile Stockton and Burlington Railway for a mine owner who needed to transport coal to port. Copying existing tramroads, Stephenson set the iron rails 56.5 inches apart, and that's still the standard railroad guage in Britain and the United States. Some engineers designed engines; others built the tracks. Stephenson did both and made the whole power-package an industrial success, forever changing the way we travel. Even his genes were mighty. In 1830 his son Robert built "The Rocket," the best engine yet, giving the golden age of rail another burst of steam.[2]

United States after the Civil War

The groundwork for a great leap in US steel production was actually laid before the US Civil War. Low-phosphorus hematite mines yielding sixty percent iron content were linked by rail to Lake

Superior and a shipping canal at Sault St Marie to the lower great lakes region in 1857. Low phosphorus content facilitated a rapid growth in US steel production from 1875 to 1880, before the widespread commercial introduction of the Thomas–Gilchrist method for dealing with acidic ores. Rapid growth waited until the second half of the 1870s. This was because the United States could not capitalize on its great coal and iron resources to take the lead in global steel production until after the delayed post-Civil-War financial panic of 1873.[3]

As shown in Table 6.1, US iron and steel production fluctuated with economic conditions around an average rapid exponential growth curve for forty years after 1876. Annual steel production rates of about 23–30 million tons per year were attained by the United States in the four years before the onset of the Great War in Europe in 1914.

Table 6.1.   US pig iron and steel (millions of long tons).

Year	Pig Iron	Steel
1870	1.6	0.0
1874	2.6	0.4
1878	2.7	0.9
1882	4.6	1.5
1886	5.4	2.4
1890	9.0	4.2
1894	6.5	4.3
1898	12.1	8.8
1900	13.6	10.1
1902	17.7	14.8
1904	15.1	13.6
1906	25.4	23.1
1908	16.4	14.1
1910	18.6	25.8
1912	31.4	30.2
1914	23.7	23.4

Source: Coal, Iron, and War (Eckel, 1920, p. 44). Fig. 3.
A long ton weights 2240 pounds and has a mass of 1016 kg = 1.016 metric ton.

The Struggle of Nations

"If ever there is another war in Europe it will come out of some damned silly thing in the Balkans." — attributed to Otto von Bismark.[4]

Before turning to the events of "The Struggle of Nations"[5] during WWI, it is worth briefly recapitulating the events that led to the war. Control of trade and territory in Europe played roles in the events that led to war. Nevertheless, the start of the war itself was an example of monarchs' preoccupation with imperial prestige overriding national economic and security interests.

WWI was itself triggered in 1914 by a demand that Austria made, but Serbia found, unacceptable. The unacceptable part of Austria's 1914 demand was that Serbia turn over everyone with complicity in the 1914 assassination of Archduke Ferdinand, the heir to the throne of the Austro-Hungarian empire. A reason that this was unacceptable to Serbia is probably because the responsibility for the assassination sat not just with anarchists but also with the support from the Serbian secret service itself.[6,a] The events described concentrate only on the Balkan portion of a more complicated global context, since the Great War was most directly sparked by events in the Balkans.

A convenient starting point is the Serbo-Turkish War of 1876–1878. That war was precipitated by a revolt of Christian inhabitants of Herzogovina and Bosnia against the Ottomon Empire. Serbia at the time was an "autonomous state within the Ottoman Empire." Serbia declared war on Turkey on the basis of a promise of Russian aide, which then failed to materialize. This and the ensuing Russo-Turkish War of 1877–1878 eventually led Britain to press for the Congress of Berlin. This conference gave Bosnia and Herzegovina to Austria–Hungary and gave independence to Serbia, Montenegro, and Romania. Austria took on the role of the protector of Serbia. This

---

[a] The events described here follow passages in the referenced wars listed alphabetically in Kohn's *Dictionary of Wars*.

prevented a Bulgarian takeover after Serbia failed to prevail militarily with its demand for a piece of what Bulgaria annexed in what became Southern Bulgaria.

The more immediate source of the troubles between Austria and Serbia, however, was the settlement of the "Pig War" of 1906–1909. This war was explicitly over tariffs. In particular, Austria closed its borders in retaliation for Serbia starting to import French rather than "tariff-laden" Austrian pork and for the 1905 customs union between Serbia and Bulgaria. Russia supported Serbia. Then, "war between Austria-Hungary and Russia was averted only because of a German ultimatum (1909) demanding the cessation of Russian aid to Serbia".[7] Serbia and Austria developed a new commercial treaty (in 1909), but Serbia covertly stirred up trouble among the southern Slavs in the newly Austrian-annexed Bosnia and Herzegovina.

In principle, the problems in the Balkans could have been settled by the outcomes of the Italo-Turkish War of 1911–1912 and the first (1912–1913) and second (1913) Balkan War. The result of these wars was a redistribution of the western parts of the Ottoman Empire. Italy gained Libya as a colony as well as Rhodes and the Dodecanese Islands. In the Balkan wars, Greece and Montenegro prevailed against the Turks. There were some remaining problems, but hardly enough to justify a major war involving all of Europe and beyond. In particular, "the Serbians were distressed over the failure to secure an Adriatic seaport, and the Montenegrins were vexed from giving up Scutari to the newly formed state of Albania".[8] This festering Serbian discontent led to the critical event that precipitated world war.

With these preliminaries in hand, it is time to turn our attention back to coal and iron. In his chapter on "The Struggle of Nations," Eckel presents the view outlined below of the role of coal and iron in the "Great War".[9] This viewpoint is all the more interesting for his not being able to look back at the period through the prism of the cold war and the WWII. Eckel's vision is sympathetic to the plight of industrial workers but not constrained by Fascist or Communist ideology that sits poorly with many 21st century readers. He is overtly protectionist, but what he had seen concerning the importance of national industrial power to warfare makes this understandable in the context of his times. Remember that Eckel wrote this work a decade before the 1930 Smoot–Hawley tariff, which was eventually credited by some for helping to pitch the whole world into deep depression and an even more global military conflict.[10,b]

Eckel makes a particularly interesting observation about French views of the strategic importance of the Lorraine steel production areas remaining in France at the onset of the Great War.[11] France wanted to make sure that Britain and others would clearly see France as the aggrieved party and come to its aid in case of war. So, French troops ceded the Lorraine mines and steel works to Germany by withdrawing ten kilometers away from the border, making it clear that it was the German rather than the French forces that initiated hostilities at the border. This withdrawal helped substantially swing the balance of Allied and Central Powers' iron production in favor of the Central Powers, until the United States finally entered the fray with its even larger capabilities. Nor, according to Eckel, did the Allied forces and Belgium initially seem to fully understand the strategic importance of preventing Germany from taking over Belgian and northern French coal fields. In the first days of the war, Germany occupied French territory responsible for 30 million of France's 41 million tons of 1913 coal production.[12] Those additional resources would tip the balance of coal production noticeably in favor of the Central Powers through to 1917.

Figure 6.1 shows the location of what were considered to be the useful portions of the Lorraine iron fields at about this time.[13] Also shown is the approximate location of the Western Front as it stabilized after German forces regrouped in the September of 1914 after failing to capture Paris. Major battles at *Ieper* (Ypres) near *Passendale* (Passchendale) in 1915 failed to dislodge Germany from the steel industry areas in Belgium and Luxembourg. Similarly, massive casualties at Verdun in 1916 failed to dislodge Germany from the major iron-producing areas in the "Lorraine Annexée" area it held from before the war through to 1918.[14] It is true that France had other

---

[b] Rankin (1990) contests the importance of the Smoot-Hawley tariff in precipitating the Great Depression.

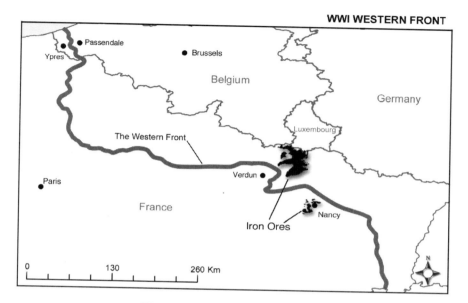

Fig. 6.1. Western front in WWI.

major iron-producing areas. However, the iron ore areas in Lorraine Annexée were not only located very near the Saar coal deposits to their west, but they were also particularly important to Germany because they yielded over twice as much iron as mines in Germany outside Lorraine in 1909. The Lorraine iron mines under German control became increasingly important over the next several years.[15]

To put the situation in perspective, Table 6.2 collects Eckel's figures on allied and Central Powers' iron and steel production just before WWI, and then after the Central Powers' advances on the Western Front.[16] The numbers in bold type in Table 6.2 tell the essence of the story. Before the Central Powers' early advances, annual allied output exceeded central by 75 Mton (million ton) of coal and by 1 Mton of steel. After these advances, central coal output exceeded allied by 45 Mton, and central steel output was 28 Mton vs 17 Mton for the allied powers.

Moreover, in 1913, production of 87 percent of Russian coal and 74 percent of Russian pig iron was concentrated in the Donetsk region

Table 6.2.   Coal and steel production in 1914 (millions of tons).

July 30	Coal	Steel
UK	320	11
UK + Russia	360	15
UK + Russia + France	405	20
UK + Russia + France + Belgium	**430**	**23**
Germany	305	19
Germany + Austria	**355**	**22**
US	570	31
US + Canada	585	32

September 30	Coal	Steel
UK + Russia + France	**375**	**17**
Germany + Austria + occupied France	395	26
Germany + Austria + occupied France + Belgium	**420**	**28**
UK + Russia + unoccupied France + US	1005	60

Source: Coal, Iron, and War (Eckel, 1920, pp. 78–80).

of southeastern Ukraine and southwestern Russia.[16] The Donestk region was far from the war front, and "the crippling distances over an insufficient rail system and the main centers of population and industrial production caused an acute coal crisis and nullified any attempts to increase output".[17] Thus, Russia's vast coal reserves were not able to be mobilized during the war to make up for the Central Power's production advantage before Russia withdrew from the war altogether as a result of its 1917 revolution.

North America's strong trading relationship with Britain eventually precipitated German attacks on transatlantic shipping. This brought the United States into the war on the side of the allied powers. When combined with the allied powers this provided 60 Mton/year vs 28 Mton/year Central Power's steel production at 1914 levels, even after the Central Powers' advances in the September of 1914. This precedent would help lead to a provision of the Geneva Convention proscribing the exploitation of an occupied country's resources for the benefit of the occupier. This was widely ignored during much of the 20th century, but came back to fuel controversy over the control of Iraqi oil in 2003.

The coal production totals in Table 6.2 before the entry of the United States into the war make it look like the Central Powers had a slight advantage, particularly in light of the difficulties Russia had making best use of its remotely placed coal fields. However, Germany also had difficulties with coal production, not apparent from the overall totals. Before the war Germany's coastal regions had been supplied by coal imports from Britain. Their replacement by coal from the Ruhr in the west and Silesia in the east put a strain on Germany's already overloaded rail transport system.[18] Thus, effectively available Allied and Central coal production was roughly in balance during most of the war.

In light of the overall imbalance that resulted, it was clearly folly for the Central Powers to take on the powers formally allied against them and the United States as well. However, it was the German command's intention to repeat the success of the war by quickly bringing Paris to its knees. Had this succeeded, which it nearly did, the involvement of the United States would not have entered into the question.

To understand how the Central Powers stumbled into fighting an alliance that included the United States and its vast industrial capacity, it is worth looking in detail into why plans laid down earlier by General von Schieffan failed to take Paris in the first two months of the war. The key to this was delay in reducing the impressive Belgian fortifications at Liège. For this purpose, the German Krupp armament works had produced 98-ton 420-millimeter howitzers. (These were nicknamed *dicke Bertha* after the first name of the Krupp heiress.) After accepting defeat of the city of Liège itself, General Ludendorff called for these cannon to concentrate on raining destruction on the surrounding circle of forts. This was what occurred:

Two days after Lundendorff's desperate order the enormous howitzers were still squatting in Essen, surround by yelping Offiziere and grunting Kruppianer. On the night of August 9–10 they were hoisted, levered, winched, craned, jacked, windlassed, pried, and clawed aboard freight cars, and the rails to Belgium were cleared. The following night they raced across the frontier, but twenty miles beyond that the locomotives came to a grinding halt; the Belgians had blown a tunnel. *The Times* of London reported that the Kaiser's assault on Liège "has been very handsomely beaten," and indeed S.M. *(Seine Majistät Kaiser Wilhelm II)* had gone over to the defensive; everything depended upon the flatulent, tumescent, unlovely but unquestionably deadly fat Berthas.

The demolished tunnel was at Herbesthal, twenty miles from the fortress. The saboteurs had achieved a stunning success. Repairs were impossible, and at midnight offloading began, starting with the yard-long shells. This was worse than Essen, because the engineers lacked heavy moving equipment. Trucks broke down. Uhlan steeds were pressed into service; their harnesses snapped. Since the guns had a range of nine miles, they need to be advanced only eleven, and the roads were good. Nevertheless the backbreaking struggle continued all night and through the next day with a combination of motor vehicles, horses, and detachments of soldiers inching the gun carriages of the Kruppstahl giantesses forward. Late in the afternoon of August 12 one of them was assembled and in position, the brutal black mouth gaping skyward. Its two hundred attendants swarmed over it and then, wearing special padded equipment which protected their vital organs, they huddled on the ground three hundred yards away. At 6:30 P.M. came the command: *"Feuer!"* An electric switch was turned. The Belgian defenders felt a jarring in the earth so alarming that some wondered what hell had risen. A Busy Bertha emerged from the bore's dark mouth, sailed up a mile and, after remaining airborne a full minute, struck its target, Fort Pontisse, dead center. Moments later a spiraling cloud of concrete, steel, and human flesh and bone was boiling a thousand feet overhead.[19]

Krupp's new cannon succeeded in destroying the previously impenetrable forts around Liège. Unfortunately for the German war plan, the delay in transporting the cannon left just enough time for British reinforcements to provide breathing room for Paris to organize its defense. Thus, on the thin thread of the skill of the saboteurs of the tunnel at Herbesthal hung the balance between a quick repeat of the Franco-Prussian War and a long and deadly struggle of nations that would ultimately bring the United States and its vast coal and steel production into the war.

This history helps explain why the Central Powers took the risk of eventually being outgunned by an alliance with superior industrial resources. The question remains why France did not give put utmost importance to the defense of these resources during mobilization. Obviously France was well aware of the importance of overall German economic power in 1914, just as Louis Napoleon had feared the implications of more extensive unification of Germany, forty-five years earlier. Nevertheless, WWI did not start out as an allied attempt to regain the energy resource losses of the Franco-Prussian War (considering here quality iron ores as essentially equivalent to an energy resource), even if that was in fact the eventual outcome. Given this mindset, France was willing to put political considerations ahead of direct military imperatives for controlling production assets.

Despite and perhaps because of the tactical and strategic mistakes on both sides concerning the importance of coal and steel production, WWI cemented into the European consciousness the idea that how energy resources are dealt with is a critical element in the balance between war and peace. Thus, when the dust finally settled on the world wars of the first half of the 20th century, the enclosure of France and Germany in a Coal and Steel Union that would evermore prevent such struggles was on the top of the Western European agenda. Before pursuing this, attention is turned here across the Pacific and onto northern China, whose energy resources would also turn out to pivot a critical chapter in the story of how all of this worked out.

Endnotes

[1] Gottlieb *et al.* (1998).
[2] Gottlieb *et al.* (1998).
[3] Eckel (1920, pp. 41–43).
[4] Stockton (1999).

5 Eckel (1920).
6 Kohn (1999).
7 Kohn (1999, p. 371).
8 Kohn (1999, p. 51).
9 Eckel (1920).
10 Rankin (1998).
11 Eckel (1920, p. 78).
12 Jensen (1968).
13 Roesler (1921).
14 USMA (1986, map 11).
15 Roesler (1921, p. 86).
16 Encyclopedia Britarnica (2006).
17 Jensen (1968).
18 Jensen (1968).
19 Manchester (1968, pp. 319–320).

Chapter 7

Coal in Asia before WWII

From 1405–1433, the Chinese sent out a massive naval fleet for exploration and trade around the rim of nearly all of the Indian Ocean.[1] Thereafter, both China and Japan resisted trade with the outside world until forced to due so under the onslaught of growing 19th century western naval power. By the end of the Opium War II in 1860, Western powers had succeeded in establishing trade rights in China. By 1860 Japan had also emerged from its isolation and had even purchased screw-drive steam warship from the Netherlands and sent it on a mission to the United States.[2]

The US Pacific conquests of the late 19th century and German naval ambitions of the time were connected to rivalry with Britain, Russia, and Japan over whether China would be a free trade area or be divided into exclusionary trading zones. Japan eventually took a direct interest in controlling Manchurian resources and production of industrial materials in addition to providing *Lebensraum* (living space) for its previously chronically, marginally fed population. Coal, as a source of naval propulsion, played a major role in the Pacific up to WWI. However, control of coal resources in Asia was a peripheral issue except insofar as it was subsumed in a broader Japanese quest for territory in Manchuria between WWI and WWII.

Transpacific Cable and US Naval Coal

At the end of the 19th century, the United States was interested in Manila as a transpacific cable terminal and a coaling station, not for the Philippines' coal resources. Accustomed as we are to thinking of global telecommunications as the flowering of something new, it is remarkable to reflect that the Manila terminus of copper cable stretching all the way across the Pacific was already considered to be an important strategic asset at the end of the 19th century. This is one of the primary Pacific assets that Thomas McCormick credits for the US interest in the origins and settlement of the 1898 Spanish-American War.[3] Naval stations and associated coaling depots that were also of course of interest, made all the more valuable through connection with the transpacific cable. However, there is no indication that the 1898 war was over control of Philippine coal deposits. After the United States acquired the Philippines, it sent an Army major there who surveyed its coal resources. A book written on this in 1901 makes it clear that the United States had essentially no idea about these indigenous energy resources before the war.[4] For the US naval operations in the Pacific during the Spanish-American War, the unavailability of local supplies led Commodore Dewey to use the coal that came all the way from Wales.[5]

In the same year the Spanish-American War, coal was discovered in Alaska. In 1903, US President Teddy Roosevelt endorsed a plan to build a coaling station in Alaska's Aleutian islands.[6] This was one of the fifth in a chain of Pacific coast coaling stations stretching back through Sitka, Puget Sound, San Francisco, and San Diego. From 1912 through 1925, the US Navy explored using coal from mainland Alaska for naval propulsion.[7] However, Alaskan coal is not of as high quality as obtainable elsewhere[8] and did not prove attractive for naval propulsion. So, the Alaskan naval coal project never took off, and was abandoned altogether in 1925 under the pressure of naval fleet conversion to oil. As with Britain, for the United States quality for naval use trumped resource location on this decision about where to obtain fuel.

German Naval Pipedreams

Germany also had an interest in projecting naval power in the Pacific before WWI. German Admiralty Chief of Staff Büchsel recommended "direct pressure on the American east cost...a merciless offensive designed to confront the American people with an unbearable situation by the spread of terror and by damaging enemy trade and property," in the case of war with the United States.[9] Germany had plans for attacking US port cities even in the Pacific Northwest, even if the United States with its large iron and coal production became allied with Britain! Admittedly, the French also acted in 1914 as if they did not fully understand the strategic importance of iron and coal production capability. But, German naval planners appear to have been completely "out to lunch" when it comes to the idea of cowering a blooming industrial giant like the United States by shelling coastal cities without any plausible hope of damaging its enormous retaliatory capability.

Some hold that WWI was an inevitable outgrowth of Germany being largely shut out of the colonial game as a latecomer and primarily a land power. Certainly, Germany was concerned about leveraging access to China, and it also took what opportunities it could to establish a presence in Africa as well as the Pacific. However, if making a serious threat of a land war in Europe to gain a larger share of the global colonial power was really its goal, then Germany does not seem to have communicated this effectively. Neither did Germany have a serious chance of success against Britain in the colonial arena by threatening countries on the continent rather than Britain directly.

Germany's Kaiser Wilhelm II acceded to the throne at the comparatively early age of 29 upon the death of his grandfather and father in 1888. The young monarch was much taken with the military trappings of his position, dressing in uniform and spending time with military officers. In 1890 the new Kaiser dismissed his grandfather's long-serving Chancellor Otto von Bismark. The German monarchy never again had a comparably strong and sober balancing influence on foreign policy. Wilhelm II was at the minimum committed to the idea of enhancing German prestige. He also undoubtedly wanted to avoid allowing the balance of power to be upset by the certain defeat that Franz-Josef would face by single-handedly taking on the triple alliance of Britain, France, and Russia. As an older man he did not embrace the rush into WWI as earnestly as some of his military command, but his early approach to foreign and military policy had already set the stage. Neither was the Social Democratic majority in the German legislature and effective balancing force, even though its cooperation was needed to authorize war funding. Having gradually emerged from an earlier marginalized legal status, the Social Democrats wanted to be viewed as supportive of monarch and country, even if this meant cooperating with the execution of a war of which some of them were skeptical.[10]

Based in part on its plans for global naval reach, there has been endless discussion on whether Germany stumbled into WWI or simply took the earliest opportunity to execute the Schlieffan plan. This was a plan for marching through neutral Belgium as discussed in the previous chapter — a plan that the German high command had had on the shelf for over a decade. Whether the war was a deliberate or more accidental miscalculation by Germany is of little importance, for here, the primary concern is international struggle over energy resources. Even if Germany welcomed war with the hope of leveraging a broader colonial role out of European battlefield advantage, this was not to import energy resources from overseas. Indigenous colonial coalfields potentially acquirable by Germany were not suitable for this in terms of the quality of the resources for steamer coal. Neither was the internal transport necessary to get industrial coal to market cost-effective to develop abroad, nor the overseas shipping costs to Germany remotely competitive with domestic coal production costs in any case. As for oil, even the conversion of the British fleet was just starting at the onset of the war. With Germany lagging behind in naval use of oil, it seems highly unlikely that Germany's long preparation and eventual decision to engage the war was based on a prescient understanding of the future importance of this newer non-domestic energy resource.

Given its battle plans and their execution, it is quite possible that Germany well understood, ahead of and during the war, the strategic importance of *European* energy resources. However, the Central Powers' resources were already comparable to the allies they faced, and those Germany were completely adequate for its own industrial development. The only reason they might have been inadequate is if the European allied powers had used their own initially very marginally larger resources to attack and defeat Germany. But, as evidenced by the behavior particularly of the French at the onset of the war, this appears to have been the farthest thing from their minds. Thus, for Germany to launch a war over European energy resources alone was absurd. No war over energy was necessary in the absence of war in the first place; so, the sensible energy-oriented policy was simply to sit tight. In any case, Germany's role in Asia was very marginal. Rather, it was the emergence of Japan as a major force in Asia at the beginning of the 20th century that would be most important in East Asia.

Manchuria

While Germany had control of massive indigenous coal and iron resources after 1871, the same cannot be said of Japan. By 1905, however, Japan had occupied Manchuria in Northern China and had control of the very considerable energy resources there. The sequence of events leading to this outcome can be traced back to the Sino-Japanese War of 1894–1895. Japan and China intervened in 1894 to suppress a revolt against the Korean monarchy and stayed on to fight each other. This led to the defeat of China and the transfer to Japan of Taiwan (under the name Formosa). As a result of military victories in the 1904–1905 war with Russia over "special interests and economic privileges in Manchuria and Korea",[11] Japan occupied Korea and much of Manchuria. This led to conversion of Manchuria to a puppet state called Manchoukuo.

The Japanese interest in Manchuria had not only to do with iron and steel, but also with the broader question of trading rights — and perhaps also the question of *Lebensraum* that will be taken up later when dealing with Germany's precipitation of WWII. We now know that the Japanese entry into Manchuria eventually drew it into a maelstrom that ended in total defeat, just as the German Kaiser's military adventure in Europe sowed the seeds of an even greater disaster for Germany than the Great War. Eventually, the control of coal and iron resources would virtually vanish as a significant factor in international warfare, but only after the question of how it would be dealt with had played an important role in triggering a complete transformation of the governance of Europe.

Endnotes

[1]   Viviano (2005).
[2]   Warinner (1963).
[3]   McCormick (1963).
[4]   Becker (1901).
[5]   McSherry (2003).
[6]   *New York Times* (1903).
[7]   Merritt (1986).
[8]   Yanity (2006).
[9]   Overlack (1998).
[10] Schorske (1955).
[11] Kohn (1999, p. 414).

Chapter 8

Coal, Steel, Customs, and the EU

The European Coal and Steel Community was the harbinger of the European Community and European Union. These institutions durably put to rest a long history of violent competition amongst their members. This finally ended military struggles between the eventual EU member states over the distribution of Western Europe's land, trade, and originally coal-driven industrial production. This history is of interest because one of the central questions on a more global basis for the first half of the 21st century is whether a mechanism can also be found for eliminating violent international conflict connected to oil.

Prelude to the European Coal and Steel Community

In September 1944, the US design adopted for dealing with the German economy after the war was the so-called Morgenthau plan, named after Roosevelt's Secretary of the Treasury:

> His proposal was un-blurred by ambiguity: What it demanded was quite literally the dynamiting of all factories and the flooding of all mines. Nothing was to be left standing or rebuilt. As Morgenthau saw it, no choice remained but to restore the economic conditions of 1860. Protestations that thirty million fewer Geremans *(sic)* had lived at the time left him unmoved. Nor was he touched by the spectacle of their being doomed indefinitely to a soup-kitchen existence, troubled by the high costs his plan would inflict upon the United States and United Kingdom, or even particularly concerned

that without the Ruhr Europe would be condemned to endure another decade or two of depression.[1]

Although it remained official policy while Roosevelt was alive, the Morgenthau plan was never actually implemented. This is attributed to the opposition of Roosevelt's Secretary of War, Henry Stimson. In the end, the Russians stripped their sector in eastern Germany of factory equipment, but only the British made even much of an attempt at this in the western occupation zones. Moreover, a serious attempt at breaking up the previous German cartel companies into much smaller units was almost completely blocked despite James Martin's 1946–1947 efforts as the chief of the US Decartelization Branch. The decartelization plan and its leader had fallen victim to red scares in the United States by May 1947. The Morgenthau approach was killed off by concerns about the potential of the severe European winter of 1946–1947 for stirring social unrest in Germany. By June 1947, several hundred million dollars in aid had already gone to Germany. As a result of the shift of mindset precipitated by the events in 1947, by April 1948 the Marshall Plan agency was set up. Gillingham explains this as follows:

> Its origins date from winter of 1946–1947, the worst in a century. From December to the end of March chilling winds, hard freezes, and repeated heavy snowfalls brought rail and barge traffic to a standstill and production to a halt for whole weeks at time in much of northern and western Europe. The war, it seemed, had done more damage than previously suspected; recovery was perilously fragile, living standards in jeopardy, and the possibility imminent that Europe would be plunged into revolutionary chaos...[2]

As it turned out, however, the absence of capital investment during the war in France had helped leave it in worse shape to rebuild its industry than heavily bombed and defeated Germany. This gave Germany increasing economic leverage, even as the proto-government led by Konrad Andenauer chafed under the formal restrictions of the occupation. In the end, the Germans agreed in principle to an unprecedented change in trade relationships for coal and steel in order to be able to launch the new Federal Republic of Germany in the western sectors. The new trade relationship was to be embodied in the European Coal and Steel Community (ECSC). The news was broken to the French by their foreign minister:

> On 9 May 1950, Foreign Minister Robert Schuman interrupted the regularly scheduled broadcasts of French radio to make a historic announcement: In order to end the decades-long-struggle over coal and steel, France was ready to become partners with its recent enemy, and other nations, in a new West European heavy industry community organized in such a way as to make war politically unthinkable and economically impossible. Little more than a month later negotiations for the coal–steel pool began. Joined by the three Benelux countries in addition to France and Germany, they would end eleven months later with the Treaty of Paris by the foreign ministers of "The Six" on 18 April 1951...[3]

From ECSC to the EU Enlargement of 2007

The ECSC treaty entered into force for a fifty-year period in 1952. In fact the ECSC never functioned as a fully effective customs union in the way that had been envisioned in May 1950. Nevertheless, it broke the ice on an evolution from a limited-scope customs union with six members in 1952 to the broader-scope European Community. The ECSC members in 1957 were Belgium, France, Germany, Italy, Luxembourg, and the Netherlands (Fig. 8.1). The European Community instruments were signed in 1957 and entered into force on January 1, 1958. Norway and Switzerland held out, but seven European Free Trade Association (EFTA) countries joined the European Union in stages after the resignation of French president De Gaulle in 1969 allowed the enlargement process to start in 1973. By the time that the ECSC had been transformed to the European Economic Community (EEC) in 1973, Denmark, Ireland, and the United Kingdom had been brought in. By 1981 it was called the

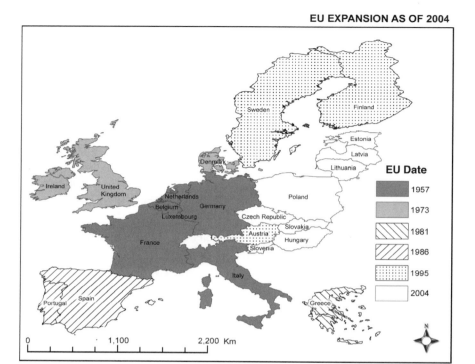

Fig. 8.1.   From the 1957 ECSC to the 2004 EU.

European Community (EC) and also included Greece. In 1986, the EC added Spain and Portugal.

By 1995 the European Union (EU) had been formed, and the end of the cold war allowed the inclusion of its formally neutral new states, Austria, Finland, and Sweden. In 2002 France's President Chirac and Germany's Chancellor Schröder agreed on a critical revision of EU common agricultural policy and eliminated the final major economic barrier to the March 2004 entry of about 70 million more people into the EU. Most of these came from countries that had been behind "iron curtain" during the cold war. The 2004 expansion of the EU included Cyprus, the Czech Republic, Estonia, Hungary, Latvia, Lithuania, Poland, Slovakia, and Slovenia.[4] At the beginning of 2007, Romania and Bulgaria joined as well. This brought the EU to the 27-member countries envisioned under the Treaty of Nice, which entered into force in 2003.[5] Croatia and the former Yugoslav Republic of Macedonia were formal candidates for admission as of 2006. This could occur within the framework of the Lisbon Treaty if its 2007 text is eventually approved by all of the EU members despite the setback of its narrow defeat in an Irish referendum in June of 2008.[6]

Entry of Turkey into the EU could eventually have significant ramifications for the future politics of oil. This would bring the EU up to the border of Iraq. It would give Kurds in Turkey access to the European Court system and make the poorer Kurdish majority regions in Eastern Turkey eligible for economic development assistance within the EU. All of this would probably significantly change the dynamics of the ongoing tension between Turkey and Iraq over the Kurdish question. However, there is considerable resistance within some member states to the joining of Turkey with the EU. If this does in fact happen, it is likely to be a long time in coming.

The ECSC was not only a customs union. Its institutional structures formed the prototype and nucleus for the European Community (EC) and European Union (EU). After its expiration in 2002, the assets of ECSC were transferred to the EU to continue supporting steel and coal research and development.[7] Coal and iron had long played a large role in domestic strife, and the ECSC also strove to deal with this problem after WWII. Chronic worker indebtedness in company towns, harsh and dangerous working conditions, periods of declining wages, strikes, and violence had plagued the coal and steel industries for over a century. The ECSC strove to implement mechanisms that would mitigate the impact of labor force downsizing on workers while keeping the industries internationally competitive. For the steel industry in the member countries, this appears to have been quite successful. The coal industry in Europe has had a rougher ride, but downsizing has been accomplished without large-scale casualties from internal violence.

An interesting question is whether the success that Europe had in dealing with the historically contentious issue of solid mineral resources can be emulated in the future to any degree for oil, natural gas, or both. Toward the end of the Clinton administration there were hints that this might be possible. At that time the US Secretary of Defense toured members of the resurgent Organization for Petroleum Exporting Countries (OPEC) and elicited an understanding that the United States and OPEC might cooperate to keep oil prices within a band around $25/barrel. This was well over what would result from unconstrained competition, but below the prices of $30/barrel or more that have since been reached during times of especial market uncertainty. By 2003 OPEC had established a target price range of $22–28/barrel,[8] but difficulties with production in Iraq, Venezuela, and Nigeria[9] relieved other OPEC countries of the discipline[10] on production levels needed to keep prices up. Since the major oil consumers still lacked an effective mechanism for negotiating production or prices with OPEC, there was still question about the long-term stability of oil prices once pressing problems were dealt with in OPEC's most troubled member, Iraq. This question and its possible broader international political and security implications will be taken up in Part V of this book.

Endnotes

[1]   Gillingham (1991, p. 101).
[2]   Gillingham (1991, pp. 115–116).
[3]   Gillingham (1991, p. 228).
[4]   CNN (2003).
[5]   Secretary-General (2001).
[6]   Lyall and Castle (2008).
[7]   c.f. European Commission Delegation to Australia and New Zealand (2002a,b).
[8]   Romero (2003a).
[9]   Fleischer (2003); AP (2003); Sengupta and Banerjee (2003); Sengupta (2003b).
[10]   Adelman (1995).

Chapter 9

Conflict over other Solid Mineral Resources

Coal and iron are not the only mined resources that have played important roles in internal or international conflict. A long history of conflict over other mineral resources has led some to conclude that such struggles are endemic to the nation–state system. To frame the previous discussions of gold, silver, iron, and coal in a broader context, this chapter has a survey of conflicts over other solid mineral resources. An exception is uranium which, as an energy resource, is taken up later. Here the focus is on international war, but some internal conflicts had effects that spilled over across international borders. The basic question here is whether international wars, where control over solid mineral resources play a major role, are a thing of the past. The conclusion will be that they are, qualified by the caveat that provincial revolts aimed at reaping benefits from regional mines still have potential for receiving outside support that leads to international military conflict. This is still possible in principle. However, there are no clear cases where this appears likely to happen in the readily foreseeable future.

In the post-Napoleonic era, nitrate resources stimulated international conflict in the 19th century. Later, phosphates and copper played roles in internal conflicts, sometimes with outside interference. Recently, conflict over diamonds has played a role in wars that have inflicted much misery in Africa. However, coal and oil played much larger roles in 20th century conflict than did solid non-fossil minerals. By the middle of the first decade of the 21st century, residual international disputes over control of solid non-fossil minerals played a minor role compared to that of oil.

Seven different arenas involving non-fossil minerals are examined here: (1) The role of nitrate deposits in the 1879–1884 War of the Pacific between Chile and Bolivia. (2) The role of phosphates relevant in the Polisario's struggle for independence from Morocco in the Western Sahara. (3) How control of copper mines affected the governance of Chile and the Bougainville island's push for independence from Papua New Guinea. (4) US government policy in the 1990s concerning strategic stockpiling of non-carbon minerals. (5) Conflict over diamond resources in Africa. (6) The effect of the 1999–2000 tantalum market price spike on the Congo. (7) Whether a policy aimed at reducing conflict over oil could lead to conflict over South African platinum reserves.

Nitrates and the War of the Pacific

The history of nitrates along the South American Pacific coast is a classic example of how a natural resource can both transform the economy of a country and lead it into disastrous international conflict.[1] The backdrop for this is the breakup of the Peru–Bolivia confederation in 1839 after three years of war over trade issues that involved Argentina and Chile. Peru bounced back with an economic boom. This boom was based on the depletion from the 1840s to the 1870s of over $600 million at then-current prices of nitrogen-rich off-shore island bird droppings that had accumulated over millennia. However, in the 1860s and 1870s, Peru borrowed heavily to finance railroad expansion and then was left a burdensome debt service when the island guano deposits were exhausted. When Peru then turned to nitrate deposits in the south, it got caught up in a long-standing competition between Chile and Bolivia over access to mineral deposits around the coastal city of Antofagasta. In the ensuing 1879–1884 War of the Pacific, Chile captured the Peruvian capital.[2] Chile forced Bolivia to cede its Antogasta province and Peru to give up the nitrate-rich Atacama desert farther north (up to about 19° south latitude). Chile also occupied areas even farther north around the cities of Arica and Tacna and promised a plebiscite on their fates. The plebiscite was never held, but finally in 1929 an agreement settled the dispute by

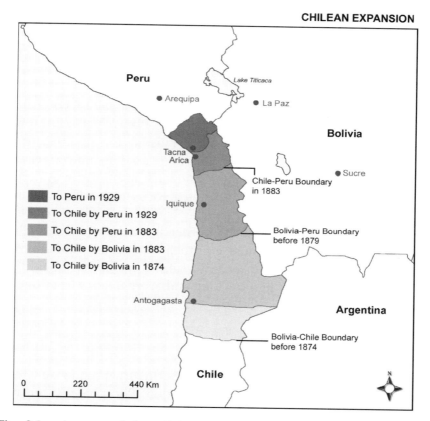

Fig. 9.1. Areas awarded to Chile at various times, and area awarded to Peru in 1929.

giving the coastal city of Arica and the area south of it to Chile, and the area north of Arica to Peru (see Fig. 9.1). The current border runs just north of Arica as it traces northeast from the coast toward Lake Titicaca in the Andes.

"Between 1819 and 1900, the export of nitrates from Chile increased from 125,000 tons to almost 1,250,000 tons".[3] Then an electric discharge process was commercialized for fixing nitrogen from air using hydroelectricity on a useful scale in 1905.[4] In 1909 this was done using the 1909 Haber process to react nitrogen with hydrogen at high pressure and temperature.[5] These alternatives put a ceiling on the value of these depleting deposits. In this sense, nitrates became an energy-equivalent resource, first directly in terms of electrical power and then indirectly in terms of the energy used to produce the hydrogen used in the Haber process to make ammonia.

As discussed in Chap. 2, metals had precipitated conflict in South America much earlier. This included Pizarro's 1532 duplicitous coup of obtaining a huge gold ransom for the Inca ruler Atahuallpa and then killing him. However, gold and silver eventually ceased to be a cause of international wars in Latin America. Similarly, nitrogen came and went as a focus of warfare in Latin America, albeit with considerable delay between the climax in 1873 of the War of the Pacific and the border settlement between Chile and Peru in 1929. So it must eventually be for all economically important deposits that are readily available in limited quantities, the primary question being how long and at what cost the struggles over them continue.

Phosphates

Phosphate is extracted from the ground rather than requiring a high energy input like industrial nitrogen fixation. Phosphate is thus not directly equivalent to a fossil energy source. There is some connection between phosphate and energy sources in that uranium production is sometimes a byproduct of processing phosphate ore, but this has not been done on a large enough scale to itself provoke disputes over access to phosphate resources. While the connection between phosphates and energy is more tenuous than between nitrates and energy, a discussion of phosphates is included here to begin rounding out a general examination of solid mineral resources and conflict. The focus of this discussion is the proposed state of Western Sahara, shown in Fig. 9.2.

The population of Western Sahara is listed as 382,617,[6] its area as 266,000 square kilometers, and its recent exports as 62% phosphates.[7] Other products are fruits and vegetables grown in the few oases, and camels, sheep, and goats kept by nomads. Morocco as a whole,

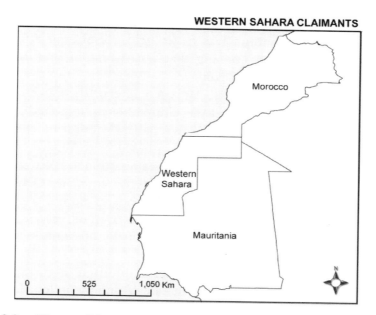

WESTERN SAHARA CLAIMANTS

Fig. 9.2. Western Sahara and its former and current claimants, Mauritania and Morocco.

including the Western Sahara region it controls, exported 21.5 million metric tonnes (Mt) of phosphate for $431 million in the year 2000, of which an "amount estimated to be 1.5Mt" came from Western Sahara.[8] Estimating the Western Saharan portion of gross phosphate sales revenues to be proportional to its production, this amounts to $30 million or just over $100 per capita of Western Sahara's population.

In the course of the 1976–1991 Spanish Saharan War, Morocco seized the southern third of the former Spanish Sahara in the Western Sahara from Mauritania.[9] When Mauritania abandoned sovereignty claims in a 1980 treaty with the Western-Sahara's pro-independence Polisario Front, the Western Sahara conflict formally ceased to be a struggle between two nations from Morocco's point of view. The Polisario Front in the region was recognized by 1981 by more than forty nations and fought a war for independence from Morocco. "In 1991, the war was suspended after an agreement between Morocco and the Polisario to hold a UN-supervised referendum." The referendum was never held, despite an attempt in 1998 to get settlement moving that was mediated by former US Secretary of State, James Baker.

After September 11, 2001, Morocco agreed to cooperate in the struggle against al Qaeda, and the United States suggested an alternative with autonomy for the Western Sahara without independence from Morocco. Also in 2001, the US-based Kerr-McGee company signed a contract for oil and natural gas exploration in Western Sahara territorial waters with the Moroccan state oil company ONAREP.[10] The issue of control of revenues from phosphates did not reignite the conflict from 1991 to 2001, but control over oil resources then started to cast a shadow over resolution of the question of Western Saharan sovereignty.

In June of 2001, James Baker submitted a "Framework Agreement" calling for Western Saharan autonomy under Moroccan sovereignty. This was rejected by the Polisario and Algeria in 2003. Then the United Nations adopted a resolution called for a five-year transition period of semi-autonomy for Western Sahara. This was to be followed by a referendum on whether to extend this arrangement or opt for independence or integration with Morocco. "Polisario signalled its readiness to accept, but Morocco rejected the plan, citing security concerns. Envoy James Baker resigned in June 2004 and the UN process remained deadlocked".[11] "The Security Council passed Resolution 1720 in October 2006 reaffirming commitment to self-determination but stopped short of coercing Morocco to grant independence. In February 2007, Morocco advised France, the United States, Spain, and Great Britain on its plan for autonomy and submitted a written proposal to the Security Council in April 2007. UN-mediated talks outside of New York during the summer 2007 ended inconclusively, with Polisario rejecting any solution short of a referendum for independence".[12] Thus, the situation remained deadlocked. The UN Security Council was formally committed to Western Saharan self-determination but unwilling to take actions that might force Morocco to allow this.

Copper, Counterrevolution, and Secessionists

George Kohn's *Dictionary of Wars* entry on the Chilean Revolution of 1973 notes how the US Central Intelligence Agency reportedly helped plan and finance a plot that overthrew the elected Salvadore Allende government after Chile nationalized copper mines.[13] Concerning copper mining elsewhere, Mark Graffis provided an update on a nine-year conflict over control of the Papau New Guinea Island of Bougainville, which he says was "sparked by a dispute over royalties from the rich Panguna copper mine owned by Australian mining giant RTZ-CRA".[14] Although politically significant and both having international overtones involving the United States and Australia, respectively, these Chile and Bougainville cases are both classifiable as internal struggles. Thus, they are not part of the subject of primary interest here, even though the demand for copper is driven in significant measure by its use for electrical energy transmission.

Copper (and diamonds) also played a role in various conflicts over Congo.[a] The Congo conflict is a complex topic that is taken up below in connection with diamonds, the mineral tantalum, and also French policies in Africa.

Other Non-Carbon Minerals

During the cold war, the United States stockpiled the minerals shown in Table 9.1.[15] It also maintained stocks of copper, industrial diamonds, gold, and minor amounts of a few other minerals.

The principles behind the US stockpiling program are defined in a comprehensive 1979 Revision of the Strategic and Critical Materials Stockpiling Act, Public Law 96–41.[16]

(1) The purpose of the National Defense Stockpile is to serve the interest of national defense only. The National Defense Stockpile is not to be used for economic or budgetary purposes.

---

[a] "Congo" is used throughout here for simplicity for all incarnations of the country containing the territory formerly called Zaire and later the Democratic Republic of Congo; see Edgerton (2002).

Table 9.1.   US Government "strategic" mineral stockpiles.

Material	Units	Uncommitted		Committed	Total	Cost and Value in 2002	
		1996	2002	2002	2006	Unit cost	Value (M$)
Antimony	ktonne	28	3	1	0	$3/kg	80
Bauxite	Mtonne	16	2	7	0	$21/tonne	300
Chromium	ktonne	8	0	7	0.3	$6/kg	50
Cobalt	ktonne	20	7	0.2	1	$15/kg	300
Fluorspar	ktonne	545	7	109	18	$500/tonne	300
Germanium	tonne	68	42	0	24	$1/g	60
Iodine	ktonne	2	2	0	0.5	$13/kg	30
Iridium	kg	900	800	0	123	$24/g	20
Mica	ktonne	2	3	0.1	0	$50/kg	100
Palladium	tonne	39	7	0.2	1	$11/g	400
Platinum	tonne	14	0.6	0	3	$18/g	200
Quartz	tonne	237	105	0	7	$600/kg	140
Silver	ktonne	1	0	0	0	$145/g	100
Talc	Mtonne	2	2	0	0.002	$110/tonne	200
Tantalum	ktonne	1	1	0	0.1	$66/kg	90
Tin	ktonne	130	45	8	9	$7/kg	900
Titanium	ktonne	24	15	1	0	$8/kg	200
Zinc	tonne	300	100	0	13	$88/kg	20

Source: Mineral commodity summaries (Cunningham, 2004).

(2) The quantities of materials stockpiled under this act should be sufficient to sustain the United States for a period of not less than 3 years during a national emergency that would necessitate total mobilization of the economy of the United States *for a sustained conventional global war* of indefinite duration (emphasis added).

Minor amendments in 1987 left these basic principles intact. In the use of the term "conventional" war, these principles implicitly acknowledge the existence of nuclear weapons. What the legislation ignores is that well before 1979 nuclear weapons holdings had made it completely implausible that there would be a "total mobilization of the economy of the United States for a sustained conventional global war" for three years or more. In the 1970s, NATO and the opposing Warsaw Pact nominally still sized their conventional forces as if an all-out conventional war between them were plausible, despite the enormously larger firepower that had been built up in their nuclear arsenals. In practice Soviet forces were more likely sized to make it obvious that armed rebellion in Eastern Europe was hopeless, while other Warsaw Pact forces had equipment, command and control apportioned to make them useless for revolt. Moreover, after 1973, US forces were reconfigured for large-scale intervention in the Persian Gulf region, with support as needed from bases in Europe. As it turned out Iraq had effectively lost Soviet backing by 1990, so the full might of NATO forces was not used for the intense fighting phase of either of the two Gulf Wars. Nevertheless, this was their most likely large-scale use in practice from the mid-1970s through the First Gulf War. Preparing for war with the Soviets in Europe remained in principle the main focus of US troops stationed in NATO allies. In practice, for much of the cold war, their only likely practical full scale use was for possible support for operations in the Persian Gulf area.

The language in the Strategic and Critical Materials Stockpiling Act, on preparing for supply interdiction during an extended conventional global war during the 1980s, is a graphic illustration of how the mindset of current leaders can be stuck back in the operational experience of a previous generation. It was in fact completely implausible that during a major war in 1980s the Soviet Union would have interdicted for over three years' supply of any minerals that were chosen for stockpiling. In any case, after the cold war it was soon realized that sources were adequately diversified and industrial substitutes so widely available that no significant "strategic" stocks of these minerals were needed. So by 1994 they were already being sold off, albeit mostly at a relatively low rate to avoid overly perturbing markets. Since the sell-off proceeded at a modest pace, readily available stockpile amounts for 1996 listed in Table 9.1 give a reasonable feel for the scale of the various stockpiles that were maintained through the cold war.

A rough idea of how much some of the 1996 stocks might have been worth if they had been held until 2002 can be obtained by multiplying 2002 prices by the 1996 stocks for each mineral. For this purpose Table 9.1 uses the larger available price for a few cases where more than one form of the material has a different price. Also, some of the material remaining in the stocks was of lower than maximum grade. Thus, the resulting numbers are rough and generally a maximum limit. They are correspondingly only listed to one significant figure (in millions of dollars). These figures nevertheless make the point that the overall economic value was very small compared to gross national product, to the value of oil imports for a single year, or to the cost of launching a major international war.

There are a few minerals, such as chromium, which were held in US government stockpiles in other forms than those included in Table 9.1. The value of these is at most comparable to the forms shown and thus does not change the basic picture. By 2002, most of the US stockpile holdings for the minerals listed in Table 9.1 had been sold off, and the remaining committed holdings were minor. By 2006 the liquidation of most of these stockpiles was still in process but almost complete.

Several materials that have been directly or indirectly related to conflict are not included in Table 9.1. One of them is copper, which has been cleared from the stockpile. Another is gold. This is held in national treasuries as a holdover from the time when it was widely used as a monetary standard. However, gold is of increasingly marginal importance as a currency reserve. Government gold reserves have been gradually released to private holders, taking care not to collapse the market by dumping large amounts at once.

In view of the fact that no significant tantalum mining has occurred in the United States since 1959 and the market instabilities described below in the section on "coltan," the United States was still stockpiling tantalum in 2003. "To ensure supplies of tantalum during an emergency, various tantalum materials have been purchased for the National Defense Stockpile (NDS). At year-end 2003, the NDS tantalum inventory consisted of about 628 tons of tantalum contained in tantalum materials valued at about $34 million, all of which was authorized for sale by the Defense Logistics Agency".

Industrial diamonds were still stockpiled in modest amounts after most other "strategic" mineral stocks were cleared. However, it is primarily gem diamonds, rather than industrial diamonds, that have been important in recent conflicts.

The US government has sold off most of its mineral stocks despite the fact that the country relies on imports of many minerals for the majority of the country's consumption. Table 9.2 gives a list of minerals that are at least 70 percent imported, along with the principle countries where the imports come from.[17]

The drawdown of many of these heavily imported materials from the US government stockpiles resulted from a decision to treat them simply as commodities, not strategic commodities. Since the markets for many minerals are very volatile, this deprived the government of an opportunity to try to dampen market fluctuations by selling off stocks only when prices are high and then replenishing them when prices are low. For better or worse, such an approach was incompatible with US government policy. The point was that neither military nor economic considerations any longer convinced US policymakers that heavily imported materials widely used in both the military and civilian sectors need to be viewed as strategic materials.

Conflict Diamonds

Setting aside the question of control of existing copper mines in Congo, diamond is the solid mineral resource which has most recently played a dominant role in some conflicts with international overtones. The struggle over control of diamond production areas in Angola eventually devolved primarily an internal conflict. However, the broader struggle over Angola involved Portugal, Cuba, the Soviet Union, and South Africa from the 1961–1974 Angolan War of Independence to the Angolan Civil War of 1975–2002. The Sierra Leonean Civil War of 1991–2002 also involved a struggle over control of diamond production and had impacts that spilled over into neighboring countries.[18]

The "Kimberley Process" establishes an international mechanism to try ensure that violent exploitation of diamond miners does not continue to fuel conflict. The process itself "requires that each shipment of rough diamonds being exported, and crossing an international border, be transported in a tamper-resistant container and accompanied by a government-validated Kimberley Process

Table 9.2.   Net US import reliance for selected nonfuel minerals.

Commodity	% Imported	Major sources (2002–2005)
Arsenic (trioxide)	100	China, Morocco, Mexico, Chile
Asbestos	100	Canada
Bauxite and alumina	100	Jamaica, Guinea, Australia, Brazil
Columbium (niobium)	100	Brazil, Canada, Estonia, Germany
Fluorospar	100	China, Mexico, South Africa, Mongolia
Graphite (natural)	100	China, Mexico, Canada, Brazil
Indium	100	China, Canada, Russia, Japan
Manganese	100	South Africa, Gabon, Australia, China
Mica, sheet (natural)	100	India, Belgium, China, Brazil
Quartz crystals (industrial)	100	Brazil, Germany, Madagascar, Canada
Rare earths	100	China, France, Japan, Russia
Rubidium	100	Canada
Strontium	100	Mexico, Germany
Thallium	100	Russia, Belgium
Thorium	100	France
Vanadium	100	Czech Republic, Switzerland, Canada, Austria
Yttritum	100	China, Japan, France, Austria
Gallium	99	China, Japan, Ukraine, Russia
Gemstones	99	Israel, India, Belgium, South Africa
Bismuth	96	Belgium, Mexico, China, UK
Platinum	95	South Africa, UK, Germany, Canada
Stone (dimension)	89	Italy, Turkey, China, Mexico
Antimony	88	China, Mexico, Belgium
Rhenium	87	Chile, Germany
Tantalum	83	Australia, Canada, China, Japan
Barite	82	China, India
Diamond (natural industrial)	81	Ireland, Botswana, Ghana, Belgium
Palladium	80	Russia, South Africa, UK, Belgium
Cobalt	79	Norway, Russia, Finland, Canada
Potash	75	Canada, Belarus, Russia, Germany
Tin	79	Peru, Bolivia, China, Indonesia
Chromium	75	South Africa, Kazakhstan, Zimbabwe, Russia
Titanium (sponge)	72	Kazakhstan, Japan, Russia
Titanium concentrates	71	South Africa, Australia, Canada, Ukraine

Source: USGS (2007).

Certificate".[19] Under this system "all buyers and sellers of both rough and polished diamonds must make the following affirmative statement on all invoices:"

> The diamonds herein invoiced have been purchased from legitimate sources not involved in funding conflict and in compliance with United Nations resolutions. The seller hereby guarantees that these diamonds are conflict free, based on personal knowledge and/or written guarantees provided by the supplier of these diamonds.[20]

As recent as the beginning of 2003, it appeared that the Kimberley process was facing an uphill battle against the strong financial incentives that exist for harvesting and smuggling diamonds out of conflict areas. As of December July 31, 2003, not included in the Kimberley Process were diamond producers Ghana and Guinea, Liberia, and Sierra Leone.[21] Liberia and Sierra Leone had been involved in serious conflict with international overtones where diamond production was a significant factor. However, three African diamond-producing states had recently met, at least, the minimum standards of the Kimberley Process Certification Scheme: Central Africa Republic, Tanzania, and Zimbabwe.

Diamond producers were not the only early holdouts. Belgium, which has the world's traditionally leading diamond-processing center in Antwerp, was also not a formal participant in the Kimberley process as of the beginning of 2003. According to Belgian Minister of Foreign Affairs Louis Michel, "The Kimberley system was based largely on the Belgian diamond certification system which aims to keep so-called 'blood diamonds' out of the lawful diamond trade."[22] However, at the time of this statement Belgium evidently still had concerns about the possibility of Antwerp being put at a competitive disadvantage under the formal restrictions of the Kimberley Process.

By March 2006, however, the European Commission (EC) had agreed to spearhead the Kimberley Process Certification Scheme (KPCS) and was reporting considerable progress from a review of the process. To a questionnaire requesting a response by January 31 of that year, the EC noted that 69 countries were participating in the

Kimberley Process (KP). These included Belgium as well as the Central African Republic, Ghana, Guinea, Liberia, Namibia, Sierra Leone, Tanzania, and Zimbabwe, and the Democratic Republic of the Congo (DRC).

> The EC strongly believes that the findings of review visits carried out in the peer review system of the KP provide substantial evidence that the KPCS has had a very positive impact in countries affected by conflict diamonds, and has dramatically reduced the incidence of illicit production and trade. This is further borne out by the dramatic increase in the proportion of trade and production carried out through legal channels in countries such as the DRC or Sierra Leone...[23]

In 2007, the Kimberley Process showed signs of maturing into a durable feature of the international landscape. By then there had been formal visits under the Kimberley Process auspices to the majority of the participants in the process. Those labeled as "progressing" in Table 9.3 received generally favorable reports, in most cases with some recommendations for improvement.[24] Botswana and Brazil were particularly singled out as exemplary participants. A few countries, such as Tanzania, were cooperating well at an official level but had small scale artisan level diamond industries not fully covered by their formal procedures.

The major Kimberley Process problem cases were in coastal countries of West and Central Africa. Côte d'Ivoire (Ivory Coast) was banned from the international diamond trade in 2005 under UN Security Council Resolution 1643 in connection with the ongoing internal struggle there. Côte d'Ivoire was only beginning, in 2007, to recover from this upheaval. Many of the major concerns expressed by visits to countries with otherwise satisfactory Kimberley Process compliance involved transit of diamonds originating in Côte d'Ivoire, particularly via Ghana.

Following the end of the Sierre Leone's civil war, that country was admitted as a participant in the Kimberley process in 2007. Liberia

Table 9.3. Kimberley process participants.

No Visit	Progressing	Problematic
Angola	Australia (2007)	Central African Rep. (2003)
Armenia	Botswana (2004)	Congo Dem. Rep. (2007)
Bangladesh	Brazil (2005)	Côte D'Ivoire (2005)
Belarus	Canada (2004)	Guinea (2005)
Croatia	EU (2004)	Liberia (2007)
Germany	Ghana (2007)	Sierre Leone
Indonesia	Guyana (2007)	
Laos	India (2004)	
Namibia	Israel (2994)	
New Zealand	Republic of Korea (2006)	
Norway	Lebanon (2006)	
Thailand	Malaysia (2006)	
Turkey	Mauritius (2004)	
Ukraine	Russian Federation (2005)	
Venezuela	Singapore (2006)	
	South Africa (2004)	
	Sri Lanka	
	Switzerland (2004)	
	Tanzania (2006)	
	Mauritius	
	Togo (2005)	
	United Arab Emirates (2004)	
	USA (2005)	
	Vietnam (2006)	
	Zimbabwe (2004	

Source: Kimberley Process (2007).

was also admitted to the Kimberley Process in 2007. Problems in the Congo precipitated a temporary expulsion in 2007.

The Kimberley process appears to have been taken more seriously by the international community than early skeptics expected it to be. While inevitably, not completely, leak proof, it focuses attention on the problem of conflict diamonds and creates incentive for countries to be certified as cooperating participants. There were other reasons that the series of conflicts along the southern cost of West Africa began to stabilize and stop spilling over into adjacent countries recently. However, the Kimberley Process can be expected to play a part in discouraging revenue from conflict diamonds fueling a resurgence of violence.

Coltan

In the year 2000, there was a brief large spike in the price of the tantalum for use in cell phones and other electronic equipment. Then technology innovations and market slowdown quieted demand. Tantalum can be obtained from columbo-tantalite, a mixture of minerals containing the elements niobium and tantalum. As for surface outcrops of diamonds and the "placer deposits" the early 1849 US prospectors panned for gold, for a brief period profits well over prevailing wages could be briefly obtained from coltan in central Africa with small scale and low technology methods.

> The industry term columbo-tantalite has been shortened to 'coltan' in central Africa. There, the dense tantalite sand forms placer deposits that can be mined with pans and sluices little different from the low-tech devices used by the Forty-Niners. All you have to do is cut down a swath of jungle, dig up the ground, and wash all the dirt in a river. At the end of a day you have a pile of dead trees, a large hole in the ground, a muddy river and one handful of shiny black coltan. When the price of tantalite spiked, you could sell that handful for maybe 20 bucks.[25]

There has been a steady base production of 2.1 million pounds per year of tantalum from two mines in Western Australia that had more than twenty years of identified surface reserves at that production rate. There are additional resources in the area of these mines for possible expansion. "The only underground mine working is in Canada, although it produces relatively little compared with ten or fifteen years ago, now less than 5% of world output. Other mines are open cut. There are several mines in Brazil, and some in China, notably the Yichun mine. There are traditional sources in Africa, such as those in

Nigeria, Democratic Republic of Congo and Rwanda, which have supplied minerals for half a century, in variable quantities".[26]

The burst of tantalum production in eastern Congo that drew the attention of foreign armed groups was short lived.

> The Congo's 'coltan phenomenon' of 1999–2001 was remarkable, both for its intensity and its short duration. The DRC did not even figure in published statistics of world tantalum production before the year 2000, when suddenly it surged from nowhere into second place with 130 tons, over one seventh of total world production, only surpassed by Australia. Almost all of this came from the Kivu and Maniema provinces. Yet production fell away quickly — to 60 tons (2001 and 2002), 15 (2003) and recovering slightly to 20 (2004). The world market price for tantalum slumped from $220 per pound in 2000 to $37 in 2001, reaching a low of $22 in 2003 before recovering slightly since. Even though such statistics are notoriously unreliable, it can be calculated that with both production and prices sinking to a tenth of their peak, the DRC's coltan export earnings in 2003 cannot have been much more than 1% of those of 2000.[27]

The Tantalum–niobium International Study Center (TIC) is an industry group with about 90 members from over 20 countries. The TIC has a policy on conflict tantalum similar to but less formal than the Kimberley process. According to the TIC Secretary General:

> In the Democratic Republic of Congo the mineral is columbite-tantalite, known locally as 'coltan', and it has been the subject of trading by militias in the civil war. The TIC continues to call on its members to take care in purchasing minerals in Central Africa, as harm to local populations, wildlife or the environment is not acceptable. The mining and trading of minerals is a way of producing an income, and Central Africa has exported tantalum minerals for many years, so putting an embargo on all such trade is not the whole answer. Supply from DRC is probably not more than 10% of world mine output.[28]

The collapse of tantalum prices and Congo production after the year 2000 and an uneasy peace deal reduced but did not eliminate the temptation for Rwandan military intervention in Congo. In December 2004, suspicions of another incursion were reported:

JOHANNESGURG, Dec. 2 — The United Nations reported Thursday that thousands of civilians had fled a battle zone in the eastern Congo near the Rwanda border, heightening fears that the Congo war, which as claimed as many as three million lives, may be erupting once more. But the Rwandan government, which played a crucial role in the hostilities that began in 1988 and, officially at least, ended early last year, rejected what United Nations observers called "collaborating clues" that its troops had entered eastern Congo, defying a recent international peace agreement. The United Nations mission in Congo told news services that it had aerial photographs and ground sightings indicating that Rwandan troops had crossed the border into Congo. The evidence included encounters with soldiers who appeared to carry Rwandan military gear and the sighting of a group of about 100 soldiers that appeared to be of Rwandan origin … Twice before, in 1996 and 1998, Rwanda's Tutsi-led government has sent troops into Congo for the stated purpose of routing Hutu rebels, at least some of whom are former Rwandan soldiers who participated in the massacre of 800,000 Rwandan Tutsi in 1994. The United Nations has mounted an effort with Congolese and Rwandan officials to disarm the Hutu rebels, but Rwandan officials say the disarmament effort has moved too slowly. Some private analysts say, however, that Rwanda wants to promote instability in the region to increase its control of the area's rich natural resources, which include diamonds, gold and coltan, a crucial ingredient in cellphone circuit boards. The United Nations has accused Rwanda, Uganda, and Burundi of stealing vast quantities of coltan from Congo, which holds some 80 percent of the world's know reserves of the mineral. Mr. Sezibera, the Rwandan president's adviser, dismissed those accusations as part of what he said was a smear campaign by Western analysts and Congolese officials against the Rwandan government.[29]

Despite the collapse of the tantalum bubble, serious problems remained with control of diamond production in the Congo.[30] The diamond problem was addressed internationally on a commercial basis through the Kimberley process discussed above. At least from 2003–2007, struggles over control of Congo resources were not promoting major international war, albeit in part due to the continuing presence of 17,000 UN peacekeepers at a cost of a billion dollars per year.[31] However, violence persisted into 2007 in the eastern Congo in conflicts with "warlords".[32] As of early 2008 peace talks aimed at ending the bloodshed were still in progress.[33] Thus, major international war was still held at bay, but internal instability persisted. This has been the largest UN peacekeeping effort; and if it had to engage regularly in active hostilities its presence would come closest to the definition of a major international war on any ongoing UN troop deployment.

Historical Legacy and the Future of Platinum

Some minerals have been viewed as especially important because they are found in their concentrated and readily extractable form in comparatively few locations. Gold and silver have the longest history in this regard, and were, of course, major focal points for conflict in pre-industrial times. Both now have alternatives in terms of finance, and the development of digital photography has recently further suppressed the demand for silver. Likewise copper wire now faces competition from fiber optics, and copper sources are widely enough distributed that large-scale conflict over as-yet-undeveloped copper resources does not seem very likely.

Spilling over very visibly from WWII into the US Strategic and Critical Materials Stockpiling Act is the idea that certain minerals are so important that normal market mechanisms might not guarantee adequate availability. What is interesting about this act is the very military-oriented lens through which these materials were viewed. What was specifically excluded in the act was the use of stockpiles to provide market stability, or to serve the national financial interest, by using stockpiles to "buy low and sell high." This may be an inheritance from strong post-war viewpoint in the Eisenhower years against the type of government meddling in markets used during WWII. (This viewpoint also led to a partly privatized US nuclear energy market in a manner much different from the French experience discussed below.) Thus, for non-energy minerals the US government did not make use of its stockpiling program to stabilize mineral market prices. These prices have in many cases been quite volatile. This volatility has had very small macroeconomic consequences for most industrialized countries, but it has sometimes caused difficulties for modest-sized producer countries that are heavily dependent on a particular mineral export for revenue.

The idea that "strategic" reserves are only meant for times of military-related crisis has also spilled over into the management of the US national petroleum reserve. In this case, however, the implications of the lack of a mechanism for stabilizing prices have been consequential for consumers and producers alike. It has been suggested that it could be more economical and a better contribution to US security interests to use a "buy low, sell high" approach to managing the US national petroleum reserve.[34] For most other materials extracted from the earth, this question does not arise, because the concept of maintaining "strategic" stockpiles seems to have been nearly abandoned by the end of the cold war.

In principle, one can imagine a potentially important exception to the increasing marginalization of the importance of non-fuel minerals. This exception is platinum, which could be in greatly increased demand because it is so far the only candidate for a practical catalyst for fuel cells for passenger cars. In principle, fuel cell cars could be phased in rapidly in order to help remove oil as a source of international conflict. This in turn would generate an enormous surge of demand for platinum. This increased demand for mined platinum should be temporary because fuel cell platinum can be very efficiency recycled. Nevertheless, a rapid tool-up phase could conceivably substitute conflict connected to control of platinum resources for conflict connected more directly to oil resources.

In practice, cars using a hybrid of internal combustion engine and an electrical motor driven by conventional rechargeable batteries appear to be a more economic solution than fuel cells for increased fuel efficiency for passenger cars. This is certainly the case in the short-to-medium term. Even in the longer term, it may be more economic to rely on plug-in hybrids recharged using non-fossil electricity sources and obtaining most of the internal combustion energy from bio-fuels. Even if a combination of security and environmental concerns were to provide great incentives for increased auto fleet fuel efficiency, it is likely that the contribution of fuel cells to the fleet would grow slowly enough to avoid generating conflict over platinum resources. For with a modest rate of growth in demand for new platinum, expansion of new mines and development of technology for efficient extraction of lower grade resources should allow the supply to be met through normal market mechanisms.

To gain more insight into the platinum question, it is useful to examine some reserves estimates. Palladium and platinum can substitute for each other in catalytic converters for exhaust pollution control, so reserves are of these are lumped together here. Distribution of production, reserves, and reserve base for 2005 for platinum and palladium are given in Table 9.4.[35] In 2005, the United States' imports of platinum group metals included comparable amounts of platinum (89 tonnes) and palladium (103 tonnes) and much smaller

Table 9.4.   Global platinum group metals production and reserves (tonnes).

Producer	Production in 2006		Platinum group metals	
	Platinum	Palladium	Reserve	Reserve base
United States	4	14	900	2000
Canada	9	14	310	390
Russia	29	98	6200	6600
South Africa	170	85	63,000	70,000
Other countries	9	13	800	850
Total (rounded)	221	224	71,000	80,000

Source: Mineral commodity summaries (production from USGS (2007) and reserves from USGS (2006)): The reserve base includes those resources that are currently economic (reserves), marginally economic (marginal reserves), and some of those that are currently subeconomic (subeconomic resources).

amounts of rhodium (14 tonnes), ruthenium (24 tonnes), iridium (3.6 tonnes), and osmium (50 kg).

Ignoring the reserve base and estimating only half of the platinum group reserve to be platinum itself, the reserve to production ratio is still over a century. Thus, the most relevant limitation may be on the rate of expansion of production. With a strong anticipated market, an annual growth in production of five percent is very likely reasonable, leading to a doubling in 14 years. At 20 g of platinum per engine, this doubled capacity would support production of about a quarter of what global automobile production was 1993 (which was 34 million cars). This corresponds to about half of the recent car and light truck market in the United States.[b]

Ramping up to a doubled platinum mining level over 20 years and continuing it for 40 years to build up a platinum stock for the global auto fleet would still leave the rest of the reserve base, plus additional resources very likely to be prospected in the interim. Generally, substantially larger resources of rare minerals are to be found in modestly lower ore grades once it becomes economic to search for and exploit them.

In principle the kind of scenario just described could lead to an effective South African monopoly on a critical element of the global transportation system. This in turn could conceivably lead to a implicit or explicit military pressure on that country to moderate plat-inum prices. In practice a more likely outcome is a much lower rate of fuel cell utilization for automobiles, since alternative technologies are likely to be competitive for many decades to come. These include hybrid cars with conventional gasoline engines and compressed natural gas for pollution-sensitive uses such as urban taxi fleets. Thus, it is in practice unlikely that platinum will, in the readily foreseeable

---

[b] This level of platinum per 15 kW engine would require hybrid technology with an additional storage battery to recapture otherwise wasted kinetic energy. It would also require sustained integrated fuel cell engine performance at a kW/g platinum level that had only been demonstrated in a piecewise basis under laboratory conditions. At a production level, a 40 kW fuel cell still required over 100 g of platinum by 2006. For background information, see Batteries News (2006); DoD Fuel Cell ERDC/CERL Programs (2003); Krempel and Pleumper (1999); Michigan State Senate (2003).

future, become an exception to the rule than non-carbon minerals are no longer treated as "strategic" materials.

Endnotes

[1] Clayton and Conniff (1999).
[2] Kohn (1999, p. 348).
[3] Clayton and Conniff (1999).
[4] Waltham (2001).
[5] Columbia Encyclopedia (2001c).
[6] CIA (2007a).
[7] Infoplease (2003).
[8] Szczesniak (2002).
[9] Kohn (1999).
[10] Knight (2005).
[11] BBC News (2006).
[12] Global Policy Forum (2007).
[13] Kohn (1999).
[14] Graffis (1997); for another view, see Havini and Havini (2003).
[15] USGS (2006) and USGS (2007).
[16] USDA (2003).
[17] USGS (2007).
[18] Kohn (1999).
[19] World Diamond Council (2003).
[20] World Diamond Council (2003).
[21] Global Policy Forum (2003).
[22] Michel (2002).
[23] see "submission" at EC (2006).
[24] Kimberly Process (2007).
[25] About Geology (2006).
[26] Wickens (2004).
[27] Johnson and Tegera (2005).
[28] Wichens (2004).
[29] Wines (2004).
[30] Johnson and Tegera (2005).
[31] Africa Week (2006).
[32] Polgreen (2007).
[33] AP (2008).
[34] ACIDS (2004).
[35] USGS (2006, 2007).

Chapter 10

An End to Cross-border Warfare over Solid Minerals?

So far considerable progress has been made here in examining the role of resources in the origins and outcome of major international wars. The focus has been on wars that involve international movement of many tens of thousands of troops. These are the wars that grab the attention of entire nations and the world at large, that require substantial fractions of national public sector spending to prepare for, and that sometimes decisively alter the course of world events. Internal conflicts and less ambitious peacekeeping missions can also be of critical importance to the directly affected populations. However, their global impact is generally incremental, particularly on energy markets, and they lie largely outside the realm examined here.

Every major international war has an economic dimension, if only in terms of how the participants on both sides are equipped and sustained. As social organization and technology have evolved, so too have the economic dimensions of warfare and how they interact with ideological and psychological factors. Plunder, often including taking slaves, was a commonplace economic factor in warfare from ancient times up to the early industrial revolution. Gradually this largely gave way to struggles over control of the bounty of the land, which coexisted with control of trade as a major economic motivation for and requirement of success in war. By the end of the 20th century, plunder was greatly discouraged by the global community and only played a significant role in situations where order had already broken down for other reasons. Plunder during breakdown of order remained occasionally spilled across borders during unrest on the southern coast of

West Africa into the present century, sometimes resulting from guns finding their way into the hands of children. For example, "gangsterism" spilled over from Liberia to Côte d'Ivoire in 2003, with heavily armed minors running out of control of the people who armed them.[1]

As the industrial revolution proceeded, some of the important bounties of the land came to be heavy industry materials, most notably coal and iron. Thus, the struggle for *Lebensraum* to provide agricultural land for burgeoning populations was complicated after the Franco-Prussian War by a growing understanding of the importance of controlling coal- and steel-producing areas. This became especially apparent during the course of WWI. Then came the re-unification of China, the integration of western European trade policies, the invention of nuclear weapons, the culmination of transition to near-zero population growth in developed countries, and the disintegration of the Soviet bloc. After these events, grasping direct control over land for its agricultural production or solid mineral resources became a thing of the past for advanced industrial economies. The ultimate irony in this transition was illustrated when a tiny and densely populated country like Singapore developed a substantially higher per capita gross domestic product than a vastly materially endowed behemoth like Russia.

Concerning control of trade, mercantilism gave way to colonialism, and then colonialism perished amid a global ideological struggle between communism and capitalism. Eventually a global regime dedicated to the pursuit of free trade in market goods emerged, with a few notable exceptions. Concerning nonrenewable resources, the most notable exceptions in the 1990s were French policies toward uranium, the role of diamond mining in Africa, and oil. The uranium story will be taken up in Part IV, along with a discussion of natural gas as the greatest current competitor for new nuclear electric power production capacity.

With respect to diamonds, many of the dominant producing and consuming nations have at least accepted an important principle, that is, an international cooperative mechanism was needed to reduce economic motivations for the control of diamond resources to lead to violent conflict. The same cannot yet be said for oil. Because of this, and because oil is the leading internationally traded nonrenewable resource, an extensive discussion of this commodity will be taken up in Part III.

This book does not deal in any depth with nonrenewable underground aquifers, the other major nonrenewable fluid mineral resource. To date aquifers have also played a minor role in generation of *international* conflict (although they played a subsidiary role in the Israeli-Palestinian conflict). Part IV will briefly examine renewable resources both as proposed incentives and antidotes for conflict. In both cases their role is likely to be peripheral in the future when it comes to major international war. With the other issues either dealt with or set aside for the moment, the stage is now set for an examination of fluid fossil fuels and uranium.

Endnote

[1] Sengupta (2003a).

Part Three

OIL

Chapter 11

Oil and Commerce

Oil has played an important role in international conflicts since the beginning of WWI. By converting its navy to oil firing starting just before WWI, Britain gained a significant advantage at sea over Germany. By the final year of WWI, internal combustion engines were playing a major role in the land war as well as powering nascent air forces. Control of oil resources played a central role in the outcome of WWII. As the British later withdrew from military operations east of Suez in the 1960s, the United States allied itself with Israel as a counterweight to the perceived danger of the expansion of Soviet influence in the oil-rich Middle East. Pushing directly for the control of other countries' oil, Iraq tried to seize some of Iran's oil production in 1980 and to annex Kuwait in 1990. From 2003 through and beyond 2007, the major unresolved economic issue in Iraq was how its oil revenues would be distributed. These are some of the key events that shape current perceptions of connections between oil and national security.

From the conversion of the British fleet through to WWII and beyond, governments, not surprisingly, took a keen interest in the oil industry. Commercial and national interests were sometimes aligned and at other times at odds with each other. The starting point for this interplay in the United States was an oil industry that was heavily monopolized at the end of the 19th century. The global industry remained dominated by a handful of mostly large US companies up to 1973. Thereafter, effective cartel action organized through the Organization of Petroleum Exporting Countries (OPEC) played an important role from 1973–1986 and started again in 1998. The story of oil and security is intimately intertwined with the commercial evolution of the oil industry. This story begins with the phenomenal growth of a trust that became synonymous with the idea of monopoly: Standard Oil.

Monopoly and Cartel

Since the first drilled oil well in the United States in 1859, economies of scale have been available for conducting transport, refining, and even sales operations in the oil industry. This is particularly true of pipeline transport. Even if two parallel pipelines with smaller cross-sectional area were as efficient as one with the same total cross-sectional area (which they are not), it would be considerably cheaper to lay and operate one pipeline instead of two competing ones.

Another feature of oil that initially promoted monopoly, and later international cartel, is the intense geographic concentration of the most inexpensively extracted resources. Oil is not a commodity like wool, which can be grown in many regions and is hard to monopolize. Instead, inexpensive oil resources with ready access to market have often been concentrated in a few locations. This made it easier to monopolize one or more critical aspects of the oil industry under the control of a single trust or to form a cartel amongst several producers to influence supply and prices.

Given 5 to 10 years of high oil prices, the market responds with greater efficiency of oil use, substituting other energy sources. However, in the shorter span of a year or two, oil consumption levels hardly budge when prices double or even triple. That is, the demand for oil is very inelastic in the short term. Oil production levels have sometimes also been very unresponsive to price changes. During oil boom years, the incremental cost of pumping on wells already drilled was sometimes low enough to encourage production to continue full out, no matter how low the market price was. During lean years, collusion amongst oil producers has sometimes limited output despite high prices. Even without collusion to limit production, it can take several years to locate and exploit new oil fields. Especially during the seventy years after the first use of drilling, this combination of features of the oil business helped produce "boom and bust" cycles that allowed better buffered larger concerns to drive out marginally capitalized smaller producers.[1]

Standard Oil

The 1860 Pennsylvania oil boom was not the first example of distilling petroleum into kerosene for wick lamps. Kerosene, or white naphta (*naft abyad*), had been distilled from petroleum since 850 AD in what the Arabs called an *al-inbiq* (alembic in English). "Essentially, the alembic consisted of three parts: a gourd-shaped lower flask called the cucurbit in which the crude oil was heated; a colled, spouted condenser that sat atop the cucurbit and received the vapors that rose from the oil; and a receiver at the end of the condenser's spout in which the clear distillate was collected".[2] Oil had other uses as well before 1860:

> Several large oil pits were operating in Iraq and nearby areas in the eighth century. So vast and strategically important was the pit at Dir al-Qayyara (near Mosul) that at one time it had to be guarded day and night. It provided not only crude oil but most of the bitumen used by the state to pave roads. In the early 13th century, the geographer Yaqut described in detail how "asphalt" was made in those days from the pit and used to build roads. In Europe, roads paved with anything but flagstones or cobbles were unknown until 1838, when asphalt was first laid on a street in Paris.[3]

Potential demand for kerosene for lighting was already in hand in 1860, particularly given the depletion of whale stocks that supplied a useful but increasing hard-to-come-by lamp oil. Oil had been drilled for before in China and Russia, but not on the commercial scale for the production of kerosene that followed first drilling in the Pennsylvania in 1859.[4] The fundamental innovation used in Pennsylvania was the adoption of brine drilling techniques to extract petroleum. Before this, "a small oil industry had developed in Eastern Europe — first in Galicia (which was variously part of Poland, Austria, and Russia) and then in Rumania. In Rumania, peasants dug shafts by hand to obtain crude oil, from which kerosene was refined. A pharmacist from Lvov, with the help of a plumber, invented a cheap lamp suited to burning kerosene. By 1854, kerosene was a staple of commerce in Vienna, and by 1859, Galicia had a thriving kerosene oil business, with over 150 villages involved in mining for oil. Altogether, European crude production in 1859 had been estimated at thirty-six thousand barrels, primarily from Galicia and Rumania. What the Eastern European industry lacked, more than anything else, was the technology for drilling."[5]

As seen in Table 11.1, the 36,000 barrels (about five tonnes) of oil produced in 1859 was dwarfed a single year later by an explosion of production from the United States.[6] (The designation tonne is again used here for what is sometimes called a metric ton, which is a thousand kilograms or 2205 pounds.) In fact the United States provided the majority of all world oil production through 1950, an outcome that would have important strategic military consequences.

Table 11.1.   Crude oil production up to 1910 (ktonne/year).

Region	Year					
	1860	1870	1880	1890	1900	1910
Canada	0	33	47	106	122	42
US	66	701	3504	6110	8482	27941
Central America	0	0	0	0	0	541
South America	0	0	0	4	38	171
Europe	0	0	1	16	52	149
OECD Europe	1	12	48	146	597	3096
Former USSR	4	28	559	3751	10342	9541
South Asia	0	0	0	16	144	818
Southeast Asia	0	0	0	0	311	1523
Japan	0	0	4	8	114	257
World	71	774	4163	10157	20202	44079

Source: General oil production estimates for period 1900–1800 (RIVM, 2002). OECD = Organization for Economic Cooperation and Development; ktonne = 1000 tonne; tonne = metric ton = 1000 kg = 2205 pounds.

From 1860 to 1911, the essential battle over oil was a commercial one. John D. Rockefeller understood the large profits that could be made by applying economies of scale to refining petroleum. Living modestly compared to other successful industrialists, by extracting lower shipping rates from the railroads than his competitors he enticed or forced almost all of them to sell out to his company at a modest price or face bankruptcy from failure to meet costs in times of oversupply. When "independent" competitors banded together to build the first oil pipeline to evade this strategy, he built his own pipeline and eventually extended it to a network connecting Pennsylvania to new oil finds in Ohio.

Retaining effective control, Rockefeller eventually prepared for the possible death of shareholders through a trust arrangement with other owners, many of which had been brought in through acquisitions. In 1892, the trust shares were transferred to twenty companies as a result of an Ohio court decision, but in 1889 a holding company for them was established as Standard Oil of New Jersey, with a capitalization of $110 million.[7] By 1895 Standard Oil controlled "between 85 and 90 percent of the oil in Pennsylvania and Lima-Indiana...and effectively determined the purchase price of American crude oil...".[8] Since US oil production was larger in this time period than the rest of the world's, this made Standard Oil the most important player in the industry overall. This was, however, before the internal combustion engine made oil so much more important in the overall global economy. As this was beginning to happen, the commercial dominance of a single company was replaced by the dominance of a somewhat larger number of major oil companies.

Origins and Fate of the "Seven Sisters"

The beginning of the end of the Standard Oil monopoly came in 1902, through a series of articles by Ida Tarbell on Standard Oil that began appearing in *McClure's* magazine. This preceded the compilation of these articles and additional documentation in her *History of The Standard Oil Company*.[9] Tarbell was the daughter of an oilman who had been saddled with debt struggling against "the Octopus," as Rockefeller's many-armed business enterprise was eventually characterized by cartoonists of the time.

Tarbell's exposé was grist for the mill for Teddy Roosevelt, elected president on an anti-trust platform in 1904. This allied the force of the presidency with the derision of trusts that appeared in the popular press. By 1911 Standard Oil had been broken up into seven companies.[10] The largest pieces were Standard Oil of New Jersey (later Exxon) and of New York (later Socony and then Mobil). There was also Standard Oil, California (later Chevron), Standard Oil of Ohio (later Sohio) and of Indiana (later Amoco), and also Continental (later Conoco) and Atlantic (later part of Arco and eventually Sun).

By 2002 these entities had evolved into pieces of the six largest oil companies in the world.[11] The 1998 merger of Exxon–Mobil merger created the largest oil company. The second largest company in 2002, Shell, was not derived from Standard Oil but rather formed as a result of a 1902 merger with Royal Dutch, prompted by fear of a takeover of Royal Dutch by Standard. Third largest in 2002 was Chevron (which took over Gulf in 1984 and separately merged with Texaco). Fourth was BP (British Petroleum, originally Anglo-Persian and later Anglo-Iranian), which had previously taken over Sohio to have an American arm. British Petroleum then acquired Amoco, Arco, and Burmah-Castrol from 1998–2000. The French Total and Elf and the Belgian Fina merged, being the world's fifth largest oil company in 2002. Conoco and Phillips, "merged in 2002 to form the sixth largest company." A subsequent agreement for merger of Russian oil companies Yukos and Sibnet provided for the fifth largest daily sales, with TotalFinaElf sixth, ENI seventh, an ConocoPhillips eighth.[12]

An opening volley in the expected commercial skirmish among the major oil companies for work on increasing Iraq's production was made in 2004, when ConocoPhillips paid $1.988 billion for a 7.59 percent share in Lukoil, Russia's second largest oil company. "Concophillips and Lukoil said they wanted to join in developing the West Qurana oil concession in Iraq, which Lukoil won during

Saddam Husseins' regime and was later taken away".[13] This gave
Russia a potential pathway for access to Iraq.

> "Lukoil is afraid they will be shut out of Iraq because Russia didn't
> participate in the war," said Roger Diwan, head of markets and
> countries research for PFC Energy, a consultant in Washington.
> "Conoco gives them an entry pass with the new government — if
> there is one."[14]

Mergers related most directly to the history of Standard Oil are summarized in Fig. 11.1. The names listed in italics at the left in Fig. 11.1
are pieces of Standard Oil resulting from the 1911 antitrust ruling.
Much later, British Petroleum acquired several of these pieces and
renamed itself "BP." The partnership between Royal Dutch and Shell
in Britain in 1907 was stimulated by competition from Standard Oil
but did not actually get approved as a merger into fully unified management company format until 2005. Figure 11.1 is useful for connecting historical oil company names to more recent company names.

The mergers just described are comparatively recent. For much of
the period of interest here the international oil industry was dominated by the French national CFP company and the so-called "Seven
Sisters" during an intermediate stage in the dissolution and partial
reconstruction of the original Standard Oil company. The Seven sisters included four US firms that cooperated to form Aramco in 1947
to develop Saudi oil: Jersey (later Exxon), Socony-Vacuum (later
Mobil), Standard of California (later Chevron), and Texaco. The
other three of the Seven Sisters were Gulf, Royal Dutch/Shell, and
BP. These three cooperated in bringing Kuwaiti oil to market after
WWII.[15] The term Seven Sisters was coined by Enrico Mattei of
Italy's Ente Nazionale Idocarburi (ENI). Although considerably
smaller than the larger six, ENI was apparently the world's seventh
largest oil company in 2002.[16] Chapter 14 summarizes the pivotal
developments when ENI and the major oil companies cooperated
with an embargo of Iranian oil exports after Iran nationalized Anglo-
Iranian's assets in 1951.

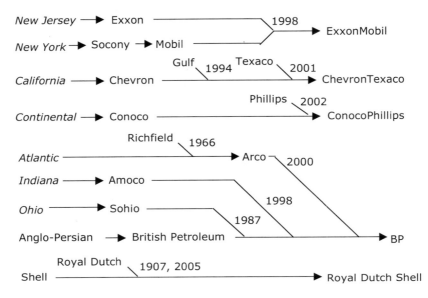

Fig. 11.1. Mergers directly related to the history of standard oil.

For the first half of the 20th century, Standard Oil and its US off-spring dominated the national and international petroleum industry. After WWII, the four US firms that joined to form Aramco helped to forge an enduring relationship between the governments of the United States and Saudi Arabia and provide a financial foundation for the reign of the Saudi monarchy for decades to come. The major competitors of US firms before and shortly after WWII were Shell and what became British Petroleum. The United States largely cooperated with Britain to try to protect the financial interests of these companies. By the beginning of the 21st century, however, US oil production was a much smaller fraction of the global market, Persian Gulf producers had established national firms, and new Russian oil firms had become more internationally significant.

Four Chinese oil firms were also becoming increasingly important in the early 21st century: China National Petroleum Company (CNPC), Sinopec, the Chinese National Offshore Oil Company (CNOOC), and PetroChina. Chinese firms became much more active internationally.[17] CNOOC went so far as to make an attempt to take over the US-based firm Unocal before being blocked by political pressure in the United States.[18]

Amoco, one of the large Standard Oil spin-offs with "America" part of its name no less, has in effect even been taken over by the foreign company British Petroleum. Lying behind all of these company formations and mergers was a broader internationalization of the operations, staff, and stockholders of major oil companies. This left a range of corporate actors in international petroleum markets with policies variously parallel, tangential, or even potentially at odds with the national policies of their countries of historical origin.

Endnotes

[1] C.F. Yergin (1991); Economides and Oligney (2000).
[2] Zahoor (1997).
[3] Zahoor (1997).
[4] San Joaquin Geological Society (2002).
[5] Yergin (1991, pp. 23–25).
[6] RIVM (2002).
[7] Yergin (1991, pp. 97–98).
[8] Yergin (1991, p. 54).
[9] Tarbell (1904).
[10] Yergin (1991, p. 110).
[11] See Thomas (2003) for the following post-1980 information, and Yergin (1991) for information on the earlier events.
[12] Tavernise (2003a).
[13] Arvedlund and Timmons (2004).
[14] Arvedlund and Timmons (2004).
[15] Yergin (1991, p. 503).
[16] According to Thomas (2003).
[17] People's Daily Online (2004).
[18] Barboza and Sorkin (2005); Collier (2005).

Chapter 12

Oil from WWI to WWII

The decision just before WWI to convert the British fleet to oil was indeed a milestone in the history of energy and security in the 20th century. Oil played an increasingly important role during that war. Near the beginning of the war the Paris taxi fleet was commandeered to move troops to the defense of the city. By the end of the war an armada of motorized vehicles made critical contributions to pushing back Germany's advances. After the war most of the Arab Middle East moved from Ottoman to British and French control. The importance of this for energy and security was only to become fully apparent after WWII, since through the interwar period the western hemisphere provided the great majority of the world's oil.

Oil and War From 1911 Through WWI

The year 1911, when Standard Oil was broken up, is also the year that Winston Churchill became First Lord of the Admiralty and initiated the conversion of the British fleet to oil. His decision was confirmed by advice from a British Royal Commission in March 1913.[1] A 1912–1914 oil-fired building campaign followed the unwelcome sailing of a German gunboat into the Moroccan port of Agadir. To help ensure that oil supplies would be available at a "reasonable price," Churchill insisted on government aid for Anglo-Persian to counterbalance the partly foreign-owned Royal Dutch/Shell.[2] Direct British government involvement in the Anglo-Persian oil company would eventually help precipitate a reaction in Iran that would reverberate into the 21st century.

Germany entered WWI with a great advantage over the Allies in motorized vehicles and airships. A total of 70,000 motorized vehicles followed the German army advance in the west in 1914.[3] The British expeditionary force that faced the German army had just 827 motorcars and 15 motorcycles.[4] In 1914 Germany had 384 planes and 30 dirigibles as compared to 186 planes and 10 dirigibles for France and Britain combined.[5]

The Germans were nevertheless surprised and dismayed in four ways by the role that oil played in WWI. The first surprise was the French General Galleini's commandeering of Paris' taxi fleet to ferry soldiers to the front. This happened when the city seemed about to fall and the war to end with France repeating the humiliation of the Franco-Prussian War. Germany was able to regroup and then maintain trench defenses in front of the Belgian and Lorraine sources of steel for most of the war. Eventually, however, the Allies brought the internal combustion engine to bear in tanks that could traverse the stalemated trenches. A massive infusion of trucks, cars, and motorcycles helped the Allies follow up on these advances. This was particularly the case after the United States brought 50,000 trucks to France in 1917, supplementing British army vehicles including "56,000 trucks, 23,000 motorcars, and 34,000 motorcycles".[6] This was an enormous increase compared to the beginning of the war.

The other major surprise of WWI connected with oil was the role of the airplane.

The war constantly pushed the pace of innovation. By the last months of the struggle, the speed of the most advanced aircraft had more than doubled, to over 120 miles per hour (about 200 km/hr), and they operated with a ceiling of nearly 27,000 feet (about 8 km). In the course of the war, Britain produced 55,000 planes; France 68,000; Italy 20,000; and Germany 48,000. In its year and a half in the war, the United States produced 15,000 ...[7]

By 1918 the British Royal Air Force had 22,000 aircraft available. Despite having produced over twice this number during the war,

Germany never managed to field more than 4000 aircraft at a time in the western theater.[8]

Increasingly dogging Germany as the war proceeded was a shortage of oil supplies and production, which limited the amount and utility of internal combustion engine machines that it could field. In 1913 Germany imported 1.3 million tons of oil. Nearly a million tons of this came from Russia and sources outside of Europe that were not reliable in wartime. On the other hand, French oil imports increased from just over a quarter million tons in 1914 to a million tons in 1918, with seven-eighths of the latter coming from the Western hemisphere.

In the only major surface naval engagement of the war, the coal-fired German fleet managed to escape a trap set for it by the more maneuverable oil-dominated British fleet at the Battle of Jutland in May 1916. With only 28 oil-burning cruisers, Germany's surface navy could not hazard venturing out into the open ocean. Germany did score tactical success with submarines against transatlantic shipping supplying the European Allied Forces during WWI. By 1916 Germany had 68 submarines available and 151 under construction.[9] Had Germany anticipated the length of the war and the importance of oil, it might have put much more emphasis on its advantage in submarine construction. Relying on stealth rather than speed and high tonnage, diesel-electric submarines were both less greedy oil consumers and better at sinking oil tankers. In the end, what success Germany did have with sinking ships supplying the Allies constituted a pyrrhic victory because they helped bring the United States into the war, with critical impact on the Western Front.

Given the growing importance of petroleum, toward the end of the war in desperation the Central Powers tried to advance to take the Russian oil-producing region of Baku on the Caspian Sea. This effort failed, and Germany was forced to sue for peace on terms far different than it had envisioned at the beginning of the war. In preparing for the WWII, the lesson of the importance of oil-driven machinery was not lost on Germany. However, the importance and difficulty of securing adequate and enduring supplies of petroleum was again to be underestimated, with militarily catastrophic results.

Romania's Miscalculation

In 1914 and 1915, Romania produced an estimated sixty-three percent of all of the oil in Europe outside of what would become the Soviet Union. As oil became increasingly militarily important, Romania was caught in the cross fire. Romania had the option of sitting out the war and selling its oil to the highest bidder, and initially it looked like the country might do just that. However, Romania's King Charles felt betrayed by Russia after supporting it militarily during the Russo-Turkish War of 1877–1878. After that war, Russia refused to let Romania participate in the 1878 Congress of Berlin, where Russia gained southern Bessarabia from Romania in exchange for the barren southern land of Dobruja. As a result, Charles signed a secret mutual defense treaty with Austria-Hungary, Germany, and Italy in 1883 and renewed it in 1913. When the leader Ionel Bratianu of the pro-French Liberal Party became the Romanian premier in 1914 and WWI broke out, he insisted that Charles' treaty did not obligate Romania to defend the Central Powers. This was on the grounds that it was Franz-Joseph's impossible demand on Serbia that started the war. So far, so good. However, fearful of Germany and promised the predominantly Hungarian-speaking region of Transylvania by the Allied Powers, Romania declared war on Austria-Hungary in the August of 1916. By December 1917, Bucharest had been occupied by the Central Powers after Russian support for a Romanian counter-offensive failed to materialize.[10]

On December 5, 1917, the British burned about 800,000 tons of petrol at Ploietsi, 35 miles (56 km) north of Bucharest in the Wallachia region of southeastern Romania[11] Hot on the heals of the British, the Germans occupied and repaired the oil fields, pumping about a million tons of oil by the end of the war.[12] The contribution that Romanian oil had made in WWI was not forgotten at the beginning of the next world war, when Germany would make sure earlier on that Romanian oil was under its effective control.

Table 12.1 summarizes casualty totals for the various combatants in WWI.[13] After disastrous battles and a long retreat, Romania had by far the largest fraction of its mobilized soldiers killed. Romania's

Table 12.1. Casualties in World War I (millions).

Country	Mobilized	Died	Wounded	Other	Total casualties	Casualties mobilized	Died mobilized
Austria-Hungary	7.80	1.20	3.62	2.20	7.02	0.90	0.15
Belgium	0.27	0.01	0.04	0.03	0.09	0.33	0.04
British Empire	8.90	0.91	2.09	0.19	3.19	0.36	0.10
Bulgaria	1.20	0.09	0.15	0.03	0.27	0.23	0.08
France	8.41	1.36	4.27	0.54	6.16	0.73	0.16
Germany	11.00	1.77	4.22	1.15	7.14	0.65	0.16
Greece	0.23	0.01	0.02	0.00	0.03	0.13	0.04
Italy	5.62	0.65	0.95	0.60	2.20	0.39	0.12
Japan	0.80	0.00	0.00	0.00	0.00	0.00	0.00
Montenegro	0.05	0.00	0.01	0.01	0.02	0.40	0.00
Portugal	0.10	0.01	0.01	0.01	0.03	0.30	0.10
Romania	0.75	0.34	0.12	0.08	0.54	0.72	0.45
Russia	12.00	1.70	4.95	2.50	9.15	0.76	0.14
Serbia	0.71	0.05	0.13	0.15	0.33	0.46	0.07
Turkey	2.85	0.33	0.40	0.25	0.98	0.34	0.12
United States	4.73	0.12	0.20	—	0.32	0.07	0.03
Total	65.42	8.53	21.19	7.75	37.46	0.57	0.13

Source: (Infoplease 2006).
"Other" = taken prisoner or missing.

civilian population also suffered greatly as a result of the war, and its economy was badly and enduringly damaged.

Oil after WWI

Britain's initial primary objective in the Middle East during WWI appears to have been securing the Suez Canal. So important was this objective that the forces allocated to it helped not only to turn back the Turks, but to chase them out of Palestine and Mesopotamia as well. At the start of the war oil production in Persia was reasonably secure and just getting off the ground, while the oil discoveries of

1927 in Iraq lay in the future. The *possibility* of oil discoveries else-where in the Middle East was acknowledged in 1912 when the pre-cocious and technically trained Armenian–Turk Calouste Gulbenkian's brainchild, the Turkish Petroleum Company, obtained an exclusive concession for the Ottoman Empire. Nevertheless, the British incursion into the Palestine and Mesopotamia area reflected short-term tactical aims as well as possible long-term interest in the oil potential of the region.

Well before the first drilling struck oil in Iraq in 1927, the poten-tial importance of oil in Gulf areas other than Persia was evident to the British. Even during the war, France and Britain were jockeying for influence over the spoils of the Ottoman Empire during negotia-tions leading to the Sykes–Picot agreement:

> The 1916 Sykes–Picot Agreement was a reflection of evolving sce-narios that set the stage for dividing up Turkey and its processions in the Middle East in the event of an Allied victory in WWI. The strongest player by far in the Sykes–Picot Agreement was Great Britain. France came in as a distant second while Italy's imperialist claims were stifled. Russia had been a partner in these evolving sce-narios but withdrew from the understandings when the Bolsheviks took power in October 1917. In the earlier Sykes–Picot maps, the northern Mesopotamian town of Mosul, with its flowing oil seeps, was clearly marked within the area to fall under postwar French influence (i.e., it was considered more Syrian than Iraqi). However, when hostilities north of the Arabian Peninsula came to an end in early 1918, France had less than 10 000 troops in the entire theater, and Britain was able to dictate its terms at will. In exchange for granting France's long-sought power over Syria (including Lebanon at the time), Britain was able to add Mosul to its own mandate domains of Mesopotamia...[14]

Remarkably, even after the demise of the Ottomon Empire, persist-ence and a delicate balancing of rival interests allowed Gulbenkian to maintain a five percent interest in all of the oil extracted from Turkey and the Middle East between Egypt in the West and Persia and Kuwait in the East. The remaining ninety-five percent was apportioned in four equal parts to Royal Dutch/Shell, Anglo-Persian, the French, and "the near East Development Company, which was created to hold the interests of the American companies".[15] Named after a curve Gulbenkian traced in color on a map to enclose the region shown in Fig. 12.1, this became known as the "Red Line Agreement."

Massive new oil finds in Mexico, Venezuela, and Texas followed WWI. So well into the 1930s, the difficulties of finding and exploiting the massive Saudi oil fields left that venture a money-losing proposition. Thus, 1940 found world oil production heavily concentrated in the Western Hemisphere, as shown in Table 12.2.[16]

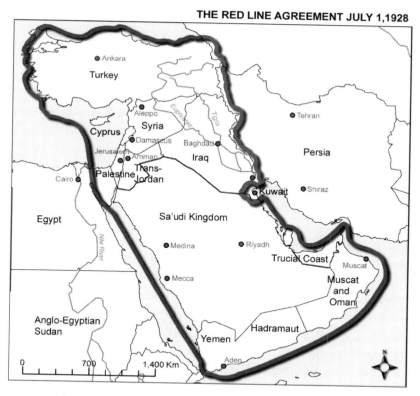

Fig. 12.1.   Region included in the Red Line Agreement.

Table 12.2.   Crude oil production from 1910 to 1950 (Mtonne/year).

Region	Year 1910	1920	1930	1940	1950
OECD Europe	0.1	0.1	0.3	1.6	3.8
Eastern Europe	3.1	1.9	6.5	6.8	6.0
Former USSR	9.5	3.9	18.5	31.1	37.9
N. Africa & Middle East	0.0	1.9	6.4	12.9	87.0
S., E. & S.E. Asia	2.3	3.7	7.0	11.0	12.0
Japan	0.3	0.3	0.3	0.3	0.3
Western Hemisphere	28.7	87.6	156.3	229.4	372.3
World	44.1	99.3	195.3	293.1	519.2

Source: History Database of the Global Environment (RIVM, 2002).
Mtonne = million metric tons; OECD = Organization for Economic Cooperation and Development.

Indeed, in 1940, about eight-tenths of global oil production was in the Western Hemisphere, with just over one-tenth in Russia and the rest primarily in South East Asia (at 10.0 Mtonne/year) and Eastern Europe. Japan was not even close to self-sufficient in oil, getting about ninety percent of its oil from the United States before access to practical financing mechanisms for its purchase was cut off by the United States in July 1941. Japanese dependency on US oil was to have fundamental implications both for the course of WWII and for attitudes about the strategic importance of oil for long thereafter.

In preparation for the next war in Europe, Germany laid and started executing plans for making up for its shortage of oil resources by making synthetic fluid fuels from coal. The first commercially available process for making liquid fuels from coal was the Bergius process developed in Germany in 1913. This process used hydrogen under pressure at elevated temperature to convert lignite or coal tar into lighter hydrocarbons like gasoline. An alternative developed later was the Fischer–Tropsch method, with used coke or crushed coal and uses hydrogen from the water molecules in steam to make gasoline.[17]

These processes recover less than half of the input thermal energy in the product and use either five tons of hard coal or ten tons of lignite to make one ton of synthetic fuel.

The prospects for a commercially self-sufficient synfuels industry had collapsed in 1931 with plummeting market prices for gasoline. To reduce its reliance on imports, Germany placed an import duty on oil that increased its cost in the domestic market by about a factor of six. This simulated the construction of fourteen synthetic fuel plants in Germany by 1939. By 1939, total German oil production from all sources was 3.7 million tons. The original German plan for the next war called for just over 3.1 million of a total of five million tons of annual oil use to come from synthetic fuels. However, in 1938, the future head Hermann Göring of the German armed forces set a revised target of 9 million tons of synthetic fuel production out of a total of 11 million tons for 1944. This target was never met.

Endnotes

[1] Kamal (2005).
[2] Yergin (1991, pp. 154–160).
[3] Jensen (1968).
[4] Yergin (1991).
[5] Jensen (1968).
[6] Yergin (1991, p. 171).
[7] Yergin (1991, p. 172), with parenthetical comments added.
[8] Jensen (1968).
[9] Jensen (1968).
[10] Sudetic (2005).
[11] Duffy (2001).
[12] Keegan (1998).
[13] Infoplease (2006).
[14] Kamal (2005).
[15] Yergin (1991, p. 204).
[16] RIVM (2002).
[17] National Academy of Engineering (2006).
[18] Jensen (1968).

Chapter 13

Oil and World War II

From an economic point of view, WWII was motivated by a quest for reconquest of lost empire by Italy, *Lebensraum* by Germany, and *Lebensraum* and resources such as coal and iron by Japan. This was complemented by Fascist ideology in Europe and militarism in Japan. During the course of the war, however, oil was to play a dominant role. Japan's fateful attack on Pearl Harbor and the evolution of Germany's ultimately catastrophic military campaigns both revolved around oil. These events would cement in the mind of at least one generation the idea that oil is a strategically critical resource. Some important events were: (1) An oil embargo could have forced Italy out of Ethiopia, but Franklin Delano Roosevelt (FDR) refused to cooperate; (2) Germany gained control of Romanian oil, but Romanian troops were unreliable allies; (3) At great cost, Germany failed to gain useful control of Soviet Union's oil; (4) Rommel's failure to get enough fuel to take Suez led to disaster in North Africa; (5) Japan attacked Pearl Harbor to protect Japan's access to oil, but lost WWII.

Italy in Africa

Italy's attacks on Africa were "Johnny come lately" colonialism. The key events are given in the following timeline.[1]

- The 1889 Treaty of Ucciali made Menelek king of an Italian protectorate in what is now Ethiopia, but he then fought Italy.
- Italy lost to Ethiopia at the 1896 Battle of Adwa (Adau, see Fig. 13.1). 100,000 Ethiopians defeated 25,000 Italians and killed 6000.[2]

- In 1914 Mussolini joined the nationalist *fascistii* break-off from the socialists and then pushed the idea that Italy's "natural frontier" includes Libya.
- From 1921–1926 Fascists moved from 35 to 374 votes in parliament, and then on to dictatorship using intimidation and murdering a leading Socialist to handily win a critical election.
- From 1926–1934 Italy supported Albania, Croat rebels, and a pre-*anschluss* fascist Austrian regime, but Italy also sent arms to the Soviet Union in exchange for oil.
- From 1934–1935 Italy took over Ethiopia (and used mustard gas), defied League of Nations condemnation, and avoided a UK-proposed oil embargo.

The United States supplied about half of non-US global oil in 1936. President Roosevelt opposed an embargo of oil to Italy despite that country's invasion of what is now called Ethiopia (formerly included in "Abyssinia"). The French were reluctant to "rock

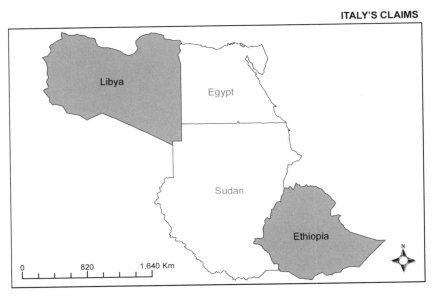

Fig. 13.1.   Former Italian claims in Africa.

the boat." Britain was not willing to "use its boats" on its own to block Italian use of the Suez Canal. Mussolini later told Hitler:

> If the League of Nations had followed (British Foreign Minister) Eden's advice on the Abyssinian dispute, and had extended economic sanctions to oil, I would have had to withdraw from Abyssinia within a week.[3]

Sources of WWII in Europe

Italy's colonial recidivism and the internal struggles between fascists, socialists, and communists in Europe provide the backdrop behind the struggle that WWII would spread beyond the European subcontinent. For insight into why this happened, it helps to take broader view of the imbalance of economics, ideology, and psychology that precipitated oil-powered attacks and counterattacks around the world.

First, consider the role of economics. About 1920, when fascism took off, birth rates were still much higher than death rates, and mass emigration to New World was no longer available. This presumably led to the idea that there was a need for more *Lebensraum* (living space) for German-speaking peoples.

Second, consider the role of ideology. The fascist ideologies espoused by Hitler and Mussolini had two important features. The first feature was nationalism. The German fascists wanted to redress perceived humiliations of the 1917 Versailles and 1925 Lucarno agreements, which respectively outlined and finished off the expected consequences of Germany's defeat in WWI. Italian fascists wanted to redress the humiliation of Italy's defeat by Ethiopians at Adwa (Adua) in 1896. The second feature was racism. In varying degrees the fascists dehumanized Slavs, Jews, and Blacks to justify brutality in pursuit of *Lebensraum* for Germany and colonialism for Italy.

Third, consider the role of psychology. Hitler and Mussolini personified many in their generation. They were physically damaged during WWI military service and perhaps psychologically damaged by earlier career failure. They both embraced collective coercive action in the pursuit of power.

The tilt toward war that resulted from the confluence of these factors created a self-sustaining momentum. Limited German militarization of the Rhineland (in 1936) and unopposed *"anschluss"* occupation of Germanic Austria (in 1938) and the occupation of Sudetenland in western Czechoslovakia were not enough for the Third Reich. Hitler and German foreign minister von Ribbentrop presumably were willing to go on to risk the 1939 attack on Poland that brought France and Britain into WWII for three reasons. First, Germany had a non-aggression pact with the Soviet Union. Second, they underestimated Britain's resolve and the performance of its air force. Third and most important, they did not count on Japan bringing the United States into WWII in 1941.

Germany's plans were facilitated by Romania seeing the handwriting on the wall and signing a mutual cooperation pact with the Axis powers in 1940. At 7.2 million tonnes per year, Romania had been the second largest oil producer in Europe and the world's seventh largest oil producer in 1937. Table 13.1 shows that in 1940 Romania accounted for nearly seventy percent of all of the oil production in the European countries that would come under Axis control.[4] Unfortunately for the German war effort, this was only two percent of global oil production. Nearly half of the oil production in the Eastern Hemisphere lay deep in the Soviet Union. The majority of the rest of the oil production in the Eastern Hemisphere was in the Persian Gulf region, beyond the Suez Canal.

As had happened repeatedly throughout history, though, Romania turned out to be the loser when caught up in struggles between major powers.[5] Romanian troops not only fought alongside the Nazis at Stalingrad, but they ended up being a weak point in the defense that allowed Soviet troops to surround Axis forces and turn the tide of the war. Then on August 1, 1943, US bombers severely damaged the Romanian oil fields at Ploiesti and with it the Axis powers' last supply of petroleum in Europe.[5] Being off the beaten path between the Soviet Union and Europe, Romania emerged from the war with a communist government that became somewhat of a

Table 13.1. Percentage of world oil production in 1940.

Country/**Region**	% of Region	% of World
USSR	99	10.6
United Kingdom		0.0
India and New Zealand		0.1
UK and Allies		**10.7**
Germany		0.4
Romania	69	2.0
Axis-Controlled Europe		**2.9**
Egypt	7	0.3
Iran	67	3.0
Iraq	19	0.9
Saudi Arabia	5	0.2
Middle East and North Africa		**4.5**
Brunei	8	0.3
Burma	10	0.4
Indonesia	73	2.7
Japan	3	0.1
Far East		**3.7**
USA	80	62.2
Venezuela	12	9.3
Western Hemisphere		**78.0**

Source: History Database of the Global Environment (RIVM, 2002).

maverick in the Soviet bloc, but its economy remained severely undercapitalized and its modest oil resources proved to be an inadequate compensation for decades of economic mismanagement.

France was quickly overrun using a *Blitzkrieg* strategy based on the rapid and unconstrained mobility provided by internal combustion engines. Germany then tried to establish air supremacy, but lost the "Battle of Britain" air war for two reasons most pertinent to the story here. The main reason was that Germany was not prepared for US supplies Britain to point of UK insolvency (and beyond, with the March 1941 "Lend-Lease" law). A subsidiary but here highly pertinent reason is that the oil-distillate used by UK aircraft fuel provided a speed edge for its aircraft, compared to German synthetic fuels made from coal.

Thanks in part to its stranglehold over Romania, Germany had adequate liquid fuels for its operations in western continental Europe. However, the qualitative limitations of the liquid fuels it used for aircraft in the Battle of Britain could have been a hint of catastrophic quantitative problems to come when Germany turned its attention eastward.

Why did Germany Repeat Napoleon's Catastrophe?

Having failed to fully subdue the United Kingdom, Germany decided to try to hold it at bay while turning the Third Reich's attention toward a goal more central to its economic and ideological aspirations. Germany attacked the Soviet Union in June 1941 because:

- Enslaving or killing Slavs and taking their land was the basic goal of *Lebensraum* ideology.
- Germany needed Baku oil in the Soviet Union for its broader war program. Since the United States was not yet in the war to mass troops in England and Africa, Hitler decided to address the oil supply problem while trying to hold the United Kingdom at bay, rather than concentrating all resources on another attempt on Britain.
- *Blitzkrieg* transport difficulties in the east were underestimated, with twice as much oil use per kilometer traveled for the attack on the Soviet Union compared to the invasion of France.

Another point of view on this is that Soviet expansionism made a conflict with Germany inevitable. Thus, despite its obvious risks, Germany's attack in the summer of 1941 was the best it could do under the circumstances. Throughout the cold war, this point of view about the Soviet Union had obvious resonance with the idea that large conventional and nuclear forces were needed to ward off ingrained Soviet expansionism. In fact, with the result of enormous Soviet losses during 1941, Stalin appears to have initially been unprepared even to fight a defensive war against Germany, much less to launch a serious attack.[7] Whatever one's view of the underlying politics, however, it is clear from the point of view of military strategy that the control of oil supplies proved to be decisive.

Why Did the Tide of War Turn in 1942?

At the start of WWII in 1939, Germany had stocks of 0.48 million tons of aviation fuel, 0.35 million tons of gasoline, 1.07 million tons of diesel fuel, and 0.05 million tons of fuel oil. Its 1939 pact with the USSR brought it 0.9 million tons of Soviet Union oil, and with its conquest of France, Germany obtained nearly another 0.8 tons of various types of liquid hydrocarbons. However, the oil consumption of German armed forces increased from 3.0 million tons in 1940 to an average of 4.6 million tons per year (Mton/yr) for 1941–1943. An additional 1.9–2.7 Mton/yr was used for the rest of the German economy from 1940–1943. With these consumption rates, the stocks available in 1940 did not last long. Germany's annual production of synthetic fuels was not adequate to achieve military superiority. This production increased steadily from 1.1 Mton/yr in 1939 to 2.9 Mton/yr in 1943, before falling to 1.7 Mton in 1944. This helps explain why Germany took the tremendous gamble of breaking its pact with the Soviet Union and trying to push its armed forces all the way to the Baku oil fields.

The Allies' emphasis on broad-based bombing of German industrial cities suggested to Jensen[8] that they did not fully grasp how critical the oil supply was for the German war effort. For the Ruhr valley synthetic fuel plants were easier targets than others that so many allied aircrews lost their lives and equipment in attacking. Even so, Germany simply could not produce or commandeer enough oil to succeed in the era of fully mechanized warfare in which it had itself taken the early lead.

Attacking the Soviet Union and battling Britain, and the United States starting in December 1941, led to Axis oil supplies being spread too thin. Inadequate oil supplies stalled Rommel's troops at El Alamein in June 1942 and thus doomed the southern route thrust. Diversion of effort to an unsuccessful northern route attack toward the Baku oil fields nevertherless proved insufficient to keep German forces adequately supplied at the turning-point flank battle at Stalingrad at the end of 1942 (Fig. 13.2). Moreover, the direct and hard-fought German drive straight into the Caucasus to capture Soviet oil facilities found them demolished and useless all the way to

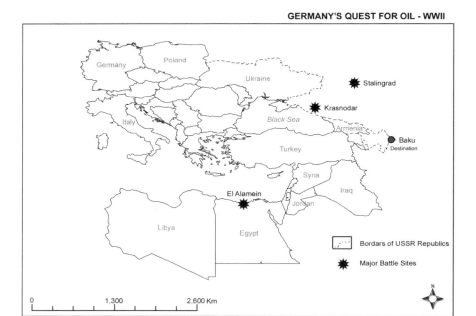

Fig. 13.2.   Stumbling blocks on Germany's drive toward Baku.

and including Krasnodar in present-day Russia.[9] The Germans never even made it to Grozny in Chechnya, north of eastern Georgia, and thus they never made it to Baku (on the Caspian Sea in Azerbaijan). But, for the timing of the United States' explicit entry into the war after the December 1941 Japanese attack on Pearl Harbor, Germany might still have been able to stave off collapse. Since the Pearl Harbor attack also led to military catastrophe for Japan as well as Germany, it is useful to review the central role that concern over oil supplies played in Japan's decision to launch that attack.

Why Did Japan Attack Pearl Harbor?

The interplay between economics, ideology, and psychology is also evident in the Japanese decision to attack Pearl Harbor. Economics: It was a protectionist era; Japan had never had adequate agriculture, and in the 20th century it wanted to control Manchurian coal and steel industry. Ideology: Japanese nationalism and broader "co-prosperity sphere imperialism" was based on a version of manifest destiny, albeit with less emphasis on redressing grievances than for Germany and Italy. Psychology: A militarist ethic at the center of power (occupied by General Hideki Tojo) tolerated putting the population in danger in a very risky venture.

Manchuria was occupied for economic reasons. Then, a power vacuum seduced Japan to expand farther south. Reaction to the effects of brutal militarist ideology and psychology and concerns about Japanese designs on Southeast Asia accelerated President Roosevelt's decision to cut off oil financing. As can be seen in Table 13.1, Japan's own oil production was very small. Over eighty percent of the oil production in the Far East in 1940 was in Dutch East Indies (now Indonesia and Brunei), with about half of the rest in Burma. In Japan, fatalism about the inevitability of conflict with the United States over access to oil in Southeast Asia led to a preemptive attack despite the risk of prompt and total mobilization of the US economy for war. Unfortunately for the Japanese and German war efforts, Japan's attack on Pearl Harbor bought them an implacable enemy with nearly ten times as much oil production as ever came under the influence of the Axis powers. That the attack on Pearl Harbor was dysfunctional was clear at the time to its commander Admiral Yamamoto, who had earlier traveled extensively in the United States ostensibly as a student. This raises the question of why his warning on this to the Japanese military staff went unheeded.

"Process Theory" for Organizational Dysfunction

An analogy to Japan's and Germany's fatal choices of attacking the United States and the USSR is a group of back-country skiers who take a wrong turn. They then plunge over a precipice at the end of an ever-increasing slope rather than face the humiliation and discomfort of discarding their skis and trudging back up the mountain. Whether they be real national leaders or these hypothetical foolish skiers, individuals make decisions in the context of day-to-day interactions with their peers. Organizations (e.g. nations) suffer the consequences of powerful individuals' decisions made in peer-interaction context. In both types of situation, win/win choice options lead to inertia, caution, and missed opportunities. Lose/lose choice options lead to hyperactivity, risk-taking, and sometimes to catastrophic outcomes that could have been avoided.

Europe's fascist leaders lived in a culture of fervent ideology and organizational terror. In this context, they plunged toward the precipice of invading the Soviet Union. They failed to halt the war even when all was clearly lost. When US oil became effectively unavailable, Japan's militarists were on a slippery slope that even Admiral Yamamoto's warning about the dangers of pulling the US dragon's tail could not dissuade them from. Psychologically unable to stop even himself from sliding down the slippery slope, Yamamoto not only acquiesced to the attack on Pearl Harbor, but also planned and commanded it.

Perceptions of the Military Importance of Oil

How did perceptions of the military importance of oil evolve between the Paris taxis episode of 1914 and the United States and Soviet H-bomb explosions in 1952–1953? Before WWI, only Churchill and the British Navy seem to have taken much substantive action based on prescience about the military importance of petroleum. When it later decided to make serious preparations for WWII, Germany had by then fully understood the tactical implications of the use of petroleum for *Blitzkrieg*. Japan was also preoccupied with its need for a source of petroleum to pursue its war aims. That both underestimated the difficulty of obtaining adequate supplies to prevail militarily only reinforced the concept that geological oil resources are critical militarily strategic commodities.

It is thus not surprising that the origin of the cold war is sometimes identified with a confrontation between the United States and the Soviet Union over Iran. After WWII, the Soviet Union sent tanks into northern Iran. A British and a US observer noticed the growing deployments and worked together to convince their governments that this was indeed occurring.[10] At the beginning of WWII, Iran had accounted for two-thirds of total oil production in North Africa and the Middle East (c.f. Table 13.1); so it is not surprising that deployment of Soviet tanks in that country was taken seriously. Then United States issued a demarche demanding their withdrawal, which occurred in 1946. "The Soviet government agreed to withdraw Red Army units from Iranian Azerbaijan in exchange for Iranian reforms in the region and the establishment of a Soviet-Iranian oil company which would operate in northern Iran. The last Soviet troops evacuated Iran on May 9th"[11] Not surprisingly, given its historic and continuing interest in Iranian oil, Britain backed the US demand for Soviet withdrawal from Iran.

Nuclear explosions completely changed the military significance of oil, but this took a long time to sink in. Concerning this sinking-in process, attributed to Albert Einstein is the observation that, "The unleashed power of the atom has changed everything save our modes of thinking and we thus drift toward unparalleled catastrophe".[12] Through 1948, however, only fission-based explosives were available, and these only in limited numbers. Indeed, in 1948, Yale Professor Walt Rostow and the new US National Security Resources Board suggested that the United States should save its own oil resources for possible wartime use by importing large amounts of Middle Eastern oil to reduce use of domestic resources in peacetime. Clearly at that point the idea that nuclear weapons had changed everything had not fully sunk in.

The massive thermonuclear ("hydrogen bomb") tests by the United States and the Soviet Union starting respectively in 1952 and 1953 should have made it clear that a protracted war between major industrial states was no longer a realistic possibility. Even with their very limited available supplies and sweeping attack plans, it took well over a year for Japan and Germany to run into militarily crippling oil supply difficulties. The concept of nuclear-armed major industrial powers taking massive conventional war casualties for such a long time without one side threatening use of nuclear weapons to avoid this looks implausible from a present-day perspective. Indeed, after a trip to Korea in December 1952, president elect Eisenhower's advisors prepared the end of the Korean war by leaking word of a "new strategic plan" for ending it, after receiving recommendations from military officers for the use of atomic munitions.[13] This was a clear enough indication of a major power's limits on casualties from conventional combat, and it does appear in fact to have been sufficient to bring the combat in Korea to a fairly quick end.

However, before the 1962 Cuban missile crisis the world had yet to look the consequences of a war between nuclear powers squarely in the eye. Moreover, the McCarthy-era controversy over the "loss" of China to communist control and how the Soviets "got the bomb" was followed by a national US crisis of confidence in 1957 when the Soviets put a satellite in orbit before the United States. Ironically, fears about the possibility of a major war were thus enhanced by the very events that propelled the cold war nuclear arms race to a point where a long and large-scale petroleum-dependent military encounter between industrial powers became implausible.

As the cold war progressed, the major powers converted some key assets in their naval fleets to nuclear propulsion. Moreover, after 1973, the United States finally established a petroleum reserve more than adequate to supply its military forces in any likely conflicts if the military were given priority for use of available oil supplies. It is true that the pre-positioning abroad of refined petroleum products remained a significant component of an overall logistics strategy, and in some cases petroleum distillates for the military might also be derived from material refined abroad. Nevertheless, control of the extraction of foreign petroleum resources from the ground became militarily marginalized during the first half of cold war. Before long the impact of potential and actual interruption of petroleum supplies in connection with a war also turned out to have only economic and political consequences. Direct limitations on the amount of petroleum products available to the largest operational military forces were no longer in the cards. This was to become apparent through events that culminated in the Yom Kippur War of 1973, as will be discussed later.

Endnotes

[1] USD (2002).
[2] Historylearningsite (2003).
[3] Yergin (1991, p. 332).
[4] RIVM (2002)
[5] Sudetic (2005).
[6] Reynolds (2004).
[7] Weinberg (1994).
[8] Jensen (1968).
[9] Economides and Oligney (2000, p. 75).
[10] McDonald (2005).
[11] League of Nations Photo Archive (2002).
[12] Lewis (1987).
[13] Lewis and Litai (1998, p. 13).

Chapter 14

Before the Iran–Iraq War

The years from WWII to 1980 saw a general trend toward more economic power and independence on the part of the countries that eventually became part of the Organization of Petroleum Exporting Countries (OPEC). This period culminated in a brief period of panic buying in energy markets after the Iranian revolution in 1979. While WWII convinced a generation that oil was of major military strategic importance, the postwar experience through 1980 reinforced the idea that oil was also of fundamental economic importance. Six milestone events occurred in this period. (1) Iran's elected government was overthrown after demanding a fifty percent share of oil profits. (2) President Eisenhower did not support Israel during the 1956 Suez crisis. (3) Oil companies' price reductions in 1959 lead to the formation of OPEC. (4) An attempted oil embargo failed during the 1967 Six-Day War despite contemporaneous war affecting oil production in Nigeria. (5) The United States provided crucial support to Israel in the 1973 Yom Kippur War. (6) A revolution deposed the ailing Iranian Shah in 1979.

Oil Demand and Supply

An increase from twenty-six million to forty million cars in service in the United States from 1945 to 1950 was a harbinger of sustained exponential growth in oil use until 1973. This stimulated interest in Saudi Arabian oil. Unbelievable as it may now seem, transport and other difficulties had made oil exploration in Saudi Arabia a money loser from 1933 to 1946 for Socal and Texaco's joint venture American Arabian Oil Company (Aramco). For help with development capital and distribution they turned to Standard Oil of New Jersey. This broke down an International Petroleum Commission "Red Line" agreement partitioning different parts of the Middle East among various oil companies. The French objected because the "Iraq Petroleum Company and the Red Line Agreement constituted their sole key to Middle Eastern oil".[1] Arabian King Ibn Saud wanted nothing to do with the British and their Anglo-Iranian oil company and thus agreed to help outmaneuver French legal objections.

Another US company, Gulf Oil, had a deal with Anglo-Iranian to avoid selling Gulf's Kuwaiti oil in India. So Gulf Oil turned to the Royal Dutch/Shell Group for marketing in Europe instead. Moreover, the United States and Britain had cooperated to pressure Stalin to remove Soviet troops from the Azerbaijani area of northern Iran in 1946. The next year Anglo-Iranian, Standard Oil of New Jersey, and the American Socony oil company signed a 20-year contract for Iranian oil. Thus did the United States get enmeshed in the Persian Gulf well before the 1953 Iranian counterrevolution and the 1956 Suez crisis that would enhance the United States role over that of the British.

The Arab league attacked the new state of Israel in 1948 after the United States and the USSR quickly recognized Israel's sovereignty. This started the first of four 20th century Arab–Israeli wars. The 1948 partition war had little immediate impact on oil, and indeed construction on a 1040-mile (1666 km) oil pipeline from Saudi Arabia through Lebanon proceeded apace.

Remembering Mexico's expropriation of the United States and British oil interests in 1938, the oil companies gradually agreed to set host countries' taxes about equal to company profits, in most cases by 1950. Previously, Aramco's take had been closer to 75 percent than 50 percent, when the Saudis were keen to get their oil industry developed and even 25 percent of rapidly increasing revenues looked substantial. However, Anglo-Iranian temporized on a 50 percent deal and had its Iranian holdings expropriated 1951 by Iran under the leadership of Prime Minister Mossadegh. Britain, then, launched a retaliatory embargo to shut down Iranian oil production. Fearing Mossadegh's overthrow by communists, the United States tried but failed to broker a deal near the end of 1951. With his country in an increasingly desperate financial situation, Prime Minister Mossadegh moved away from democratic procedures and courted the USSR. At this point, Churchill and the Americans hatched a successful plot to overthrow the Iranian government and reinstall thirty-three-year-old Shah Mohammed Reza Pahlevi as ruler of Iran. With anti-British sentiment in Iran still running high enough to make Iranians suspicious of an exclusive arrangement with the Anglo-Iranian oil company, several oil companies agreed to cooperate with the Shah and a new National Iranian Oil Company.

Suez Crisis and Second Arab–Israeli War

The hundred-year British concession for use of the Suez Canal obtained at its completion in 1869 had enormously simplified Britain's far-flung Indian Ocean operations. By 1955, the Suez Canal was the conduit for two-thirds of Europe's oil. Following a 1952 military coup in Egypt and the takeover by Col. Nasser in 1954, the United States abruptly cancelled a loan for the gigantic Nile River Aswan Dam in 1956 after Egypt bought Soviet arms and recognized China. Nasser responded by expropriating the Suez Canal. Doubting that Britain and France could sustain a pliable alternative government in Egypt following military intervention, a cautious US President Eisenhower refused to support military action when Britain and France launched it in cooperation with Israel. The United States pressure then forced a cease-fire and withdrawal from the Suez Canal, which remained closed until April 1957.

The Suez crisis played a critical role in the turnover from a predominantly British to predominantly American influence in the Arabian Peninsula and Persian Gulf. J. E. Peterson puts this in a broader context:

> The slowly emerging American insinuation into the Peninsula occurred simultaneously with a gradual British retrenchment from the existing position in the Gulf and Middle East. This phenomenon was only the local manifestation of a broader process involving the

dismemberment of the British Empire and the cumulative relin-
quishing of long-held East-of-Suez responsibilities. The Peninsula
and Gulf constituted the tail end of a retreat punctuated by exits
from India in 1947 and Egypt in 1954, the Suez debacle in 1956,
the Iraqi revolution in 1958, the surrender of Aden in 1967, and
finally withdrawal from the Gulf in 1971.[2]

OPEC

Under price pressure from the large discoveries of the 1950s, the oil
companies understandably reduced prices in 1959, but they neglected
to consult ahead of time with the host governments whose revenues
would be seriously affected. This led to the formation of the
Organization of Petroleum Exporting Countries (OPEC), albeit with
little practical effect until 1973.

Of more immediate consequence were challenges to the major oil
companies' market dominance. This started fitfully with a challenge
by the Italian national company ENI until its chairman died in 1962.
It gathered momentum as the opening up of new Libyan production
to Occidental and other independent oil companies put further
downward pressure on the price of oil through the 1960s. Resultant
lower oil prices facilitated conversion from coal to oil for transport
and other purposes in the United States and Europe, despite continuing European coal mining subsidies harking back to the strategic
role of coal and the political importance of miners' unions earlier in
the century.

Third (Six-Day) Arab–Israeli War

Preempting an Egyptian military build-up following Nasser's expulsion of UN peace observers from the Sinai in 1967, in May of that
year Israeli forces raced across the Sinai all the way to Suez. Israel also
occupied all of Jerusalem, what became the West Bank occupied territories, and the Golan Heights in Syria. Coincidentally, Nigerian
action against the attempted secession of Biafra removed 500,000
barrels per day of oil from the world market. Under American threat

of refusal to share oil, a producer sharing arrangement within the Organization for Economic Cooperation and Development (OECD) countries reconstituted arrangements like those that had helped them weather the 1956 Suez Canal closing, and an Arab oil embargo collapsed. By August total Arab production was actually eight percent higher than in May. However, due to rapidly rising consumption, the new oil glut was so short-lived that substantial sums were spent in preparing an expensive trans-Alaska pipeline. Environmental concerns postponed an expected 1972 start-up, but oil was soon to become valuable enough to provide a resolution to this impasse.

The actual halt to the glut-induced slide in oil prices following the 1967 Six-Day War occurred after a coup in Libya led by Colonel Khadafi in 1969. This resulted in Libya's revenue share increasing from the traditional 50 percent to 55 percent, and in an increase in oil prices. The 55 percent share soon became the minimum, and posted prices increased by a then-substantial ninety cents per barrel. Host countries also started acquiring participation shares in oil operations. Moreover, excess production capacity margins had shrunk to a nominal one percent (i.e. virtually zero) by 1973. However, up to this point the idea of the need for direct US military intervention to guarantee access to oil had evidently not recovered from Eisenhower's reluctance, judging by the neglect of suggestions to this effect from the US embassy in Iraq in 1970.

Fourth (Yom-Kippur) Arab–Israeli War

On the Yom Kippur Jewish holiday on October 6, 1973, Egypt attacked and drove the Israelis out of positions on the eastern bank of the Suez Canal. This happened just as OPEC had been unsuccessfully pressing oil companies for a doubling of oil prices. Having rejected an impromptu summit overture by Soviet Premier Leonid Brezhnev on preventing Middle Eastern war three months earlier, US President Richard Nixon and Secretary of State Kissinger found themselves in a bind. They felt forced to supply Israel against Egyptian military advances while the USSR conversely resupplied Syria against Israeli gains. Saudi Arabia responded by escalating a previous plan for monthly 5–10 percent Arab production reductions to an all-out embargo on export of oil to the United States. Coincidentally, on October 20, Nixon's Attorney General resigned over the sacking of the Watergate scandal prosecutor. Within six days Brezhnev mobilized to intervene to save Egypt's Third Army from an Israeli counter attack, and US nuclear forces went from a first to third or higher stage of alert. There was then a ceasefire in the Middle East, but the oil embargo remained in place. This was then replaced in March of 1974 with general production limits to raise prices, with only Syria and Libya against lifting the complete embargo. Posted prices of a benchmark crude oil barrel went from $1.80 in 1970 to $2.18 in 1971 to $2.90 in mid-1973 to $5.12 in October 1973 to $11.65 in December 1973. (This is all in then-current prices. There was a major round of overall price inflation after these events. Accounting for this and subsequent inflation to 2008 prices, from the middle to the end of 1973 oil jumped from $14/barrel to $53/barrel.)

Adjustment, Second Shock, and Great Panic

The response to higher oil prices was highlighted by the approval in 1975 of the Trans-Alaska Pipeline, which had been reconfigured for better environmental protection. The US legislation in that year also established standards for doubling auto fuel efficiency. A strategic petroleum reserve was established but filled too slowly to be a useful tool in fighting further skyrocketing of prices in the early 1980s. North Sea oil also started flowing into Britain in 1975.

None of these measures made up for the withdrawal of Iranian oil exports following the overthrow of the Iranian Shah in 1979, the flight of foreign oil company personnel from Iran, and the start of the Iran–Iraq War. Ending a "mini-glut" that had been heading toward slumping prices, global production fell by 4–5 percent. This was enough to trigger panic buying that by 1981 had driven oil prices to about $76/barrel in terms of 2008 purchasing power, as shown in Table 14.1.[3] Lines at US gas stations reinforced the panic mentality. Although of little short-term importance for energy supplies, the partial commercial nuclear reactor core meltdown at the Three Mile

Table 14.1. Saudi Arabian light crude oil prices ($/barrel).

1970 to end of first cartel period			1987–2008		
Year	Nominal $	$US2008	Year	Nominal $	$US2008
			1987	16.15	30.09
			1988	17.52	31.37
			1989	13.15	22.50
			1990	18.40	29.92
			1991	24.00	36.94
1970	1.35	7.40	1992	15.90	23.85
1971	1.70	8.85	1993	16.80	24.41
1972	1.90	9.58	1994	12.40	17.57
1973	2.10	10.22	1995	16.63	22.92
1974	9.60	**42.68**	1996	18.20	24.42
1975	10.46	**41.59**	1997	22.98	29.92
1976	11.51	**42.88**	1998	15.50	19.87
1977	12.09	**42.81**	1999	10.03	12.64
1978	12.70	**42.09**	2000	24.78	30.41
1979	13.34	**40.46**	2001	20.30	24.02
1980	26.00	**69.23**	2002	17.68	20.68
1981	32.00	**76.20**	2003	27.39	**31.23**
1982	34.00	**74.69**	2004	27.08	**29.46**
1983	34.00	**72.02**	2005	34.05	**36.33**
1984	29.00	**58.96**	2006	55.01	**57.75**
1985	29.00	**56.95**	2007	55.12	**57.49**
1986	28.00	**52.93**	2008	91.00	**91.00**

Source: Information for the beginning of year oil prices icomes from the US Energy Information Agency (USEIA, 2003a; USEIA, 2006a; USEIA 2008b), with the consumer price index used to adjusted beginning of year prices to 2008 purchasing power from the US Bureau of Labor Statistics (USBLS, 2008).

Island nuclear plant in March 1979 certainly did not help calm concerns about alternative future energy supplies.

Until 1980, the primary focus of the British and US concern over what kind government controlled Persian Gulf oil resources had been on Iran. But the center of attention was in the process of shifting to Iraq. In fact, trouble for the Anglo-American partnership in Iraq had been brewing ever since the fall of the Ottoman Empire.

Gertrude Bell, a British foreign service officer, had played a major role then in combining the Kurdish, Sunni, and Shia-dominated Ottoman administrative districts into a single country.[4] The policy preference was for this country to be dominated by the Sunni minority, since the Shia proved resistant to British demands.[5] In 1920, British air and ground forces put down a rebellion in Iraq at the cost of over six thousand Iraqi casualties. They then installed a foreign Sunni king in 1921 and finalized Iraq's borders in 1922. Iraq was granted independence in 1932, but British troops remained and eventually deposed a pro-German government in 1941. In 1952, an uprising against the monarchy was put down, but in 1958 a military coup was successful. By 1963 an anti-leftist coup had installed the Ba'th party in power, leading shortly thereafter to the dictatorship of Saddam Hussein.[6] His attack on Iran after its 1979 revolution would lead to a new chapter in the history of oil in the Persian Gulf.

Endnotes

[1] Yergin (1991, p. 414).
[2] Peterson (2002, p. 22).
[3] USEIA (2003a, 2006a, 2008b); USBLS (2008).
[4] Wallach (2005).
[5] Youssef (2006).
[6] Everest (2004).

Chapter 15

Iran and Iraq

After the fall of the Iranian Shah that the United States had helped to install, US–Iranian relations were so soured that the United States actually provided important support to Iraq after its attack on Iran in 1980. It is ironic that Iran's first post-Shah revolutionary leader was thwarted in his one critical demand for ending the Iran–Iraq war before the point of mutual exhaustion: that Saddam Hussein step down from power. Two enduring enmities may have had a significant psychological impact on the outcome of the Iran–Iraq war. One of these was the bitterness engendered in both the US public and its foreign service by the holding of hostages in the US embassy in Tehran after the revolution. The other was the bitter hatred that Iran's supreme leader Ayatollah Khomeini held for Saddam Hussein.

Iran and the United States

Troubled relations among Iran, Iraq, and the United States have dominated the global relationship between energy and security since 1979. The poisoning of US–Iranian relations dates back to well before Ayatollah Khomeini took over from the Shah as the supreme power in Iran in 1979. With the formation of the National Iranian oil company and subsequent US Central Intelligence Agency (CIA) support for the ouster of Iranian Prime Minister Mossadegh in 1953, the United States inherited the bitterness of Anglo-Iranian relations from WWII and before. It certainly did not help that the murder of Khomeini's eldest son in 1977 was attributed by some to the Savak, the secret police organization that supported the Shah.[1]

161

In October 1979, the administration of US President Carter made a portentous mistake by finally succumbing to lobbying by Henry Kissinger, David Rockefeller, and others to allow the cancer-ridden Shah into the United States to be treated. "Though he was checked into the New York Hospital, Cornell Medical Center, under a pseudonym, which just happened to be the real name of the US Undersecretary of State David Newsom, to the latter's discomfort, his presence was immediately known and widely reported".[2] Suspecting this to be another ruse, the Iranian government stood by while young people occupied the US embassy in Tehran and retained fifty hostages for a siege that would go on for 444 days. Nightly US national news broadcasts counted the days and often showed Iranian crowds chanting "Death to America." This poisoned US–Iranian relations until well after the two countries by Machiavellian logic should have had common cause against Iraq.

Then in December 1979, the USSR sent troops into Afghanistan to try to save a relatively new secular communist government there. In response, the US president's 1980 State of the Union Address contained a statement that came to be known as the Carter Doctrine:

> Let our position be absolutely clear: An attempt by any outside force to gain control of the Persian Gulf region will be regarded as an assault on the vital interests of the United States of America, and such an assault will be repelled by any means necessary, including military force.[3]

Carter's personal commitment had catalyzed peace between Egypt and Israel, and his approach to the Western Hemisphere helped pave the way for democracy and respect for human rights. He weathered the Soviet incursion into Afghanistan, but his country's sheltering of the dying Iranian Shah and his response to the siege of the US embassy in Tehran combined to cost him his reelection and cast an enduring shadow over US–Iranian relations.

Iran–Iraq War

Iran–Iraq relations were also poisoned by historical events. The most directly important of these was a boundary dispute over the Shatt-al-Arab waterway, which connects to the Persian Gulf at the boundary between the two countries. Iraq exported much of its oil through the Shatt-al-Arab and had claimed sovereignty over the whole channel. In 1975, the Shah got Iraqi President Saddam Hussein to agree to split the channel in return for Iran halting support for separatist Kurds in Iraq. In 1978, Iran also got Iraq to expel Iran's future supreme leader Ayatollah Khomeini, who had been living in Iraq for fourteen years as an exile from Iran. Another source of tension was Hussein's suspicion of the half or so of Iraq's population from the Shia branch of Islam, which is the dominant sect in Iran.

There was an assassination attempt against Iraq's Deputy Prime Minister in April 1980. Saddam Hussein then ordered the execution of the most prominent Shi ayatollah in Iraq and the ayatollah's sister. Hussein thereafter referred to Iran's supreme leader with demeaning insults and as a "Shah dressed in religious garb".[4]

However, the ultimate source of enmity on the Iraqi government's side was not just cultural or personal. Rather, the ruling Iraqi group relied on high oil prices to provide a sizeable and quiescence middle class with consumer goods while the country still invested heavily in its military. Other producers' contributions to a "mini-glut" of oil production and slumping prices were threatening this approach, and revolution and purges in made Iran into Iraq's most tempting target for shutting down or taking over the competition. Combined perhaps with simple opportunistic greed, there were thus underlying motivations connected with international economics and maintenance of the internal power structure that provided impetus for an Iraqi attack on Iran.

On September 23, 1980, Iraq attacked Iran's oil facilities, and Iran counterattacked and cut off almost all Iraqi oil exports. Hussein's goal was evidently to revisit Iraq's historical claim on the Shatt-al-Arab and its (Iranian) oil production facilities at the minimum, and perhaps to annex or control Iranian Khuzistan, which contained ninety percent of Iran's oil reserves and a very substantial Arab Shia population. However, Iranian Shia did not welcome the Iraqi invasion. Iraqi hopes for a quick victory were frustrated in a bloody war that Khomeini refused to end even when Western support for Iraq left no hope of a decisive outcome.

> The Arabs of Khuzistan showed no desire to be liberated by Iraq and did not welcome the Iraqis as "brothers," but rather saw them as invaders. The Iraqis were unprepared for the "human wave" assaults they encountered on the battlefield. Hundreds of thousands of young people, drawn by the Shiite version of martyrdom, and with little thought for their own lives, advanced on Iraqi positions in front of Iranian troops...[5]

The further loss of oil production accompanying the Iran–Iraq war drove prices to a new peak. However, increased global oil production elsewhere, a combination of inflation and US recession termed "stagflation," conservation measures, and inventory draw-down limited the price rise. Moreover, these measures set up the world for a new oil glut even before Iran-Iraq production started to recover. In 1983, OPEC cut prices by fifteen percent. Prices continued to slide, and in 1986 they suddenly plummeted. By the beginning of 1987 the benchmark price was $30/barrel, substantially lower than the $40/barrel price that preceded the Iranian revolution (both in terms of 2008 purchasing power).

In 1986, Iran captured the Fao Peninsula bordering Kuwait in the south (see Fig. 15.1). Then in response to an Iraqi counterattack Iran stepped up attacks on shipping out of Kuwait and on third-country tankers carrying Iraqi oil exports. Iran also launched a few missile attacks on Kuwait itself. Kuwait asked for assistance not only from the United States but also from the USSR. The Reagan administration then insisted on a sole US role in reflagging eleven Kuwaiti tankers under US naval escorts. Thus, despite Iraq's use of chemical

OIL FIELDS

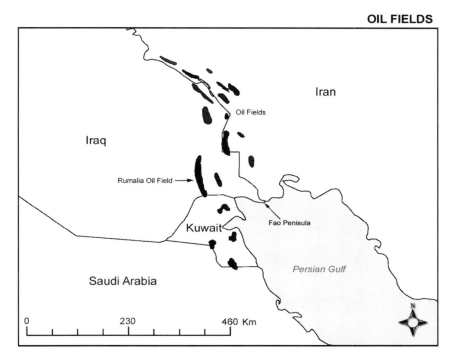

Fig. 15.1.   Oil fields in Kuwait and near the Iran–Iraq border.

weapons against Iran in 1988, the United States helped its soon-to-be enduring foe prevail against Iran and forced a dying Khomeini to accept peace short of his long-stated goal of removing Hussein from power in Baghdad. In the process, a United States destroyer mistakenly shot down an Iranian Airbus and thus killed 290 passengers, further sowing seeds of bitterness between the United States and Iran. As a result of combined Soviet and Kuwaiti support and the West's lean toward Iraq, by 1989 Iraq had been allowed to buy military equipment worth $56 billion in then-current dollars on credit in the hopes that renewed oil exports would eventually allow repayment. What was to be done about this debt would plague international relations involving the lenders even after the US-led occupation of Iraq in 2003.[6]

Endnotes

[1] Smitha (1998).
[2] Yergin (1991, p. 700).
[3] Carter (1980).
[4] Yergin (1991).
[5] Yergin (1991, pp. 710–711).
[6] Smith (2003b; Bumiller, 2003).

Chapter 16

Gulf War I

By 1990, the collapse of cartel-controlled oil pricing, accumulated military spending faced Iraq with an impending fiscal crunch that it tried to sidestep by invading Kuwait. Concerns about Iraq's nuclear program were used to mobilize support for a US-led counterattack. This led to an enduring commitment to keep Iraq from possessing nuclear, biological, or even chemical weapons. Although the lethality of these unconventional weapons varies widely from one type of chemical or biological agent to another, these were collectively referred to as "weapons of mass destruction." Attempts to enforce this ban could use aerial bombardment, limited ground incursions, or full scale invasion and occupation. The Clinton administration chose the first of these. Three questions are addressed here in connection with these events: (1) Why did Iraq occupy Kuwait? (2) What was the state of Iraq's nuclear program before it occupied Kuwait? (3) How did Iraq's suspected nuclear program relate to the US decision to counterattack?

Kuwait

Iraqi hopes for avoiding austerity measures after the 1986 oil price slump were to be dashed by a creditors' meeting in Paris in 1990 to consider Iraq's credit worthiness in light of continuing stagnation of global oil prices. This put the revenue stream that propped up middle class consumption in Iraq at risk. Saddam Hussein tried to preempt domestic political and international economic problems by invading Kuwait and seizing its gold reserves and oil production capacity. The United States had in-depth military capability as a result of building up forward deployment bases farther south along the Persian Gulf to support the Carter Doctrine. However, previous leaning toward Iraq and antagonism toward Iran left the US authorities in a mind-set that allowed them to be caught flat-footed diplomatically by Iraqi troop movements toward the Kuwaiti border. The United States failed even to issue a clear warning about what would happen in case Iraq invaded Kuwait.

Within a year, to prevent the destruction of the remaining assets of his "elite Republican Guard", Hussein had been forced to accept a hastily arranged cease-fire agreement. This agreement called for the start within fifteen days on a process of inspections and dismantling weapons of mass destruction. There were also reparations due to Kuwait and payments to the United Nations for overseeing control of Iraqi oil sales and disarmament inspections. After a long cat-and-mouse game, Iraq's nuclear arms program was evidently thoroughly dismantled; but in 1998 Hussein refused further cooperation with biological and other weapons inspections. Iraq was then subjected to a reinvigorated and ongoing air defense suppression campaign by the United States and the United Kingdom. Meanwhile oil prices had collapsed to just over $10/barrel in then-current prices by 1998. Oil prices had nearly tripled by 2000, after events in Venezuela catalyzed renewed effective OPEC action. At that point, the US Secretary of Defense "jawboned" prices down a bit temporarily while US Congressmen implicitly threatened lack of future military support in the Persian Gulf in case oil prices remained high. The quarterly oil prices shown in Table 16.1 illustrate how low prices had sunk before OPEC came alive again in 1999.[1]

Iraqi Unconventional Weapons before 1990

The situation in Iraq before and after Gulf War I illustrates both the limitations and some of the uses of the Nuclear Nonproliferation Treaty (NPT) and associated International Atomic Energy Agency (IAEA) inspection protocols. Iraq ratified the NPT and was subject to safeguards inspections under standard IAEA procedures up until the attack on Kuwait. For some time, Iraq operated a small nuclear

Table 16.1. Turn of the century crude oil prices ($US2008/barrel).

Year	Quarter			
	1st	2nd	3rd	4th
1997	30	24	24	26
1998	20	16	15	19
1999	13	17	21	29
2000	29	29	35	35
2001	26	28	29	24
2002	22	29	27	31
2003	31	28	29	29

Source: US Energy Information Agency (USEIA, 2003b).
Price are for the first Friday in each quarter for "Saudi Arabia Light Spot Price FOB" (freight on board) adjusted using the US consumer price index to purchasing power at 2008 prices.

reactor named Osirak. This reactor used fuel supplied by other countries that had uranium highly enriched in the weapons-usable isotope uranium-235 (^{235}U).

Iraq's Osirak reactor was destroyed by an Israeli bombing raid.[2] Iraq recovered nuclear fuel from the facility after this attack. Well before Iraq's attempted annexation of Kuwait, there was evidence that the bombing of the Osirak reactor had not terminated Iraq's nuclear weapons program. For example, two Iraqis were arrested at London's Heathrow airport early in 1990 for attempting to smuggle out capacitors reportedly suitable for use in triggering nuclear explosions.[3] Beyond continuation of IAEA inspections under the NPT, various countries that were simultaneously supporting Iraq's other military activities showed relatively little active concern at the time about Iraq's nuclear program. For example, one of British Foreign Secretary Hurd's comments on the smuggling incident was, "I can see considerable risk and damage by breaking off diplomatic relations…and no actual advantage".[4]

Iraq then turned to acquiring uranium enrichment technology, as had Pakistan, South Africa, and Brazil. In the decade after the Osirak bombing, Iraq did not succeed in manufacturing a nuclear weapon using this technology, despite an estimated ten billion dollar expenditure on its nuclear weapons program.[5] There are several reasons for this lack of success. Iraq had to deal with technology export controls established under the NPT. Compared to simply importing a complete technology, this made the process more difficult. Even under the best of circumstances, high-level enrichment of uranium in large enough quantities for a nuclear weapons program is a technically difficult exercise. This was made all the more difficult by an 8-year war with Iran that created alternate demands for resources.

Iraq's pursuit of multiple paths to nuclear weapons materials, rather than emphasizing larger-scale production with a single technology, split its resources and slowed down each path; but Iraq had no other viable alternative. Setting up large-scale nuclear materials production with a single technology might have been easier to detect. This might have encouraged Iran to attack Iraq even more vigorously in the 1980–1988 war before Iraq could produce nuclear weapons. A more transparent Iraqi nuclear program might also have undermined international support for Iraq during the Iran–Iraq war. This support included international transfers of an estimated $46.7 billion worth of conventional military equipment at then-current prices.[6] This was despite the buildup of a debt of comparable magnitude that, of course, became operationally in default during the war on Kuwait. Imminent Iraqi nuclear weaponization could also have prompted another attack on Iraq by a third country, at a time when Iraq could ill afford this.

Well before its annexation of Kuwait, Iraq had acquired a substantial chemical warfare capability using technology from West Germany and other countries. Although potentially quite dangerous, this was not uncommon. Many other countries had similar capabilities. Chemical weapons were reportedly used by Iraq against Iranian troops, and were used with catastrophic effect on thousands of Kurds in Iraq. By whom in specific cases has been disputed,[7] but it is commonly accepted that Iraq used chemical weapons to kill thousands of Kurdish civilians. There were no comparable mainline press reports of military use by Iraq of bacterial toxins or infectious agents.[8]

Nuclear Threat Justification for Countering Iraq

Since Iraq was a signatory to the NPT and nominally in good standing with the IAEA before the attack on Kuwait, Iraq's declared nuclear facilities were subject to occasional IAEA inspections. At the end of 1990, the latest such inspection had taken place that November. "According to the Associated Press, the IAEA made a routine visit November 19–22 to Iraq's two research reactors, a storage and fuel-producing plant, and 'found no evidence that Baghdad is developing atomic weapons for its arsenal' ".[9] On November 16, 1990, New York Times reporter Malcom Browne also wrote that Iraq had invited IAEA inspectors "to verify that Iraq's small stock of highly enriched uranium has not been made into a nuclear weapon".[10] According to Browne, the enriched uranium consisted of 27.6 pounds (12.5 kg) of weapons grade uranium (at about 93% ^{235}U) salvaged from the Osirak reactor after its destruction in 1981. Browne also reported that "in the last year Western intelligence operations have stopped various clandestine attempts by Iraq to import materials, machinery, and expertise that could be used for making nuclear fuel suitable for warhead explosive." The net effect was that the time was very short between the last IAEA inspection and the disruption caused by the intense bombing of Iraq associated with the 1991 Desert Storm campaign. According to the report supplied to the Nuclear Threat Initiative by the Monterey Institute for International Studies Center for Nonproliferation Studies, the bombing campaign disrupted a crash program aimed at the difficult task construct an implosion-driven nuclear bomb from the limited amount of uranium salvaged from the Osirak reactor.[11]

Meanwhile, the US administration had succeeded in obtaining a UN Security Council resolution authorizing the use of force against Iraq. However, according to Thomas Friedman, the US administration was still searching for "a rationale to convince the American public of the need to commit hundreds of thousands of troops for a possible war to free Kuwait from Iraq".[12] Toward the end of the Fiscal Year 1991 budget debate, the Senate Minority Leader, Robert Dole, had declared that the military build-up in the Persian Gulf was about one thing: "oil".[13] While noting that this had earlier been disputed by the US administration, Friedman reported in this same article that in November US Secretary of State Baker had recently linked the gulf operation "directly to oil supplies and the health of the American economy." Baker was very specific about this. "'If you want to sum it up in one word, it's jobs,' Mr. Baker said. 'Because an economic recession, worldwide, caused by the control of one nation, one dictator, of the West's lifeline will result in the loss of jobs on the part of American citizens.'" Various measures of public and Congressional opinion found considerable skepticism about initiating war in this context, as noted a week later by *New York Times* reporter Michael Gordon. Concerning rationales for military action in the Persian Gulf, Gordon reported in an article dated November 25:

> The Bush Administration today stepped up its effort to raise American concern about Iraq's ability to develop nuclear weapons, saying Baghdad might be able to produce a crude nuclear device within a year. Defense Secretary Dick Cheney and Brent Scowcroft, the U.S. national security adviser, said in separate appearances that the Iraqi nuclear weapons program was advancing despite the embargo, and they provided intelligence intended to buttress President Bush's statements about Iraqi's emerging nuclear ability made during his Thanksgiving visit to Saudi Arabia. President Bush's statements, and the remarks by the two officials, were clearly intended to add weight to the Administration's argument that the situation in the Persian Gulf must be brought to a decisive turn in the coming winter.[14]

Referring to the other rationales for military action discussed above, this article went on to report:

> None of those rationales for possible military action against Iraq appears to have decisively swayed public opinion. In contrast, in a recent New York Times/CBS Poll, 54 percent of the respondents said they believed that preventing Iraq from acquiring nuclear weapons

was a good enough reason to take military action against Iraq. An Administration official said the survey results had been noted by the White House, which is also looking for an argument that will sway the public. Another Government official, who insisted that he not be identified, said the Administration's statements today that Iraq could produce a bomb in a relatively short time was unduly alarmist, considering the difficulties of the technical processes.

Despite concerns that had recently been expressed about Iraq's nuclear potential, two former Joint Chiefs of Staff appeared before a Senate committee on November 28, 1990, and "urged the Bush Administration today to postpone military action against Iraq and to give economic sanctions a year or more to work".[15] One of those making this statement was the then most recent Joint Chiefs Chairman, Admiral Crowe.

It was in this context that three articles appeared concerning the significance of Iraq's nuclear potential with respect to the then-current military situation in the Persian Gulf.[16] One was a submission by Richard Rhodes, who had recently authored an award-winning book on the early history of the US nuclear weapons program. Rhodes' commentary appeared on the day before the former Joint Chiefs' testimony. Another by essayist William Safire appeared two days later. A third by Tom Wicker of the *New York Times* appeared on December 5.

All of these articles agreed that Iraq's theoretical short-term potential for constructing a single nuclear explosive from IAEA-inspected uranium was not militarily significant. Rhodes applied to Iraq the argument "that nuclear weapons are useless militarily, precisely because using them would trigger nuclear retaliation." Safire agreed that "one crude device would be a suicidal demonstration, not a serious means of turning back an attack." Concerning the 12.5 kg of highly enriched uranium recently inspected by the IAEA, Wicker noted:

That's less, moreover, than the 15 kilograms usually required for a single bomb such as the "primitive" weapon dropped on Hiroshima 45 years ago. A bomb made from 12.5 kilograms would have to be more sophisticated; that would require an advanced design and technology, of which Iraq probably is not capable. Even if it is, diversion of the fuel to make a bomb would not be easy or quick (though perhaps technically "matter a months") and probably not secret. Only one bomb could be made and it almost certainly would not be used.[17]

Concerning the longer term, there was a much wider difference of opinion among these three commentators. Safire inferred: "If he can explode a test device by one means in months, it would be dangerously foolish to think he could not explode a weapon built by another means in a few years." This is a nonsequitur, since the possession of a small quantity of enriched reactor fuel has no technical connection to the problems confronting Safire's eventual presumption[18] that Iraq intended building a nuclear weapon using indigenous uranium ores. Such an action was possible, however, and Wicker used the example of Pakistan to get an idea of how long this might take.

> To get from Iraq's current stage of nuclear development to weapons production took Pakistan about 11 years, and Pakistan had a more advanced scientific and technological establishment, as well as the tacit willingness of the US to let the effort proceed. Iraq, in sharp contrast, has been almost entirely dependent on Western technology and must now go ahead, if at all, against a Western blockade and under the threat of war.[19]

Instead of speculating on the actual timing, Rhodes made the observation that the essential problem was "to provide Saddam Hussein *and his successors* with security guarantees sufficiently robust to convince them not to go nuclear as soon as they can manage to do so" (emphasis added).[20] Rhodes' more cautious approach avoided the embarrassment of being caught out by the later revelation that Iraq had been successfully concealing research on an alternative approach to enriching uranium, the calutron. Each calutron is a low-throughput device. Operation of enough of them to produce a single bomb over the course of a substantial period of might well have become apparent through operation of the previously identified power lines needed to supply them and possibly also the electromagnetic fields or power dissipation created by their operation. Nevertheless, Iraq's success in keeping its calutron program secret was a wake-up call for the IAEA, which targeted 1992 as a starting point for a major effort to tighten up its overall approach to nuclear safeguards.

Options for Keeping Iraq Disarmed

Rhodes' observation concerning the inheritors of Iraq's governance points out an essential and continuing problem concerning Iraq and the nuclear proliferation question in general. With respect to Iraq, there remained three possibilities concerning its long-term potential for constructing weapons of mass destruction. (1) This potential could be constrained by threat of the use of force. (2) Some negotiated or implicit agreement could be obtained for voluntary restraint. (3) Programs to develop such weapons could proceed with no restraints except perhaps standard protocols for IAEA inspections. In the end, the George W. Bush administration chose the first of these options in 2003, though as it turned out a combination of the other two had already put Iraq's nuclear weapons development program on ice.

One possibility for threat of the use of force in the 1990s was aerial bombardment of any facilities that could reasonably be expected to lead imminently to production of nuclear, biological, or chemical weapons. This was the option prepared during the Southern and Northern Watch air defense suppression campaigns before 1998 and then exercised in that year when inspections ceased. However, it was questionable whether this would have ultimately been effective against hardened and/or dispersed facilities — unless perhaps the hypothetical possibility of repeated nuclear attacks on Iraq were allowed for. It also put the enforcing countries effectively in a state of permanent limited war against the target country. An indefinite continuation of this state of affairs is what the Bush administration wanted to escape from after the events of September 11 in 2001 provided an opportunity.

A second possibility for the use of force was to be prepared for ground operations connected with specific facilities, as opposed to an invasion of the country as a whole. In her summary of a proposal for "Coercive Inspections," Jessica Matthews looked at backing up an inspections program with military force as needed.[21] In this report, retired Air Force general Charles Boy looked at military issues, Rolf Ekeus looked at intelligence sharing, and others examined the politics and technical and legal basis for such an approach. However, risking continuing substantial casualties from engaging an enemy without being able to effect a conclusive military victory ran counter to post-Vietnam and especially post-cold-war US military doctrine. This approach also turned out to be incompatible with the clear focus on "regime change" that had solidified within the Bush administration after September 11, 2001.

A third possibility was supposed to end up like the solution adopted at the end of WWII. Here, the target countries gave up their sovereignty and were militarily occupied until a culture and treaty obligations evolved which indefinitely postponed their acquisition of weapons of mass destruction directed at the occupiers. This option became politically conceivable in the United States only after the attacks on its eastern seaboard on September 11. Even after an invasion of Iraq, it remained unclear whether the United States would have the staying power, if needed, to forcibly restrain the reintroduction in Iraq of chemical, or biological or even nuclear weapons production.

It might be inferred from the above discussion of justifications for US military action in the Gulf War I that use of force to constrain Iraqi nuclear capabilities was the policy of the first President Bush's administration as well as that of his son. In the first week of 1991, however, then-President Bush indicated that this is not the case when he said that Iraq would not be attacked if it complied with UN Security Council resolutions concerning the invasion of Kuwait.[22] Indeed, it turned out that promptly and thoroughly dismantling Iraq's nuclear and chemical weapons programs was not a high enough priority for President George H. W. Bush to keep a ready invasion force in place until this was accomplished. Thus, the Clinton administration inherited an awkward situation, which it managed with a juggling act involving sanctions and inspections.

Endnotes

1 USEIA (2003b).
2 Lewis (1991a).
3 AP (1990a).
4 AP (1990b).
5 Lewis (1991b).
6 Klare (1991); Grimmett (1989, p. 51).
7 Pelletiere (2003).
8 Browne (1991).
9 Wall (1990).
10 Browne (1990).
11 NTI (2005).
12 Frriedman (1990).
13 Dole (1990).
14 Gordon (1990a).
15 Gordon (1990b).
16 Rhodes (1990); Safire (1990a); Wicker (1990).
17 Wicker (1990).
18 Safire (1990b).
19 Wicker (1990).
20 Rhodes (1990).
21 Matthews (2002).
22 News–Gazette Wire Services (1991).

Chapter 17

Sanctions and Inspections

An early period of heavy international sanctions produced limited Iraqi cooperation with weapons inspectors through 1995. This gave way to a later period through 1998 where Iraq's nuclear program had been dismantled and some additional progress was made uncovering its chemical and biological weapons programs. In 1998, the inspections regime broke down after disputes over espionage. Then, the OPEC cartel again became effective at limiting production and increasing oil prices. This set the stage for a substantial increase in oil revenue to Iraq outside of the purview of nominally complete United Nations' control of Iraq's oil exports.

What Iraq Actually Had in 1990

What occurred in the decade after the events described in the previous chapter had a significant impact on subsequent international approaches to Iraq. First, during Gulf War I there was a large-scale bombing of Iraqi facilities. This used mostly traditional munitions but also a large number of precision guided munitions. The bombing was intended, amongst other things, to destroy Iraq's facilities for producing unconventional weapons. Under the subsequent cease-fire agreement, Iraq nominally acceded to inspection of all such facilities. In practice, Iraq initially attempted to frustrate the inspections just short of the point of outright resistance to the inspection procedures.

A significant event during the earlier part of this period was the discovery of an illuminating set of records in a building in Baghdad. These records outlined the Iraqi nuclear weapons program.[1] A particular concern expressed by the Iraqi government at the time was that the documents might reveal information about program personnel. Most of the records were removed by the time IAEA inspectors arrived, but enough remained to give an overview of the Iraqi program. Together with other inspection activities, the following was discovered.

In addition to previously suspected uranium enrichment activities, the Iraqis had also done some work on plutonium reprocessing and had a sizable electromagnetic separation program under way for uranium enrichment. The electromagnetic separators are called "calutrons" since they were pioneered by the University of California scientists during the Manhattan Project for the final stages of enrichment of weapons uranium. The Iraqi adoption of the calutron approach came as a surprise because the low throughput rate of these devices makes them less suitable for earlier stages of enrichment that the Iraqis also had to go through.

After Gulf War I, it was discovered that much of the Iraqi nuclear facilities had survived the intense aerial bombardment of the preceding conflict.[2] A number of foreign companies, including several in Germany, had supplied materials useful for the Iraqi effort. Iraq reportedly had also enriched lithium, indicating an interest in thermonuclear fusion.[3]

There were implications of these discoveries for future weapons inspections. First, the limited nature and possible shortcomings of the original goals of IAEA inspections became more apparent. The basic goal of IAEA inspections before the attack on Kuwait was to give some advance warning of approach to production of weapon materials in critical amounts at inspected facilities. The inspections did not fail to do so. Indeed, what the IAEA operationally defined as a "significant quantity" of fissile material had not actually been produced or converted to weapons. However, the inspections evidently did fail to detect production of a small amount of plutonium at the Tuwaitha experimental reactor facility on the Tigris river a short distance southeast of Baghdad.[4] Also, the well-known problem of dealing with weapons program activities at undeclared facilities was highlighted.

Second, the extent of involvement of foreign suppliers indicated a need for improved unilateral and international efforts, if restricting supply of information and technology is to be as effective as possible in slowing nuclear weapons programs. Third, these events highlighted the relative inefficacy of remote intelligence and intense aerial bombardment in destroying much of the weapons complex. In a country where covert foreign intelligence had been frustrated or inadequately pursued, aerial bombardment did not prove completely effective.

Fourth, technical personnel generally survived the bombardment and were presumably available to resume the weapons program if so directed. In this regard, a United Nations resolution was developed that "would require Iraq to adopt laws making it a punishable offense for any citizen to try to develop weapons of mass destruction or possess or manufacture forbidden materials".[5] Indeed early in 2003 Iraq did finally adopt domestic laws against production of weapons of mass destruction, but only under threat of invasion, not of economic sanctions. It took this long for Iraq to even formally comply with this UN resolution despite the reported tripling to quadrupling of Iraq's infant mortality rate with reportedly 1,000,000 children undernourished and 120,000 severely undernourished under the sanctions regime.[6]

Sanctions and Inspections: 1995–1998

The first President Bush had built a domestic and international coalition to counterattack Iraq on the basis of the limited goal of restoring the political *status quo ante*. This was not consistent with occupying Iraq to enforce disarmament. Dismembering Iraq as a means of allowing most of its population to escape domination by a secular subgroup of its Sunni Arab minority had also been precluded. Thus, even though Iraqi military resistance collapsed within days of the onset of allied ground force movements, Bush called a halt to the killing as soon as Iraqi armor had been shattered and an armistice could be arranged.

The *status quo ante* strategy was soon challenged by the sight of huge numbers of Iraqi Kurds moving toward the northern mountains to escape retribution from the Iraqi military. This desperate exodus was taking place despite a lack of shelter and increasingly harsh weather. Also, southern Iraqi Shiite Arabs who had been encouraged to rise up against Saddam Hussein's forces were abandoned to a continuing campaign of oppression and environmental assault on some of their difficult-to-penetrate marshlands. These events produced a political necessity to intervene in the north, and an opportunity for the United States to declare "no-fly zones" in the north and south delimited by latitude lines. The operations to enforce this and suppress interfering antiaircraft capabilities came to be know as Northern Watch and Southern Watch.

Under both President Bushes, there was still no appetite for partitioning Iraq in a way that would provide independent control for either the northern Kurds or the southern Shiite Arabs of the oil sources in their regions, perhaps leaving the mid-latitude Sunnis with some oil near the Iranian border. The US "Iran allergy" was still too strong at the end of Gulf War I to allow Iraqi Shiites control of substantial oil resources, even if they were of Arab rather than Persian descent. Also at this time there was still substantial violent strife occurring in Turkey over the Kurdish question. Turkey was a US ally in NATO and adamantly opposed to establishment of an independent Kurdistan. Thus, even though an effectively autonomous northern Kurdish region was established in Iraq, the Iraqis were eventually allowed to divide and partially conquer rival Kurdish groups.

As noted above, Iraqi unconventional weapons in general, and nuclear weapons potential in particular, had essentially been brought in as an afterthought to the arguments for expelling Iraq from Kuwait. This was to persuade a reluctant public and US Senate that there was more to reconstituting a privileged and undemocratic absentee Kuwaiti regime than just keeping them rather than the Iraqis in control of Kuwait's oil. (When the occupation occurred, many of the wealthiest Kuwaitis were absentees in the sense that they were out of the country on customary vacation to escape the seasonal heat, and remaining high government officials fled before the occupation could be completed.) The terms of the armistice dealing with weapons of mass destruction were similarly ad hoc. The armistice included a promise that all such weapons would be destroyed within a few months. In terms of compliance and enforcement, this commitment was evidently not taken literally by either side. This is evidenced by subsequent Iraqi intransigence and by the standing down of US expeditionary forces without compliance yet having been enforced.

Economic sanctions were left as the primary tool for enforcing the terms of the armistice. Revenues from Iraq's remaining oil production were to be controlled by the United Nations to pay primarily for reparations to Kuwait and for the UN's own weapons inspections and operations. Initially this and import restrictions simply left insufficient revenues to provide for Iraqis' public health and welfare. Then Iraq reluctantly recognized the durability of sanctions and accepted an "oil for food" program that at least provided for a minimal level of sustenance and some other essentials.

Meanwhile, the oil export sanctions proved increasingly leaky, early on at less than a billion dollars per year, but rising eventually to an estimated three billion in 2002. This included overland smuggling in the northeast and also some shipping via Iran. To obtain access to oil, companies also paid surcharges to Iraqi sources that were not supposed to be allowed under the sanctions regime. None of Iraq's neighbors that profited from this had an immediate economic incentive to suppress oil smuggling. While the Iraqi regime thus obtained substantial revenues that could in principal have been used to supply immediate human needs, in practice substantial sums were spent on building a network of "presidential sites" off limits to UN inspectors.

The possibility of sanctions being lifted from Iraq was undoubtedly reduced by continuing unfavorable reports on Iraq's cooperation with biological weapons program monitoring by the United Nations through 1995.[7] Reluctance to lift sanctions was perhaps reinforced by criticism of Iraq's approach to human rights issues.[8]

End of the First Round of Inspections

After the UN weapons inspectors' breakthrough on Iraq's biological weapons program in 1995, the inspection program became increasingly contentious. What had been left out of the sanctions regime requirements was repayment of the billions of dollars each that Hussein's government owed to France and Russia for previous imports. Russia and France became increasingly restive about the prospects of an endless sanctions regime under these conditions. Perhaps looking forward to a revised "smart sanctions" approach that would restore commerce and debt repayment without complete resolution of questions about compliance with inspections, Russia and France were more tolerant than the United States of Iraqi restrictions on inspectors' activities.

As the inspectors paid increasingly close attention to so-called presidential sites, Iraq claimed that this was in aid of espionage. Iraq reacted is if it felt this might lead to activities that could endanger the life of its President. That this was a serious concern was later claimed by an inspection team leader named Scott Ritter but denied by non-nuclear inspections project leader Richard Butler, both of whom wrote books on the matter.[9] The Clinton administration gave the distinct impression that sanctions were expected to continue indefinitely as long as Saddam Hussein remained in power. Since Clinton appeared to have too little motivation or domestic support for an effective military campaign to enforce Iraqi disarmament, there was little incentive on Iraq's part to continue cooperating with weapons inspections.

In 1998, following a series of disputes over the espionage issue, the weapons inspections teams were withdrawn and President Clinton ordered a brief series of attacks on suspected Iraqi weapons facilities. Suppression of anti-aircraft defenses in the no-fly zones continued, and was briefly extended northward of the southern zone after President Bush took over the White House from Clinton following the closely contested election in the year 2000. Thus concluded a decade of what would turn out to be a war interregnum of continuing strife over an incompletely enforced armistice. There was no lasting accommodation or deterrence relationship established between Iraq and the United States and its primary ally in the matter, the United Kingdom.

After the 2003 invasion of Iraq, over a billion dollars was spent looking for weapons of mass destruction. No evidence was found that Iraq had such weapons in 1998, or made them, afterward. Nor was there any substantial support for speculations that chemical or biological weapons had been moved to another country such as Syria. This was despite the fact that Iraq at the least had previously possessed thousands of mustard gas shells. Much of the former senior Iraqi leadership was eventually taken into custody. Still, little useful information has been released on why Iraq was so thorough in eliminating its chemical weapons and biological weapons research program but refused US and UN demands to make this more transparent.

One hypothesis is that the Iraqi leadership had concluded that a US invasion was inevitable, and would again be promoted on the basis of the threat Iraqi weapons of mass destruction. By leaving enough ambiguity for the invaders to walk out on this plank but also thoroughly scrubbing its chemical and biological programs, collapse of the justification for the invasion would then leave the invaders more diplomatically isolated and publicly embarrassed. This is indeed what occurred. However, the timing of the Iraqi scrubbing program does not appear compatible with such a nuanced plan. According to Gordon and Trainor, the ambiguity posture was indeed meant to create what Iraq's Second Republican Guard Commander Raad Majid al-Hamdani reportedly dubbed "deterrence by doubt."[10] However, Saddam Hussein is supposed to have come quite late to the realization that the United States was actually going to attack,[11] far too late for a last minute attempt to reach a deal to avoid an invasion to have any chance of success.[12] Instead, Hussein was trapped in his own kind of generational lag, a fixation on Iran as being his primary enemy.

> His political strategy was to keep Tehran in check by maintaining some measure of ambiguity over Iraq's WMD, what Hamdani had dubbed "deterrence by doubt." While a decade of sparring with

United Nations inspectors over the fate of his past weapons programs meant that Iraq faced economic sanctions, Saddam saw value
in not letting the world know that his officials had disposed of his
chemical and biological arsenal.[13]

Thus, it is more likely that after the 1995 revelations the Iraqi leadership simply decided that making nuclear weapons under such intense
scrutiny was impracticable, and maintaining active chemical or biological weapons programs under such circumstances was more trouble
than it was worth. After all, in connection with Gulf War I Iraq had
been fairly explicitly threatened with nuclear retaliation if it used chemical or biological weapons. As long as the sanctions on Iraq remained in
place, the only plausible attack on Iraq would be led by the nuclear-
armed United States. Without nuclear weapons, the possession of
chemical or biological ones was thus militarily useless for Iraq.

What was likely the case was that Iraq wanted to maintain the
potential to reconstitute its weapons of mass destruction programs,
and retaining key personnel in country was part of a strategy of maintaining the needed infrastructure. A simpler explanation is that the
Iraqi leadership had concluded that no amount of cooperation would
be sufficient to satisfy US demands, and the demand for Iraqi personnel to be taken out of country was simply the last straw.

Saddam Hussein refused a UN and US demand in 1998 that
chemical and biological weapons program personnel and their immediately families be taken outside of Iraq in connection with interviews with weapons inspectors. One possibility is concern that the
results of these interviews would be used to augment suspicion over
Iraq's weapons programs without drawing a distinction between current and previous activities. However, this refusal is also consistent
with the idea that Hussein wanted to perpetuate ambiguity about
whether or not they still existed. Knowledge about the disposition of
Iraq's chemical weapons was so compartmentalized that some Iraqi
commanders may have thought that others still had access to chemical weapons. Indeed, according to US weapons inspection team
leader David Kay, by 1997–1998 Iraq had plunged into such a "vortex

of corruption" that "Iraqi scientists had presented ambitious but fanciful weapons programs to Mr. Hussein and had then used the money for other purposes."[14] Not surprisingly, this situation was known to relatives of Iraqi scientists. More interestingly, it was also known to participants in a "a secret prewar CIA operation to debrief relatives of Iraqi scientists," set up in response by a push by assistant director for collections Charlie Allen for other sources of information after UN weapons inspectors were withdrawn from Iraq in 1998. Rather than "writing reports that accurately reflected the information they had" and providing an assessment of the possibility that what had been heard was part of a coordinated disinformation campaign, the intelligence agents did not circulate information that could have challenged the conventional wisdom that Iraq still had unconventional weapons.[15] Upon leaving his job in charge of the post-occupation search for unconventional weapons, David Kay summarized the situation:

> "The whole thing shifted from directed programs to a corrupted process," Mr. Kay said. "The regime was no longer in control; it was like a death spiral. Saddam was self-directing projects that were not vetted by anyone else. The scientists were able to fake programs."[16]

This situation served the policy of maintaining ambiguity well. There is no better basis for convincing someone else of something that is not true than to be convinced of it oneself. A mirror of this phenomenon occurred in much of the senior US leadership, many of whom appear to have actually convinced themselves that Iraq did still possess substantial stocks of chemical and biological weapons in the absence of any credible evidence whatsoever that this was actually the case. This ambiguity apparently deliberately created by Iraq thus left room for doubt in the minds of permanent US and British intelligence staff not to directly contradict US and British officials and their political appointees making strong, but untrue, claims about Iraq's possession of weapons of mass destruction.

Impact on Palestine and Iran

After the Palestinian Liberation Organization sided politically with Iraq during the war over Kuwait, it lost much of the support it had previously enjoyed from Saudi Arabia and other Arab states that had chosen the other side. This proved an important catalyst for the establishment of a "peace process" highlighted by Yasser Arafat and Israeli prime minister Rabin shaking hands in front of a beaming President Clinton in Washington on September 13, 1993.[17]

The Israelis and Palestinians then managed to "snatch defeat from the jaws of victory" in their peace process by hanging up otherwise more-or-less complete negotiations on practical issues on the largely symbolic question of the political status of Jerusalem. Following a provocative visit to a religious site by a former Israeli defense minister skeptical of the peace process, Ariel Sharon, the death toll escalated as Israeli forces exchanged fire sometimes even with the Palestinian police with whom they were meant to be cooperating.

Had nothing at all been learned from the past, the history of 1973 would have been poised to repeat itself, with Arab countries threatening a new oil embargo in support of the Palestinians. In practice, Saddam Hussein appeared isolated among Arab leaders, albeit not among all of Arab populations, in hinting of such possibilities.

The prospects for a more orderly producer–consumer cartel bargaining over stabilization of oil prices within an agreed $22–28/barrel range were unsettled by these events. At the same time, an incipient Iranian counter-revolution, supported by many of those born in the high fertility 1973–1980 period, was at least temporarily muffled by Iranian theocratic leaders' control of the legal system and press laws. A pro-reform faction had substantial support in the elected legislature but lacked the ability to override veto of reform by Iran's theocratic establishment. Prospects for a rapprochement along any two sides of the US–Iran–Iraq triangle of bitterness thus remained in limbo. Prospects for a more stable energy and security nexus in the Persian Gulf then vanished, at least for quite some time to come, under the gathering clouds of war in 2002.

Endnotes

1   Lewis (1991); Albright and Hibbs (1992).
2   Schmitt (1991).
3   Broad (1991).
4   Wines (1991).
5   Lewis (1991a).
6   Tyler (1991).
7   Reuters (1995); Crossette (1995b, c); New York Times (1995).
8   Crossette (1995a).
9   Ritter (1999); Butler (2000).
10   Gordon and Trainor (2007).
11   Shanker (2004).
12   Risen (2003).
13   Gordon and Trainor (2007, p. 74).
14   Risen (2004a).
15   Risen (2004b).
16   Risen (2004a).
17   BBC (2006).

Chapter 18

Iraq After 9/11/01

After the first Bush administration left office, former Secretary of Defense Cheney and others revisited previously rejected suggestions to effect "regime change" in Iraq. This was justified by embracing a goal of enforcing disarmament in order to achieve détente with a democratized Iraq. In principle, the goal was to avoid a choice between disengagement from dependence on imported energy or an enduring deterrence relationship with the holder of the world's second largest oil reserves. The hope that Iraq, after the removal of Saddam Hussein, would peacefully embrace democracy and manage economic reconstruction using its own oil revenues turned out to be wildly optimistic. From the invasion of Iraq until he left office, George W. Bush and his defense secretaries would be overseeing a fight against an insurgency that they could neither fully defeat nor disengage from.

Regime Change: From Heresy to Shadow Cabinet Policy

The reasons why the US President stuck as close as possible to the goal of restoring the *status quo ante* after Gulf War I seemed clear enough at the time. First, commitment to this goal was essential for mobilizing the regional and global consensus and support that facilitated the counterattack. Second, the situation with the Kurds in Turkey at the time had not evolved to the point that the United States could countenance independent or autonomous Kurdish control of northern Iraq's oil resources. This concern persisted into the Clinton administration, which allowed Iraq to divide and marginalize its

Kurdish population while the northern Iraq oil wells remained under the control of the central government. Third, the United States' "Iran allergy" was so strong that the United States failed in the end to support a Shiite revolt in southern Iraq. This abandonment would lead to the death of thousands and complicate the occupation after Gulf War II. At the end of Gulf War I, the possibility that Iraq's southern oil resources might come under the control of an independent or autonomous Shiite majority apparently looked too risky.

Certainly, the primary excuse that was used to launch Gulf War II was already available almost immediately after the first one. Within weeks of its Gulf War I ceasefire promise to cooperate fully with nuclear disarmament, Iraq was already transparently refusing to carry out these obligations. Had the coalition forces been willing to "stick around," there would have been the possibility of either gaining full apparent Iraqi cooperation with disarmament or renewing military engagement against the clearly outgunned remnants of Iraq's army. For the reasons just described, however, this was not to be.

There was shortly to be disenchantment with this state of affairs amongst a small group, whose views ultimately won the day. In February 1992, Republicans still held the White House. Paul Wolfowitz was deputy defense secretary and Dick Cheney was the secretary of defense. At that time, staffers for Wolfowitz "drafted an American defense policy that called for the United States to aggressively use its military might. The draft made no mention of a role for the United Nations.[a]" Moreover,

> The proposed policy urged the United States to "establish and protect a new order" that accounts "sufficiently for the interests of the advanced industrial nations to discourage them from challenging our leadership," while at the same time maintaining a military dominance capable of "deterring potential competitors from even aspiring

---

[a] Bunch (2003), for this and the following quotes in this section.

to a larger regional or global role." The draft caused an outcry and was not adopted by Cheney and Wolfowitz.

By the spring of 1997, a new group called the Project for the New American Century (PNAC) had formed to revisit the kind of approach that had been disowned under Cheney's leadership at the Pentagon in 1992.

> In addition to Cheney, Rumsfeld and Wolfowitz, early backers of the group included Jeb Bush, the President's brother, Richard Armitage, now deputy secretary of state, Robert Zoellick, now U.S. trade commissioner, I. Lewis Libby, now Cheney's top aide; and Zalmay Khalizad, now America's special envoy to Afghanistan.

By 1998, the PNAC had started to argue publicly for regime change in Iraq. In January 1998, it wrote to President Clinton[b]:

> "We urge you to enunciate a new strategy that would secure the interests of the U.S. and our friends and allies around the world," stated the letter to Clinton, signed by Rumsfeld, Wolfowitz and others. "That strategy should aim, above all, at the removal of Saddam Hussein's regime from power."

This effort continued with an approach to Congress:

> "We should establish and maintain a strong U.S. military presence in the region, and be prepared to protect our vital interests in the Gulf — and, if necessary, to help remove Saddam from power," the group wrote to Rep. Newt Gingrich and Sen. Trent Lott in May 1998.

This suggests that even before he had been chosen as George W. Bush's secretary of defense, Donald Rumsfeld in particular had already decided about the desirability of "regime change" in Iraq, even at the

---

[b] The full text of the 1998 PNAC letter to President Clinton is in Abrams *et al.* (1998).

expense of military action if necessary. For his first seven months on the job though, Rumsfeld would have to bide his time.

Smart Sanctions

Before September 11, 2001, the advocates of Iraqi regime change within the younger President Bush's administration were eclipsed as the US State Department tried to come to agreement with France and Russia over implementation of a policy of "smart sanctions." Recognizing the increasing political and practical difficulty of maintaining complete UN control over Iraqi oil exports, this policy would have essentially re-created the export control and deterrence relationship that existed between NATO and the USSR during the latter stages of the cold war. Had the smart sanctions policy been implemented and effective, Iraq would have forgone access to militarily relevant imports but gained the freedom to trade oil at will for other goods and services. Having also to revoke its denial of liability for previous debts in the process, Iraq would of course also have had to begin repayment on those debts in order to establish credit with the international financial system. This was a matter of obvious interest to France and Russia as substantial holders of Iraqi debt.

Regime Change Becomes Policy

On September 11, 2001, US Secretary of Defense Rumsfeld immediately recognized an opportunity to sweep away the smart sanctions policy in favor of a thrust toward regime change in Iraq.[1] The CBS news organization reportedly obtained information that Rumsfeld promptly sketched notes calling for information on such a policy change only a few hours after he had rushed to survey the damage to the Pentagon from the September 11 attack:

> Rumsfeld wrote, according to a later CBS News report, that he wanted "best info fast. Judge whether good enough (to) hit S.H. at same time. Not only UBL" — meaning Osama bin Laden. He added: "Go massive. Sweep it all up. Things related and things not."[2]

In light of the first of the two 1998 PNAC letters quoted from above, the immediacy with which Rumsfeld apparently connected the September 11 attacks with unseating Saddam Hussein (S.H.) suggests that this policy might be pursued irrespective of whether any significant functional connection came to light between Saddam Hussein and the perpetrators of the September 11 attacks. Indeed, this would prove to be the case, despite President Bush reportedly having been told point blank by "his top counterterrorism advisor" Richard Clarke that it was al Qaeda that was responsible for the attacks of the previous day, when the president asked Clarke to "see if Saddam did this."[3] While the president did insist on attacking Afghanistan before Iraq, his interaction with Clarke was already a hint that he would prove easy to convince to go to war with Iraq as well, even though his very experienced Secretary of State remained deeply skeptical.[4]

A few months later, in his next state of the union address, President Bush made his widely controversial claim that North Korea, Iran, and Iraq constituted an "axis of evil." What was not as much noticed at the time was the accompanying complaint that Iraq had flaunted its hostility toward the United States. Based on a new unilateralist foreign policy concept, this complaint foreshadowed a military build-up to effect the desired regime change in Iraq.

Presenting the Case for War

British Prime Minister Tony Blair was a potentially useful ally for the US attack on Iraq. An April 3, 2003, program called "Blair's War" on the Public Broadcasting System (PBS) program "Frontline" examined how Britain was brought into line with the US plan for occupying Iraq. In 2002 Blair reportedly privately agreed to provide military support for an attack on Iraq if needed, if Bush would agree to seek UN approval for the threat of use of military force.[5] Following comments by Blair on September 7, 2002, the program narrator said, "Bush had agreed to take Blair's route through the U.N., but he exacted a high price." Matthew D'Ancona continued, "By the time Bush committed to the U.N. route, he had obtained a private assurance from Blair that he would go to war with him, pretty much no matter what." While participation in the war did not become as controversial in Britain as in the United States, it was from the outset more broadly unpopular in the United Kingdom and did domestic political damage.[6] that Blair never completely recovered from.

Initially it appeared that Blair's ploy might be successful, as the UN Security Council passed Resolution 1441 calling for Iraq to face serious consequences if it failed to cooperate with a more stringent inspections regime than Iraq had previously rejected. Thereafter, the Iraqis repeatedly met some but not all of the United Nations' demands.

In response to Iraqi foot-dragging on cooperating with the renewed inspections, Colin Powell went before the UN Security Council on February 5, 2003. There he tried to make a case that Iraq had an active program involving the pursuit of nuclear weapons, the retention of chemical weapons, and the use of about seven mobile truck laboratories to manufacture biological weapons.

Powell claimed that Iraq had imported aluminum tubing specially suited for uranium enrichment centrifuges. This claim was soon refuted by the IAEA Director, who was in charge of nuclear inspections in Iraq. Powell also displayed photographs purporting to show that chemical weapons had likely recently been moved from an Iraqi storage facility. This was soon given a more benign interpretation by Hans Blix. This attracted notice because Blix was in charge of the chemical and biological inspections. Finally, an artist's rendition of mobile bioweapons laboratories was said to be based only on a human intelligence source. There was no way for Powell's audience to assess whether this report might have been influenced by financial or other incentives to provide an obviously politically convenient claim. The value of British government spokespersons' confidence in US claims was undermined in some eyes by a British government's report on the question quoting a nongovernmental source without clear attribution.

Powell also claimed that Iraq had been cooperating with al Qaeda. This claim was reiterated by CIA Director George Tenet during congressional testimony on Febuary 11,[7] even though professional US intelligence analysts had serious doubts about it.[8] The majority of UN Security Council members were not persuaded that this provided sufficient additional reason to sanction a prompt military attack on Iraq. Of course, Iraq was well known to have made major violations of human rights. However, having tolerated this in many other countries without intervening militarily (and even reportedly turned over suspects for interrogation in countries with documented records of human rights abuses), the United States was hardly in a position to convince others that this alone constituted grounds for overturning national sovereignty.[c]

Given all of this, and the long history of oil-related Anglo-American involvement in the Middle East described above, it is hardly surprising that many governments and peoples in the Middle East and around the world were very skeptical of the United States and British governments' credibility and intentions as they prepared an attack on Iraq.[9] That this Anglophone alliance sought and was then forced to abandon obtaining a second UN Security Resolution actually authorizing the attack only added insult to injury.[10]

Re-Examining Powell's Case for War

An August 2003 Associated Press (AP) re-examination of the claims Powell made on February 5, 2003, suggested that questions about the credibility of these claims turned out to be well founded.[11] This report examined the questions of satellite photos, audiotapes, hidden documents, anthrax, bio-weapons trailers, "embedded" capability, "500 tons" of chemical agent, chemical warheads, and deployed weapons. Powell had said that at two sites, "trucks were 'decontamination vehicles' associated with chemical weapons." Later, "Norwegian inspector Jorn Siljeholm told the AP on March 19 that 'decontamination vehicles' UN teams were led to invariably turned out to be water or fire trucks." The AP report dismissed two supposedly incriminating audiotapes as vague and said of a third:

> The third tape, meanwhile, seemed natural, an order to inspect scrap areas for "forbidden ammo." The Iraqis had just told U.N. inspectors they would search ammunition dumps for stray, empty chemical warheads left over from years earlier. They later turned over four to inspectors.

Concerning hidden documents:

> Powell said "classified" documents found at a nuclear scientist's Baghdad home were "dramatic confirmation" of intelligence saying prohibited items were concealed in this way.
>
> U.N. inspectors later said the documents were old and "irrelevant" — some administrative material, some from a failed and well-known uranium-enrichment program of the 1980s.

Powell had said that UN inspectors had estimated that Iraq could have made up to 25,000 liters of anthrax, but none had been "verifiably accounted for." The August 2003 AP report says:

> No anthrax has been reported found. The Defense Intelligence Agency (DIA), in a confidential report last September, recently disclosed, said that although it believed Iraq had biological weapons, it didn't know their nature, amounts or condition. Three weeks before the invasion, an Iraqi report of scientific soil sampling supported its contention it destroyed its anthrax at a known site, the U.N. inspection agency said May 30.

Powell also showed artist's conceptions of mobile bio-weapons laboratories.

> After the invasion, U.S. authorities said they found two such truck trailers in Iraq, and the CIA said it concluded they were part of a production line. But no trace of biological agents was

found on them, Iraqis said the equipment made hydrogen for weather balloons, and State Department intelligence balked at the CIA's conclusion...

"Powell said Iraq produced four tons of the nerve agent VX...Powell didn't note that most of that four tons was destroyed in the 1990s under U.N. supervision...Experts at Britain's International Institute of Strategic Studies said any pre-1991 VX most likely would have degraded anyway. No VX has been reported found since the invasion." Powell also reportedly said, "We know that Iraq has embedded key portions of its illicit chemical weapons infrastructure within its legitimate civilian industry."

> No "chemical weapons infrastructure," has been reported found. The newly disclosed DIA report of last September said there was "no reliable information" on "where Iraq has — or will — establish its chemical warfare facilities." It suggested international inspections would be able to keep Iraq from rebuilding a chemical weapons program.

Powell reportedly said, "Our conservative estimate is that Iraq today has a stockpile of between 100 and 500 tons of chemical weapons agent." Based on the AP report, it was apparently inaccurate to describe this as a "conservative estimate" if this was based on intelligence information consistent with what the AP reporter had become aware of from the previous year:

> Powell gave no basis for the assertion, and no such agents have been found. An unclassified CIA report last October made a similar assertion without citing concrete evidence, saying only that Iraq "probably" concealed *precursor* chemicals to make such weapons. The DIA reported confidentially last September there "is no reliable information on whether Iraq is producing and stockpiling chemical weapons" (emphasis added).

"Powell said 122-mm chemical warheads found by UN inspectors in January might be the 'tip of an iceberg'." However, chief UN inspector

"Blix said on June 16 the dozen stray rocket warheads, never uncrated, were apparently 'debris from the past,' the 1980s. No others have been reported since the invasion. Powell also reportedly said, "Saddam Hussein has chemical weapons. ...And we have sources who tell us that he recently has authorized his field commanders to use them." The AP reported concluded, "No such weapons were used, and none was reported found after the US and allied military units overran Iraqi field commands and ammunition dumps."

Left out of Secretary of State Powell's February 5 address was a bogus claim, included in the US President's state of the union address immediately beforehand, that Iraq had recently attempted to buy uranium from Niger. Just before the August 10, AP review of Powell's claims, this had drawn considerable press — until the US government announced the killing of Saddam Hussein's sons and then issued a stream of reports on the continuing hunt for Saddam Hussein himself. Thus, well before the final report of the team sent into Iraq to look for weapons of mass destruction, it was clear that the case that Powell had made about them was full of holes. While *post facto* analysis after the fact obviously could not undo the invasion itself, it did play a role in the gradual unraveling of widespread U.S. public support for the war. Despite a thorough debunking in the mainstream press of the primary rationale cited for the war, the US President and Vice President continued to hold the view for months thereafter that weapons of mass destruction might eventually be found in Iraq, which further undermined their credibility as the occupation effort proved to be much more difficult than they had anticipated.

Initial Outcome of the Occupation of Iraq

The US/UK/Australian attack on Iraq did not go completely smoothly,[d] but Iraq was so outgunned that the intense first phase of the war was over in less than a month. However, interactions between

---

[d] Extensive reporting by Michael Gordon (2003b–2003n) concentrates on strategy, while that by Patrick Tyler (2003b–2003s) focuses more on tactics.

occupying forces and Iraqis were not as smooth[12] as had been anticipated by senior US administration officials who had pressed for war.
In Baghdad initial defiance transitioned to chaos and looting rather
than the hoped for orderly transition to a new regime, and there was
a breakdown of order elsewhere in the county as well.[13] In an incident
that may have been a critical tipping point for the occupation, on
April 15, people were killed by US soldiers at an "anti-American rally"
in Fallujah, northwest of Baghdad.[14]

Another problem that plagued the occupation during 2003 was
that, with the northern front lacking the mass of US forces that had
been blocked from deploying through Turkey, Saddam Hussein and
his sons readily managed to go to ground as US forces advanced on
Baghdad from the south. The younger son, Qusay Saddam Hussein,
took with him about a billion dollars in cash from the Iraqi central
bank.[15] Saddam Hussein's sons were killed in a gun battle in July,[16]
but it would not be until December 13, 2003, that the former Iraqi
president himself would be run to ground.[17] The lingering fear in Iraq
that having these people at large inspired[18] and the fact that the US
lead-up to the war had put so much emphasis on demonizing Saddam
Hussein as a dangerous individual made it even more difficult to draw
down occupation forces in Iraq with the country in chaos and any of
them at large. Nevertheless, on May 1, the US president was flown
onto an aircraft carrier to declare victory in front of a large sign that
said "mission accomplished."[19] As it would turn out, the mission had
barely begun, and the question of who would control Iraq's oil
remained contentious throughout.

In an interview the previous November, dealing with the confrontation with Iraq, Rumsfeld had been asked, "what do you say to
people who think this is about oil?" His reply was: "It has nothing to
do with oil, literally nothing to do with oil."[20] Superficially, a case
could be made for this claim. Some of the key architects of the invasion had a broader goal than simply putting a more friendly government in control of Iraq's oil. This broader goal was in essence to
demonstrate the efficacy of American power. Amongst the key people
involved, the reasons for doing this may have variously included ideal-
ism about promoting the spread of democracy, providing a showcase

for theories about the importance of a purported revolution in military affairs, taking advantage of an opportunity to strike down the most likely looking enemy, and demonstrating forcefulness as a leader. Nevertheless, it was no accident that the country with the world's second largest inexpensively extractable oil resources was chosen as the laboratory for an attempt to execute the demonstration of the efficacy of American power. There were at the time serious ongoing crises in Liberia and Sudan, and also fallout from previous US interventions in Somalia and Afghanistan that would continue to fester for years to come.[21] There was no shortage of other available venues. Indeed, the worsening situation in Liberia would by July get to the point of a US show of force off the Liberian coast.[22] The disconnection between approaches to the Persian Gulf and trouble spots elsewhere was highlighted when Joint Chiefs of Staff Chairman Richard Meyers invoked the so-called Powell Doctrine in defense of advice not to intervene militarily in Liberia. Given the approach being taken at the time to US military involvement in Iraq, and Afghanistan, the irony of General Myers' comments on criteria for military action in Liberia will no doubt not be lost on the reader:

> "I'm concerned like, like you," General Myers said, "that whatever we do, that we have a very clear mission, we understand the mission we're asked to do; that we have an idea of when the mission is going to be over — in other words, when can we come out of the mission? And that we have sufficient force to deal with the security situation.[23]

Whatever motivation one assigns for the invasion of Iraq, the war came to center on oil as soon as coalition troops crossed the border. Rumsfeld's expectation had been that Iraqi oil revenues would pay for reconstruction after the invasion. This would reprise the situation in Gulf War I, where other countries had picked up most of the bill for the actual military operation (albeit not for the trillions of dollars the United States had previously invested in developing and maintaining the requisite military capability).

A first order of business for the troops moving in to occupy Iraq was to secure the southern oil fields.[24] A day after the Iraqi oil ministry was hit by an air strike and subsequently looted, US marines secured the building. Almost everything else was left vulnerable to uncontrolled looting, including earliest artifacts of civilization from Babylon and other ancient Mesopotamian sites in the national archives and museum.[25] The question of who had control of oil was still up in the air a month after the invasion.[26] By August, there were riots reported sparked by the inability of Iraq's energy industry to even provide enough fuel to maintain basic services in southern Iraq.[27] The United Nations, whose oil for food program had been the previous mechanism for dealing with distribution of Iraq's oil revenues before the occupation, was effectively forced out of the picture after its Baghdad headquarters were demolished in a suicide bombing on August 19, 2003. Not surprisingly, a proposal to mimic the use of the Alaska permanent fund by distributing a substantial part of earnings from Iraq's oil sales on directly to Iraqi citizens[28] was completely untenable given the domestic political situation, not to mention the investment needs for repairing devastation of the country's public infrastructure.

Tension over who would have control over oil would continue through five long years of debilitating insurgency and civil war. A report in early 2007 that Sunni-dominated areas in Iraq's Anbar province might contain large previously untapped oil resources[29] only further complicated the issue. Draft legislation "that would govern the development of Iraqi oil fields and the distribution of oil revenues," that was submitted to the Iraqi cabinet in February 2007 was opposed by Sunnis and Kurds[30] and had yet to be enacted into law a year later.[31] A renewed attempt on this was made by the cabinet in July 2007, as had been demanded by the US Congress.[32] However, this attempt ran into opposition from the Kurds.[33] A legal solution to the fundamental problem of control of Iraq's oil had yet to be enacted into law a year after the February 2007 draft was sent to the Iraqi cabinet. On February 14, 2008, the Iraqi Parliament did follow weeks of acrimony by passing a budget for the year, but the resulting uncertain compromise did not solve the problem of how oil resources and revenues would be controlled in the longer term.[34]

Going back to the initial situation with the occupation, a UN official had been reported as noting that the Geneva Convention was incompatible with coalition forces alone controlling revenues from resources from an occupied state. US sources had occasionally been reported as expecting that Iraqi oil revenues would be important in paying for reconstruction, but it was unclear how companies were to be convinced that contracts for delivery of Iraqi oil revenues would be viewed legally on an international basis. UN sanctions were formally in place, and the UN-controlled oil for food program was only operationally suspended rather than formally terminated. In its initial roughly $80 billion special war appropriation, the US Congress only included about $2.5 billion dollars for reconstruction of the massive damage in Iraq.[35] Despite British griping about its secretive assignment to a US firm, of this a $600 million contract was promptly made to Bechtel, including money for port and airport reconstruction.

With few of the fifty-odd top Iraqi leadership initially accounted for and no weapons of mass destruction uncovered to that date, some US administration sources were credited with suggestions that one or the other may have moved to Syria. The sanctions-busting oil pipeline to Syria, which had previously been left untouched, was shut off. Syria was warned in public statements to curtail support for terrorism. Syria reportedly denied suspicions that it had weapons of mass destruction, but agreed to inspections to verify this if it would also apply to others in the region (i.e. Israel). Syria subsequently became cooperative on the question of senior Iraqi Ba'th functionaries, and as more of these were apprehended in various places, the US administration toned down its rhetoric on Syria.

A fundamental problem was that no prior plans had been made for an extended occupation.[36] US Defense Secretary Rumsfeld had concentrated his attention on the idea that intense firepower and highly mobile forces could bring down the regime quickly. Overjoyed at the fall of Saddam Hussein, as many Iraqis were, the country's people were supposed to use its oil revenues to organize a friendly government, so that all but 30,000 US troops could leave by the end of the summer.

All the King's Horses

Over the strenuous objections of the State Department, January 20, 2003, Presidential Directive No. 24 turned the occupation of Iraq over to an Office of Reconstruction and Humanitarian Assistance (ORHA) under the Defense Department. The designated ORHA director, retired Lt. Gen. Jay Garner, was given seven weeks notice to pull about a hundred officials together to oversee the occupation. They met at the National Defense University on February 21 and 22. "The danger of looting was discussed, but the planning officers sent over from Centcom [Central Command] had been instructed not to respond to such 'post-conflict' issues, in part because the invasion force lacked enough troops to address them."[37] Barbara Bodine from the State Department was given the job of administrator for Baghdad and central Iraq.

> When Bodine briefed Rumsfeld on the administration of Iraq after the fall of the regime, she emphasized the need to pay civil servants immediately in order to head off chaos or resistance. Rumsfeld saw no hurry — the Iraqis could wait a couple of weeks, or even a couple of months. More important was the fact that the American taxpayers shouldn't have to pay the bill. As for the possibility of disorder in the cities, the secretary of defense suggested that this could be used to persuade the countries of old Europe to chip in troops.[38]

The reference to "old Europe" here was a phrase that Rumsfeld had used to contrast the reluctance of western continental European allies to provide troops to the war with the cooperation of those in eastern Europe, most notably Poland.

Saddam Hussein's statue was famously toppled in Baghdad's Firdos Square on April 9, but looting and general chaos kept Garner's team from arriving in Baghdad until April 23. Garner arrived in Baghdad with no coherent plan for how Iraq was to be governed, a distrust of the Pentagon's favored exile Salem Chalabi, and inadequate military security support for staff to move about Baghdad safely to consult with local Iraqis. Not surprisingly, his tenure was short. Iraq had crashed as hard as Humpty Dumpty, and Garner's small and hastily assembled team was nowhere close sufficient to put it back together again, no matter how hard he tried. By May 6, President Bush had already announced that "former diplomat and counterterrorism expert L. Paul (Jerry) Bremer III would replace Jay Garner in Baghdad."[39] By the end of May, in 2003, it had already become clear that a rapid drawdown of US forces in Iraq was not in the cards.[40] By July, Tommy Franks, the departing leader of US Central Command, said that a large occupation force would need to remain in place in Iraq. The monthly cost was estimated at $3.9 billion in then current dollars, twice the figure that had been envisioned three months earlier.[41] By October, the US Congress would pass another $87 billion special appropriation, with $67 billion for military operations in Iraq and Afghanistan.[42] This was despite a growing skepticism amongst the US public. A national opinion poll in early October reported that disapproval of the president's handling of foreign policy exceeded the approval rate. This was a drastic change from the point of the end of 2001 through the time storming of Baghdad, throughout which the approval had ranged from 60–75 percent and disapproval had ranged from 15 percent to just under 30 percent.[43]

As the occupation ground on, the minor contributors to the participating "coalition of the willing" started to lose what initial enthusiasm they had. The most spectacular departure was Spain. Facing an imminent election, the Spanish government had initially jumped to the conclusion that Basque separatists had been behind the deadliest attack on civilians in Europe since WWII, which had just occurred in Madrid.[44] When it became clear that this was not the case, it undermined the credibility of the government and apparently precipitated an upset victory by the opposition Socialists.[45] The Socialists had been apposed to Spanish participation in the war in Iraq and soon made good on their promise to withdraw their 1400 troops.[46]

Garner had earlier hoped that the Iraqis would figure out for themselves how to form a government, but Bremer decided that more outside guidance was needed. With the help of the UN Secretary General's special representative Sergio Viera de Mello, Bremer established a twenty-five-member Iraqi Governing Council in July. However, key decisions continued to be made by Bremer as head of the Coalition Provisional Authority (CPA). Three of these decisions proved to be critical.[47] First, plans proposed by Iraqi civil servants for an abbreviated census that could have supported a voter registration list were ignored. The idea of systematically holding local and regional government elections in more secure areas before setting up a national government was also overlooked in favor of a hodgepodge of occasional informal local councils with no real authority or reliable source of financing. Second, the Iraqi army was disbanded rather than just being stripped of its senior officer corps. This threw hundreds of thousands of disgruntled men with military training into a collapsing labor market. Large stores of Iraqi ordnance were also left unguarded and thus potentially available to the resistance. Third, a "de-Ba'thification" program denied employment to tens of thousands of civil servants. Many of these had only joined the party as a necessity of holding their jobs. The result was to strip the government of much of the talent needed to run education and other public services, even before the security situation degenerated to the point where women in particular were often too fearful to venture forth to their jobs.

Never fully under control after the killing of ninety-five people in the bombing of a Shiite mosque in August 2003 marked an escalation of sectarian violence,[48] the security situation in Iraq took a potentially irretrievable turn for the worse just a year after the invasion. On March 31, 2004, the charred corpses of four American civilians were hung from a bridge in the central Iraq city of Fallujah, west of Baghdad.[49] This city had been a focal point of resistance to the occupation and too insecure for occupation troops to establish a permanent presence. Upon orders from Washington, US marines fought their way into the city on April 8. Larry Diamond writes that residents claimed about 600 Iraqis were killed.[50] This probably included many people who were simply trapped in the city before a one-day ceasefire was ordered on April 9. The toll of forty-eight US casualties was the highest weekly total since the end of the invasion. At the same time there was an uprising in response to an attempt to disarm Shia forces in the south loyal to Muqtada al-Sadr, the son of a well-known martyred Iraqi ayatollah.[51] It soon became clear that the occupation coalition would abandon the attempt to arrest al-Sadr on murder charges.[52] After a major assault on insurgents in Fallujah in November 2004,[53] occupation forces then turned over security in Fallujah to an Iraqi militia later called the Fallujah Brigade. "Within a month, the Fallujah Brigade would be camped outside the city in tents and the police would be cowering in their patrol cars while masked insurgents ran the city."[54]

Given the ever-dicey security situation, efforts to establish a constitution and a functioning government were an uphill struggle.[55] The occupation forces could not even provide adequate security to allow the rank and file people assigned to the CPA the freedom of circulation in Iraq. This made it impossible to be fully effective at assisting political and economic reconstruction. At a formal level, an interim constitution was approved, and the CPA eventually turned over sovereignty to an appointed government on June 28, 2004. A constitution was ratified in a vote on October 15, 2005, but only because the terms for ratification made it almost impossible for a majority of the Sunni minority to block it. A permanent Iraqi National Assembly was elected in December 2005 to replace a temporary one, but it took until the following June to fill the most important security-related cabinet posts.

Perhaps, the most fundamental problem with the occupation of Iraq was the steady erosion of trust between the occupying forces and the Iraqi populace. Telling glimpses of this story have been told from the point of view of interviews with Iraqis[56] and one example of a US National Guardsman's experience.[57] Even the first press reports from Iraq after the invasion reported a frequent theme from some Iraqis: thanks for getting rid of Saddam Hussein; now please go home. Nevertheless, there was initially considerable hope that the United States' enormous resources would be brought to bear to maintain order and repair the damage of years of decay, the initial attack, and even the subsequent looting. But it was not just the failure of this to materialize that soured Iraqis on the occupation.

Even in the first summer, acquaintances returning from central Iraq reported that the population gave US soldiers a wide berth whenever possible. This is hardly surprising. The top of the US military chain of command had long-stressed war fighting rather than nation building as its proper calling. Given an expectation that most of the invading forces would rapidly be rotated out, scant attention had been paid to useful training in Arabic for the soldiers who ended up patrolling the streets. As the resistance stiffened, occupying forces ended up shooting at approaching vehicles that did not follow instructions, and miscommunication led to occasional civilian casualties.

Some local military commanders made progress with stabilization and reconstruction using the limited funds at their command, but these funds were easily exhausted. Rapid rotations broke up relationships where trust had been established, sometimes with catastrophic consequences for Iraqis due to miscommunication with replacement forces. A particular problem was the incarceration of thousands of Iraqis caught up in sweeps aimed at arresting wanted persons from the previous regime or suspected insurgents. Inevitably, this resulted in incarcerating many people who would later be released for lack of reason to hold them. In the meantime, relatives and friends inquired in vain about their fate, due to a policy of providing no such information until well after these incarcerations. The well-known prisoner abuse at the Abu Ghraib facility was only the tip an iceberg of resentment, provoked by this common counter-insurgency practice.

Not surprisingly, occupation forces occasionally came across suspicious stashes of cash, some of which had been salted away before the invasion and others maybe infiltrated afterward to fuel the resistance. Also not surprisingly, in some cases assets were confiscated that were not connected to the resistance, apparently without a systematic accounting procedure to compensate families for this when it turned out to be inappropriate.

On the occupying forces' side, patrolling in full gear in temperatures well over a 100°F (38°C) through even the first summer was trying enough. Since an extended occupation had not been planned for, state-of-the-art individual and vehicle armor was in short supply. With increasing insurgency use of improvised explosive devices, patrolling became dangerous and nerve-wracking. Some units' morale suffered as deployments were extended against soldiers' wishes. Inevitably, many occupation forces out in the field came to look at the people they needed rapport with as potential enemies. In some areas this gradually produced a deadly spiral of mutual suspicion.

The occupying forces increasingly had their hands full just trying to protect themselves. During the Coalition Provisional Authority period, this left the people charged with the political and infrastructure reconstruction effort increasing holed up in the heavily fortified former presidential palace "Green Zone" in Baghdad.[58] The security overhead also severely hampered the freedom of movement and effectiveness of private contractors. Bremer's top–down approach and the difficulty of building up lasting relationships with Iraqis at the local level made it hard to effectively replace foreign contractor reconstruction efforts with Iraqi labor. The resulting high unemployment and underemployment rates amongst Iraqis further contributed to disillusionment amongst the populace.

After the Coalition Provisional Authority period, both the occupying forces and the nascent Iraqi government faced a dilemma. One the one hand, Iraqi security forces were not well developed enough to counter the insurgency and protect government officials themselves from attack. This is evident from the statistics for May 2005 shown in Table 18.1.[59] On the other hand, resentment of the occupying forces provided a lightning rod for strengthening the resistance. Attempts to strengthen Iraqi security forces were plagued by the danger of retribution faced by recruits and by suspicion that Sunni and Shia recruited into these forces were involved in sectarian vendettas. This led to a stalemate where the Iraqi government was reluctant to press for an end to the occupation. This meant that the occupation could only end either with a seismic shift away from internal strife or a growing weariness of the US public leading to the election of a government committed to withdrawal. As the occupation ground into its third year, neither of these escape routes seemed imminent. The security situation in Iraq was just beginning to be stabilized by some measures of Iraqi security force operations. However, the situation deteriorated substantially from May 2005 to May 2006 with respect to kidnappings and killings of Iraqi civilians, much to the discouragement of the population. The situation in 2006 overall was substantially worse than in 2005, with a UN estimate based on official sources alone averaging over 2800 Iraqi civilian deaths from the conflict in 2006.[60]

Table 18.1.   Iraq occupation progress metrics.

	May 2003	May 2004	May 2005	May 2006
Iraqi civilian deaths	250	1,000	1,000	2,500
Iraqi army and police fatalities	10	65	259	149
Coalition troop fatalities	41	84	85	78
Monthly incidents of sectarian violence	5	10	20	250
Multifatality bombings	0	9	36	56
Daily attacks by insurgents	5	53	70	90
Estimated number of insurgents	3000	15,000	16,000	20,000
Estimated number of foreign fighters	100	300	1,000	1,500
Iraqis kidnapped per day	2	10	25	35
Iraqis optimistic about future (percent)	75	51	60	30
Voting rate in last free election (percent)	0	0	58	71
Oil production (million barrels per day)	0.3	1.9	2.1	2.1
Grid electric power (GW)	0.5	3.9	3.7	3.8
Telephone subscribers (millions)	0.8	1.2	3.5	7.5
Real per capita GDP ($US2006)	550	1,000	1,075	1,100
Iraqi security forces in top two tiers	0	0	20,000	60,000
Actionable tips from Iraqi civilians	100	300	1,700	4,400

Source: Kamp, O'Hanlon and Unikewicz (2006).

What progress there was toward forming an Iraqi government that could even begin to restore a sense of security and economic normalcy was glacial compared to what was envisioned at the onset of the occupation. For example, in May 2006 Iraqi oil production remained well below the prewar value of 2.5 million barrels per day, which itself was about a third of Iraq's share of global production based on its fraction of global reserves. The slow progress toward normalcy in Iraq was in large part due to a fundamental disagreement over how oil revenues would be shared. The Shia majority naturally preferred simple majority rule without any prescribed revenue-sharing arrangements. The Kurds were willing to put up with anything short of outright independence only if they had control over oil in the north. This included oil-rich areas where the Kurds were in the process of reversing the ethnic cleansing that had been going on for decades under the previous Iraqi regime. The Sunnis resented resistance to a revenue-sharing arrangement for fear that this resistance would constitute revenge for the government having focused investment and developed in central areas of the country. Thus, no matter what had precipitated the occupation of Iraq, in the end the control of oil became a central focus of the war.

The Surge

US Secretary of Defense Donald Rumsfeld resigned the day after the election results in November 2006 that transferred control of the US Congress to the Democrats.[61] Rumsfeld had long opposed sending more troops to Iraq and had selected commanding generals who would not vigorously protest this policy. Table 18.2 gives various sources' estimates of US troop levels in Iraq at various times.[e] The numbers in Table 18.2 do not include many tens of thousands of nonmilitary expatriate personnel doing tasks in Iraq connected with the occupation.

Under Rumsfeld, military operations in Iraq had only sporadically paid attention to lessons from the few previous successful campaigns against dedicated insurgencies. An oft-cited example is the Malay Jungle Wars of 1948–1960. However, the British tactic of strictly controlling food supplies to leave rebels a choice between surrender and starvation was unlikely to be applicable in Iraq.[62] By 2008, the US Army would finally draft "a new operations manual that elevates the mission of stabilizing war-torn nations, making it equal in importance to defeating adversaries on the battlefield," although "some influential

---

[e] Global Security 2007; Kube 2007; Reid and Burns 2007. The numbers in Table 18.2 should be understood as rough estimates. Definitive estimates of the effective number of deployed troops were difficult to make as troops rotated in and out.

Table 18.2. US troop levels in Iraq.

Month	US Troops
March 2003	130,000
October 2005	152,000
December 2005	160,000
March 2006	133,000
June 2006	127,000
August 2006	133,000
November 2006	152,000
August 2006	162,000
November 2007	167,000
May 2008	155,000

Source: Global Security (2007); Kube (2007) for August 2007; Reid and Burns (2007) for November 2007; Luo and Whenton (2008) for May 2008.

officers" were "already arguing that the army still needs to put actions behind its new words, and they have raised searching questions about whether the Army's military structure, personnel policies and weapons programs are consistent with its doctrine."[63]

The appointment of Admiral William Fallon as head of Central Command and Lt. Gen. David Petraeus to command US forces in Iraq in January 2007 coincided with both the application of a revised military strategy and a commitment of additional troops that had been dubbed the "surge option" during Pentagon studies the previous November.[64] In December 2006, former Democratic Vice Presidential candidate Joseph Lieberman and future Republican Presidential candidate John McCain endorsed increasing the number of US troops in Iraq through this approach by as many as 35,000.[65] This approach was adopted even though a "blue-ribbon" panel study supported by the US government's Institute of Peace had recently cautioned against such an approach.[66] The context for this was continuing attacks on US forces and what amounted to an ethnic cleansing campaign, with particular impact on a sizeable Sunni population being driven out of neighborhoods by Shiite militias in Baghdad.[67] As can be seen from Table 18.2, the increase in US troop deployments in Iraq during the "surge" was not all that dramatic, even less so when accounting for small draw-downs of forces of other countries in the occupation coalition.

Initially, it seemed that there was enough widespread skepticism about the wisdom of the surge strategy[68] that its failure to quell the violence might stimulate the Democrats to make good on its claim that the public had given them back control of the US Congress in order to end the war. However, by the summer it appeared that the US casualty rate was declining, and at least in Baghdad the overall level of violence appeared to be reduced. In late summer of 2007, Petraeus and US Ambassador to Iraq Ryan Crocker gave Congressional testimony on the situation in Iraq.[69] There was controversy about the meaning of the statistics compiled for Petraeus, some of which are given in Table 18.3.[70] In particular, the drop in reported monthly Iraqi fatal civilian casualties was primary in Baghdad, where the surge activity was concentrated through the end of 2007. At least according to Multinational Force Iraq official source statistics, there was also a substantial drop in the rate

Table 18.3.   Casualties and attacks in Iraq from May 2006.

| Month | US Military | | Iraq civilian deaths (1000s/Month) | 1000s of attacks | |
	Wounded	All Deaths		Attacks/ Week	IEDs/ Month
July 2006	525	43	2.6	1.2	2.7
August	591	65	2.1	1.2	2.7
September	790	72	2.3	1.4	3.0
October	781	106	2.5	1.6	2.6
November	548	70	2.6	1.4	2.7
December	702	112	3.0	1.4	2.8
January 2007	640	83	2.8	1.5	3.0
February	517	81	1.8	1.6	3.0
March	617	81	1.8	1.5	3.3
April	650	104	1.8	1.4	2.9
May	655	126	2.1	1.5	3.0
June	749	101	1.5	1.7	3.1
July	614	78	1.9	1.5	2.7
August	565	84	1.5	1.2	2.1

Source: USDOD (2008); Petraeus (2007) (for numbers in thousands, with total attack numbers for the midmonth week and IED = improved explosive device).

of violent civilian deaths overall in the late fall of 2007.[71] The reduction in US military force casualties was even more pronounced later, averaging thirty-seven per month for the ten months starting with August of 2007. Thus, despite controversy about the statistics and some subsequent small revisions in the numbers shown in Table 18.3, by the beginning of 2008, it was fairly widely accepted that the intensity of violence in Iraq had somewhat recovered from the intensity of mid-2006 through mid-2007. Accordingly, attempts to put teeth in limits on funds for the war collapsed near the end of 2007 amongst horse trading about the overall appropriation process. The decline in the level of violence in Iraq did not continue in the first half of 2008. Nevertheless, the Congressional budget process in 2008 did not force the US administration into any substantial changes in military strategy in Iraq. Thus, President Bush would have his way with the Congress on troop deployments in Iraq until the day he left office.

The changed US military strategy was not the only factor affecting levels of violence in Iraq in 2007. Other possible factors are completion of ethnic cleansing campaigns that separated Sunni from Shia populations, a decision by Shia militia to "lay low" for a while, relocation of Sunni resistance forces out of the Baghdad region for a while, reaction of less fundamentalist oriented regions, northwest of Baghdad to forces loosely identified as al Qaeda in Iraq, and a general war weariness that evolves in almost any region where intense conflict has been going on for a long time.

One thing to which the apparent drawback of violence in Iraq in the last half of 2007 could not be attributed was an increase in the number or capabilities of fully formed Iraqi security forces compared to the situation a year earlier. According to Petraeus' charts, the only increase in numbers of Iraqi security forces over the previous year was in the number of units in the process of being formed. Nor did Ambassador Crocker have much concrete Iraqi political progress to report on. On the most central economic question, five years after the start of the occupation Iraq had still not managed to pass long-awaited legislation dealing with management of oil revenues. Concerning this and other hoped for legislation, Crocker noted, "what is difficult about these laws is that they take Iraq another step down the road toward a federal system that all Iraqis have not yet embraced."

The essential impediment to political progress in Iraq under the occupation was pinpointed in an August 2007 news analysis in the *New York Times* by Damien Cave.[72] He quotes Iraqi Shiite member of Parliament Qasim Dawood as saying "There are people living on the crisis, gaining their power through the crisis." That is, much of the Iraqi economy became controlled by forces working in ways incompatible with a well-functioning and orderly government. Even Iraq's oil industry was not immune from lack of accountability under the nose of the occupation, with a draft US report estimating that from 0.1–0.3 million barrels per day over a four year period was unaccounted for. An unknown part of this discrepancy not simply resulting from overstatement of production could have been siphoned off through "corruption or smuggling."[73] To expand on Cave's observation to consider the role of the occupiers, they provide both a substantial source of funds and protection for members of the Parliament and government that continues to get paid but does not resolve underlying problems. If they do resolve those problems, then both the source of money and their physical security will be compromised as occupation forces withdraw. Thus, there is a stalemate in Iraq that is most likely to come to an end, quite possibly a very messy end, when and only when the United States tires of the occupation and decides to withdraw. It is in this sense that economic motivations underlie the sectarian and nationalist strife that perpetuates violence.

Of course, to focus exclusively on an economic cause for violent conflict is to overlook other important dimensions. There was also sectarian division and tension in Iraq over the role of Islam in the legal system. Kurdish nationalism had deep roots and engendered a sense of national identity that had a potential to transcend economic interests, even if this urge was kept in check by the political necessity of treading carefully in pursuit of the quest for control of oil (and avoiding an invasion from Turkey). There was also no shortage of inherited personal grudges and individual ambition that from time to time seemed to get in the way of pursuit of broader group interests. Nevertheless, without an understanding of the geography and politics of oil, no sense can be made of the enormous difficulties facing the Iraqi National Assembly and its people as they struggled to form a functional government.

The likely future for Iraq and other troubled oil-producing regions will be taken up in Part V of this book. For now, Chapter 19 reflects on what can be learned by looking back at the history pertinent to energy and international war reviewed so far.

Endnotes

1 USDOD (2002).
2 Bunch (2003).
3 Clarke (2004); Lichtblau (2004).
4 Jehl (2004).
5 WGBH Educational Foundation (2003).
6 Cowell (2003a); Hoge (2003; 2003b).
7 Johnston (2003).
8 Regan (2005).
9 Barringer (2003); Preston (2003).
10 Tagliabue (2003); Weisman and Barringer (2003); Sanger and Hogue (2003); Weisman (2003); Sanger and Hogue (2003b).
11 Hanley (2003).
12 Filkins (2003b–2003t); Sanger (2003); Santora (2003a); Smith (2003a).
13 Burns (2003a–2003q); Chivers (2003a–2003b); Smith (2003b–2003c); Fisher (2003a); Jehl (2003); Santora (2003b); Gordon (2003).
14 Fisher (2003b).
15 Filkins (2003u).
16 MacFarquhar (2003).
17 Sachs (2003).
18 Burns (2003r).
19 Bash (2003).
20 USDOD (2002).
21 Butler (2003); Pike (2005a); Yager (2006).
22 Schmitt (2003b).
23 Marquis and Shanker (2003).
24 Dao (2003).
25 Riedlmayer (2003); C.F. Andrews (2003).
26 Tavernise (2003b).
27 Oppel Jr. and Worth (2003).
28 Tierney (2003)
29 Glanz (2007a)
30 Wong and Stolberg (2007).
31 Glanz (2007b).
32 Rubin (2007).

[33] Glanz (2007d).
[34] Rubin (2008).
[35] Firestone (2003).
[36] Gordon and Trainor (2007).
[37] Packer (2005, p. 123).
[38] Packer (2005, p. 126).
[39] Parker (2005, p. 144).
[40] Gordon (2003p).
[41] Shanker (2003a).
[42] Firestone (2003).
[43] Purdum and Elder (2003).
[44] Sciolino (2004a).
[45] Sciolino (2004b).
[46] Simons (2004).
[47] Diamond (2005, p. 294).
[48] MacFarquhar and Oppel Jr. (2003),
[49] Gettleman (2004).
[50] Diamond (2005, p. 235).
[51] Burns (2004a); Gettleman and Jehl (2004); Hauser (2004).
[52] Burns (2004b).
[53] Filkins and Glanz (2004).
[54] Diamond (2005, p. 239); C.F. Williams (2004).
[55] Stephenson (2007).
[56] Glantz (2005)
[57] Crawford (2005).
[58] Diamond (2005).
[59] Kamp, O'Hanlon and Unikewitz (2006).
[60] Tavernise (2007).
[61] Stolberg and Rutenberg (2006).
[62] C.F. Kohn (1999).
[63] Gordon (2008).
[64] Cloud (2006).
[65] Burns (2006).
[66] Baker and Hamilton (2006).
[67] Tavernise (2006); Tavernise and Worth (2007).
[68] Shanker and Cloud (2007)
[69] CQ Transcripts (2007).
[70] USDOD (2008); Petraeus (2007).
[71] Gordon (2007).
[72] Cave (2007).
[73] Glanz (2007c).

Chapter 19

Oil and War

In 1870 coal and iron entered the international scene in a way that would have decisive impact on the course of war. Churchill's 1911 decision on conversion of the British fleet and the increasing use of oil for land and air operations during WWI initiated a similar process for oil. If history repeated itself with precise timing, then the resolution of conflict over coal and iron that began with the European Coal and Steel Union four decades after 1912 would have been mirrored shortly after Gulf War I by a similar mechanism for avoiding conflict over military capabilities and the form of governance in major oil producers. However, this was not to be.

Why were the lessons of history on coal and iron through WWII not applied to the Persian Gulf region after the United States yet again mounted a decisive expeditionary force to end a war between other parties? The underlying conceptual problem that prevented this in the case of Gulf War I is clear enough. During the 19th century, the major European powers pursued a balance of power strategy. Only after this balance broke down in WWI and could not be reconstructed to prevent WWII did they devise a fundamentally different form of economic and political order for Europe. For decades after the Suez crisis, the US–UK alliance similarly pursued a balance of power strategy in the Middle East. First Britain tried to set up compliant and nominally constitutional monarchies in the region, while western oil companies leveraged as much profit as possible out of oil concessions. The ultimate result of these policies following the breakup of the Ottoman Empire was that Persian Gulf states' cooperation on cartel pricing would be fragile rather than organized under a single political authority.

The role of outside powers in the devastating 1980–1988 Iran–Iraq war was a classic example of balance of power politics. Despite Iraq's initial aggression, its war effort was given some support by the United States. However, this support went only to the point of preventing the removal of the Iraqi regime, not beyond this to allow that regime to regain ground against Iran. The subsequent Iraqi move toward Kuwait in 1990 caught the western powers unprepared to issue an effective demarche. Nor were these powers able to follow up their military success in Gulf War I with an alternative to the *status quo ante* while their expeditionary armies were still deployed in force. Partition of Iraq and its oil resources would have been preferred to the actual outcome, at least by both the Kurds in the north and by the Shiite rebels in the south whose supporters died by the thousands. A limited autonomy, without control of the major oil fields, was eventually allowed to some of the Kurds. However, fear of the consequences of allowing the southern Shiite Arabs out from under thumb of the Ba'th regime stayed the hand of the United States from providing effective assistance to them, even after it provided verbal encouragement of their rebellion.

After the first Bush administration left office, a new vision was formulated with the participation of some of that administration's former senior officials. That vision called for exercise rather than simply balance of power. Surprisingly, by 2003 this vision had been given an opportunity to be executed due to flukes of history. These included a stained dress not being sent for dry cleaning,[1] the outcome of what was consequently a toss-up election, and intelligence failures leading to three airplanes being crashed into buildings by people armed with small cutting tools and trained in the United States to fly the planes but not to land them. Thus it happened that, five decades after the occupation of Germany, the occupation of Iraq again in principle provided an opportunity to reshape the economics and politics of the world's predominant energy resource. Historical precedent suggested, however, that even if this could be managed it would not happen overnight.

Unlike Athena out of the head of Zeus, the European Union was not immediately born full-grown out of the German defeat in WWII.

Several years of painful learning and the threat of chaos were required to transition from the draconian Morgenthau plan to the European Coal and Steel Union. Many more years were needed to transition on through the European Community to the EU. Similarly, establishing a new stable social and political order in Iraq proved elusive in the years following the initial occupation in 2003. Only after a period of economic chaos and deteriorating security did the US government realize that the occupation could not be successfully financed by Iraqi oil revenues, but would instead require large additional congressional appropriations. Both historical analogy and the immediate difficulties at hand made this hardly surprising. A crucial question was whether the alliance that had so quickly crumbled the Iraqi military could also be effective in establishing a lasting peace. One commentator who took a broad view of such matters was Wendell Berry. He made the following comment during the lead-up to Gulf War II:

> Authentic peace is no more passive than war. Like war, it calls for discipline and intelligence and strength of character, though it also calls for higher principles and aims. If we are serious about peace, then we must work for it as ardently, seriously, continuously, carefully, and bravely as we now prepare for war.[2]

Stated US administration goals after Gulf War II, presumably supported by the UK government, were that Iraq should be a democracy and that its oil revenues should be used for the benefit of the Iraqi people — and that the development of democracy in Iran should be encouraged. Such goals were of course not realized from 1951 to 1991. During this period Anglo-American goals instead focused first on oil companies' interests and then on thwarting Iraqi attempts to influence or control regional oil production. The backwash from nearly a century of mistrust and support for undemocratic regimes stood in the way of the newfound stated goals of the Anglo-American alliance for the outcome of regime change in Iraq.

After a nominal twenty-six days of active combat and five years of occupation of Iraq, there were still three major challenges. The first concerned the future of the regional and global oil markets. How

222 Energy and International War

plentifully and how fast would Iraqi oil return to the global market, and under whose control? What would be the impact on oil prices and the second effective OPEC cartel period? In the longer term, would oil prices continue to fluctuate by a factor of two or more, or would a mechanism be found to provide more price stability?

A second major unresolved question was the future of security in the Middle East. In the spotlight of international attention before the onset of Gulf War II hostilities, the US administration had floated the idea of resolving the Palestine question within three years. Moreover, with Kuwait no longer facing the possibility of Iraqi armored divisions massing on its northern border, the occupation of Iraq substantially altered the need for basing of US forces in Saudi Arabia. The stationing of US forces in the land of Mecca and Medina had already arguably been more trouble than it was worth after the end of the Gulf War I. With the US operational command set up in Kuwait, the net value of having US forces in Saudi Arabia after the occupation of Iraq was even more questionable.

The removal of western forces from the country of Islam's holiest cities and an end to the occupation of Palestine had been Osama bin Laden's primary two original demands. For the September 11 attacks, nothing but an all-out "war on terrorism" had been promised as a US response. Ironically, however, by using the September 11 attacks as a springboard to change US policy on Iraq, the proponents of this change ended up potentially facilitating the meeting of one of bin Laden's two primary demands — the removal of US troops from Saudi Arabia. This, of course, is nothing new. In Northern Ireland too the non-state purveyors of violence for political ends were tracked down relentlessly, but the final settlement allowed for the possible emergence of majority Catholic control if current demographic trends continue. So also has order emerged from chaos elsewhere, but whether it will actually work out this way in the Middle East in the foreseeable future is far from clear.

A third major unresolved question is whether Gulf War II will turn out to be the last major international war, or at least the last one where control over energy resources looms large in the background. In light of much conventional "wisdom" concerning how endemic such wars purportedly are to the human condition, this might seem like a remarkable question to even pose. However, all of the material covered here so far should make it clear why this is an interesting question. The Franco-Prussian War and World War I left unsettled the question of how to deal with the increasingly important influence of coal and steel resource holdings on the balance of power. It took the cataclysm of WWII to lead to a solution of this dilemma, but the solution has been an enduring one. Control of uranium resources once was arguably viewed as playing an important strategic role, at least with respect to French policy toward Africa. Now uranium is traded widely on a global market; known resources appear to be sufficient that run-up in uranium ore prices will play a negligible role in determining energy prices for many decades to come; and a major war over control of uranium mines seems a remote prospect indeed. Natural gas resources are broadly diversified and traded largely between friendly partners. For at least the next decade or so, control of natural gas resources or pipeline routes appears headed for a peripheral rather than central role in international conflict.

Not even counting the war in Lebanon where the United States unsuccessfully intervened in 1983–1984, there were six post-WWII international wars in the Middle East before Gulf War II. Counting the UN vote to partition Palestine as the *status quo ante*, in each of these conflicts before 2003 the goal of the United States as was to support that status quo. Like in WWII, in Gulf War II the stronger coalition opted instead for all-out military victory and subsequent occupation. If the United States and its allies were able to rise to the challenge, then their ultimate goal could be that the result of Gulf War II occupation will do the same for oil and natural gas that the occupations following WWII did for coal and steel.

In a book title, the liberation of Arab states from Ottoman Turk rule after WWI has been called *The Peace to End All Peace*.[3] This is a play of words on the earlier hope that WWI would be the "war to end all wars." In light of the above survey of events in the Middle East since 1914, the reason for the irony in the title of a book on the post-Ottoman Middle East should be clear. Nevertheless, WWII did indeed turn out to be the "war to end all wars" in Western Europe (i.e., excluding the Balkans). Accomplishing this was, however, no easy matter. The route from the potentially ruinous Morgenthau plan through the European Coal and Steel Union to the European Economic Community was a long hard road that involved years of occupation of Germany, however much of a formality the occupation became toward its end. If an analogous outcome can be achieved at all concerning Iraq, its neighbors, and oil, then a different path to this end will no doubt be necessary. If not, then the United States and the world may have to make a major adjustment to the outcome of a very problematic policy.

Part V of this work examines the questions just posed. How will supplies and prices of oil be negotiated in the future? Can stability and peace be achieved in the Middle East? If so, will this signal an end to wars involving the shipping of many tens of thousands of troops abroad to project an attempt to occupy foreign territory if unacceptable political demands are not met? In other words, in that sense is it possible that Gulf War II could in fact turn out to be the war to end all major international wars? If not, what opportunity will have been lost, and why?

Before addressing these questions, Part IV first takes a look at uranium, natural gas, and renewable energy. Electricity production is the most rapidly growing from of energy use, and at times uranium and natural gas have had the fastest growth in use for production of electricity. Thus, building a more complete picture requires examining their competition with renewable resources as well as with coal and oil.

Endnotes

[1]   Van Natta and Broder (1998).
[2]   Berry (2003).
[3]   Fromkin (1989).

Part Four

URANIUM, NATURAL GAS, AND RENEWABLES

Chapter 20

France and Uranium

In the four decades after WWII, France developed an independent military nuclear force and became the only large country that obtained most of its electrical power from nuclear energy.[a] As long as effective control was required over the uranium supplies needed for these policies, limitations on its own uranium ore resources and nuclear fuel breeding programs led France to have a strong predilection toward neocolonial policy in the West African region that provided the remainder of its supplies. France's 1998 ratification of the Comprehensive Test Ban Treaty heralded a changed policy on security of uranium supply. Henceforth, France would be content to rely on the global uranium market for imports. This liberated France's foreign policy from being tethered to a perceived need to retain preferential access to African uranium supplies.

French Security Strategy

Cementing a peaceful trading relationship between France and Germany within the European Community was a key element of the French security strategy after WWII. With the wisdom of hindsight, it is clear how successfully this relationship evolved into an enlarging European Union. In hindsight, this strategy was evidently sufficient for guaranteeing that France would never again repeat its disastrous

---

[a] The information given here on nuclear electrical power comes from the French atomic energy authority, the *Commissariat à l'énergie atomique* (CEA, 2002; 2006a, 2007). Except as otherwise noted, the information on French policy in Africa generally comes from Pederson (2000).

struggles against German steel and munitions. However, from the perspective of the early post-WWII period when Charles de Gaulle held so much sway over French security strategy, it was not so obvious that European integration was sufficient to guarantee France's security. So France pursued two back-up options. These were meant to ensure that the French would never again have to be reliant on Anglophone allies whose aid had twice in the 20th century proven inadequate to repel attack without France first sustaining calamitous damage.

At the core of both of France's major back-up security strategies was the newly illuminated power of nuclear fission. From a military perspective, for a decade France invested a remarkably large portion of its military expenditure in building an independent military nuclear force, the *force de frappe*. By maintaining this independent nuclear force and refusing to integrate its military fully into NATO, France guaranteed itself an independent deterrent against a potential attack from the Soviet Union and "all other directions" (*tous azimuts*). In principle, this deterrent covered even France's own NATO allies including Germany, in case of some catastrophic disintegration in the West. From a 21st century perspective, insisting on *tous azimuts* capability seems odd. However, when looking at the issue from the perspective of de Gaulle and others much closer to the disasters of WWI and WWII, the psychology behind this policy is easy to understand.

From an industrial perspective, France's other major military back-up strategy was to make its growing electrical power production nearly independent of imports of German coal or any other fossil fuel source. After WWII, French industrialists had decided that the British and early American strategy of smashing the foundation of the old German coal and steel cartels was not feasible. The reason for this decision was that the badly depreciated French industrial base needed to trade with the German Ruhr rather than duplicate and try to complete directly with its capabilities using a less appropriate French mineral base. Rather than becoming heavily dependent on fossil fuel imports for the critical area of electricity production, however, France evolved a centrally planned approach to eventually obtain about three-quarters of its electrical energy from nuclear power plants.

France's heavy reliance on nuclear power for electricity production did not completely free it from reliance on fuel imports. For France's endowment of reasonably good quality uranium ores was limited. Given its desire to retain greater freedom of action in foreign policy than its other European NATO allies, France was reluctant to rely on North American resources for the uranium needed for its military and civilian back-up security strategies. Nor was the Soviet bloc a suitable source once the cold war became the predominant French security concern. Australia had long-standing concerns about nuclear weapons testing in the Pacific and about the potential global impact of uranium exports in general, so it too was not an attractive source. Ironically, in pursuit of energy independence France set off toward becoming the only major user of nuclear power to exhaust its own inexpensive uranium ore resources. The only suppliers that France initially felt it could rely on to slow the depletion of its own uranium resources were in Africa.

For over two decades after the beginning of the last quarter of the 20th century, after a major buildup in its military and commercial use of nuclear energy, France relied only on Gabon and Niger in West Africa for uranium imports. France wanted these imports because it could readily domestically produce only about half of what it used. This situation changed as France halted nuclear weapons testing and then promptly ratified the Comprehensive Test Ban Treaty after it was opened for signature in 1996. This signal event marked the end of a one and one-quarter century history of military struggle intertwined with solid mineral energy resources. This story had its origins with Germany's decision to redraw its border with France around the surface outcroppings of the Lorraine iron ore fields after the Franco-Prussian War. It ended when France decided to turn to purchases and investments in the global uranium market to secure future uranium supplies.

Until France was willing to rely on the global market for security of uranium supplies, it was inextricably committed to a unilateralist and interventionist approach to Africa. Afterward, France adopted a more multilateral approach to Africa. France also developed greater emphasis on fostering representative governance in parts of Africa where it had previously propped up what were in effect one-party dictatorships.

In addition to its broad-based and enduring influence in Francophone North and West Africa, France has repeatedly been involved in catastrophic events on the fault line between this region and that of the predominantly Anglophone elites in more southern and southeastern regions of Africa. Along this fault line French policy has also recently been freed from its previous constraints.

French Nuclear Electricity

As just noted, France assigned a critical role to uranium-dependent technologies and had a long-standing reliance on Africa as a sole and major source of imported uranium. An understanding of French uranium use is thus necessary, albeit by no means sufficient, for understanding the relationship between control of natural resources and conflict in Africa. In particular, it is useful to understand why France's uranium use rate is likely to be fairly stable for the foreseeable future. Also, aggregate global annual uranium use over the next several decades is not likely to be high enough to increase the price of mined uranium enough to have a significant effect on the cost of electricity generation.[1] Compared to previous periods of rapidly expanding military and then civilian demand for uranium, and in light of a post-cold-war assessment of global uranium reserves,[2] this understanding allows France to anticipate an adequate future uranium supply without necessarily relying on domestic supplies or those of other countries entwined in a uniquely French sphere of influence.

France has the largest commercial nuclear power system in the world except for the United States. As of 2007 France's nuclear electric power capacity was stable, with no plants on order or under construction and no more shutdowns scheduled for at least ten years. France's oldest pressurized water reactor plants, Fessenheim-1 and -2 at 0.92 gigawatts gross electrical power (GWe) each, entered service in 1977. Barring mishaps, all of France's 63 GWe net power of installed pressurized water reactor capacity as of 2007 should continue to operate for another decade. France's long-term plan has been to replace old plants as they shut down. This nominally includes a 1.47 GWe Penly-3 plant in 2013 and five additional plants of about the same capacity after 2014. Should this policy persist, it is likely to continue for at least a decade France's position of operating about a sixth of global installed nuclear capacity, which totaled 369 GWe for the whole world in 2007.

The stability of France's pressurized water nuclear electricity plant planning is indicated by the fact that the only two French orders for nuclear power plants were ever cancelled.[b] By contrast, between 1970 and 1994 in the United States 138 nuclear plant orders for 150 GWe of gross electrical power were cancelled. This can be compared to 95 GWe of net US nuclear operating capacity, with no new plant orders placed after the partial meltdown of the Three Mile Island plant in 1979.

Given the decimation of French industrial capacity by fighting in WWII and the German occupation, it is hardly surprising that France lagged about a decade behind the United States in the initial growth of its nuclear power program. Eventually, however, France built a system of fifty-eight high-capacity pressurized water reactors situated at nineteen locations, almost all on rivers or the coast. A comparison of the resultant French nuclear electric generating capacity to that of the United States is given in Table 20.1. Part of the reason that France's nuclear electric generating capacity appears more stable than that of the United States is simply that much of France's is younger and thus not scheduled for decommissioning in the next two or three decades.

In the year 2004, France obtained 78.5% of its electricity from nuclear energy, as opposed 32% for the European Union. In other regions, the percentages were 18.5% for former Soviet republics, 18% for North America, 4% for Asia, and 2.5% for Latin America and

---

[b] France cancelled two 1.0-GWe boiling water reactors in 1975, only 2 years after they were ordered. This simplified the construction and regulation of France's nuclear power system compared to the other largest nuclear power users by limiting all of France's water-cooled electricity production reactors to the pressurized water type; cf. CEA (2006a).

Table 20.1.   US and French installed nuclear capacity (GWe).

Year	The United States	France
1965	2	0.3
1970	8	2
1975	39	3
1980	55	16
1986	88	45
1991	102	57
1996	102	60
2001	95	63
2005	98	63

Source: Commissariat è énergie atomique (CEA 2002, 2006a).

Africa.[3] France's reliance on nuclear energy for electricity production is thus in a class by itself, despite its being nearby extensive British and German coal deposits and within economic piping distance of vast natural gas supplies. Nor has France's commitment to obtaining most of its electricity from nuclear power been tempered by the fact that it has exhausted its own economically competitive uranium ores without being able to provide the majority of uranium supplies for its own reactors.

France's nuclear electric production system is more centrally coordinated than that of other countries that had capitalist economies during the cold war. Aside from the primarily research-oriented Phenix breeder reactor, France uses only pressurized light water reactors. (These have a heat exchanger to raise steam for drive turbines, so that any radioactive water coming from the reactor core never comes in direct contact with the turbine blades, as opposed to the case for boiling water reactors.) By contrast, all other nations with more than 20 GWe of net installed nuclear electric capacity use a mix of pressurized water and other reactor types. (This includes the United States, Japan, Germany, and Russia.)

France's nuclear power plants are run by a single state-dominated organization, *Électricité de France* (EDF). Of the twenty-four global nuclear electrical energy producers with a net output of more than

30 TWh in 2001, however, EDF's operational capacity factor was 73%, making it only one of three with an average capacity factor of less than 77%. (The capacity factor is the actual output divided by the output that would result from running all the time at the maximum rated production rate.) By 2003, EDF's capacity factor had risen slightly to 76% but was still below that for all of the producers of large amounts of nuclear power with a few exceptions. These exceptions included slightly lower capacity factors for Russia and Canada and a much lower capacity factor for Japan, whose boiling water reactor fleet operated only at 35% capacity due to a sudden unmasking of safety concerns. France's comparatively low earlier capacity factors may reflect a historical lack of commercial pressures on performance, as perhaps was also the case for Japan and Taiwan, the only other such producers with capacity factors of less than 80% in 1999. However, EDF's capacity factors continued to increase in 2004 and 2005 and stabilized in 2006, bringing closer to some of the higher values achieved elsewhere. The net result was that by 2007 France was operating nuclear power reactors at an apparently reliable and predictable pace.

Uranium for France

Corresponding to France's *ca.* one-sixth of installed world nuclear capacity, that country has recently generated about one-seventh of global demand for uranium. (The difference between the 1/6 and 1/7 ratios is due to differences in capacity factor, uranium use per unit energy in pressurized water versus other types of reactors, and a small amount of French use of plutonium from reprocessed spent fuel as a replacement for part of the uranium in new reactor fuel.) To extrapolate this trend, Table 20.2[4] uses the lower of two projections for French and global uranium requirements.[5] The figures are in thousands of metric tons (ktonne) of elemental uranium.

In the 1990s, France reported having a very modest fraction of the world's reasonably assured reserves of uranium, amounting to 12 ktonne out of a global total 2,515 ktonne for countries reporting

Table 20.2. Annual reactor-related uranium requirements (ktonne).

Year	France	World
1998	8.2	60
2001	8.6	64
2005	7.2	55
2010	7.4	70
2015	7.4	75
2020	7.4	74
2025	7.7	82

Source: Uranium: Resources, production and demand (IAEA 1999, 2001, 2005).

to a 1999 IAEA summary.[c] Through 1992 France nevertheless spent the third largest amount on domestic exploration at $0.86 billion, versus $0.96 billion for Canada and $2.63 billion for the United States. (These figures are in terms of sums of face value dollar outlays in the year of expenditure, not adjusted for inflation).

In 1998, France ratified the Comprehensive Test Ban Treaty draft that was opened for signature the year after the 1995 Nonproliferation Treaty Extension and Review Conference. Before this, France had

---

[c] IAEA (1999). From 1985 to 1990, the great majority of uranium exploration by countries was domestic (totaling within 10% of $150 million/year in then-current dollars), compared to a slide in foreign exploration from about $70 million/year to less than $40 million/year. After the collapse of the Soviet Union and consequent availability of former Soviet republics' uranium supplies on the global market, domestic uranium exploration evaporated altogether in France. In the 1990s total global uranium exploration expenditures also declined for five years, recovering largely through Canadian efforts at just over $40 million in 1997 and 1998. This recovery resulted in opening of new mines and partly closed up a continuing post-cold-war gap between production and consumption. This gap, amounting to a substantial 26 ktonne in 1998, was made up by a depletion of cold war military and civilian stocks that had helped depress prices from about $75/kg in 1982 to about $30/kg in 1998 in then-current prices. Especially since they do not appear to be corrected for inflation, these values represent a remarkable price drop. France was the leader in non-domestic uranium exploration expenditures from 1992 on except for 1995, when its $10 million spent on this was eclipsed by Japan's $15 million.

obtained its uranium domestically[d] and from Gabon and Niger in the former French West Africa. French domestic uranium production reached a plateau of about 3 ktonne/year from 1983–1998, having been overtaken by production in Niger in 1979. From 1996 to 1998, French domestic uranium production declined from 0.9 ktonne/year to 0.5 ktonne/year, while that of Niger remained within about 6% of 3.5 ktonne/year. Production in Gabon had long been comparatively small, comparable to its value of 0.6 ktonne/year in 1996. By 1999, underground and open pit uranium mining from sandstone deposits in Gabon was being phased out.

Of particular interest is the ownership pattern for the Somaïr and Cominak uranium mining concerns in Niger, which were listed, respectively, as *ca.* 36% and 31% domestic in both the 1991 and 1999 IAEA reports.[e] Niger's uranium mining is concentrated along the Algerian border just west of the *Aïr Massif* about equidistant northeast of Niamey, northwest of Lake Chad, and southwest of Libya.

In 2001, Cogema merged with Framatome and CEA Industrie to form Avera. In France, Cogema's Lodève uranium mine at Le Bosc, Hérault was shut down in 1977. Its last mine in France, Le Bernardan at Jouac, Haute-Vienne, was shut down in 2001. This completed the transition to France relied solely on foreign sources of uranium.

France's reliance on uranium for electricity production is indeed unique, and its reliance for a long period on a narrow base of uranium

---

[d] IAEA (1999). Uranium production in France has been concentrated in the *Massif central* in the south-central part of France. There are also an additional six mined-out sites in a narrow a leucogranite (mica-containing granite) formation running along the Atlantic coast into *Bretagne* (Brittany). In 1999, environmental management at mining sites was a significant activity, dominated by seven million dollars at the Hérault site and about four million dollars at La Couzille, phasing down to about two million dollars at each site in the year 2000. This heritage has left France with depleted domestic uranium mines and a well-established system for handling mine tailings and other forms of low-level radioactive waste.

[e] IAEA (1991); IAEA (1999). In 1999, the remaining ownership for Somaïr was listed as 57% French and 7% for the German-origin firm Urangesellschaft. For Cominak the remaining ownership had evolved to 36% for the French Cogema concern, 25% Japanese, and 10% Spanish.

resources is remarkable. It is, thus, worth inquiring in more detail how this state of affairs evolved, and what consequences it had for the region France turned toward to complement its own uranium resources.

What Motivated de Gaulle's Nuclear Policies?

France's cold war nuclear policies were in essence put in place by President Charles de Gaulle in the 1950s. The decision to construct an independent French nuclear force was taken in secret, essentially at the discretion of the president. The decision to commit the country so heavily to reliance on nuclear energy for electricity production obviously required a broader enduring consent on funding, but this die was also basically cast by de Gaulle.

In the WWII, the luster of previous western European continental dominance by France was for the third time in 135 years tarnished by a terrible military defeat on its own soil. Charles de Gaulle's response to these events can be understood both in terms of his own role in the war and the broader context of the following notable developments in French history. France had dominated continental western Europe militarily under the long 1661–1715 autocracy of Louis XIV. Conceptually this harked back to the reuniting of the Franks under Charlemagne (771–814), but in practice it resulted from the French gradually prevailing in its struggle with England and other European powers from the 1066 Norman invasion of England through to 1457. Following Louis XIV there was a long and gradual decline in French preeminence, punctuated by a number of key events:

- Louis XV fumbled the 1740–1748 War of Austrian Succession and lost French continental New World possessions in the Seven Year's War of 1756–1763.
- Napoleon (briefly) flaunted "*La gloire de France*" and modernized France's top-down "*département*" governance system.
- Counterrevolution after the 1848 revolution was followed by the presidency and then enthroning Louis Napoleon, who later fumbled the Franco-Prussian War.

These events were followed by Paris' narrow escape in WWI and then rapid collapse under the German *Blitzkrieg* in WWII. In summary, France had a long history of struggle to obtain preeminence in western continental Europe under Louis XIV and briefly regain it under Napoleon. But then it was repeatedly trounced by Germany. In WWI and WWII alliances with Britain and the Soviet Union proved inadequate to forestall catastrophic losses, and the United States intervened in both cases only in its own good time.

Moreover, with France militarily crushed in WWII, General de Gaulle as leader of this once great nation was inevitably marginalized within Dwight Eisenhower's unified allied command. After WWI, it turned out that France could not count on reliable and affordable access to British coal; and after WWII France and Britain again had different interests and policies when it came to establishing terms for facilitating economic reconstruction in Germany. Further estrangement from the United States resulted from Eisenhower's letting France fall to another embarrassing defeat with Britain and Israel in the 1956 Suez crisis. While France and its allies, in the Suez misadventure, made a putative blunder of failing to consult with Eisenhower adequately ahead of time, the net result was that the United States again appeared to be an insufficiently reliable ally from a French point of view.

In this context, it is hardly surprising that de Gaulle was loathe to defer to the United States and Britain on the *sine qua non* of major power military might and prestige in the post-WWII period: nuclear weapons. Similarly in the civilian context, entwining Germany economically and eventually politically in the European Economic Community was one thing, but being reliant primarily on German coal for the increasingly industrially central supply of electricity was quite another matter. France thus chose from the beginning to push both military and civil uses of nuclear energy extremely hard. Up to half of the military budget for about a decade during the build-up of the *force de frappe* was consumed by nuclear arms programs. Concomitantly, the nuclear intensity of the French electrical industry became nearly complete while many other countries still relied much more heavily on coal.

For the uranium to support its military and civilian programs, France decided to supplement its own domestic resources with those from Niger and Gabon, as noted above. By extension of the reasons noted above for the military sphere, France did not want to be reliant upon the United States for its civilian uranium supplies either. By the early 1970s Canada was the largest noncommunist producer aside from the United States, but for a variety of reasons France decided not to try to rely on Canada either during the cold war. Obvious generic considerations are that Canada had strong US economic ties, and a close strategic cooperation with the United States that included early warning radar detection of possible trans-arctic Soviet nuclear weapons delivery. In both of these partnerships Canada clearly held a junior position potentially subject to US pressure on nuclear policy issues.

More specifically, there was a failure to realize a closer Canadian–French nuclear connection that could have followed the movement of the scientist Frédéric Joliot-Curie from Paris to Montreal after he fled in front of the Nazi occupation with his then-rare uranium stocks. Joliot's communist sympathies doomed any prospects for his direct participation in the US nuclear bomb construction Manhattan Project resulting from this move, and indeed set Canada off in a completely different direction on nuclear power than France. As compensation for his cooperation, Joliot-Curie was enrolled in developing a reactor using heavy water, which was technically interesting but was correctly expected to proceed too gradually to have a military impact during WWII.

The difference between heavy and light water is that the hydrogen nuclei in the heavy water have a neutron attached to their proton, and they are thus very much less likely to absorb another neutron. As a result of this lower neutron absorption in the water, heavy water reactors can tolerate the greater neutron absorption per nuclear fission event than occurs in natural as opposed to enriched uranium. While heavy water reactors took longer to develop, they do thus allow practical nuclear power production without the need for a nuclear-weapons-relevant uranium enrichment program.

Canada relied on the US military nuclear umbrella and thus did not feel a compelling need to develop uranium enrichment capacity. France instead took the fast route of graphite-moderated nuclear reactors for weapons plutonium production. Then, France abandoned the dead end of graphite-moderated natural uranium reactors after producing electricity in its handful of such reactors for a maximum of twenty-four years each. France thus ended up with a light water reactor fleet for electricity production while Canada settled on heavy water. Even had the French corporate culture in early stages in this field encouraged joint transatlantic ventures, which it did not, the French and Canadian nuclear industries were consequently not a natural match.

During the cold war, the Soviet Union insisted on control of all uranium resources in the Eastern bloc. While the French Socialist–Communist coalition after de Gaulle nominally had an "all horizons" generic nuclear deterrence policy, in practice the size of France's "minimal" intermediate range nuclear weapons delivery capability was set to overwhelm the Moscow missile defense system. Thus, France would hardly have been likely to rely on communist countries' uranium during the cold war, even if some of those countries had been in a position to sell.

Australia entered the uranium mining game in a noticeable way in 1975, and became the world's second largest producer after 1994 (followed by Niger in third place). For example, in 1996 production in thousands of tonnes of elemental uranium was 11.7 for Canada, 5.0 for Australia, 3.3 for Niger, 2.6 for the Russian Federation, and 2.4 each for Namibia and the United States. However, before 1995 France was not willing to shift reliance for uranium imports from Africa to Australia. The reason was continued French nuclear weapons testing. The origin of Australia's antipathy to nuclear testing may have roots in initially secretly planned British nuclear explosions on Australian islands and subsequent continued atmospheric testing in the Australian outback.[6] For whatever reason, Australia developed a strong antipathy toward nuclear explosives testing in the Pacific.

French nuclear testing was in fact confined to Pacific islands thousands of miles from Australia. The testing nevertheless continued to raise the issue in Australia (and New Zealand) of whether Southern

Hemisphere countries should have any truck at all with courting the prospects of radioactive fallout from Northern Hemisphere nuclear powers contaminating the Southern Hemisphere either in peacetime or during a possible nuclear war. The Australian Labor Party initially favored a complete end to uranium mining and then while in power established a policy of limiting production to three mines. In the face of global competition for this limited supply, France was thus also not willing to rely on Australian uranium mines. France's concern was the possibility of threat to supplies in case of growing disagreement, which did in fact materialize, over French nuclear testing in the Pacific. Political difficulties also made it difficult for France to rely on the South African apartheid regime, which also held sway over Namibia. Thus, France initially turned to West Africa to supplement production from its limited domestic uranium resources.

Endnotes

[1] Rethinaraj (2005).
[2] Singer (1998).
[3] CEA (2006b, p. 32).
[4] IAEA (1999, 2001, 2005).
[5] IAEA (2005).
[6] Grabosky (1989).

Chapter 21

French Neocolonialism in Africa

Strife in Africa convinced France to turn in the early 1960s to a neocolonialist policy in the vast area of West Africa over which it had increased its direct colonial rule for a century through to 1929. During the neocolonial period, France repeatedly intervened militarily on the side of one-party rulers in a number of countries, including uranium producers Gabon and Niger. France signed the Comprehensive Test Ban Treaty (CTBT) in 1996 and ratified it in 1998. This helped give France confidence in its ability to freely access the global uranium market outside of Africa. After that, Niger managed to make a start on transition to civilian rule.

French Colonialism and Neocolonialism in Africa

France was effectively shut out from colonial control outside of Africa in the 19th century (aside from its ultimately ill-fated venture in Southeast Asia). France thus turned to Africa for restoration of its empire after recovery from the Napoleonic wars. France occupied Algeria in 1830 and formally annexed it in 1848. After his country's 1871 defeat at the hands of Germany, the French philosopher Charles Bernard Renouvier publicized the notion of France's *mission civilisatrice* to civilize the supposedly benighted peoples of Africa.

French dominance in all of West Africa was not easily imposed before the age of troop airlifts. Compared with much of the New World, West Africa had a heritage of more militarily capable kingdoms that had in many ways rivaled that of western Europe until the late Middle Ages. In Niger for example:

> During the Middle Ages the western part of present-day Niger formed part of the Songhai empire, established during the 7th century by Berbers, and had accepted Islam by the 11th century. Much of eastern Niger belonged to the state of Kanem-Bornu (14th–19th century). In the south city-states arose (c. 14th century) among the Hausa and became southern termini for trans-Saharan commerce. During the early 19th century the Hausa states were conquered by Fulani under the Muslim reformer Usman dan Fodio. In the 1890s the French signed treaties with the rulers of the Say, Gaya, and Dosso states, but Niger did not become a formal French colony within French West Africa until 1922.[1]

Nevertheless, France gradually moved from alliances with cooperating local rulers to outright colonialism, completing the process in 1929. The 1954–1962 War of Algerian Independence helped convince France that its colonialism in Africa should be replaced by a more nuanced neocolonial approach.

> Faced with increasingly pressing demands for independence in the early 1960s, France moved to include in its new special economic relationship with former African colonies the treatment of uranium as a strategic material. This in some ways paralleled old mercantilist arrangements in spheres of influence before outright colonial annexation. To make sure of the establishment and continuity of such relationships, France did not shrink from sending military forces into the countries shown in Fig. 21.1. These include Gabon (in 1962) and Niger (in 1963), as well as into nearby countries (Cameroon in 1960–61, Mauritania in 1961, and Niger's neighbor Chad between 1960 and 1963).

France intervened east of Gabon in Congo in 1960 and 1962 as well. As noted by Pederson:

> France also intervened again in Gabon in 1964. This was after a coup briefly interrupted the leadership of Leon Mba, who had negotiated

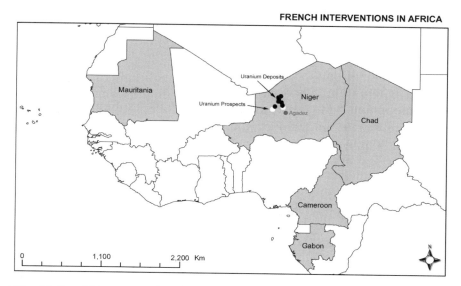

Fig. 21.1. African countries where France intervened militarily from 1960–1964.

independence for Gabon in the context of maintaining a special relationship with France and subsequently moved to set up a one-party state.[2]

Over 600 French soldiers intervened to put down the 1964 coup in Gabon. There were other resources and political alliance relations in Gabon that may have helped to precipitate this intervention, but uranium was likely on de Gaulle's mind in the process. Again as noted by Pederson.

It was in 1961 that the Gabonese company Compagnie des Mines d'Uranium de Franceville (COMUF) began to actively mine uranium in the Mounana region of Gabon. Production in the Mounana region stayed at around 500 tonnes per year for over ten years before a sharp drop-off in 1972.[3]

Niger

Under Prime Minister Diori Hamani, Niger also effectively established a one-party state after independence in 1960. France retained a particularly strong relationship with Niger, maintaining a garrison in the capital at Niamey and intervening in 1963 to put down a military uprising and settle a border dispute with Dahomey (now known as the Republic of Benin).

While uranium mining did not start in Niger until Hamani's second unopposed win of the presidency in 1970, exploration for uranium was started in 1956 by the French *Commissariat à l'énergie atomique* (CEA) and later taken over by the French nuclear fuel company Cogema. Hamani was removed in 1974 in a coup following discontent over governmental officials' corruption. At that time, France's presidency was caught in an interregnum between the sudden death of de Gaulle's successor Georges Pompidou and the subsequent installation of the actively interventionist Valéry Giscard d'Estaing. France did not intervene militarily in the events of the 1974 coup in Niger.

Despite continuing civil strife in Niger from an attempted coup in 1976 through to a five-day national strike in 1991 that shut down uranium mining and led to the first multiparty free national election in 1993, Niger's uranium output evidently remained adequate. Given the continuing output of the uranium mines through to 1991 and the successful resolution of the crisis in Niger that year, France chose not to intervene directly with military force. Nor did interruptions of civilian rule by coups in 1996 and 1999 provoke French military intervention.

US policy under the Clinton administration was to suspend development aid in response to the Niger coup of 1996. In Niger, a country with a per capita income of less than $300 in 1995 and a population of about ten million in 1997, loss of even the just twenty million dollars of annual US development aid available before 1995 may have been enough to grab the attention of the political leadership (see USAID, 1998). After the 1999 coup, a National Reconciliation Council effected a transition to civilian rule in December of that year. Furthermore, the country and international financial organizations have worked on development plans.[4] While France remained part of the donor pool, the transition from unilateral French military intervention to international cooperative action on democratization and development exemplifies an overall evolution of French policy toward Africa. Even in the 2003 French military intervention in Côte d'Ivoire[5] received UN and US approval.

France's Africa Policy after the CTBT

The complex of motivations behind the evolution of French African policy in the 1990s and the role of uranium therein will no doubt remain controversial. Here, it suffices to note that the train of nuclear-related events from the end of the cold war to French ratification of the Comprehensive Test Ban Treaty was necessary for the evolution of a new French Africa policy, but not in itself sufficient.

Although it is not yet complete, there has been a striking transformation from a unilateralist French African policy emphasizing military intervention in support of nondemocratic governance to a more multilateral approach constrained by concerns about fostering more broadly representative political systems. There are many reasons for this transformation. These include economic globalization inimical to special national spheres of commercial influence, the integration of France into common European economic and foreign policy, and the passing of the neocolonialist old guard and bureaucratic reorganization of African affairs in the French foreign ministry.

There may also have been some impact from international exposure of the mess left over after the death of Zaire's dictator Joseph Mobutu ended his cozy relationship with France. French policy has weathered such embarrassments before. However, the estimated over three million (mostly indirect) casualties from the consequent regional war[6] through 2003 was comparable even to the effects of prolonged regional conflict in Southeast Asia. Since the causalities reached that number, the death rate in the Democratic Republic of the Congo continued to be unusually high as that country coped with a ravaged infrastructure and continued regional violence.[7]

More timely, and more telling because of the timing and eventually transparent involvement in arms shipments, was French support for the Hutu dominance in Rwanda. This continued up to and through the 1994 Hutu genocide that killed an estimated 75% of the 657,000 Tutsi minority in the country.[8] Previous French involvement in zones of mass death in Biafra and Zaire in the Anglophone/ Francophone transition area in Africa were less domestically transparent. However, an unusual public inquiry in France drove home the catastrophic consequences of ineffectual meddling in this realm in the case of Rwanda.

While the reasons for the reformulation of French African policy in the 1990s were varied, it remains hard to imagine that this could have proceeded as it did had France remained frozen in its cold war dependence solely on West Africa for half of its uranium supply. During the cold war and even as late as 1995, French nuclear policy spiraled itself into a hole of global isolation when it came to alternate sources of uranium supply. Supporting the myth of French as the world's preeminently beautiful and culturally significant language helped tie the Francophone African elite to the French both commercially and politically. However, France's language-oriented foreign policy also may have irritated relations with what became the world's largest uranium producer, Canada, because of concerns a separatist movement in Canada's Francophone Quebec province. French nuclear testing in the Pacific helped develop and modernize France's nuclear arsenal independently of NATO. However, that testing seriously complicated relations with what became the world's second largest uranium producer, Australia. France's commitment to an independent military nuclear force also made it politically infeasible to import uranium from the United States or the eastern bloc, which were the other major producers outside of Africa.

The decision to make almost all of the country's electricity from nuclear power made France less dependent on imported coal. However, an emphasis on subsidizing domestic uranium production in the name of energy independence ironically led France to be the only major nuclear electric producer to substantially deplete its significant domestic uranium resources. Initially, France planned to stretch out its own domestic uranium resources up to about a hundred-fold using breeder reactors with massive loadings of plutonium metal to produce additional plutonium from the isotope uranium-238.

(This isotope constitutes 99.3 percent of natural uranium and is otherwise of very limited value.) In the end, France was not able in the 20th century to demonstrate that it was technically feasible to breed plutonium in an economically attractive manner. It was a fluke that the then tiny French Green Party was needed to keep a Socialist-led coalition government in power for a short time after the end of the cold war. As a result, the French Greens managed to precipitate the shut-down of the technically troubled 1.2 GWe net power Superphenix breeder reactor by 1998. With this, France's breeder reactor program died in practice, even if some people in France's nuclear establishment continue to hope it may be reborn like the mythical creature its breeder reactors were named after.

France continues to reprocess spent light water fuel to recover plutonium for conversion to oxides for a second round of burning in light water reactors. This practice potentially augments its uranium supplies by a factor of about one-third, but the dream of uranium self-sufficiency through breeder reactors was clearly in trouble by the 1980s. This dream effectively died with the decision to shut down Superphenix. Thus, through to the end of nuclear weapons testing in 1995, France's drive for military and commercial nuclear independence effectively locked it into a policy of preparing for unilateralist military intervention in West Africa no matter what, to forestall any serious threat to continuity of uranium imports from there.

France's ultimately enthusiastic embrace of a global end to nuclear testing provided the final key to unlocking its sole dependence on West African uranium imports.[9] This came on top of Australian domestic reforms on environmental impact of uranium mining and relations with aboriginal peoples. In this context, France's apparently permanent abandonment of nuclear weapons testing cemented an enduring French participation in expansion of Australian uranium exports and foreign mining operations ownership. Meanwhile, France's fences were mended with Canada, and the evaporation of barriers around the former eastern bloc promoted overall globalization of uranium markets. Given the diversity of supplies and the static nature of its uranium demand for the foreseeable future, France thus gained the opportunity to view access to uranium on the global market like any other industrially important material. Thus, a neocolonialist policy for securing uranium supplies was no longer of unique strategic importance to France. In short then, France's liberation from sole dependence on African uranium imports appears to have been a necessary albeit not sufficient condition for an important evolution in its foreign policy.

Endnotes

[1]   Cordell (2003).
[2]   Pederson (2000).
[3]   Pederson (2000).
[4]   see UNCDF (2004); IMF (2002).
[5]   New York Times (2003).
[6]   Lacey (2003).
[7]   Addario (2008).
[8]   Kolodziej (2000)
[9]   Pike (2005c).

Chapter 22

Natural Gas Resources and Transport

Readily extractable natural gas resources are found in similar but broader and more plentiful distribution than readily extractable oil. Even so, the growth of natural gas use has been slower than that of oil. This is due in part to the greater convenience of oil distillates as transportation fuels. Early technical and continuing political impediments to shipping natural gas long distances by pipeline and the expense of liquefying it for tanker shipment have also made oil a more attractive energy source. Nevertheless, large national and international gas pipeline networks grew up in parts of the northern hemisphere. By 2008 some gas pipelines were in place in South America and an extensive north–south continental network was under consideration.[1] There was also increasing interest in extending gas pipelines in Asia to India, Korea, or Japan. Despite the growing importance of natural gas pipelines, however, major international wars over control of natural gas exports by pipeline are unlikely.

National Systems and Regional Cooperation

It is easy to see why natural gas security was not a major concern in the 20th century. Before WWII, natural gas pipelines were local or regional systems designed largely to supplement and gradually replace synthetic gas made locally from coal. During the first quarter century after WWII, international natural gas trade by pipeline grew, but primarily within security alliances in North America, Western Europe, and the Soviet-dominated bloc. Thereafter, Italy and then Germany started importing Russian natural gas, but Russia ended up being more dependent on European Union countries' cash flows than the importers were on a secure flow of natural gas. South America came later to the game of building a continental-scale gas pipeline network.

Throughout most of the 20th century, expanding use of natural gas and the consequent motivation for more international trade in natural gas remained throttled by regulatory restrictions in North America and Europe. In the 1990s the United States liberalized its regulatory environment. The European Union later became poised to follow its own liberalization path. Thus, the early 21st century is likely to see heavier use and depletion of the most easily extracted regional stocks. These trends are providing stronger incentives for long-range international trade in natural gas.

This chapter describes the impediments to more rapid development and use of advanced natural gas technologies in the 20th century. This will form the basis for the discussion in the next chapter on incentives for the expansion of long distance international trade in natural gas in the coming decades. Much of this expansion will involve pipeline shipments from Russia, which is likely to long remain economically dependent on natural gas revenue source but immune to major military incursions by importers. It will also be seen that the expansion in liquefied natural gas trade is unlikely to unfold substantial risks of major international war, especially if mechanisms can be developed to avoid major international wars connected to international trade in oil.

Natural Gas Deposits

Building an understanding of the role of natural gas logically starts with an examination of how and where its deposits were formed. Natural gas is normally extracted from deposits that formed at high temperatures from deeply buried material over the course of millions of years. On a logarithmic scale, typical deposits are closer to a hundred million years old than to ten million or a billion. It typically takes about a hundred million years for oil deposits to form at temperatures from 40 to 100 degrees centigrade and for gas deposits to form at temperatures from 100 to 350 degrees centigrade.[2] Longer exposure at higher temperature produces "dry gas" from "wet gas," which contains more easily condensed hydrocarbons like propane and butane. At higher temperatures, for such extended periods, gas tends not to last in the form of readily extractable deposits while coal remains intact at very high temperature. The difference in these temperature ranges partly explains why there is a thought to be a comparable but somewhat larger amount of conventional natural gas at a given depth than oil, and a considerably larger amount of coal.

Only a small fraction of the overall geological endowment of oil and natural gas can be extracted by "simply" pumping it out of the earth. For readily usable reservoirs to exist, fluid material must have been transported out of the matrix of material it was originally embedded in and trapped against geological formations such as folds, salt domes, or slipped faults.[3] Beyond the most readily extractable deposits of this kind, there remains an enormous amount of "unconventional" oil and natural gas for which other technologies can be used (at a cost) to liberate it from sands, shale, or coal beds. There is also a vast amount of methane originally directly produced by live organisms at moderate temperatures. Some of this gas can be liberated (albeit usually at very high cost) from its entrapment in ice as a "methane hydrate." What all of this means is that the world will never "run out of natural gas." Rather, as for oil, alternative energy technologies will eventually evolve that perform the same function at a lower overall cost than extracting ever more difficult to recover resources, leaving the remainder untapped.

Large deposits of cheaply extractable natural gas abound in western Eurasia and around the North African fringe of the Mediterranean, and also in North America and Venezuela. There are additional substantial such resources in the East Indies and Nigeria. There are also smaller resources in or near Australia, Argentina, and Bangladesh and India. However, India's resources are comparatively modest in view of its large population.[a]

---

[a] For websites with maps showing the location of natural gas resources, see Masters *et al.*, 2002.

Oil deposits commonly have *associated* natural gas. Originally this was considered to be a nuisance, and was burned in flares to avoid accumulation of an asphyxiation or explosion hazard. Before systems were developed to make better use of natural gas, its larger resource base occurring independent of oil was simply left in the ground.

Where oil is valuable and natural gas is not, one alternative to gas flaring is to re-inject the oxygen-free natural gas into the ground to maintain oil well pressure. Re-injection to maintain oil well pressure requires an oxygen-free gas like methane or carbon dioxide where avoiding underground combustion is important. "Some oil producers in Ohio instituted gas re-injection as a method of *secondary recovery* in 1903, but it was not until the 1930s and 1940s that this approach became widespread" in the United States.[4] In the following comment on flaring in 1984, the abbreviation tcf stands for trillion cubic feet of natural gas. In energy content, this is equal to the accuracy needed here to the quadrillion British thermal units ("quad") used by many US sources, and to the metric unit exajoule, as detailed in Table 22.1.[5]

> Fully three-fourths of the known gas in the United States is *nonassociated* with oil. Oil, however, is rarely found without gas, and if it is, it might as well not exist. For methane, an expandable vapor, provides the motive lift that drives oil upward through a well in defiance of gravity. One of the great tragedies that accompanied the birth of the petroleum industry was the tremendous resource waste. Not only were huge volumes of natural gas vented into the atmosphere (probably upward of 50 tcf have been flared in the United States), but much of the original oil in place was stranded as a result and is still inaccessible.[6]

Due to the widespread occurrence of *nonassociated* resources, globally conventional natural gas is more diversely distributed geographically than conventional oil. Defining the "reserves" as identified resources that can be extracted roughly at current global average extraction costs with current technology, 66 percent of global oil reserves but only 34 percent of global natural gas reserves have been estimated to lie in the Middle East.[7]

Table 22.1. Energy content equivalents.

Definition	Abbreviation	Comments
Commercial units		
British Thermal Unit	Btu	Heats one lb. of water from 58.5°F to 59.5°F
Million Btu	"mmBtu"	Some use "mm" in place of "M" for "million"
thousand cubic feet	"mcf"	This much natural gas has 1.026 million Btu
therm		For residential bills $1/therm = $10/million-Btu
barrel of oil	bbl	Burning 1 bbl of oil releases 5.8 million Btu
Metric system units		
billion	G (or "b")	A (US) billion is a thousand million
gigajoule	GJ	One million Btu is 1.056 GJ
cubic meter		Cubic meter of natural gas has 36 million Btu
tonne (metric ton)	t (1000 kg)	1000 kilogram natural gas has 50 million Btu
Macroeconomic units		
quadrillion Btu	quad	$billion/quad = $ per million Btu
exajoule	EJ	Exajoule = billion billion Joules = 0.948 quad
gigawatt electric	GWe	Large plants make billion Joule/second = GWe
gigaWatt year		0.1 quad fuels 1 GWe, year at 32% efficiency
Mass/energy equivalents		
Gtonne natural gas		A billion tonnes natural gas yields 50 quads
Gtonne oil equivalent	Gtoe (btoe)	A billion tonnes of oil yields 42 quads
Gtonne coal equivalent	Gtce (btce)	A billion tonnes of coal yields 28 quads

Sources: The Natural Gas Industry: Evolution, Structure, and Economics (Tussing and Barlow, 1984) Table 2.2, p. 16; *Energy in a Finite World: Paths to a Sustainable Future* (Häfele 1981, p. 211). The energy content for a given volume of natural gas is varies with the composition of the gas and has slightly different values quoted in different references.

US Regulatory Constraints

Going back to before WWII, a number of factors combined to delay the realization of the full potential of natural gas. Back when petroleum was useful primarily for making lamp oil, there were initially difficulties with long-distance transport of a competing fuel that was gaseous at room temperature. "Town gas" did compete for lighting in urban areas, but this was generally made by local gasification of coal. By the time pipeline technology had developed to the point where natural gas could have been supplied over a large area for lighting, competition by electricity was rapidly displacing both lamp oil and gas as light sources in developed countries.

By WWI, transportation was providing a growing demand for fluid fossil fuels, but here again petroleum distillates had a major advantage over natural gas by virtue of their higher volumetric energy density. As long as oil was cheap and its pollution byproducts not a major concern at pre-WWII use levels, natural gas had little chance to compete in the transportation market.

Clean-burning and convenient natural gas did become increasingly competitive as a heat source. In urban environments pipeline networks increasingly brought gas directly to consumers at the turn of a nozzle, and in rural environments liquid propane condensed under pressure from wet gas sources could conveniently be used in the same sorts of appliances. As US customers became increasingly reliant on gas for everyday energy needs, wild fluctuations in pre-WWII oil markets and the command economy of WWII set the political stage for a post-war regulatory environment that would discourage application of natural gas to electricity production.

The US regulatory structure for natural gas had its roots in the idea of natural monopoly. A natural monopoly on distribution of a product is a business that is difficult and inefficient to divide between competing firms once one of them has set up a distribution infrastructure. Examples other than gas piping are water mains and electrical power and telephone lines. For such systems governments came to either manage the systems directly or set up public utilities or public service commissions to prevent owners from extracting more than a "reasonable rate of return" on investment. New York and Wisconsin set up commissions in 1907 that became involved in regulation of gas distribution. All but a few states eventually followed suit, had public utilities, or both.

Before 1925, US natural gas shipping was intrastate with the exception of transfers out of Louisiana, Indiana, and West Virginia to nearby states. In 1930 pipe diameters were limited to less than 20 in (0.5 m) and pressures to 500 pounds per square inch (34 atm) of pressure differential between the inside and outside of the pipe.[8] The strength and diameter of pipes had been gradually increased by oxyacetylene welding in 1911 and by electric welding in 1922. Pressure gas welding and metallurgical improvements were developed during WWII. By 1948 diameters were available up to 26 in (and over 50 atm pressure), increasing to 36 in or 0.9 m (and nearly 70 atm) in 1960, and 42 in (and nearly 90 atm) in 1975. By 1980 it was possible to make 56 in (1.4 m) pipe for pressures of 2000 pounds per square inch (136 atm). These are major technical advances. For at a given pressure drop per unit pipe length, friction reduction increases flow rate *more* rapidly than pipe cross-sectional area as the area increases. However, the cost of laying the pipe increases significantly *less* than proportionately to the pipe's cross-sectional area. That larger and stronger pipe can hold larger pressures and flow speeds at a given diameter further helps to increase achievable flow rates for a given spacing of pumping stations. The net result is that modern trunk pipelines became far more cost effective for moving natural gas than their early 20th century precursors.

The early stages of these advances facilitated a boom in US pipe construction in the late 1920s. However, at this point pipeline service areas in Southern, Midwestern, Western, and Eastern regions were each served by a single long-distance pipeline. At this point, long-distance piping was thus still subject to concerns about monopoly pricing if left unregulated.

The great depression halted long-distance pipeline construction until the WWII. During that war one longer distance gas pipeline was built from the south to the east coast. Moreover, afterward came the conversion to natural gas of two similar long-distance oil pipelines that had been built to avoid putting tankers at risk from German submarines.

During WWII there was, of course, no question of deregulating transport of energy resources deemed important to national security. Even during the post-war pipeline construction boom, interstate transmission continued to be regulated under the New Deal Congress' 1938 Natural Gas Act, as amended in 1942.

> The act instituted federal oversight of rates charged by interstate gas-transmission companies. The Federal Power Commission, which owed its existence to the Federal Water Power Act of 1920, became the administrating agency. In addition to rate regulation, the FPC held limited franchising powers. Nobody could build an interstate pipeline to deliver gas into a market already served by another gas pipeline without first obtaining FPC approval. In 1942, an amendment rounded out those powers by requiring commission certification of facilities penetrating new markets as well.[9]

Franchises were evidently readily granted, and by the 1960s the system was mature even to the point of several pipelines coming from Canada into western US states and all the way to the east coast. "By 1966, natural gas was available to consumers in all of the forty-eight conterminous states. Today [written in 1984], the nationwide network is so interconnected that if direction of flow and institutional barriers were of no concern, practically anybody who sells gas could send it to anybody who buys gas, regardless of location".[10]

Such flexibility was not to be realized in practice, however, until after 1993. Unlike common carrier US oil pipelines open to all sources, gas pipelines were long owned by companies that did not have to take others' shipments, even if interconnections were readily manageable. Further constraints on system expansion resulted from new federal interest in more regulation in the 1960s, despite the growing redundancy of the interstate system that could have allowed it to be non-monopolistic if deregulated. The 1960s thus saw a slow-down of the natural gas boom of the 1950s:

> System maturity was not, however, the only reason for the down-turn. The incoming Kennedy administration effected huge changes in regulatory policies. A more consumer-oriented Federal Power Commission monitored profits and looked for ways to trim the pur-ported fat off pipeline tariffs. These actions prompted Mutual Fund companies to dump interstate pipeline stocks from their portfolios between 1960 and 1962.[11]

Federal expansion of regulation also included controls on wellhead production for interstate sale. With intrastate production and sales freer to accommodate consumers in states such as Texas, this led to two markets. In important intrastate markets gas was cheap in the 1960s, and there was little incentive to develop more efficient tech-nology to use it to produce electricity. Meanwhile, the interstate mar-ket was approaching a supply crunch. Discovered reserves began to decline in 1967 as exploration became less attractive in the face of price ceilings.

Switches from oil to gas in face of increasing oil prices after the 1973 OPEC production limits forced a change to a national US nat-ural gas price ceiling twice the prevailing rates of the 1960s. However, political pressures kept Congress from deregulating prices until after a serious supply shortage developed. "During the winter of 1976–1977, interstate pipelines were unable to fulfill about one-fourth of firm demand, with some individual pipelines in considerably worse shape".[12] Since supplies to residential customers in the cold Northeast could not be interrupted, this had serious consequences for industrial customers and for overall production and employment.

The resulting Natural Gas Policy Act of 1978 was a compromise implemented "by phasing out price controls only on additional sources of supply, and extending the phasing over substantial periods of time".[13] What followed was a brief "glut" of gas on the market dur-ing a period of limited economic growth, followed by a gradual increase in production with slight dips in 1986 (when competing oil prices fell sharply) and a very slight drop during an economic slow-down from 1990 to 1991.

The "energy crises" of 1973 and 1977 prompted a rash of government investments in expensive alternative technologies, including production of gas and liquid fuels from coal and oil from shale. Also, ironically, "the Fuel Use Act of 1979 curtailed industrial demands by requiring that power plants not add to generation capacity with natural gas as the fuel source. With new capacity dedicated to coal and nuclear fuel-based generation, new gas demands in the power sector were reduced to low levels".[14] The irony is that this policy delayed the development and deployment of combined cycle natural gas plants that use gas turbine exhaust to raise steam for a second cycle of electricity generation. These plants achieve an overall thermal to electric conversion of about 50 percent, as opposed to the 32–38 percent range for older coal and newer coal and nuclear power plants, respectively. By cutting off the combined cycle gas option, the 1979 Fuel Use Act precluded the introduction of an alternative to some expensive nuclear power plants. It also precluded the adoption of fossil-fired electricity production giving off less than half as much atmospheric carbon emissions per unit electrical power output than the ongoing use of coal.

The process of partial US federal deregulation of natural gas that was initiated in 1978 took major additional steps in 1989 and 1991. Wellhead price controls were eliminated by an act of Congress in 1989. In 1991, the Federal Energy Regulatory Commission ordered that the natural gas industry "restructure itself into separate production, transmission, and distribution service industries".[15] With vertical integration of these three functions prohibited and multiple competing paths available from wellhead to "city gate," the door opened to widespread application of commodity market procedures to trading in natural gas futures. With the end of the era of new nuclear plants coming online in the United States, nuclear power output had very limited growth. Nuclear power plant managers only gradually learned how keep their plants producing electricity a larger percent of the time. New coal capacity was hard to site and had to meet stricter emissions standards than existing plant, so comparatively low natural gas prices provided an attractive alternative for electricity generation. Given heavier early investments in base-load capacity, much of this new investment was instead for peaking plant where the low capital and maintenance cost of simple open-cycle gas turbines was particularly attractive. However, technology for combined cycle plants also matured to the point where they would look increasingly attractive for base-load capacity if gas prices remained stable.

Then chaos struck. California made the mistake of deregulating energy supply markets without deregulation consumer prices. At the same time drought put pressure on California's hydroelectric supplies from the state of Washington. Trading companies took advantage of the complexity of new energy markets to run up prices dramatically, and the effect on natural gas prices rippled across the continent. The huge upstart Enron company deliberately restrained supplies to elevate prices, and then the company spectacularly collapsed after exposure of its faulty accounting practices. By 2003 natural gas prices had partly subsided down to about five dollars per gigajoule. However, in December of that year futures prices rose to over seven dollars per gigajoule. (See Table 22.1 for conversions to British thermal units, therms and cubic feet of natural gas.) The New York Times then reported that "the frenzied climb in prices has led to calls for investigations by politicians and executives of gas-dependent industries into whether traders have improperly manipulated natural gas markets... Several large energy companies, including Duke Energy of Charlotte, N.C., and Dynegy Inc. of Houston, have recently paid millions of dollars in fines to settle federal charges that they tried to manipulate prices of natural gas contracts improperly".[16] At the same time natural gas inventories of three trillion cubic feet (about 3 EJ) were up seven percent from the same time the previous year. The chairman of the Senate Judiciary Committee announced hearings to look into the possibility of natural gas market manipulation, and Federal Reserve Chairman Alan Greenspan called for increased imports of liquefied natural gas. The market background was this:

Gas drilling has increased, mainly in the Rockies and Texas, but much of it has come from fast-depleting wells. Imports of natural gas from Canada, meanwhile, have grown less reliable than in past years as demand for the fuel has also increased in that nation...[17]

US natural gas prices remained high through 2008. Even the construction of new liquefied natural gas (LNG) receiving terminals failed to provide the expected price relief in the United States, as global production bottlenecks kept world LNG prices above US prices beyond the beginning of 2008. With residential and commercial uses continuing, there was also strong demand for natural gas for production of chemicals, ammonia, fertilizer, and electricity. These developments certainly produced strong incentive to increase both natural gas production in Canada and facilities for importing LNG. What effect this will have on global markets depends on how natural gas markets develop elsewhere, particularly in Europe and Asia. These are now discussed in turn.

Europe Approaches Deregulation

Not surprisingly given the political situation from WWI through WWII, long distance shipping of natural gas was slower to develop in Western Europe than in the United States. After WWII, international piping of natural gas gradually became feasible in Europe. Italy put particular emphasis on natural gas, enlarging its small wartime system to 700 km of transmission pipe by 1950. The growth in Italy in the three succeeding decades was by 3900, 4400, and 7000 km, respectively, covering most of the country by 1980. For a diversified feed to this system, Italy began importing by pipeline from Russia and Holland in 1974, and under the Mediterranean from Algeria in 1983 via the Transmed line. In 1996, Italy started a project to double the capacity of the Transmed. In 1997 Italy started an upgrade project to receive North Sea gas and on a six-year project for a pipeline from Libya. In 1997 it started on "a third import line from Russia...planned for completion in 2007".[18] Italy's connections illustrate the gradual evolution from a small national system to part of an interconnected network drawing gas from as far a field as Russia, the North Sea, and North Africa.

The Netherlands first tapped natural gas in 1924, but serious production began only after WWII and was limited to the eastern Netherlands until 1955. In 1996 wet gas was discovered in the western Netherlands. By 1972 "natural gas had come within the reach of nearly every household in the Netherlands".[19] In 1960 the reserves in the Groningen area were re-estimated upward, leading to a partial privatization of the state concern to bring in large energy companies. By 1965 export contracts were made with Belgium and German concerns, but the British market became unattractive after discovery of North Sea gas in the same year. With the connection to Italy in 1974, the Netherlands also became part of a much larger European network.

Germany and France were the locomotives of European integration, but each took very different approach to energy security. During the US Reagan administration years in the 1980s, Germany enlarged upon the precedent set with the Netherlands in 1965 by making an arrangement with the Soviet Union for a new east–west natural gas pipeline from Russia. As a temperate region, almost all of Europe usually had up to half a year's stored natural gas reserve to prepare for unusually cold winters. It also had the ability to turn to North Africa, the North Sea, and the Middle East over the longer term if Russian supplies turned out to be unreliable for political reasons. Thus, Germany felt reasonably comfortable with obtaining part of its gas from Russia.

Normally the German government tried to keep on the good side of the United States. This had extended even to the point of Chancellor Helmut Schmidt and his Foreign Minister Hans Genscher taking a great deal of domestic political flack over the United States plans for deployment intermediate range nuclear weapons delivery systems and "neutron" bombs.[20,b] However, even in the 1980s Genscher was remarkably prescient in his view that economic interdependence

---

[b] The so-called "neutron" bomb is controversial because its higher than usual ratio of radiation to blast energy might conceivably lower the threshold for nuclear by making it more suitable for US military forces to use as a battlefield weapon in Germany rather than just threatening the Soviet block mutually assured destruction later war.

between Germany and the Soviet Union would ultimately be good for German security. He developed this vision even further when his party switched alliance partners and managed to remain part of a new governing coalition in Germany as the Soviet Union began to disintegrate. As a result the newly emerged Russia found itself locked in an important economic relationship with Germany and thus with the enlarging European Union.

France inherited from Napoleon Bonaparte's time a more centralized approach to governance. For the reasons noted above, France also placed remarkably heavy emphasis on a centrally administered set of nuclear power plants. Not surprisingly then, after the European Union moved toward coordinated energy market liberalization starting in the late 1990s, as of 2002 France remained amongst the least enthusiastic:

> Liberalisation is intended to remove the impediments to efficient trade. This implies that the national markets have to be integrated into an international (European) market and that the national networks should be opened to third party access (TPA). In order to reach these goals, EU member countries chose different solutions…Most countries opted for regulated TPA, while others, like the Netherlands, selected a hybrid form of regulated and negotiated access. Some countries enforce a strict separation of transportation and trading activities (like the UK and the Netherlands), while others are satisfied with only an unbundling of accounts. Most EU members have already opened up the largest part of their market, while others, like France realized only the minimum targets set by the EU.[21]

According to Machiel Mulder,[22] the EU energy market liberalization was likely to lead to a period of lower natural gas prices, followed by depletion of British gas fields, and resulting price pressure and increase in imports from more distant regions. Much of the imports will come from Russia. However, it is likely that EU countries will also increasingly turn to LNG imports over the coming few decades.

Asian Gas Pipelines

There are also a few pipelines aimed primarily at bringing interior natural gas to the coasts in countries such as Australia, Iran, and Algeria. There is a modest regional pipeline network in the southern cone of South America. What has been lacking is a set of long-distance pipelines aimed at connecting vast Middle Eastern and Siberian natural gas resources to the half of the world's population that lives in South, Southeast, and East Asia.

In South Asia, political difficulties have blocked the construction of a gas pipeline across Pakistan to India. The most geographically attractive route goes from Central Asian gas resources through Afghanistan and Pakistan to India (see Fig. 22.1). Before the Clinton administration fired cruise missiles on Afghanistan in 1998 in

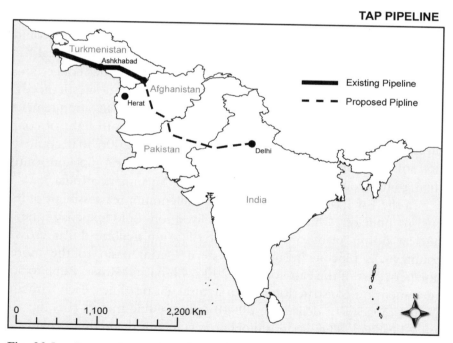

Fig. 22.1. Proposed extension of natural gas pipeline from Turkmenistan through Afghanistan and Pakistan to India.

response to bombings of US embassies in Africa, the company Unocal explored getting a concession to build a natural gas pipeline from Turkmenistan across Afghanistan to Pakistan and perhaps on to India. As of 2008, sufficient political stability had yet to be established in Afghanistan to allow pipeline construction across that country.

In addition to some progress on working toward reduction of overall tariff barriers in South Asia,[23] relations between India and Pakistan had improved by 2005 to the point where a long-stalled agreement in principle on a natural gas pipeline from Iran was reached. However, agreement on the critical detail of the price to be paid for the delivered natural gas was more difficult to achieve.[24] It took until 2008 for details of arrangements for either a 36-inch diameter pipeline from Iran to Pakistan or a 56-inch pipeline through to India had reportedly been worked out, but this left the project still a long way from successful completion.[25]

An alternative undersea gas pipeline route from Iran to India was deemed too expensive. Bangladesh has much more modest reserves that might nevertheless be profitably sold to India if a pipeline could be constructed up the Ganges valley even as far as Delhi. Unocal has shifted its interest to this project. However, uncertainties concerning the size of the Bangladesh resource, its own future domestic needs, and the political and security implications of such an arrangement with India precluded an agreement on this project. In light of continuing political turmoil in Bangladesh, by May 2006 that country was still not able to agree to a more efficient natural pipeline route than going around Bangladesh to get from Myanmar to India.[26]

In the Far East, after a turn-of-the-millennium reassessment of its energy policies, China put a short-lived on hold expensive new nuclear power plant orders in favor of a multibillion-dollar cross-country gas pipeline from the western Qarim basin to the more northern part of the east coast. In 2006, China and Russia came to an agreement on construction of two natural gas pipelines, each with an annual capacity of delivering 30–40 billion cubic meters (i.e., up to 1.4 EJ each).[27] The western pipeline was to run through an environmentally sensitive Ukok highland region, which lies southeast of Novosibirsk and is home to the endangered snow leopard.[28] What had

yet to materialize in concrete form as of 2008 was an even more ambitious plan to link to Siberia through this or a more northerly route
and pipe gas as far a-field as Japan. Should such a pipeline be routable
down through Korea, this could also provide North Korea affordable
energy supplies independent of the need to develop nuclear technology. There are, of course, both substantial political and capital-raising
problems to be overcome before a plan as ambitious as piping gas
through Korea to Japan could become a serious undertaking.

South America

Bolivia has the second largest proven natural gas reserves in South
America. Venezuela's proven reserves are much larger (*cf.* Table 22.2).[29]
However, Venezuela is much farther from the comparatively prosper-
ous southern part of the continent. This makes Bolivia a more attractive source of natural gas for shipment by pipeline to southern Brazil
and Argentina. So far at least, all international disputes over natural
gas in South America have been resolved quickly through negotiations. The re-nationalization of the Bolivian natural gas industry in
2006 was followed by negotiations in 2007 that led to a much higher
price paid by Brazil. This included a 285 percent increase, to about
four dollars per billion joules (US$4.20 per million BTU) for an elec-
trical power plant in Cuibana, Brazil.[30]

Table 22.2.   South American natural gas reserves.

Country	tcf	Exajoule
Venezuela	152.4	148.1
Bolivia	24.0	23.3
Argentina	16.1	15.6
Brazil	10.8	10.5
Peru	8.7	8.5
Columbia	4.0	3.9
Chile	3.5	3.4

Source: Bolivia: Natural gas (USEIA, 2007a).
tcf = trillion cubic feet.

Bolivia had previously privatized its natural gas industry in order to attract investment capital. Disputes over distribution of revenues from the increasingly profitable industry had provoked domestic turmoil and led to the sudden ouster of the previous government.

Gas Pipelines and Security

Here the primary purpose of looking into the details of gas pipeline development is to provide background for asking whether major international wars over security of piped gas supplies are likely. Central to this question is the role of Russia. This is because between them Russia's enormous western and eastern reserves have the potential to be piped almost anywhere in Europe or Asia.

A direct conventional military attack on Russia is not plausible despite maintenance problems with Russia's strategic nuclear arsenal.[31] Russia also has enormous dispersed stocks of "tactical" nuclear explosives that could be delivered to many of targets by a variety of means. Conversely, Russia might theoretically return to using military force to impose its favored terms of trade on those of its smaller neighbors that have not joined NATO, but the implications for Russia's relationship with Europe make this also highly implausible. In any case, disputes over a particular commodity would likely only be an excuse for an ideologically driven resurgence of Russian imperialism, even should recent economic integration and political cooperation of Russia with Europe somehow be so dramatically reversed.

Turning to the Western Hemisphere, there is a historical example of difficulty on agreeing on terms of natural gas trade between the United States and Mexico in the 1970s.[32] However, even the legacy of Mexico's early nationalization of its oil industry has not raised the slightest possibility of a US invasion. The idea of a war over energy between the United States and its North American Free Trade Association partners seems totally out of the question. Similarly, the countries trading natural gas in South America appear to be completely and durably committed to negotiation rather than use of military force over economic issues.

This is not to say that pipelines are totally disconnected from violent conflict. Security for existing and potential oil pipeline routes in Columbia, Chechnya, and Russia's southern neighbors may well be on the minds of those respectively in the United States and Russia who support military actions in those regions. Likewise, criticism of some pseudo-democratic and autocratic regimes in Central Asia by the major outside powers appears to be muted by prospects for accessing the fluid fossil fuel resources controlled by these regimes. However, not-so-benign neglect is about the most that can be expected in the former Soviet republics in Asia. Russia has no need to secure external natural gas supplies. The European Union has little inclination to intervene and has alternate and better sources of natural gas than Central Asia. These include Iran, but the United States, experience with Iraq and the large population and strong nationalism in Iran all make it clear that a European invasion of Iran to try to help secure natural gas supplies is a remote possibility indeed.

As analyzed above in detail, France's interests in Africa have deep historical roots but have changed appreciably since the mid 1990s. Nevertheless, France's continuing interest in influencing events in Algeria no doubt has something to do with Algeria's fossil fuel resources. In particular, France put its support behind an Algerian government that nullified election results and thus precipitated a long and debilitating internal conflict. However, given France's previous defeat in Algeria, the prospects of a large-scale direct French military intervention in Algeria are also very remote.

In Afghanistan, during the 1990s hopes for a possible trans-Afghanistan gas pipeline may have played a minor role in tamping criticism of the Taliban regime. Even so, the Clinton administration was in no position to take on what in hindsight is clearly the enormous task of restructuring Afghanistan simply to make it secure for gas pipeline construction. Indeed, that NATO has proven incapable of committing to the effort needed to fully stabilize Afghanistan is a reflection of how marginal that country's position in legitimate international commerce is.

So far, the major potential customers, India and Japan, have been cautious about investing in major gas pipeline projects that could bring alone potential temptation for large-scale military intervention in Afghanistan, Pakistan, or Korea. Instead they have been focusing their attention in this area on LNG, as described in Chapter 23.

Endnotes

1. Beaubeoef (2007)
2. Singer (2008a)
3. Singer (2008b)
4. Tussing and Barlow (1984, p. 26)
5. Tussing and Barlow (1984); Häfele (1981).
6. Tussing and Barlow (1984, p. 128).
7. Singer (2008c).
8. Tussing and Barlow (1984, p. 30).
9. Tussing and Barlow (1984, p. 97).
10. Tussing and Barlow (1984, p. 55).
11. Tussing and Barlow (1984, p. 55).
12. Tussing and Barlow (1984, p. 113).
13. MacAvoy (2000, pp. 58–59).
14. MacAvoy (2000, p. 61).
15. MacAvoy (2000, p. 79).
16. Romero (2003b).
17. Romero (2003b).
18. Snam Rete Gas (2003).
19. Gasunie (2002).
20. Pike (2005d).
21. Mulder (2002, p. 31).
22. Mulder (2002, p. 32).
23. AP (2004).
24. Srivastava (2006).
25. Joshi (2008).
26. Staff Reporter (2007).
27. BBC News (2006b).
28. Blagov (2006).
29. USEIA (2007a).
30. USEIA (2007a).
31. Lieber and Press (2006).
32. Tussing and Barlow (1984, pp. 150–152).

Chapter 23

Liquefied Natural Gas and Security Developments

At the end of the 20th century, liquefied natural gas (LNG) accounted for a small but rapidly growing fraction of total natural gas use. This growth raises the specter that a large global market for LNG shipped by tanker could lead to military interventions similar to those that arose after oil began to be shipped globally by tanker. To see whether this is likely to be a serious concern requires looking at three questions: (1) Where, when, and why is gas-fired electricity favored over nuclear power? (2) How much natural gas is shipped by tanker? (3) How much is LNG use likely to grow?

Historical Liquefied Natural Gas Trade

Liquefied natural gas technology started as a seasonal storage ("peak-shaving") method rather than for tanker shipping. The first such facility was built in Cleveland in 1941. In 1944, an explosion there killed 130 people. This put an end to use of LNG for peak-shaving for twenty years, until improved technology was developed. By 1982, there were over fifty peak-shaving plants operating in the United States.[1] This use of liquefaction paved the road for recovery and tanker shipping of some of the enormous volumes of natural gas that were being flared in connection with oil production. This flaring amounted to nearly five quads of natural gas (i.e. about 5 EJ) per year in 1979.

US experiences with attempts to import LNG got off to a rocky start in 1978–1982. The US government had provided over $400 million of loan guarantees covering the cost of six tankers, three of which were already in service and shipping Algerian gas by 1978. As oil prices subsequently rose, the exporter first renegotiated the price to $1.95 billion per quad ($1.85/EJ, in then-current dollars), freight on board (*f.o.b.*) at Algeria. Then Algeria asked for more:

> US approval of the new $1.95-per-mmbtu (*f.o.b.* Algeria) was granted in December 1979, but Algeria announced shortly there-after that it believed a further increase was warranted. Algeria was seeking a gas price that would achieve parity with its crude-oil exports, irrespective of the fact that tinkering, regasification, and other downstream charges would make it impossible for the LNG to compete with refined oil at the *burner tip...*[2]

In the US regulatory framework at the time, even at the higher requested price Algerian gas might still have been marketable by blending it with cheaper domestic supplies. Despite this, the United States blocked the requested price increase "fearing in part the sig-nal that acceptance of such terms would send to Canada and Mexico, who kept edging toward higher and higher prices for their own exports".[3] Algeria then cut off delivery, and the resulting total loss of $547 million amounts to well over a billion dollars in 2008 purchasing power. Shipments recommenced in 1982, but only by imposing on customers a price well over market value to help recover the large investment that had already been made in regasifi-cation terminal facilities. After that US imports of LNG remained quite modest and confined to Algeria through to the 1990s (see Table 23.1).[4]

Globally, LNG trade more than doubled from 3.2 EJ in 1993 to 8.2 EJ in 2006, (cf. Table 23.2). This was much faster than an eighteen percent increase in overall global natural gas consumption from 1989 to 1999. By 2006 global LNG shipments had jumped to 8.2 EJ. At 3.4 EJ Japan still dominated LNG exports in 2006. South Korea was a distant second at 1.3 EJ, followed by Spain at 0.9. Despite its enor-mous overall natural gas consumption levels, by 2006 the United States had years to go before greatly enlarging its LNG landing capac-ity and remained in fourth place in LNG imports at 0.6 EJ.

Table 23.1. World LNG imports by origin in 1993 (exajoules).

	Exporter					
Importer	Algeria	Libya	Indonesia	Malaysia	Other	Total
United States	0.08					0.08
Belgium	0.17					0.17
France	0.32					0.32
Italy	0.01					0.01
Spain	0.16	0.48				0.20
Japan			0.93	0.40	0.72	2.05
S. Korea			0.22	0.01		0.23
Taiwan			0.10			0.10
Total exports	0.73	0.48	1.25	0.41	0.72	3.17

Source: USEIA (2003c).
Quantities from "other" exporters to Japan include 0.05 EJ from the United States, 0.13 from the United Arab Emirates, 0.25 from Australia, and 0.29 from Brunei.

Natural Gas Depletion

In the previous chapter, it was shown that recent deregulation of the natural gas industries in the United States and Europe left both markets potentially more open to LNG imports. However, there are still a number of uncertainties about how fast LNG trade will expand. These concern the large capital investments needed and public perceptions of the safety of new liquefaction facilities and pipelines.

Replacement of depleting continental resources with LNG imports can be easier than supply enhancement. This is the case where existing pipelines can be used and there is no need for new onshore US regasification facilities. Options for the United States included placing liquefaction facilities in remote locations such as Baja in Mexico and off shore in the Gulf of Mexico. For a substantial expansion requiring long new trunk pipelines to ship inland from regasification terminals, there will be some delays and additional costs as environmental review and local opposition in affected areas.

In North America, from the year 2000 California partial deregulation fiasco through 2006, natural gas prices remained high enough

Table 23.2. World LNG exports and imports in 2006 (exajoule).

EJ	Exporter	EJ	Importer
0.07	United States (to Japan)	0.63	United States
0.63	Trinidad and Tobago	0.05	Mexico
0.91	Algeria	0.03	Puerto Rico (from Trinidad and Tobago)
0.57	Egypt	0.01	Dominican Republic (from Trinidad and Tobago)
0.03	Libya	0.16	Belgium
0.68	Nigeria	0.53	France
0.47	Oman	0.02	Greece
1.20	Qatar	0.10	Italy
0.28	United Arab Emirates	0.08	Portugal
0.76	Australia	0.93	Spain
0.38	Brunei	0.20	Turkey
1.16	Indonesia	0.13	United Kingdom
1.10	Malaysia	0.04	China
		0.27	India
		3.39	Japan
		1.26	South Korea
		0.40	Taiwan
8.24	Total	8.24	Total

Source: USEIA (Griffin, 2007).
Total omits 0.002 EJ by truck from the United States to Mexico.

to justify Alan Greenspan's enthusiasm for increased LNG imports to the United States. Nevertheless, a Congressional energy bill that contained provisions for massive investment in a pipeline from Alaska was narrowly postponed by minority action in the US Senate toward the end of 2003. In the face of rising natural gas prices, the US Congress subsequently passed the Alaska Natural Gas Pipeline Act of 2004. In February of 2006, the Federal Energy Regulatory Commission reported to the US Congress that an agreement had been reached between the State of Alaska and natural gas producers pursuant to shipping through the prospective pipeline.[5] This pipeline was expected to ship 0.8 quad/year starting in 2018 and reach full capacity at

2 quad/year in 2024. Without this pipeline, there would likely be a corresponding increase in comparably expensive LNG imports.[6]

Canadian production may also respond to demand at prevailing prices given enough lead time. An 1994 analysis by Carl Calantone of the Alberta Natural Gas Company, Ltd., detailed the likely resiliency of Canadian natural gas resources against depletion.[7] Calantone used an analysis of the Canadian natural gas resource base to conclude that its inflation-adjusted extraction cost will actually be lower in 2020 than in the year 2000 if a long established historical trend in efficiency improvement continues that far into the future. His expected well-head price range for 2000 was about 1.4 Canadian dollars per million Btu, presumably at 1994 prices, corresponding to about the same price in $US per million Btu in 2003.

The prices of Canadian natural gas *beyond* the wellhead as imported to the United States that are listed in Table 23.3 started in 1995 to reverse a long decline. Starting in the winter of 2001 this price showed large seasonal fluctuations.[8,9] The nominal price per thousand cubic feet peaked at US$9.63 in January of 2001, 7.84 in March of 2003, and 11.96 in October of 2005. These high prices were not of course due to a sudden exhaustion of cheaply extractable natural gas in Canada. Rather, they were due to fluctuations in the US market resulting from inadequately thought-out moves toward deregulation.[10] More generally, the idea that resource depletion is not likely to drive major extraction cost increases on a global basis over the next two decades is no guarantee against substantial increases in delivered price at least temporarily in some locations.

In May 2007, the US Energy Information Agency reported that the United States had five LNG receiving terminals operating with a total annual regasification capacity of 2.1 trillion cubic feet (2.3 EJ). The ongoing construction of four more such facilities would more than double US LNG landing import capacity. US LNG imports were expected to overtake those by pipeline from Canada by about 2015. The total of LNG and Canadian natural gas imports was nevertheless expected to about quarter of total US usage in 2015, and to remain so through 2030.[11]

In the European Union, market liberalization is expected to reduce inflation-adjusted natural gas prices and drive demand that would deplete

Table 23.3.   US price of Canadian natural gas.

Year	Normal $ per 1000 cu ft	CPI	$US2008 per 1000 cu ft	$US2008/GJ
1985	3.17	105.5	6.26	5.75
1986	2.42	109.6	4.60	4.24
1987	1.95	111.2	3.65	3.37
1988	1.83	115.7	3.29	3.04
1989	1.81	121.1	3.11	2.87
1990	1.91	127.4	3.12	2.88
1991	1.81	134.6	2.80	2.58
1992	1.84	138.1	2.77	2.56
1993	2.02	142.6	2.95	2.72
1994	1.86	146.2	2.65	2.44
1995	1.48	150.3	2.05	1.89
1996	1.96	154.4	2.64	2.44
1997	2.15	159.1	2.81	2.60
1998	1.95	161.6	2.51	2.32
1999	2.23	164.3	2.83	2.61
2000	3.97	`168.8	4.90	4.52
2001	4.43	175.1	5.27	4.86
2002	3.13	177.1	3.68	3.40
2003	5.23	181.7	5.99	5.53
2004	5.80	185.2	6.52	6.02
2005	8.09	190.7	8.83	8.15
2006	6.83	198.3	7.17	6.62
2007	6.83	202.4	6.54	

Source: US Energy Information Agency (USEIA, 2007b), with the consumer price index (CPI) used to adjusted beginning of year prices to 2008 purchasing power from the US Bureau of Labor Statistics (USBLS, 2008).

local resources. Even given a decade for local resource depletion to reverse a trend of decreasing prices, Russian and Iranian natural gas have enormous potential to make up the difference via pipeline deliveries. In the short term China is likely to relying on primarily on its own resources, but planning to import natural gas from Russia. In the longer term even Korea and Japan might gain access to international gas pipelines. Thus, what is really needed to stimulate major growth in LNG trade is a global depletion of the natural gas resources that are readily accessible by pipeline, not just localized depletion and temporary price instability.

On the other hand, the increase in sustained piped gas prices needed to make LNG substantially more attractive may not be all that large. A recent study cited by the Clingendael International Energy Program suggests that LNG shipping costs can complete with high-pressure pipelines only at shipping distances of over about 5000 miles (8000 km).[12] At this range most of the major markets can be connected to northern gas fields. If the wellhead cost of gas at these sources increases by a dollar per million Btu (just over $1/EJ), at 2008 purchasing power, however, then LNG from remote locations like Nigeria, Indonesia, and Australia becomes competitive with natural gas shipped by pipeline when comparing existing technology for both shipping methods.

In the United States, natural gas use had eclipsed that of coal by 1960, which had already been overtaken by oil by 1950.[13] Globally, natural gas has been taking longer to catch up with coal. That developing countries are likely to follow the pattern of gas replacing coal is part of the basis for projecting strong global growth in natural gas use even in view of uncertainty concerning sustainability of acceleration of the overall rate of energy use.

Table 23.4 gives an idea of recent annual natural gas use and one conception of how it may evolve in the future.[14] The remarkable projected growth from 26 to 62 EJ from 2004 to 2030 for the "other OECD" developing countries in Table 23.4 is broadly distributed

Table 23.4.   Annual natural gas consumption by region (exajoule).

Region	\multicolumn{5}{c}{Year}
	1990	2004	2010	2020	2030
OECD N. America	24	30	33	37	38
OECD Europe	13	20	23	26	29
OECD Asia	3	5	6	7	8
Non-OECD Europe and Eurasia	29	26	29	34	38
Other Non-OECD	11	26	34	48	62
Total	79	108	125	152	176

Source: International Energy Outlook 2007 (USEIA, 2007d).
OECD = Organization for Economic Cooperation and Development; Eurasia includes former Soviet Republic in Asia.

among them. China and India have the largest projected percentage annual consumption growth in this group, but together they only account for a quarter of its projected increase in consumption.

Based on fits to estimates from H-H Rogner,[15] the amount of natural gas used to date would need to about double in order to drive inflation-adjusted global average extraction costs up by $1 billion/EJ in year 2008 purchasing power, assuming comparable improvements in production efficiency and the economy as a whole. As of 2008 an estimated amount of just over 2300 EJ of natural gas had been used overall. At the global use rate projected for 2010 it would take 20 years for cumulative use to double. If global natural gas use rate continues to increase at the rate projected for 2010–2020 in Table 23.4, then the doubling of cumulative global use would only take just over 16 years. The resulting increase in natural gas prices can be expected to help slow the rate of growth of natural gas use. This expectation is qualitatively consistent with the lower rate of use growth for the 2020–2030 decade than the 2010–2020 decade as shown in Table 23.4.

The idea that the tripling cumulative global natural gas depletion might increase inflation-adjusted extraction costs by about $1/GJ is based on more than fits to estimates of global resource endowments versus extraction costs. This analysis also assumes that the efficiency of natural gas discovery and extraction improves at about the overall global rate of change of production efficiency in economies at large. However, the analysis by Calantone referred to above is based on the observation that efficiency improvements in the Canadian natural gas industry have occurred at a higher rate than in the economy as a whole. This has kept a lid on inflation-adjusted wellhead prices even as more readily extractable resources are depleted. If this trend persists long enough, then the time required for the production and transmission cost of gas delivered across the border to the United States to increase by the 2008 purchasing power equivalent of $1/GJ may longer than fifteen years.

LNG and Nuclear Power

One reason that use of natural gas is unlikely to increase exponentially long after inflation-adjusted wellhead prices increase by $1/GJ

($1 billion/EJ) is that such an increase in natural gas prices would likely make alternative energy technologies look more attractive. For example, the difference in capital cost between a 1 GWe nuclear electric power plant and combined cycle natural gas plant capacity of the same size is about a billion dollars in terms of year 2008 purchasing power. At the five percent differential between interest rates and inflation commonly assumed by the International Atomic Energy Agency for developed countries, the annual inflation-adjusted interest charge on $1 billion is $50 million. A $1 billion/EJ increase in natural gas prices would also increase base-load plant fuel costs for a 1 GWe gas-fired baseload combined cycle plant by about $50 million. (This assumes operation at 80 percent capacity and 50 percent thermal-to-electric conversion efficiency.) Details of such competition depend on location-dependent operations costs and licensing requirements. However, these simple estimates give an idea of the level of fuel cost increases that should make nuclear power substantially more competitive. In summary, while new nuclear power plant installation was only commercially competitive in isolated markets under recent conditions, an average global run-up in inflation-adjusted natural gas wellhead prices of $1 billion/EJ could make nuclear power competitive in a much broader set of markets.

One reason that nuclear power use was able to grow rapidly when readily extractable natural gas abounded was that for decades nuclear power technology received far larger public research and development support than natural gas. The United States and the Soviet Union took the lead in this, at first spinning small pilot nuclear electricity plants off of their military nuclear programs. Eastern Europe had little choice but to follow the Soviet lead. Germany and Japan adopted both boiling and pressurized water technologies developed in the United States. France insulated its national nuclear electric power generation from competition for the reasons described in Chapter 20. Meanwhile, there was comparatively little government support for research and development activities that could have provided a balanced test of combined cycle natural gas plants against nuclear plants. Thus, nuclear instead of combined-cycle gas plants were installed for meeting base-load electrical demand even in an era where natural gas could be delivered to many populated areas for less than \$2/GJ at 2008 purchasing power levels.

The reasons why costly nuclear power technology trumped inexpensive natural gas for new electricity generating capacity in the United States in the 1970s are more extensively analyzed in Steve Cohn's book *Too Cheap to Meter*.[16] Public funds supported not only the development of nuclear power but also the training of the work force needed to operate such a complex technology. The availability of a broad-based cadre of nuclear technologists was considered to be a national security asset in the United States and other countries. Also, putting a friendly face on nuclear energy was one tactic for diverting attention from a continually expanding nuclear arms race.

However, public subsidies alone are not enough to explain why, during the period of rapid growth of US nuclear power, private companies took the risk of making large investments in a new energy technology at an unprecedented pace. Utilities were insulated from risk by pricing regulations allowed them to pass the risk onto ratepayers, who had to pay all of the costs of electricity generation plus a reasonable profit to the utilities. Only during an era of subsequent deregulation did the so-called stranded costs of high interest payments on the more poorly performing nuclear plants come back to haunt utilities that could not convince regulators to guarantee cost recovery from customers. Even so, utilities could just have well opted for alternate technologies whose performance would clearly have been less likely to embarrass their executives. The author of *Too Cheap to Meter* chalks up the decisions of US utility executives to embrace nuclear power so enthusiastically in the years before the Three Mile Island accident to a bandwagon effect. Seduced by the prestige of a new technology, the enthusiasm of officialdom, and the decisions of their peers, the responsible executives are said to have chosen a risky alternative that would often not have resulted from a more dispassionate analysis of purely technical and economic factors.

Whatever the reasons, during a period of rapid growth in electricity use from after the Korean War to the 1973 "energy crisis," natural gas technology was not developed to the point that was feasible at the time. Then came a decade of modest growth in energy use. After this, however, developments in natural gas technology allowed it to mature to the point where, in the 1990s, no US utility executive with plant sites connectable to trunk gas pipelines would even seriously consider installing a nuclear electric power plant over a gas-fired one. This change set the stage for a situation where natural gas would not only take over from coal for direct use of heat content in developed countries, but could also capture a growing share of electricity production.

LNG and War versus Oil and War

The upshot of all of this is that liquefied natural gas is likely to continue to make inroads into and help globalize the natural gas market at and beyond the margins of pipeline distribution areas. However, market penetration by LNG will be a gradual process, perhaps not really approaching maturity until the 2020s or 2030s. At that point continued growth in the use of LNG for base-load electricity production may face increasingly stiff competition from nonfossil fuel sources. Even if use of coal is finally effectively limited due to concerns over global warming, by the 2030s nonfossil energy sources may be broadly competitive with natural gas for replacing retired coal-fired electrical production capacity. Moreover, the great majority of natural gas is still likely to come from pipeline connections direct from natural gas fields. Pipelines will continue to be able to supply a vast number of users especially on the Eurasian continent, and perhaps somewhat more into Africa as well.

Thus, the developing situation with LNG in the 21st century is very different from the history and present state of oil. Oil reserves are concentrated in a small number of comparatively weak countries, with about two-thirds of known reserves in the Middle East. This concentration allows the development of an occasionally effective oil cartel. This concentration has provided a recurring temptation for powerful consumers and other producers to resort to threat or use of large-scale military force to influence who controls oil resources. Natural gas reserves are more widely distributed, with only about one-third concentrated in the Middle East and a substantial portion of the rest found in Russia — a nuclear weapons state effectively immune from large-scale conventional military attack. Moreover, due to the high cost of liquefaction, a much smaller fraction of natural gas than oil is likely to move by tanker on a global market. Most of the major consumers will continue to have access to pipeline shipments of natural gas negotiated on a bilateral basis. Thus, although Russia's president Putin has reportedly expressed interest in the formation of an international natural gas cartel,[17] this would be more difficult to organize and make effective than for oil within OPEC.

In any case, the maturation of global LNG trade is likely to be a gradual process stretching over decades. This allows a considerable amount of time to evolve mechanisms to deal with international oil trade that avoid major international wars where control of oil plays a significant role. Should this be possible, then these mechanisms may be adopted for LNG trade as well, making major international war over natural gas all the more unlikely. Thus, when it comes to avoiding major international war over fluid fossil fuels, in essence again "it's about oil."

This is by no means to say that lesser international conflicts and even major internal conflicts where control of LNG revenues plays a role will necessarily avoided. Algeria has already seen violent internal conflict where France supported a government that suppressed election results. In 2003, there was also violent internal conflict in Bolivia, with one of the issues under contention being the proposed terms for shipping natural gas through Chile to port. This followed close on a major internal struggle in Venezuela over the distribution of benefits from its oil industry.[18] During the latter struggle, in April 2002 the US government backed off under from what initially appeared to be an approval of a faction that attempted overthrow of a democratically elected government.[19]

At the beginning of 2006, Russia very briefly reduced natural gas supplies to Ukraine as part of a campaign to force Ukraine to pay market prices.[20] Since the Soviet era, Ukraine had been importing natural gas from Russia at low prices and using some of it very inefficiently for industrial production. However, the pipeline to Ukraine also connects on to Western Europe, which was affected by the flow interruption and protested loudly. The net result was that Russia and Ukraine negotiated a price readjustment, but not before the European Union took notice of the importance of diversified energy supplies. Then on February 7, 2008, Gazprom announced an intention to halt pipeline shipment of a quarter of Ukraine's natural gas supplies in six days unless its demand was met for a settlement of "what it said was $1.5 billion in debt." This announcement "came 22 days after the Ukraine's pro-Western leaders formally applied to be put on a path to NATO membership." Gazprom is "the world's largest natural gas producer and a monopoly half-owned by the Russian government..." At a joint news conference dealing with a Ukrainian agreement to a settlement of the debt payment question, Russia's President Putin noted that if NATO deployed antimissile systems in Ukraine then "Russia could target its missile systems at Ukraine." President Viktor Yushcehko of Ukraine responded that his country "had the right to choose its own alliances and that his country's Constitution prohibited foreign military bases on its territory.[21] In these exchanges there was no hint of war over natural gas, but continuity of natural gas supplies dose apparently remain entangled more broadly with political/military tensions left over from the disintegration of the Soviet Union.

In May 2006, the recently elected populist Bolivian president nationalized his country's natural gas industry and even sent troops to occupy its natural gas fields.[22] Negotiations over pipeline supplies to Brazil were promptly initiated, so the nationalization move appeared to be more of internal than international consequence. Neither in the Russia/Ukraine nor Bolivia/Brazil cases was there any hint of an impending international military conflict. Both cases involved questions of commercial interest that were resolved by negotiation.

It is not only possible but even likely that violent internal conflict will continue to be sparked from time to time over the distribution of benefits from export or transit of natural gas. It is also likely that external powers will exert diplomatic or economic pressure to affect outcomes of such conflict, and in some cases they may also provide material support to one side or the other. What is less likely is that such conflict will broaden and escalate to the point of major international wars like those involving Iraq from 1980 through 2008. For the major providers of pipeline gas are likely to be largely immune from military intervention by their customers. Moreover, the LNG from any particular provider is likely to be a comparatively small "bit player" in overall energy markets, compared to the nearly twenty percent of global oil reserves that Iraq would have held in 1990 had it kept control of the major Iranian oil fields or all of Kuwait.[23] Internal conflicts and outside meddling in the affairs of natural gas producers are indeed expected. Beyond that, to avoid major international wars over natural gas it is likely to be sufficient and probably not even necessary that a mechanism be found to avoid major international wars over oil.

Endnotes

[1] Tussing and Barlow (1984, p. 63).
[2] Tussing and Barlow (1984, p. 69.
[3] Tussing and Barlow (1984, p. 69).
[4] USEIA (2003c).
[5] FERC (2006).
[6] Pirog (2004).
[7] Calantone (1994).
[8] USEIA (2007b); USBLS (2008).
[9] USEIA (2007c).
[10] See Economides and Oligney (2000).
[11] USEIA (2007d).
[12] CIEP (2003, p. 10).
[13] Singer (2008d).
[14] USEIA (2007d).
[15] Rogner (1997).
[16] Cohn (1997).
[17] Fattah (2007).
[18] Romero and Barrionnuevo (2005).
[19] Marquis (2002).
[20] International Herald Tribune (2006).
[21] Kramer (2008).
[22] Hauser (2006).
[23] USEIA (2006c).

Chapter 24

Hydropower

In the 20th century, hydroelectric dams produced major changes in water flows to downstream nations on several continents. Nevertheless, one may have to look all the way back to ancient Mesopotamian civilizations on the Tigris River to find an example of an "international" war fought primarily over water. Hydroelectric power has had some impact on production of nitrogen fertilizer and enrichment of uranium, but not to the point of critical impact on international war. For South America, South Asia, the Nile basin, and Turkey and its neighbors, watershed management has been arranged peacefully or as an afterthought to wars fought primarily over other issues. Internal dissention due to inadequate compensation for people displayed by dam building projects is not uncommon in developing countries, notably in India and China. However, all outstanding international disputes where construction of hydropower dams plays a role appear to be in the process of being peacefully negotiated or are beyond the reach of military influence by downstream countries.

Dams

This chapter explains why construction and control of hydroelectric dams has not led directly to international war, despite the critical importance of water flows across international boundaries. More generally, even before dams were constructed on the vast scale of some 20th and 21st century hydropower projects, international wars over water were remarkably rare. An interesting comment on this question is attributed to Oregon State University professor and "expert on international water basins" Aaron Wolf:

> The instances of nations actually going to war specifically over water are quite rare, Wolf noted. Ironically, the last full-scale war directly linked to water was 4500 years ago between Lagash and Umma on the River Tigris in what is present-day Iraq.[1]

A more accurate way of putting this would be that changing control of water resources has very rarely been the direct and primary aim of a war. The fate of water runoff has been but one of a number of issues that may have influenced how wars were terminated. What is remarkable, however, is how often competing international interests connected with international water basins have been dealt with through negotiation rather than war.

The discussion here is confined to surface runoff. In most cases underground aquifers span much smaller geographical areas than major surface watersheds. Thus, though contests over their use may be life-and-death matters in poor and dry regions, use of underground aquifers is usually an internal question that spills over at most indirectly into potential for international conflict. Chapter 29 deals with the interesting case of Palestine, where aquifer depletion and preferential access to water are but a part of a larger conflict with other causes that would likely persist even if water supplies somehow stopped being a significant problem.

Most dams that significantly affect international rivers are constructed at least in part for the production of electricity. Thus, although these dams are often also used for flood control and irrigation, focusing on hydroelectric projects continues the theme of energy and is sufficient for the present purpose. A noticeable exception is the Farakka barrage that directs Ganges waters to Calcutta and away from Bangladesh.

The discussion here starts with some brief comments on the history of hydroelectric power. It then goes on to look at a few particular water basins. The early history coincidentally touches back on the topics of nitrate production and uranium enrichment discussed in previous chapters, but only peripherally. More pertinent are the specific discussions focusing on South America, South Asia, and the Nile and Euphrates watersheds.

Early Hydropower

The first use of hydroelectric power was in Grand Rapids, Michigan, in 1880. This was followed by installation of a hydroelectric power plant in Wisconsin in 1882.[2] Canada was quick to adopt this technology on a larger scale in Ottawa. This presaged later projects on such a large scale as to produce substantial power excess for export to the United States. During the Great Depression, hydroelectric projects provided employment and electrical production capacity by government decree, in some cases before a market for the electricity was fully developed. One such case was the Tennessee Valley Authority (TVA). During, and even after WWII, the TVA had so much excess production capacity that it could readily power the very energy-intensive gaseous diffusion approach to uranium enrichment. As it turned out, the self-energized plutonium production reactor route to nuclear weapons also worked, and there were alternative locations and methods for enriching uranium. Thus, the contribution of the TVA was not crucial, but it did fix the United States on the path of an energy-intensive uranium enrichment process for decades to come.

Europe was also quick to catch on to hydroelectricity. As noted above, one of the early uses of Norwegian hydroelectric power was for an electrochemical nitrogen fixation process for a while after 1905. By this time, however, the War of the Pacific had already basically settled the fate of nitrogen deposits in western South America, so the development of process powered by hydroelectricity was more of a footnote to this episode rather than a definitive event.

France and Italy were two Allied Powers in WWI that suffered from coal shortages. France had lost most of its coal production to Germany, and other demands for British coal reduced annual Italian imports from 11 million tons in 1913 to an average of 7.5 million tons from 1915 to 1918. French hydroelectric power resources were far from the fighting front and were expanded for rail electrification and other purposes during the war. Following a reorganization period just after the war, France's hydroelectricity grew rapidly, more than doubling from 1923 to 1930. Like France, Italy's hydroelectricity grew rapidly in the 1920s, doubling from 1923 to 1930.[a]

South America

South America's geological history has left it remarkably poorly endowed with accessible coal deposits. Much of the continent's topography is dominated by the long crest of the Andes to the west and the great Amazon basin to the east. The mountains are too rugged and the basin composed of the wrong strata for coal mining. All of this is a legacy of the break-off of the continent from Africa and westward drift over the Pacific plate that throws up the Andes range.

Along with the tropical location of much of its landmass, this same topography has left South America well endowed with great volumes of water flowing over large elevation drops. There are also large deposits of bauxite, which requires electricity for conversion to aluminum. This recipe has left South America remarkably concentrated in hydropower for its electricity supply.

Another relevant feature of South American geography, in the political sphere, is that its country boundaries were mostly determined early in the 19th century along the lines of natural terrain features. This derived largely from Spanish colonial administrative practice and contrasts with the straight-line boundaries later slashed across other continents' maps by French and British colonial administrators. In many cases major rivers form parts of geographically determined boundaries in South America.

Following a protracted period of international conflict as the continent reorganized itself after the Napoleonic Wars and independence, South America's rivers and mountains ended up providing stable dividing lines between states that have shown remarkably little recent appetite for war with each other. Part of this may result from common linguistic and cultural heritage amongst the governing elites and part

---

[a] Italy's installed capacity increased only from 0.85 to 0.9 MWe from 1914 to 1918, but it managed to increase production from 2.5 GWh in 1914–1915 to 4 GWh in 1918–1919, as noted in Jensen 1968.

from the United States discouraging other outside powers from playing one side against another in potential internecine conflict between
South American states. Whatever the reason, the outcome is that
there is neither history nor prospect in South America for international warfare over control of hydropower resources, even though
these resources are centrally important to many countries' industrial
production.

An example of the type of cooperation used to develop South
American hydropower is the massive 12.6 GWe Itaipu dam project.
"The work began in February 1971, and on April 26, 1976, Brazil
and Paraguay signed the Treaty of Itaipu, the legal instrument providing for the development of the Paraná River by both countries.
A binational entity, called Itaipu, was created in May 1974 to manage
the construction of the Power Station, and the work began in January
of 1975".[3]

South Asia

The Indus and Ganges watersheds are the lifeblood of a substantial
fraction of the quarter of humanity that lives in South Asia. In addition, the water flowing off the Himalayas in Nepal has very substantial hydropower potential. The management of these watersheds has
indeed been controversial, but following the wars leading to partition
of colonial India in 1947 and Bangladesh's independence in 1971
they have been dealt with by negotiation. Indeed, the terms of the
Indus Waters Treaty have been honored even through subsequent
conflicts between India and Pakistan, including the reversal of the
1999 intrusion into Indian-occupied Kashmir at Kargil.[b]

This is not to say that India's neighbors are fully satisfied with the
way that common watersheds are managed. India's diversion of the
Indus headwaters certainly leaves less flow downstream than Pakistan
would prefer. Moreover, Pakistan probably agreed to the Indus Waters
Treaty primarily because it had little choice after being faced with a
fait accompli after partition. However, from an Indian perspective its

---

[b] The Kargil conflict is discussed in Pike (2005b).

acquisition of the Indus headwaters was a side effect rather than a cause of the decision of Kashmir's Hindu maharaja to choose India over Pakistan at partition, despite that state's Muslim majority. Likewise, the new state of Pakistan would likely have considered the loss of Kashmir to be unacceptable in any case. Thus, control of water became an issue that had to be dealt with after Kashmir was divided into Indian, Pakistani, and Chinese occupied portions. Control of water was not in itself the sole or even dominant factor precipitating war. In any case, Pakistan is in no position militarily or politically to use threat of force to change the current status quo. India could conceivably provoke a conflict by diverting substantially more Indus headwaters than allowed by the accord. However, this would more likely be a pretext for starting a war over other issues such as attacks within India blamed on Pakistani intelligence services. India has been cautious about taking such steps following Pakistan's acquisition of nuclear weapons, and this state of affairs is likely to continue.

In 1974, India built the Farakka Barrage barrier on the Ganges to divert water to Calcutta. When a series of short-term agreements guaranteeing Bangladesh a guaranteed flow of Ganges water expired after eleven years in 1988, India started taking more.[4] Finally in 1996, India and Bangladesh signed a new treaty providing for alternating the flow of the river in the dry seasons to flush the port of Calcutta periodically. Though Bangladesh may not be completely happy with the outcome, the disagreement was settled without resort to use of force. Certainly there is little prospect of a Bangladeshi military challenge to India, and India appears happy enough with the status quo not to take action itself that would perturb things to the point of military confrontation.

From 1991 until the completion of their Mahakali Treaty in 1996, India and Nepal were at odds over a very small parcel of Nepalese land to be used for protection from flooding due to a barrage on India territory.[5] Moreover, substantial Nepali hydropower potential remains untapped because India and Nepal cannot agree on terms for financing and power purchase. Here, India dominates the political impasse that supports the status quo, and India has such overwhelming military superiority that Nepal is hardly likely to start a war over water issues.

Nile Basin

Egypt has the potential for conflict with both Sudan and Ethiopia over the Nile.[6] However, Sudan has been preoccupied with internal conflict for decades,[7] and Ethiopia has so far lacked the means to undertake major water diversion projects farther upstream on the Blue Nile.

In 1999, a new mechanism called the Nile Basin Initiative was launched by the Council of Ministers of Water Affairs of the Nile Basin States. In 2002, a Headquarters Agreement was signed to "facilitate the establishment and operation of the Nile Basin Initiative Secretariat at Entebbe, Uganda…"[8] Ministers responsible for electricity in the 10 cooperating states met in 2003, following the issuance of a fifty-two-page "Nile Basin Regional Power Trade Agreement Project Document" in March 2001.[9] Subsequent meetings of the Nile Basin Initiative have concentrated on planning of joint development projects.[10] While these plans have yet to be fully implemented, these measures are signs that here too negotiation rather than international warfare is likely to be the vehicle for management of potential disputes.

Turkey

Kurds in Iraq near the Turkish border have been negatively affected by Turkey's water use. However, when northern Kurds gained a measure of autonomy in the US-imposed northern no-fly zone after its Gulf War I with Iraq, there was little chance that they would get much support on this issue from the central Iraqi government. Even after the fall of Saddam Hussein's Ba'th government in 2003, the Kurds, thinly veiled preference for an independent state left them still unlikely to get central government support for a confrontation with Turkey over water.

The completion of the massive Great Anatolia Project portends a more significant interference by Turkey with water flow into its southern neighbors. In 1999, Thomas Homer-Dixon explained the problem as follows:

> The case of the Euphrates shows how a weak and antagonistic downstream country might respond to upstream diversions. The

Euphrates originates in Turkey, and by early next century Turkey plans to build a huge complex of twenty dam projects along the upper reaches of the river. This $21 billion Great Anatolia Project, if fully funded and built, will reduce the annual average flow of the Euphrates within Syria from 32 billion cubic metes to 20 billion. The water that passes through Turkey's irrigation systems and on to Syria will be laden with fertilizers, pesticides, and salts. Syria is already seriously short of water, with an annual water availability of not much more than a thousand cubic meters per capita. Between 80 and 85 percent of the water for its towns, industries, and farms comes from the Euphrates, and the country has been chronically vulnerable to drought. Furthermore, Syria's population growth rate — at 3.3 percent per year in 1995 — is one of the highest in the world, and this adds further impetus to the country's demand for water.[11]

However, with Turkey safely ensconced within NATO, there is no prospect for either Syria or Iraq downstream to use military force to dissuade Turkey from executing its plans.

A more serious threat of invasion in the past was that the Turks would again send troops across its borders in response to what it considered to be unacceptable support for dissidents in their country. Indeed, in 1996 an international peacekeeping force of the United States, British, French, and Turkish soldiers set up in a base at Arbil in northern Iraq. The other forces subsequently withdrew, leaving this as a Turkish base until the end of 2004. After that there remained another base with an estimated five thousand Turkish soldiers nearer the Turkish border.[12]

With Turkey actively courting the European Union and with growing urbanization and economic integration of its Kurdish minority, for a while the specter of Turkish intervention in Iraq seemed to recede. During the run-up to Gulf War II with Iraq, the United States refused to bow to demands that Turkey be allowed to move into northern Iraq. This led to a very inconvenient Turkish refusal, by a close vote in the Turkish legislature, to allow an already positioned U.S. division to transit through Turkey to Iraq.[13] Moreover, Iraqi advisors to the occupying forces were able to dissuade the occupying coalition even from inviting Turkish troops into southern Iraq.

Then in 2004, an internal struggle with Kurds in Turkey resurfaced. Starting on December 16, 2007, Turkey launched a series of attacks on Kurds in Iraq. By February 4, 2008, Turkey had acknowledged five such attacks.[14] As long as Turkish integration with the European Union appears possible, this will restrain how aggressively Turkey deals with Kurds on either side of its border with Iraq. This situation is likely to change only if Turkish relations with Kurds seriously deteriorate and the European Union calls an abrupt halt to serious discussions on integration with Turkey.

Water for Agriculture

Some water resources are renewable, such as rechargeable aquifers and surface runoff. Some are not, such as nonrecharging aquifers and inland lakes whose sources have been diverted. In general, tension over aquifer depletion is an internal affair, although negative impacts on agrarian populations can spill over into neighboring countries. Problems involving water and Palestine[15] also complicate the peace process discussed below. In general, results of tension over uses of water for purposes other than hydroelectric power generation can spill over to affect international disputes, but have not been direct causes of international war for many centuries.

Population and industrial growth have been putting increasing pressure on water resources in many places where these resources are scarce. However, there has also been a remarkable increase in the overall efficiency of water use. Drip irrigation and better recycling of industrial and municipal wastewater are some of the techniques that have been used to achieve this. Increased efficiency of water use has allowed global economic growth in the face of limited water supplies, so the decline of per capita water resources has so far been a localized rather than serious global water scarcity problem.

To launch a major international war to force a change in behavior by a country sharing a water basin courts a "lose-lose" outcome and is very costly compared to negotiation. It is true that disagreements over use of water resources have aggravated tensions over other issues. Israeli restrictions on Palestinians' use of water in the West Bank are the primary case in point. However, there are no readily foreseeable prospects for the launch of a major international war over control of water resources alone. Thomas Homer-Dixon summarizes the situation as follows:

> The renewable resource most likely to stimulate interstate war is river water. However, wars over river water between upstream and downstream neighbors are likely only in a narrow set of circumstances: the downstream country must be highly dependent on the water for its national well-being, the upstream country must be threatening to restrict substantially the river's flow, there must be a history of antagonism between the two countries, and most important, the downstream country must be militarily stronger than the upstream country. Research shows that conflict and turmoil related to river water is more often internal than international; this conflict results from dams and other major water projects that relocated large numbers of people.[16]

In none of the most significant international disputes over river water are the conditions for international war set down by Homer-Dixon satisfied. Turkey's Great Anatolia Project planned to reduce annual flow to Syria from 32 billion to 20 billion cubic meters, but Syria lacks the wherewithal to launch a major international war to prevent this. The worst that Syria can do is to retaliate by supporting disaffected groups in Iraq, but such support could easily backfire to Syria's further disadvantage. Similarly, Iraqi Kurds are upset about Turkish water management, but in 2003 Turkey was blocked from a major intervention in Iraq first by failure to agree on terms with the United States and later at the insistence of the Iraqi council advising the US occupation. Ethiopia could in principle divert a substantial portion of the Nile but lacks the military capability to challenge Egypt to the point of provoking a major war. Thus, Ethiopia had to make do with negotiation of the Nile Basin Initiative instead.[17] Similarly, Bangladesh has been adversely affected by Indian construction of the

Farraka Barrage on the Ganges but has no effective military recourse. Pakistan's discontent with Indian management of Indus headwaters in Kashmir is also a sore point, but water itself is not the major bone of contention between the two countries. Finally, in a dispute related to changes in water use in 1989, Mauritania and Senegal nearly came to war after several hundred people were killed. "About seventy thousand black Mauritanians were forcibly expelled to Senegal, from where some launched raids to retrieve expropriated cattle. By 1993, diplomatic relations between the two countries had been restored, but neither had agreed to allow the expelled population to return or to compensate them for their losses".[18] Certainly the human consequences of difficulties related to water can be great, but in none of these cases does it seem likely that there will be a major international war aimed at redistributing water resources.

International War versus Internal Conflict

At first glance, there might appear to be considerable disagreement among a number of recent books that comment on water and conflict. In *Resource Wars*, Michael Klare explains how water resources *could* be a source of conflict.[19] Vandana Shiva went so far as to title her recent work *Water Wars*, but focuses primarily on internal civil strife rather than civil or international war.[20]

Thomas Homer-Dixon's *Environmental Conflict* makes a case that international war over control of water resources is both uncommon and now unlikely.[21] Generalizing from some of the specific cases discussed above, he notes that power asymmetries currently tend to make it difficult for downstream countries to reverse upstream countries' water management plans by the application of military force. More generally, the geographic breadth of watersheds has historically made military action aimed specifically at controlling them a difficult undertaking.

The closest thing to a recent war over water that is cited by Homer-Dixon is the above-mentioned dispute between Mauritania and Senegal following completion of a cooperative regional water management project.[22] This project led to the construction of a high dam upstream in Mali and a barrage connecting Senegal and Mauritania. After land values increased along the rivers, Mauritania's Moorish elite revoked and effectively expropriated the agricultural rights of non-Arab Senegalese near the river and provoked an internal conflict that spilled over into Senegal. In this case international war was barely avoided, although diplomatic relations between Senegal and Mauritania were broken off for four years. More generally, where water management is a problem contributing to violent civil strife, any international spillover can generally be expected to result from such problems rather than a direct attempt to use international warfare to determine water management policy.

Again, in this book the primarily concern is with major international wars. A reasonable definition of a major war is one with 50,000 or more troops attacking across established international lines of control. At this scale, Homer-Dixon's conclusions do not in fact appear to be contradictory to the analyses of Shiva and Klare. For Klare's delineation of possible sources of conflict is by no means identical to a prediction of future major international war. On Shiva's part, her analysis is basically directed at the deleterious effects of poor water management and how populations respond to these effects. This is not the same as a prediction that this response will come in the form of actual internal warfare, much less major international war.

Endnotes

[1]   Lowry (2003).
[2]   Bellis (2003).
[3]   IguassuFallsTour.com (2003).
[4]   Roy (1977).
[5]   DDP Secretariat (2006).
[6]   El-Fadel *et al.* (2003).
[7]   Vick (2003).
[8]   Nile Basin Initiative (2003).
[9]   Nile Basin Initiative Shared Vision Program (2001).
[10]   Nile Basin Initiative (2006).
[11]   Homer-Dixon (1999, p. 140).
[12]   Glantz (2005, pp. 98–100).

13 Filkins and Chiver (2003); Sanger and Filkins (2003), Schmitt (2003a), Filkins (2003a).
14 Torchia (2008).
15 Isaac (1999).
16 Homer-Dixon (1999, p. 139).
17 Shiva (2002, p. 76).
18 Homer-Dixon (1999, p. 77).
19 Klare (2001).
20 Shiva (2002).
21 Homer-Dixon (1999).
22 Homer-Dixon (1999, pp. 76–77).

Chapter 25

Other Renewable Resources

Newly emerging renewable sources of primary energy include the generation of electricity from wind and solar thermal energy. The replacement of coal and natural gas partly by wind and solar energy in electricity production is likely to be a very gradual and continuous process. There are still vast quantities of fossil fuel resources that can be extracted as their production costs gradually increase. Regional promotion of renewable electricity generation is thus likely to have at most an indirect and modest effect on oil price stability. From the point of view of prevention of major international war, expansion of renewable electrical energy is most useful as part of a more comprehensive coordinated approach to energy and security by oil consuming nations, rather than being very helpful when pursued on a piecemeal basis. Biotechnology innovations for making transport fuels are more directly connected to oil and security. A key question is whether a decision not to fight over oil has to come before or after the policy decisions needed for a massive shift from petroleum to other sources of energy for transportation in order to have a significant security impact.

Wind and Sun

The basic purpose of this chapter is to dispel two common misconceptions about new renewable energy sources. The first of these is the idea that the world is about to "run out" of fluid fossil fuels, so new renewable energy sources will be needed to avoid a massive shift to coal and a resultant upswing in emission of gases that trap solar energy and raise temperature of the atmosphere. The second misconception is the idea that promotion of new renewable energy resources alone can in practice precipitate international security benefits through reducing oil consumers' dependence on imports.

The comments made here are not meant to imply that new renewable energy sources are irrelevant in the longer term to the problem of carbon dioxide emissions from fossil fuels and consequent global warming. The point is rather that new renewable energy sources are not a panacea for shorter-term security problems connected primarily with oil. Indeed, focusing attention on new renewable energy resources at the expense of dealing more directly with stability of consumer–producer relations in international oil markets could even be counterproductive. On the other hand, if and when effective mechanisms are developed to produce the expectation and reality of oil price stability, then there could be some noticeable if largely indirect effect on development of new renewable energy production capacity.

At the onset it is necessary to be more precise about what is meant here by the terms "primary energy" and "new renewables." In the quantitative study of energy systems it is necessary to draw a somewhat arbitrary line between primary energy supply and efficiency of energy use. One reason for this distinction is that the solar energy shining on the land and buildings we use is far larger than measured primary energy use but nevertheless essential to life. It is neither desirable nor practical to measure the thermal energy coming through every sun-facing window and count that as primary energy use, even in the case of a structure with windows and walls designed to drastically reduce the use of fossil fuels or electricity for heating. Similarly, analysts do not ordinarily count the calorie content of the food we eat as part of our primary energy supply, so biotechnology developments that impact global food supply are not normally included in the accounting of primary energy use. Consider, for example, a simple shift in commodities like corn or sugar from use as a foodstuff to use as a feedstock for transportation fuels. Counting this as an increase in primary energy production would give a misleading picture of such how this shift had affected the overall utility of commodity production.

Here, a distinction is also made between hydroelectricity and geothermal energy as "old forms" of "renewable" energy, and production of electricity from wind and solar thermal energy as "new renewables." The reason is that these "old renewables" are well established and have contributed a nearly constant fraction of total primary energy supply over the past few decades. On the other hand, installed wind-electric power generating capacity has recently been growing exponentially. Solar electric power has evolved in technological terms to the point where it could grow rapidly given fairly modest evolution of market conditions. By contrast, using currently available technology a number of other renewable energy technologies have very modest prospects for making a significant impact on primary energy supply. These include electricity from waves, tides, and ocean thermal gradients.[1]

The word renewable is in quotes in the previous paragraph when referring to hydroelectricity and geothermal energy. This is because some geothermal energy systems draw out underground energy faster than it is replaced by nature, and some hydroelectric water reservoirs are subject to silting that may reduce their utility over the long term. By and large these are minor impacts, so the present discussion uses the term "renewable" for hydroelectric and geothermal energy.

Reserves versus Resources

Until recently it was commonplace to read that the United States and the world at large were facing an imminent crisis because petroleum reserves would soon be exhausted. Closer to the mark is what geologist Kenneth Deffeyes has to say about the definition and estimation of oil reserves:

> Oil reserves are defined as future production, using existing technology, from wells that have already been drilled (not to be confused with the US "strategic petroleum reserve," which is a storage facility for oil that has already been produced). Typically, young petroleum engineers unconsciously tend to underestimate reserves. It's a lot more fun to go into the boss's office next year and announce that

there is actually a little *more* oil than last year's estimate. Engineers who have to downsize their previous reserve estimates are the first to leave in the next corporate downsizing.[2]

If reserves had been all the oil available to the United States in 1945, then US domestic consumption would have been enough to exhaust them by about 1956. Indeed, US cumulative production has trailed cumulative discoveries by about eleven years ever since, except for a slight glitch in 1970 due to the addition of the Prudhoe Bay discovery in Alaska.

Deffeyes' comments on conservatism in estimation of reserves do not apply uniformly to the whole world at all times. In particular, the onset of the procedure of keying OPEC production quotas to each member's fraction of total reserves produced an incentive to be less conservative in estimation of reserves. Nevertheless, globally, discoveries have led production fairly consistently by about twenty-one years.[3] Thus, had reserves been the only oil left in 1970, global annual production would have halted altogether in 1991 rather than continuing to grow for more than another decade.

That reserves are defined as production using existing technology would give a misleading picture of likely actual future production even if geologists' reputed conservatism were corrected for, and as yet undiscovered resources were also estimated on the basis of broader knowledge of the geology of potential production areas. The reason is that technology continues to progress. This is particularly important if the exhaustion of more readily extractable resources puts upward pressure on prices and thus creates economic incentive for technological improvement. Even geologists like Deffeyes who try to take a broader view may underestimate the total amount of oil that is likely to be produced if inflation-adjusted prices rise substantially.

One author who tried to correct for such difficulties in estimating resources of coal and natural gas as well as oil was H-H, Rogner, writing at the time from the University of Victoria Institute for Integrated Energy Systems. He produced useful estimates of the original total global endowment of each of these fossil fuels in various categories of extraction costs up to $62/barrel of oil, $50/barrel of oil energy equivalent for natural gas, and \$24/barrel of oil equivalent for coal, all at 1990 prices.[4] Converting these to 2008 prices and dollars per billion Joules gives upper limits on Rogner's useful cost ranges of \$17/GJ for oil, \$14/GJ for natural gas, and \$7/GJ for coal. These numbers refer to globally averaged resource extraction costs, not market prices, and are considerably higher than current globally averaged extraction costs. That there are continuing substantial increases in likely resources all the way up to these cost ranges indicates that the world will not suddenly "run out" of oil or natural gas. Rather customers will gradually have to pay more and more to use them, all other things being equal.

To within the accuracy of the estimates of fossil fuel resources upto extraction costs of 7–17\$/GJ, it suffices to make linear fits to original global resource endowments as a function of cost of extraction after a given amount has been extracted. On a global basis over all history the amounts extracted are so large that it is appropriate to measure them in 1×10^{21} J, or zetajoules (ZJ). This number is so large, equal to 1000 EJ, that the designation "zeta" for this many powers of ten is not widely known. Aggregating fluid fossil fuels, from these fits one would expect extraction costs to go up by about \$1/GJ for every 2 ZJ of oil and every 2.6 ZJ of natural gas extracted.

By the end of the 20th century the cumulative global extraction of oil totaled about 6 ZJ and that of natural gas about 1.6 ZJ.[5] The global average extraction cost for natural gas was for a long time on the order of \$1/ZJ. Global average wellhead oil extraction costs per unit of energy content are higher and not too far below the value of \$2.2/GJ (\$15/barrel at 2008 prices) from the simple result inferred here from Rogner's estimates. These are incremental costs for exploration and deeper drilling over the costs of tapping the most easily found and recovered near surface deposits. Adding in these unavoidable costs gives slightly higher total current global average wellhead costs.

The point of this discussion is that, without more rapid technological progress in the fluid fossil fuel industries then in the global economy as a whole, inflation-adjusted *extraction* costs may be expected to rise fairly gradually and continually on the average, perhaps doubling as cumulative extraction doubles over the next couple of decades. By that point, global average wellhead extraction costs could still be well under $3/GJ for natural gas and below $30/barrel for oil (inflation adjusted to 2008 prices). Even with these increases, market prices at delivery for many customers would only be substantially higher if large price markups beyond the wellhead costs continue to be piled on top of them. Towards the middle of the 21st century and beyond, average wellhead prices can be expected to continue to rise even after correcting for inflation. This should gradually produce increasing incentive to switch to coal and nonfossil fuels as well as using fluid fossil fuels more efficiently. Thus, with careful attention to the underlying geology one realizes that there is no looming "energy crisis" being driven by the prospect of "running out" of fluid fossil fuels. Price instabilities and the perception of crisis are instead driven by imperfections in markets and political institutions.

Nonfossil fuels provided 4 percent of primary energy in 1967. This was mostly from hydropower. By 2000, the contribution of nuclear power on a global basis had about matched that of hydropower, while the contribution of wind-electric energy was small but growing rapidly. The pattern for nuclear power was an initial exponential growth of the fraction of total energy it supplied, followed by a leveling off as the technology matured and reached market saturation. In the late 1990s, there was a similar exponential growth in wind energy in areas with favorable regulatory and tax environments. These allowed enough production volume for so-called "learning by doing" to reduce unit costs toward the level expected for a mature technology.[6] Later, solar thermal electric power may see a similar exponential growth in sunny low-latitude desert regions near a few concentrations of high population and air conditioning loads.

Wind and solar electric power generation are referred to here as "new renewables" since they have a potential for an exponential growth phase that is unlikely to be available to already mature technologies like hydropower and geothermal power. Other new renewable technologies for primary energy production may also be forthcoming. Other renewable primary energy sources such as tides, waves, and ocean thermal electric power appear to be limited to at most niche markets. Bioengineering may become more important, but primarily in what is classified here as an energy efficiency improvement rather than primary energy production.

Unless there are strong political impediments to use of nuclear power in the distant future, it is likely that the long-term penetration of new renewables will be limited by two factors. One is the limited geographic distribution of favorable wind energy and solar thermal energy locations. Favorable winds are found in only parts primarily of mid-latitude countries. Favorable solar electricity production locations are primarily in cloudless subtropical desert regions that are in many cases sparsely populated. The second problem with these energy sources is their variable availability, both by season and time of day. Pumping water uphill or storing compressed gas in underground cavities can help smooth out the energy supply, but this is only economically attractive in a limited number of favorable locations. In the long-run the variability problem may be partly compensated for by using excess capacity as an energy source for producing hydrogen or other fluid fuels. However, variable availability is bound to limit market penetration to some extent compared to fossil and other major nonfossil energy sources. Nuclear power does not have these limitations. So nuclear power may capture a large share of the electricity production market as natural gas and coal are gradually phased out.

Renewable Energy and Security

Something all nonfossil sources of electricity have in common is high capital cost. This is true of new hydropower projects, nuclear power, and wind-electric and solar-electric power. Locations for new hydropower installations are severely limited by geography. Thus, to the extent that investment in more renewable energy supply affects use of coal and natural gas for electricity generation, the primary effect is likely to be to a modest delay in the time at which these fossil fuels reach a given level of depletion.

However, natural gas and oil will continue to be used for the purposes for which they are best suited, particularly for transportation in

the case of oil and as a convenient source of heat in the case of natural gas. In practical terms only a massively expensive coordinated continuing global effort at the more technically difficult task of
substituting new renewables for oil would by itself have much direct
security impact on "resource wars." For if only some countries make
this substitution, the primary effect should be to moderate oil prices
for others and thus stimulate their own oil consumption.

Thus, relying on regional efforts alone to subsidize new renewable sources of electricity is like trying to make a very small tail wag a
very large dog when it comes to the central problems of oil and security. There may be other reasons for pursuing such policies. However,
it needs to be well understood that only in combination with coordinated consumer-nation action to more directly attack the problem of
oil price instability are such policies likely to help effect a noticeable
amelioration of international security problems directly related to oil.

Virgin Timber and Renewable Land Use

Where virgin forests contain a century or more of useful growth, they
can be considered for all practical purpose a nonrenewable resource —
one that in many cases is harvested with enduring environmental
damage. There has been violent conflict over who will reap the benefit of such harvests, sometimes to detriment of forest inhabitants and
even the world at large. Normally such conflict has been internal
rather than international, although in the case of Congo it may have
spilled over into a broader central African war.

More common in history have been broader-based struggles over
land, especially its agricultural productivity back to the Middle Ages
and earlier, through Babylon and back to the dawn of civilization. It
was not only energy-related matters but also the (by then obsolete)
ideology of conquering *Lebensraum* that guided the course of the
WWII both in Eastern Europe and in Northeast Asia. During and
after the partition of Palestine control of agricultural land was also a
concern, especially in the early days when agriculture provided a
larger proportion of national product. There too, the process of
unlearning inherited assumptions about the relative importance of the

control of particular areas of land compared to functional integration into a global economy is still incomplete. Similar comments could be made about control of marginal land in other disputed areas. Recurring debilitating casualties from placement of troops for many years on the economically useless Siachen glacier area in Kashmir provide a particularly bizarre example of this phenomenon.

Five fundamental developments combined to marginalize control of land per se as a source of conflict in major international wars. These are the fertility transition, the industrial revolution, further globalization of trade, the development of nuclear weapons, and the evolution of transnational security mechanisms. Most fundamental is the widespread transition to lower fertility rates. For the first time in human history a peak in the population growth rate has been passed through over a wide area by the mechanism of reduced fertility rather than enhanced mortality. Moreover, the industrial revolution has marginalized agriculture as a dominant source of wealth on a global basis and in many individual countries. The development of even more efficient regional and intercontinental shipping methods means that food can be shipped in adequate quantity anywhere in the world where local security conditions allow. This means that the impact of war is only occasionally to induce famine, not to be necessary for escaping from hunger. Nations with large agricultural areas have also either been covered by a nuclear umbrella or rejected nuclear weapons (e.g., in South America) as unnecessary for the defense of their productive land in the modern global economy. It is now broadly recognized that military conquest of land *per se* is likely to be a losing proposition economically, and a global security apparatus has evolved to label this as aggression and strongly discourage it. In the concluding chapter of *Environment, Scarcity, and Violence,* Homer-Dixon summarizes the contemporary situation with respect to international conflict over renewable resources as follows:

> In this book, we have seen that environmental scarcity contributes to diffuse, persistent, subnational violence, such as ethnic clashes and insurgencies. It rarely, if ever, contributes to conflict among

306 Energy and International War

states, that is to *resource wars*. During the twentieth century there have been a number of interstate conflicts over, in part, access to nonrenewables like oil and minerals. But there are few modern examples of interstate war over renewables such as cropland, forests, fresh water, and fish. There are two explanations for this difference. First, in general states cannot easily or quickly convert renewable resources into assets that significantly augment their power. Second, the very countries that are most dependent on renewable resources, and that are therefore most motivated to seize resources from their neighbors, also tend to be poor, which lessens their capability for aggression.[7]

Biofuels for Transportation

The amount of nonsolar energy that has been used to produce ethanol from corn in the United States is nearly equal to the energy content of the ethanol produced. Because it requires so much energy to produce, corn-based ethanol has not been classified as a primary energy source here. In the current US market, ethanol production is more like an energy conversion process, much like refining petroleum.

While the solar energy input to production of ethanol from corn in the United States produces little net energy gain, it is more effective at substituting a mixture of energy inputs for petroleum. This is because only part of the primary energy used for corn and ethanol comes from oil. Natural gas and electricity are also used for processes such as fertilizer production, process heat, and machinery drive.

Under special circumstances, it is possible for a country to substantially reduce or even eliminate oil imports by using biomass to make transportation fuel. The best example is Brazil. In Brazil cars come equipped to burn different mixtures of gasoline and ethanol. When gasoline prices are low, the ethanol content can be as low as 10 percent used to prevent engine knocking. When gasoline prices are higher, up to 85 percent ethanol can conveniently be used. This works for Brazil because its per capita automobile fuel consumption is much lower than, for example, for the United States. Also, Brazil's large land mass and tropical climate are ideal for production of the sugar cane used to make ethanol. Combined with a recent large Tupi deepwater oil field discovery,[8] Brazil's approach to biofuels looks sufficient to keep that country continuing to avoid being a net oil importer if the Tupi field comes into production by 2015 as hoped for.

On a global basis, it is not practical to effect a large substitution for gasoline of ethanol made from corn kernels and sugar using currently available technology. In the face of the coming growth in global population to ten billion or more, the amount of arable land that would have to be diverted from food to transport fuel production is too large. The same applies to the production diesel fuel from edible vegetable oils. However, recent advances in biotechnology are bringing us closer to the point where structural materials from plants can be used to make alcohols for transport fuel. The process of converting nonfood plant matter into transportation fuels will be more expensive than making alcohol from cane syrup or cornstarch. This approach will thus not have much market impact unless it is heavily subsidized or given very preferential tax treatment or access to markets, unless oil prices remain unusually high.

What is needed for biomass to have a fundamental impact on petroleum use is a more profound advance in biotechnology. Bypassing industrial production processes by bioengineering plants that directly produce transport fuels in a convenient form is one theoretical possibility. Developing methods to use land not currently classified as arable to make products that substitute for petroleum is also conceivable. Even if this is possible, there will be ecological consequences likely to receive considerable scrutiny. For now, the widespread application of these kinds of advances in biotechnology is too speculative to rely on as a solution to the problem of escaping from a repeating cycle of international wars where control over oil resources plays a major role. The consequences of these observations for the future of national energy policies will be taken up here in Chapter 28.

Endnotes

1   c.f. Singer (2008e).
2   Deffeyes (2001, p. 6).
3   Deffeyes (2001, p. 148).
4   Rogner (1997, p. 254).
5   Rogner (1997); BP (2000).
6   Rethinaraj (2005).
7   Homer-Dixon (1999, p. 179).
8   Barrionuevo (2008).

Chapter 26

It's About Oil

Early after WWII, France committed to an independent military nuclear force and a large-scale nuclear electric power program. Then its colonial heritage in Africa was cemented into a unilateralist and militarily interventionist policy even after its colonies gained independence. The events connected with France's halt to nuclear weapons testing were necessary but not sufficient for the evolution of a more multilateral-oriented policy with greater emphasis on fostering representative government in former colonies, particularly Niger.

Four factors have combined to turn uranium into a standard item of international commerce rather than a "strategic" material for which the threat or use of military force to secure supplies is a plausible future outcome. (1) The globalization of uranium markets has provided diversity of supply for all of the user countries that would be capable of military intervention to secure supplies. (2) Global uranium resources are adequate to support nuclear energy use for many decades with minimal impact on power production costs. (3) All of the states capable of intervening militarily to secure uranium supplies have stopped producing fissile materials for weapons purposes. (4) The near universality of International Atomic Energy Agency safeguards procedures helps ensure that all but a few countries have access to the global uranium market.

After the lifting of sanctions on Iraq, the nominal exceptions not in good standing with the IAEA as nonnuclear-weapons states are India, Israel, Pakistan, the Democratic Peoples Republic of Korea (i.e. North Korea), and possibly Iran. Of these, only India has plans for a major expansion of nuclear power, and it has adequate domestic uranium supplies for this for the coming one or two decades at least.

Moreover, in the past India has been able to negotiate for uranium supply on a case-by-case basis as needed. In the future India is extremely unlikely to be shut out of the international uranium market if in fact it carries through with ambitious plans for nuclear–electric expansion and becomes a significant potential buyer on the international market.

Iran has hidden past activities that should have been reported to the IAEA but claims to be interested in restricting its future nuclear fuel cycle activities to those allowed by the Nuclear Nonproliferation Treaty. According to a report by US intelligence agencies, Iran suspended its direct pursuit of nuclear weapons in 2003.[1] Iran's stated plans and plausible civilian needs are indeed only to develop an industrial nuclear power capability in anticipation of future depletion of natural gas supplies to the point where it becomes uneconomic to use domestic natural gas to the exclusion of nuclear energy for its electricity production. This strategy requires only a few demonstration nuclear power plants for decades to come, without the need for uranium imports. Frustration of a need for Iran to access the international uranium market for civilian energy needs is thus in itself not a plausible cause for war in the foreseeable future. If there are military hostilities between Iran and the United States over Iran's nuclear capabilities, this will not be a result of inadequate Iranian uranium resources but rather as a result of domestically driven political miscalculation on one or both sides.

The price of natural gas as a fuel has a significant influence on the attractiveness of nuclear power for producing electricity. However, foreseeable changes in the price of uranium are likely to have negligible impact on the price of natural gas on a global basis. This is in part because natural gas has much broader uses than electricity production. This means that changes in the electricity production sector generally have comparatively small impact on the overall depletion of more readily extractable natural gas resources. More importantly, the rate of uranium depletion and the proportion of electricity production costs attributable to uranium mining are so small as to have very little impact on decisions between uranium and natural gas for fueling new electricity production capacity. Thus, from a security perspective concerning adequacy of fuel supplies, when considering natural gas one can essentially neglect concerns about run-up in uranium prices for the readily foreseeable future.

Natural gas as a whole, however, is gaining an increasing fractional share of total energy supply. Nevertheless, international trade in *liquefied* natural gas (LNG) is unlikely in the next twenty years to achieve the same level of significance as international trade in oil in issues pertinent to conflict involving movement of substantial military forces between continents (here treating Europe as a separate "continent" from Asia).

Depletion of global natural gas resources alone is unlikely to drive durably large increases in average extraction costs for those resources over the next two or more decades. For global prices to nevertheless increase enough to give natural gas resources the same security importance as oil would instead require the formation of an effective global export cartel for natural gas. Given the much greater geographic distribution of natural gas resources compared to oil, it would likely be more difficult to form and maintain an effective export cartel for natural gas than for oil. Of course, natural gas resources may continue to have the kind of occasional regional political importance concerning pipelines described above. Natural gas may also have local importance comparable to other revenue sources concentrated on particular industries in some small countries. However, major transoceanic military ventures stimulated by a radical increase in the economic importance of LNG trade over the next two decades seem unlikely. Exceptions may arise, however, perhaps as comparatively straightforward intervention in very small Persian Gulf states in case of political instability. The attitude of developed countries toward political developments in Nigeria may also be affected by concerns over the reliability of its LNG exports, although whether this would extend to direct unwelcome military intervention in such a large country is another matter.

Over the next two decades, expanded use of biofuels is likely to have little impact on this picture. Production of methane from waste biomass and production of diesel fuels from vegetable oils may have a modest impact in niche markets. Ethanol production from edible materials like corn or sugar has limited global potential in the face of an expected near-doubling of global population and its consequences for demand for food. Advances in biotechnology needed for conversion of cellulose to ethanol have the potential to cap the price oil on a free market basis probably at most in the long term.

Thus, at least for the next two decades or more, oil will remain unique in connecting energy and security. The problem of coal and steel in Europe appears to have been laid to rest. The motivation that dependence on uranium imports may have provided for interventions in Africa also appears to have evaporated due to globalization of uranium markets after 1995. Nor does natural gas appear poised to take on the same security significance as oil. So the final part of this book concentrates on the future of the interaction between oil and international war.

Endnote

[1]   Reid, (2007).

Part Five

THE FUTURE

Chapter 27

Troubled Producers

Norway has recently been the world's third largest oil exporter, but there will be no revolutions or wars over control of Norway's oil. Others in the top thirty oil exporters listed[1] in Tables 27.1 and 27.2 have not been so fortunate. Iran and Kuwait have been attacked in attempts to take over oil fields. Iraq has been occupied. The United Arab Emirates have had a militarized dispute with Iran.[2] Planning of oil export pipeline routes has been affected by conflicts in Azerbaijan and Russia. Political turmoil has disrupted Venezuela's oil production, and internal violence has plagued Nigeria's. Oil-rich Cabinda had a secessionist movement that proclaimed independence from Angola, leading to a negotiated peace in 2006.[3] A negotiated settlement of brutal dispute involving control of resources in southern Sudan helped trigger a conflict in western Sudan that led to an aborted attempt to overthrow the government in neighboring Chad.[4] Another dash from the eastern border all the way across Chad's capital city in 2008 led to more extensive fighting in the capital city and sent many of the tens of thousands of refugees across the border to Cameroon.[5]

How prone each oil exporter is to involvement in international war depends on both its external relations and internal political situation. The largest three oil exporters, Saudi Arabia, Russia, and Norway, have so far been immune to external attack since WWII. To put these at the bottom of the table, the top fifteen oil exporters are listed with the largest at the bottom in Table 27.1 With the exception of Kazakhstan and those in North America, each of the twelve countries at the top of Table 27.1 has had a recent internal conflict, militarized international dispute, or international war.

Table 27.1. Top 15 exporters' total petroleum production and exports.

Country/Years (OPEC in Bold) Units	2004 EJ/yr	2004 Total	2004 Export Million barrels/day (Mbbl/d)	2006 Total	2006 Export (Mbbl/d)	2006 Export/Total %	Change from 2004 to 2006 Total %	Change Export %	Change Total (Mbbl/d)	Change Export (Mbbl/d)
Canada	6.30	3.14	0.84	3.29	1.07	33	5	27	0.15	0.23
Kazakhstan	2.46	1.22	1.00	1.35	1.11	83	10	11	0.12	0.11
Angola	2.11	1.05	1.00	1.42	1.36	96	**35**	**36**	**0.37**	**0.36**
Iraq	4.06	2.02	1.48	2.01	1.44	72	**-1**	**-3**	**-0.02**	**-0.05**
Libya	3.18	1.58	1.33	1.81	1.53	84	**14**	**15**	**0.23**	**0.20**
Mexico	7.72	3.85	1.97	3.71	1.68	45	-4	-15	-0.14	-0.29
Algeria	3.95	1.97	1.73	2.12	1.85	87	**8**	7	**0.16**	**0.11**
Nigeria	4.68	2.33	2.30	2.44	2.15	88	**5**	**-6**	**0.11**	**-0.15**
Kuwait	5.05	2.51	2.18	2.67	2.15	80	**6**	**-1**	**0.16**	**-0.03**
Venezuela	5.73	2.86	2.30	2.80	2.20	79	**-2**	**-4**	**-0.05**	**-0.09**
UAE	5.54	2.76	2.36	2.94	2.52	86	**6**	7	**0.18**	**0.16**
Iran	8.24	4.10	1.51	4.15	2.52	61	**1**	67	**0.04**	1.01
Norway	6.42	3.20	2.95	2.79	2.54	91	-13	-14	-0.41	-0.41
Russia	18.62	9.27	6.50	9.67	6.57	68	4	1	0.40	0.06
Saudi Arabia	21.07	10.49	8.65	10.72	8.65	81	**2**	0	**0.23**	**0.00**
All of the above	105.13	52.35	38.10	53.88	39.33	73	3	3	1.52	1.22
World Crude			43.22							
World Refined			20.54							
World Total	166.91	83.12	63.76							

Source: USEIA (2007e; 2007f; 2007g for conversion to exajoules/year = EJ/yr).
UAE = United Arab Emirates.

Contested control over oil revenues is less predominant in minor oil exporters. The next fifteen top oil exporters are listed in descending order of total exports in order to place the more significant exporters at the top of Table 27.2. Some of these countries have also had internal or international conflicts, but their oil revenues have generally played a smaller role.

The information in Table 27.3 is a useful background for examining which oil exporters are most likely to be prone to involvement in international war in the future.[6] Iraq is a special case, already at war, and not included in Table 27.3. Estimates for Iraq from a different source give a population of 27.5 million in 2007, a GDP of $40.7 billion (G$US) at official exchange rates for 2006, and a ratio of 2006 purchasing power parity to 2007 population of $1479 per person.[7]

Countries with a large population or GDP are difficult to make war on. Countries with large populations are particularly hard to occupy completely or in part. For example, Iraq's attack on Iran's nearly threefold larger population was foiled in part by massively manned counterattacks. The world's preeminent conventional military power took over four years to even begin to come to grips with the task of occupying Iraq, a country with less than one-tenth of the US population. In the longer run, countries with a large GDP have the option of building nuclear facilities that give them the option of rapidly constructing a nuclear arsenal. Provided that the process of acquiring these facilities does not itself precipitate war, such countries then either have an overt or recessed nuclear deterrent, depending on whether or not they actually proceed to construct nuclear weapons. The upshot of all of this is that countries with large oil exports but comparatively small population and GDP can appear to be more attractive targets for attack. The 1990 Iraqi occupation of Kuwait is the prime example.

Internal political dynamics in oil-producing countries can also have an important influence on the probability of getting involved in international war. This is clear from the narrative histories in Part III of this book, particularly in the cases of Iran and Iraq. In particular, the origins of the 2003 occupation of Iraq can be traced back to internal conflict in the northern part of that country immediately after its

Table 27.2.   Next 15 exporters' total petroleum production and exports.

Country/Years (OPEC in Bold) Units	2004			2006			Change from 2004 to 2006			
	EJ/yr	Total	Export Million barrels/day (Mbbl/d)	Total	Export	Export/Total %	Total %	Export %	Total (Mbbl/d)	Export (Mbbl/d)
Qatar	2.10	1.04	0.96	1.11	1.01	91	6	5	0.07	0.05
Oman	1.51	0.75	0.69	0.74	0.68	91	−1	−2	−0.01	−0.01
Azerbaijan	0.64	0.32	0.20	0.65	0.52	80	104	**164**	**0.33**	**0.32**
Ecuador	1.06	0.53	0.38	0.54	0.38	72	1	**1**	**0.01**	**0.00**
Eq. Guinea	0.75	0.37	0.37	0.34	0.33	100	−10	**−10**	**−0.04**	**−0.04**
Sudan	0.69	0.34	0.28	0.37	0.28	75	8	0	0.03	0.00
Argentina	1.65	0.82	0.35	0.80	0.32	40	−3	−9	−0.02	**−0.03**
Yemen	0.85	0.43	0.34	0.38	0.29	76	−11	−16	−0.05	**−0.05**
Malaysia	1.73	0.86	0.35	0.80	0.28	36	−7	−18	−0.06	**−0.06**
Colombia	1.09	0.54	0.27	0.55	0.28	52	0	**3**	**0.00**	**0.01**
Rep. of Congo	0.47	0.24	0.23	0.25	0.24	97	5	**5**	**0.01**	**0.01**
Gabon	0.48	0.24	0.23	0.27	0.25	95	11	12	0.03	0.03
Brunei	0.41	0.20	0.19	0.22	0.21	94	8	8	0.02	0.02
Syria	0.91	0.45	0.19	0.45	0.18	40	−1	−4	0.00	−0.01
Chad	0.34	0.17	0.17	0.16	0.16	99	−7	−8	−0.01	−0.01
All of the above	14.68	7.31	5.20	7.61	5.42	71	4	4	0.30	0.22
World Crude			43.22							
World Refined			20.54							
World Total	166.91	83.12	63.76							

Source: USEIA (2007e; 2007f; 2007g for conversion to exajoules/year = EJ/yr).

Table 27.3.   Economic indicators for some petroleum exporters.

Country/Years (OPEC in Bold)	2004		2006		Per capita GDP PPP ($1000)	
Units	GDP G$US	Population million	GDP G$US	Population million	2004	2006
Chad	4.4	8.8	6.4	9.3	1.59	1.75
Sudan	21.7	34.5	37.4	36.2	2.26	2.78
Eq. Guinea	4.9	1.1	8.6	1.2	17.85	18.17
Azerbaijan	8.7	8.3	19.8	8.5	3.80	6.48
Oman	9.5	2.5	13.8	2.6	15.94	18.50
Qatar	31.7	0.8	52.7	0.8	31.61	36.63
Kazakhstan	43.2	15.1	81.0	15.1	7.41	9.57
Angola	19.8	15.0	45.2	15.9	2.46	3.54
Libya	30.5	5.7	50.4	6.0	11.18	12.85
Algeria	85.0	32.4	113.9	33.5	6.92	7.75
Nigeria	167.2	142.7	228.1	149.9	1.07	1.23
Kuwait	59.3	2.8	95.9	3.1	19.10	20.89
Venezuela	112.8	25.9	181.6	27.0	6.00	7.48
UAE	103.8	3.8	163.3	4.2	30.43	34.11
Iran	161.3	68.4	222.4	69.8	7.47	8.53
Norway	259.0	4.6	335.9	4.6	40.06	44.65
Russia	591.9	144.2	984.9	142.8	9.98	12.18
Saudi Arabia	250.7	22.5	349.1	23.7	14.74	16.51

Source: IMF World Economic Outook Database, 2007.
PPP = purchasing power parity.

expulsion from Kuwait. The US plan had originally simply been to restore the *status quo ante* without getting entangled internally in Iraq. However, concerns over internal Kurdish refugees in northern Iraq was the genesis of the over-flight programs that kept the United States involved in militarily suppressing Iraqi fighting capabilities. Thus, Gulf War I in a sense never really ended, but rather went into a lower intensity combat phase until followed by the 2003 occupation. The origin of the internal flight of Kurdish refugees in Iraq in 1991 was the imbalance of internal power and distribution of wealth in that country. Thus did internal conflict attract external attention that ultimately led to international war.

Some quantitative information on the internal distribution of political power and wealth in some oil-exporting countries is given in Table 27.4.[8] The first two columns are computed from the information on GDP and population in Table 27.3. (The GDP values used to compute the ratio of GDP in 2006 to that in 2004 are nominal, face value dollars.) The dollar price of oil more than doubled from 2004 to 2006, while a long decline exchange rate between the dollar and other major currencies paused between 2004 and 2006. Thus, countries that earned about half or more of their total GDP from oil exports and a high ratio of GDP for 2006 vs 2004 had a national income increase heavily dependent on the windfall from higher oil prices. Of the countries listed in Table 27.4, only Norway has established a permanent investment fund to smooth out the flow of oil revenues and thus avoid the boom and bust influence of variable revenues from the export of fossil fuels. Elsewhere, this has only been done on a subnational basis, in Alaska and Alberta.

For countries with a large fraction of GDP coming from oil revenue, a high percentage increase in population from 2004 to 2006 in Table 27.4 can also be an indicator of potential political problems when those revenues decline in the future. The very highest numbers for population growth may reflect an expansion of the workforce accompanying the oil boom. However, the African countries listed in Table 27.4 have high underlying population growth rates, as does Saudi Arabia.

Table 27.4. Economic and political indicators for some petroleum exporters.

Country/Years (OPEC in Bold)	2006/2004				2006			
	GDP ratio	Population growth %/biennium	$Oil/GDP (%)	Property rights 7 = least	Democracy 10 = max	Corruption 10 = least	Gini	Richest quintile (%)
Chad	1.4	5.1	49	6	1.65	2.0		
Sudan	1.7	5.1	15	7	2.90	2.0		
Eq. Guinea	1.7	5.9	78	7	2.09	2.1		
Azerbaijan	2.3	1.6	53	6	3.31	2.4	19	31
Oman	1.5	2.7	99	6	2.77	5.4		
Qatar	1.7	10.8	39	6	2.78	6.0		
Kazakhstan	1.9	0.2	28	6	3.62	2.6	34	42
Angola	**2.3**	**6.0**	**61**	**6**	**2.41**	**2.2**		
Libya	**1.7**	**4.0**	**61**	**7**	**1.84**	**2.7**		
Mexico	1.2	2.0	4	2	6.67	3.3	50	55
Algeria	**1.3**	**3.5**	**33**	**6**	**3.53**	**3.1**	**35**	**43**
Nigeria	**1.4**	**5.1**	**19**	**4**	**3.52**	**2.2**	**44**	**49**
Kuwait	**1.6**	**12.4**	**45**	**4**	**3.09**	**4.8**		
Venezuela	**1.6**	**4.1**	**24**	**4**	**5.42**	**2.3**	**44**	**49**
UAE	**1.6**	**12.4**	**31**	**6**	**2.94**	**6.2**		
Iran	**1.4**	**2.1**	**23**	**6**	**2.93**	**2.7**	**43**	**50**
Norway	1.3	0.9	15	1	9.55	8.8	26	37
Russia	1.7	1.0	13	6	5.02	2.5	34	47
Saudi Arabia	**1.4**	**5.2**	**50**	**7**	**1.92**	**3.3**		

Source: IMF (2007); Freedom House (2007); Economist Intelligence Unit (2007); Lambsdorf (2006); Watkins (2006).
$Oil/GDP = ratio of gross oil export revenues to GDP.

The last five columns in Table 27.4 report indicators of the distribution of political and economic influence. The Freedom House Property Rights Index is meant to reflect security against the state appropriating or sanctioning or tolerating the extra-legal taking of real and other properties. The Economist Intelligence Unit Democracy Index is a measure of political pluralism, ranging from a low of 2.0 for Chad and Sudan to a high of 8.8 for Norway. Lambsdorf's Corruption Perception Index, commissioned by Transparency International, gives a rough measure of the predictability of being able to conduct business within an established rule of law. The last two columns give, where available, two measures of the distribution of income. The last column is the fraction of total income accruing to the highest income earning fifth of the population. The Gini index is a similar measure weighted across the entire income distribution. Adding 8 to the Gini index gives nearly the same result as the last column in Table 27.4 in percent.

Countries with a low property rights vulnerability number, a high democracy index, a high Transparency International rating, and a small Gini index are unlikely to be prone to internal pressures towards domestic or international violence. Of oil exporters listed in Table 27.4, only Norway falls firmly in this category. Canada would also qualify, but including only Norway in Table 27.4 is sufficient to make this point. The converse is not necessarily true; a single troubling number in this table suggests potential tendency to conflict but may not be sufficient for the conflict to actually develop.

Qatar is a case with a mix of stability indicators but overall stability. With its high per capita income, "Qatar hosts one of the most extensive welfare states in the Middle East: free medical care, education and low cost housing are available for its citizens."[9] The per capita incomes in the United Arab Emirates, Kuwait, and Oman are high enough that there are no major signs of unrest, though there are substantial differences in income levels between permanent residents and imported labor in some cases. A contrasting case also with high per capita income is Equatorial Guinea. The per capita income averaged for Equatorial Guinea has recently become comparable to that of Kuwait. However, Equatorial Guinea has remained far from being smoothly governed a quarter century after a coup that overthrew its pervious leader.[10]

In some oil exporting countries there may be internal conflict that is only indirectly related to oil. Mexico is an illustration. Of the countries listed in Table 27.4 for which data was available, Mexico has the largest concentration of wealth in the highest income quintile. There has indeed been internal conflict in the impoverished state of Chiapas in southern Mexico, though with no obvious direct connection to oil. The uneven distribution of wealth in Mexico perhaps derives in part from the policies of governments dependent on oil revenues, but the conflict in Chiapas is not as directly traceable to oil as, for example, in the Niger delta region in southern Nigeria.

The type of information in Table 27.4 has been used by Kaufman, Kraay, and Mastruzzi to produce an overall instability index.[11] The recent evolution of this stability index for twenty countries of interest is shown in Table 27.5. This is a measure of overall political instability, not just of a propensity for violent conflict. In most cases shown in Table 27.5, the values of this index nevertheless track historical events connected with violence. For example, the situation in Chad has become tenser as refugees have fled the Darfur region in eastern Sudan. The violence in Darfur escalated when rebel forces there were disaffected by not obtaining settlements of their grievances comparable to those that considerably reduced the violence in oil-rich southern Sudan. This situation ratcheted the instability index for Sudan back up from a lower estimate of 1.85 for 2004.

Russia and two other former Soviet Republics, Azerbaijan and Kazakhstan, were amongst the leading eighteen oil exporting countries in 2006. Russia and Azerbaijan were both plagued with separatist movements in regions close to suitable routes for exporting oil westward from the Caspian Sea region. According to the estimate in Table 27.4, Kazakhstan remained less democratic than Russia after the cold war. However, according to the estimate in Table 27.5, Kazakhstan remained comparatively politically stable.

The ethnic Armenian majority Nagorno–Karabakh region lies near Armenia, but surrounded by Azerbaijan, on the shortest pipeline route from Baku on the Caspian Sea through Turkey to the Black Sea.

Table 27.5.   Instability index.

Country	1996	1998	2000	2002	2004	2006
Chad	0.74	1.31	1.37	1.61	1.22	1.81
Sudan	2.58	2.06	2.39	2.05	1.85	2.18
Eq. Guinea	0.39	0.27	0.03	0.38	0.16	0.15
Azerbaijan	0.64	0.72	0.91	1.27	1.37	1.07
Oman	−0.47	−0.69	−0.86	−0.85	−0.79	−0.24
Qatar	−0.33	−0.96	−1.03	−0.67	−0.91	−0.86
Kazakhstan	0.31	−0.16	−0.13	−0.09	0.15	−0.06
Angola	2.27	2.23	2.39	1.42	0.95	0.51
Iraq	2.90	2.34	1.75	1.90	3.07	2.91
Libya	1.77	1.23	0.69	0.39	−0.03	−0.24
Mexico	0.83	0.05	0.08	−0.02	0.06	0.40
Algeria	2.44	2.32	1.90	1.88	1.48	0.89
Nigeria	1.63	0.84	1.58	1.71	1.81	1.99
Kuwait	0.00	−0.35	−0.61	0.01	−0.06	−0.28
Venezuela	0.84	0.40	0.54	1.32	1.22	1.24
UAE	−0.74	−0.72	−0.80	−0.80	−0.61	−0.68
Iran	0.69	0.39	0.35	0.82	1.08	1.25
Norway	−1.22	−1.25	−1.26	−1.47	−1.34	−1.21
Russia	1.02	0.84	0.72	0.60	1.04	0.74
Saudi Arabia	0.52	0.08	−0.05	0.47	1.08	0.65

Source: The instabilty index listed here is the negative of the stability index of Kaufmann *et al.* (2007).

After a conflict that is estimated to have displaced over a million people[12], a ceasefire was negotiated in 1994, but a decade later a final resolution of the conflict remained illusive.[13] British Petroleum built the Baku–Tbilisi–Ceyhan pipeline on a longer route through T'blisi in the former Soviet Republic of Georgia and thus avoided going through Nagorno–Karabakh.[14]

The Chechnya region lies between the Caspian and Black Sea in southern Russia. A major campaign against Chechnya separatists was launched in 1999, and by 2005 the separatists had largely shifted operations out of Chechnya. The political stability index values given in Table 27.5 reflect, however, on a much wider range of issues in Russia. By 2008 a transition to a successor to Vladimir Putin had been effected. The improvement in the Russian economy from 2004 to 2006 noted in Table 27.4 was much larger than its increase in oil export revenues as a fraction of GDP. A slump in oil prices could well have a negative impact on the popularity of the ruling party in Russia, but would not be expected to be as problematic as in other countries where oil export revenues are of a much larger fraction of GDP.

The decreasing political instability indices shown for Angola and Algeria through 2006 in Table 27.5 are consistent with the gradual petering out of violence previously amounting to or verging on civil war in those countries. Angola saw a resurgence of violence in 1998 but made peace internally in 2002.[15] In Algeria however, despite the beginning of a reconciliation and amnesty plan beginning to be implemented in 2006, politically motivated violence re-emerged and persisted through 2007.[16] Libya came to an international settlement over the role of its nationals in bringing down a passenger airliner and agreed to eliminate its clandestine nuclear program. This allowed it greater access to trade with Europe, consistent with a process leading to a decrease in its assigned instability index. Iran, on the other hand, continued with a program to enrich uranium and thus remained at odds with the United States and influential members of the European Union.

Venezuela's populist president Hugo Chavez was elected in 1998 and re-elected in 2006. However, a referendum proposal to increase the powers of the president was defeated in December 2007.[17] Government takeover of the oil industry was accompanied by domestic political turmoil, as reflected in the instability index listings in Table 27.5.

Last but by no means least in Table 27.5 comes Saudi Arabia. In 1996, 19 people were killed and over 370 wounded in a bomb attack on the Khobar Towers building near Dhahran in Saudi Arabia.[18] In 2003 a series of incidents followed another set of bombing attacks that killed over 35 people in Riyadh.[19] The timeline of these events is consistent with the varying political stability index assignments listed for Saudi Arabia.

The onset and outcome of wars involving the more significant oil exporting nations are by no means determined by developments within those countries themselves. The major oil exporters have a big impact both on international oil markets and on the military balance between oil exporters. Others who are neither major oil exporters nor importers can also take actions that help precipitate wars where who has control of oil revenues is a major issue. The events that led to the 2003 occupation of Iraq are the examples of both these kinds of influences. Chapter 28 examines the role of major oil importers. Chapter 29 looks at how other actors influence events pertinent to oil and war. This will provide the background for a look ahead at the rocky road to a sustainable energy future where international wars centered on control of fossil fuels no longer occur.

Endnotes

[1]   USEIA (2007e–g).
[2]   TED (1997).
[3]   BBC News (2007a).
[4]   Vick (2003); Gettleman (2007).
[5]   Polgreen (2008a and 2008b).
[6]   IMF (2007).
[7]   CIA (2007b).
[8]   IMF (2007); Freedom House (1997); Economist Intelligence Unit (2007); Lamb's dorf (2007); Watkins (2006).
[9]   Dargin (2007).
[10] Shaxson (2004).
[11] Kaufman *et al.* (2007).
[12] CIA (2007c).
[13] c.f. Migdalovitz (2003)
[14] Darbandi (2007).
[15] BBC News (2007a).
[16] BBC News (2007b).
[17] BBC News (2007c).
[18] CNN (2001).
[19] BBC News (2008).

Chapter 28

Uncoordinated Consumers

Between them, the United States, the EU, and Japan recently accounted for two thirds of petroleum imports. The United States and its allies also account for the great preponderance of the world's conventional military power and have a long history of intervening in the affairs of a number of petroleum exporters. The past, present, and future of international wars in which control of oil resources play a major role thus depend on the policies and actions of oil importers as well as on those of oil exporters.

OPEC has a formal, albeit not rigid, structure for influencing the amount of petroleum traded internationally as market prices vary. The major oil importers do not. It is true that many of the major oil importers are members of the International Energy Agency (IEA). However, that agency serves primarily to coordinate information distribution and only has a formal role in energy markets to help re-allocate distribution of stocks in an emergency like that which followed the 1973 oil embargo. Rodney Smith explains the purpose of 1974 Agreement on an International Energy Program as follows: "It has two purposes: to limit OECD losses from future oil supply disruptions and to reduce long-term OECD dependence on oil imports from OPEC. To achieve these goals, the treaty created the International Energy Agency (IEA), which has devised a complex oil-sharing plan and imposed policies of demand restraint, import control, and oil stockpiling."[1] In practice what the IEA has done has been a far cry from forming an organized consumers union to present a coordinated response to OPEC cartel actions.

Thus, to date the commercial energy policies of the major petroleum importers have largely been uncoordinated at the broadest international level. There is some regional coordination of energy market policies in North America and increasingly also in the European Union. However, the United States and the EU have so far largely formulated energy policies independent from each other and the major oil importers in Asia.

As with Saudi Arabia amongst the oil exporters, the United States plays a key role amongst the oil importers. The reason for this is apparent from Table 28.1, which lists the top sixteen petroleum importers' oil use and shortfall (the difference between use and

Table 28.1.   Petroleum imports.

Year	1994		1996	2004	2006		
Region	Use	Shortfall = Use-Production				Use	
Units	Million barrels per day						EJ/yr
USA	17.88	8.47	9.04	12.25	12.55	20.92	41.99
EU of 2007	13.94	10.27	10.53	11.59	12.20	15.02	30.15
Japan	5.65	5.57	5.64	5.17	5.03	5.16	10.35
Chinese	4.01	1.05	1.38	4.05	4.66	8.53	17.12
South Korea	1.84	1.86	2.12	2.14	2.16	2.17	4.36
India	1.41	0.76	0.93	1.58	1.65	2.50	5.01
Singapore	0.50	0.51	0.58	0.74	0.82	0.83	1.67
Thailand	0.60	0.52	0.65	0.66	0.59	0.93	1.86
Australia	0.79	0.16	0.16	0.34	0.37	0.92	1.85
Philippines	0.30	0.30	0.35	0.31	0.32	0.34	0.68
South Africa	0.41	0.21	0.22	0.27	0.30	0.50	1.01
Pakistan	0.28	0.22	0.27	0.26	0.28	0.34	0.69
Switzerland	0.26	0.26	0.27	0.27	0.27	0.28	0.56
Ukraine	0.50	0.41	0.31	0.23	0.26	0.36	0.73
Chile	0.18	0.15	0.19	0.23	0.24	0.25	0.51
Israel	0.20	0.20	0.21	0.24	0.23	0.23	0.47
Other Shortfalls	5.20	2.13	2.30	3.12	3.07	7.02	14.09
World Total	68.86	0.27	0.29	0.79	0.10	84.73	170.02
All 2006 Importers	53.96	33.06	35.15	43.44	45.01	66.33	133.11

Source: USEIA (2007h; 2007g for conversion to exajoules/year = EJ/yr; and 2008b).

domestic production).[2] Without the leadership of Saudi Arabia as by far its largest oil exporter, OPEC would be an empty shell. Without the cooperation of the United States, which accounts for over a quarter of global oil imports, no substantive changes in the how importers deal with the global petroleum market is possible. It is thus useful to concentrate on the factors that influence US policies pertinent to petroleum imports when trying to divine what may lie in store for the future of global consumption and prices.

Energy Policy

The occupation of Iraq and a large run-up in the prices of petroleum products have recently stimulated much discussion on energy policy in the United States. The focus of much of this discussion is on what public policy initiatives can reduce the fraction of US petroleum consumption that comes from imports. As evident from Table 28.2, this fraction increased from about 47% in 1994 to about 60% in 2006.[3] What is listed in this table is actually the "shortfall" between petroleum use and domestic production. Because petroleum stocks may be built up or drawn down in any given year, the shortfall is not exactly equal to net imports, but the two are generally fairly close.

There are essentially three different ways to try to decrease consumption of anything, including petroleum imports. These are subsidizing alternatives, imposing mandates, and increasing targeted taxation.

The alternatives subsidized can be domestic oil production, production of other transportation fuels, or production of other energy sources for things other than transportation that oil is used for. Favorable tax treatment and subsidies for domestic oil production include depletion allowances and setting favorable terms for leasing of drilling rights. Subsidies of alternative transportation fuels include continuing farm price supports for biofuels feedstock like corn even as commodity prices rise. One reliable outcome from such subsidies is that people will use more energy with them in place than otherwise. The more effective subsidies are at making alternatives to oil imports more financially attractive, the more effective they will also be in promoting higher overall energy use.

Table 28.2.   Petroleum importer percentages.

Years	1994:1996	2004:2006	1994	2006	2006	
			Shortfall/ Use			Summed
Region	Growth %/Biennium				Shortfall/All	Shortfall/All
USA	7	3	47	60	28	28
EU of 2007	3	6	74	81	27	55
Japan	1	2	99	98	11	66
Chinese	31	45	26	55	10	77
South Korea	14	1	101	99	5	81
India	22	7	54	66	4	85
Singapore	15	15	101	99	2	87
Thailand	24	10	87	64	1	88
Australia	1	15	21	40	1	89
Philippines	17	1	98	93	1	90
South Africa	2	14	52	60	1	90
Pakistan	20	6	80	80	1	91
Switzerland	3	3	99	99	1	92
Ukraine	−25	9	83	72	1	92
Chile	28	6	84	95	1	93
Israel	6	4	99	97	1	93
Other Shortfalls	8	2	41	44	7	100
All	6	4	61	68		

Source: USEIA (2007h; 2007g for conversion to exajoules/year = EJ/yr; and 2008a). Chinese includes Hong Kong, Macao, and Taiwan.

Mandates have included cooperate average fuel efficiency (CAFE) standards and requirements for use of ethanol in transportation fuels. CAFE standards make the vehicles affected less expensive to drive per mile, thus reducing the financial incentive to drive less. (This would not be true if more fuel-efficient vehicles were so much more expensive to buy as to create a stronger counterincentive to increase their useful lifetime by driving them less, but this does not appear to be as important for consumer behavior as fuel efficiency.) CAFE standards also inevitably apply only to a portion of petroleum uses. By reducing petroleum use in the regulated vehicles and thus helping to push down the use and price of petroleum, CAFE standards of limited applicability inevitably also encourage the purchase of petroleum products for other uses. This became painfully apparent when light trucks and sport utility vehicles were previously exempted from US CAFE standards, producing a situation where "the average fuel economic of the nation's cars and trucks fell to its lowest level in 22 years in the 200 model year."[4] This result is reflected in increased US petroleum use in the figures for 1994 and 2006 in Table 28.1. More broadly based CAFE standards were enacted by the US Congress in 2007. While these may be more effective in reducing US petroleum use, they will also likely have the effect of stimulating a shift in the use of petroleum to aviation fuel and other purposes.

Mandates for use of larger amounts of ethanol were also included in legislation enacted by the US Congress in 2007. US ethanol production methods at the time used nearly as much energy as contained in ethanol delivered to markets near distilleries. Due to its affinity for water, ethanol cannot be pumped through oil pipelines. If ethanol is to be used broadly across the country as an antiknock agent in proportions of about ten percent in "gasohol," then there will be increased energy costs from trucking it long distances from major production areas to major consumption areas or building new pipeline capacity for shipping ethanol.

Ethanol can be used as the primary energy source in specially modified vehicles, e.g. in an 85:15 ratio with gasoline called E85. To increase the average ethanol content used in US transportation fuels well over ten percent, it could be necessary to develop a larger fleet of vehicles and pumping stations for dispersing fuels with higher ethanol content. This has already been done in Brazil on a large scale, where conditions favorable to inexpensive growth and harvesting of sugar cane make ethanol much cheaper to produce than in the United States. If US mandates succeed in raising average ethanol content in gasoline well over ten percent, the net result will be to reduce the demand for petroleum for powering the vehicles that use ethanol. This should tend to lower the price of petroleum and increase demand for its use for purposes other than mixing with gasoline.

Targeted taxation is generally considered by economists to be the most economically efficient way of discouraging use of a particular product. Partly to this end, in Europe and Israel there are much higher gasoline taxes than in the United States. There are, of course, other reasons why the European Union uses substantially less petroleum per capita and per unit of GDP than the United States. A generally milder climate is one factor, but probably the most important one is a higher population density and corresponding lower driving distances and greater use of public transportation.

To be most effective for reducing petroleum use, targeted taxation needs to be applied across the board to petroleum products, not just to land transportation uses. Even more effective at reducing petroleum imports would be a broad based tariff directly upon them. Such tariffs could be particularly effective if coordinated amongst the major petroleum importers.

If coordinated effectively enough, cooperation on setting import tariffs could even be used to induce OPEC members to adopt oil field development and production policies to stabilize international market prices on terms more favorable to importers. From the numbers in the rightmost column in Table 28.2, it will be apparent that coordinated action by the first three to six importers listed there could have a major impact on global petroleum markets. Two-thirds of global oil imports in 2006 were into the United States, the EU, and Japan. Adding to these the Chinese, Indians, and South Koreans accounts for about eighty-five percent of global petroleum imports.

A simple example of a coordinated oil import policy would be for each country to eventually join the United States in imposing an import tariff that increased each year by five dollars per barrel. For the first six years or so, this would likely merely keep the prices of imported oil at somewhere near their early 2008 high values. Otherwise, it seemed highly likely that the price of imported oil would slide downward, both because such high prices suppress demand for petroleum in the intermediate term and because there are vast supplies of conventional and unconventional oil resources outside of OPEC countries that can be recovered at well below $100/barrel. So in the short term, the primary effect of such a set of increasing import tariffs would be to signal a continuing high oil price in countries heavily reliant on imports. This "bark" by the oil importers would in turn be expected to provide a stimulus for longer-term investments needed for more efficient use of petroleum.

Looking more than six years ahead, the prospect of another decade or more of import tariffs rising faster than the rate of inflation should be enough to convince Saudi Arabia and other OPEC members that some accommodation on oil price stabilization is needed to keep exporters' revenues from oil sales continuing to fall as the import tariffs' "bite becomes more important than their bark."

In practice, even as oil prices set new record levels it seemed likely to take quite some time before coordinated punitive import tariffs would be used as an effective mechanism by importers to pressure OPEC members into production policies that would stabilize oil prices at levels more favorable to consumers. From an international perspective, there is no established mechanism for organizing a cooperation between the other major oil importers and China and India. It is true that there are memoranda of understanding on cooperation of the IEA with China, India, Southeast Asia, and Russia.[5] Also, cooperation of the IEA with China and India did rise to a new level in 2007 during a week's discussion with high-level delegations from those countries in Paris. However, this involved "convening of key IEA committees on emergency preparedness, oil markets, long-term policy co-ordination, energy research and technology,"[6] not apparently with establishing a coordinated approach to confronting OPEC with import tariffs. In any case, their much lower per capita oil use suggests that China and India are likely to want more latitude for taking advantage of falling international oil prices to increase consumption.

A possible awkwardness of using the IEA as a springboard for coordinating oil import tariffs has to do with oil exporters Canada, Norway, Mexico, and Russia. As noted in Table 28.3, Canada is a member of the IEA. Norway has a special arrangement with the IEA. Mexico is a member of the OECD, which was the framework for establishing the IEA. The IEA has also been trying to develop a working relationship with Russia. None of these potential difficulties need be insurmountable. None of these four countries are actually members of OPEC. Geographically, Canada and Mexico are natural oil suppliers

Table 28.3.   Membership of OECD, IEA, EU, and NATO in 2007.

Australia	OECD	IEA		
Austria	OECD	IEA	EU	NATO
Belgium	OECD	IEA	EU	NATO
Bulgaria			EU	NATO
Canada	OECD	**IEA**		NATO
Czech Republic	OECD	IEA	EU	NATO
Cyprus			EU	
Denmark	OECD	IEA	EU	NATO
Estonia			EU	NATO
Finland	OECD	IEA	EU	
France	OECD	IEA	EU	NATO
Germany	OECD	IEA	EU	NATO
Greece	OECD	IEA	EU	NATO
Hungary	OECD	IEA	EU	NATO
Iceland	OECD	IEA		NATO
Ireland	OECD		EU	
Italy	OECD	IEA	EU	NATO
Japan	OECD	IEA		
Korea	OECD	IEA		
Latvia			EU	NATO
Lithuania			EU	NATO
Luxembourg	OECD	IEA	EU	NATO
Malta			EU	
Mexico	**OECD**	**IEA**		
Netherlands	OECD	IEA	EU	NATO
New Zealand	OECD	**IEA**		
Norway	**OECD**	**IEA**		NATO
Poland	OECD	IEA	EU	NATO
Portugal	OECD	IEA	EU	NATO
Romania			EU	NATO
Slovak Republic	OECD	IEA	EU	NATO
Slovenia			EU	NATO
Spain	OECD	IEA	EU	NATO
Sweden	OECD	IEA	EU	
Switzerland	OECD	IEA		
Turkey	OECD	IEA		NATO
United Kingdom	OECD	IEA	EU	NATO
United States	OECD	IEA		NATO

Source: IEA (2008) notes a special arrangement with Norway. Net oil exporters in 2006 are in bold.

for the United States. Norway is similarly a geographically convenient supplier for the European Union, which takes part in the work of the IEA. It should be attractive for these oil exporters to make special trade arrangements with the United States and EU that exempt them from import tariffs aimed primarily at OPEC member states. Such arrangements might or might not be possible with Russia, but Russia has no governing role either in the IEA or the OECD.

Before even getting to the point of a serious international discussion on coordinating oil import tariffs, however, there would need to be substantial changes in domestic energy politics in some countries. Chief among these is the United States.

Politics of US Transportation Sector Subsidies and Mandates

The political feasibility of energy policies in the United States is inversely proportional to the levels of economic efficiency described above. Subsidies are easy. Mandates are harder but sometimes possible. Effective increases in targeted taxation have so far been political infeasible.

The most readily digestible subsidies are for energy research and development. These generally require a modest fraction of the federal budget and can sometimes be targeted relatively narrow at the constituencies of influential members of Congress. General support for basic research with potential practical applications can be very economically efficient. However, large research and development projects aimed promoting particular energy technologies can be problematic. A particular case in point is the attempt to jumpstart industries for using coal or oil shale to make liquid fuels, after the oil prices shocks of 1973 and 1980. The essential problem was that the timing of attempts to develop these expensive technologies was not matched to that of cyclic changes in oil prices. The attempts at demonstration projects were not mature when oil prices collapsed in 1986.

Indeed, there is in general a timing mismatch between political pressures and market forces that poses a generic risk to large government-sponsored energy technology demonstration projects. High oil costs produce a political pressure to initiate such projects, but high oil prices also produce a market response that will relieve pricing pressure. In the liquid fuels sector, the time required for commercial sector investments to apply existing technology as a market response is similar to the time needed to implement a government-sponsored technology demonstration. As a result, the market response tends to undermine the commercial viability of a government-sponsored demonstration project just before or as such a project enters an operational phase.

Government-sponsored basic research can be transformative in the longer run, however. The most likely example pertinent to the 21st century is genetic engineering. It is not out of the question that photosynthetic biological systems can be so radically re-engineered that they could produce transportation fuels at a cost that undercuts even free market petroleum. However, if this occurs, the current research that most enables such a development will be the basic investment in genetic sequencing, DNA synthesis, prediction of the functionality of novel proteins, and understanding the basic bio-molecular physiology of plants and microbes. These are technologies that are being developed primarily on the basis of their application to medicine, food production, and other commercial purposes. Their application to re-engineering entire organisms or ecosystems radically enough to completely undercut petroleum as a transportation fuel feedstock is likely to take a number of decades, and what that number is remains very hard to predict. There is little prospect, however, that the impact of government-sponsored research and development will significantly rival that of market response in influencing how oil imports evolve in the first decade following the recent reaching of record high inflation-adjusted oil prices.

Another politically popular but comparatively inexpensive form of subsidy is preferential tax incentive for adopting new technologies. Tax credits for purchasing gasoline-electric hybrid vehicles are an example. The US tax code allowed a tax credit for some such vehicles place in service starting in 2005 and purchased no later than the end of 2010. The number of vehicles eligible for full credits was limited to 60,000 per manufacturer. This had the effect of an early reduction in the availability of tax credits for popular high fuel-efficient cars, like the 60 city miles per gallon Toyota Prius. (A fuel consumption rate of 60 mpg is 25.5 km per liter, with a US gallon being 3.7854 liters). Meanwhile, smaller tax credits for much lower fuel efficiency hybrids, like the 18 city mpg General Motors Corporation Sierra pickup, continued to be fully available.[7]

If the maximum tax credit of $3150 for the Prius had applied to all 60,000 of Toyota's qualifying hybrids qualifying for the full tax credit, the total lost revenue to the US Treasury would have been $94.5 million. This and the other tax credits in this program pale by comparison to the subsidy that would be needed to make an alternative technology like ethanol from cellulose market-competitive with gasoline from oil. Making ethanol from corn is only marginally competitive even at recent peak oil prices. The cost of using cellulose was anticipated to drop from $3 to $4 per gallon of ethanol on a pilot scale to about two dollars per gallon at a commercial scale by 2009.[8] This is still about twice the cost of making ethanol from corn. Corn-based ethanol is only marginally competitive with gasoline, except as an anti-knock fuel additive, unless prices stay well over $100/barrel. If such a price penalty for cellulosic ethanol persists, pursuing a goal of 16 billion gallons per year of US cellulosic ethanol through subsidies could cost $16 billion/year. This would be on top of comparably large subsidies for corn feedstock for making an additional 21 billion gallons of fuel from biomass, including at least a billion gallons of biodiesel. If oil prices continue dropping beyond the $83/barrel expected in early 2010 by oil futures traders in early 2008,[9] then the required subsidies could be much larger.

To make taxes on petroleum products more digestible for wage earners, energy economist Phil Verleger is reported by columnist and author Thomas Friedman to have suggested using the resulting revenue to reduce payroll taxes. One suggestion was to use gasoline tax revenues to increase take-home pay by 6 to 9 percent.[10] A more effective alternative for reducing petroleum imports would be a tariff, e.g. of forty dollars of 2008 purchasing power equivalent per barrel of petroleum imported as crude oil or used to make refined petroleum products. Based on year 2006 US oil imports and expected year 2009 federal minimum wage and payroll tax rates, the resulting revenue would be sufficient to eliminate the 7.65 percent employee portion of Social Security and Medicare taxes on the minimum wage portion of 181 million full time (1800 h/year) employees, which is more than the entire United States labor force of 151 million in 2006. Alternatively, it would be enough to eliminate all federally mandated payroll taxes of $2053 (including the federally mandated portion of unemployment tax) on over 90 million full time employees, thus including more than the number of full time employees earning up to median wage. Even if special tariff reductions were allowed for more reliable pipeline imports from North America or some other non-OPEC sources, there could still be enough revenue to remove a 7.65 percent payroll tax on the minimum wage portion of all employees or all of the federally mandated payroll tax on the minimum wage portion of all employees earning up to the median wage.[11] Such an approach to avoiding a net tax increase on workers most hard hit by high petroleum prices would move closer to the present the inevitable adjustments that need to be made if Medicare and Social Security are to be put on a pay-as-you-go basis in the United States, for example by increasing the upper limit on the amount of income subject to payroll taxes. As a result, regardless of its economic efficiency, such an approach would be likely to be fiercely resisted by powerful political forces aiming to keep payroll taxes higher than Medicare and Social Security outlays as long as possible.

US Energy Bill of 2007

Given already fierce pressures on the federal budget and a deep-seated resistance to raising taxes, the 2007 US energy bill envisioned meeting its targets primarily through mandates on industry. Only a portion of the cost was authorized for funding through federal subsidies.[12]

Assuming that the required appropriations followed, a total of half a billion dollars spread over fiscal years 2008 through 2015 would be allocated for grants to encourage the production of cellulosic and other advanced biofuels not made from cornstarch. The fuel made from cellulose would most likely be nearly entirely ethanol. An additional $0.2 billion/year was authorized for research for fiscal years 2008 through 2014.

The 2007 US energy bill also provided for a subsidy of $0.25 per gallon for cellulosic fuel for any year in which projected use for the following year did not meet the target levels listed in Table 28.4. This subsidy would be larger if wholesale gasoline prices were less than $2.75 per gallon. For example, at gasoline prices of $2.50 per gallon, the cellulosic fuel subsidy would be $0.50 per gallon of cellulosic fuel. At gasoline prices of $2.00 per gallon, the subsidy would be $1.00 per

Table 28.4. US biofuels targets in 2007 energy bill.

Year	Cellulosic	Biodiesel	Advanced	Total	EJ
		Billion U.S. gallons			
2008				9.00	0.8
2009			0.60	11.10	1.0
2010	0.10		0.95	12.95	1.1
2011	0.25		1.35	13.95	1.2
2012	0.50	0.50	2.00	15.20	1.3
2013	1.00	0.65	2.75	16.55	1.5
2014	1.75	0.80	3.75	18.15	1.6
2015	3.00	1.00	5.50	20.50	1.8
2016	4.25		7.25	22.50	2.0
2017	5.50		9.00	24.00	2.1
2018	7.00		11.00	26.00	2.3
2019	8.50		13.00	28.00	2.5
2020	10.50		15.00	30.00	2.6
2021	13.50		18.00	33.00	2.9
2022	16.00		21.00	36.00	3.2

Source: Energy Independence and Security Act of 2007, Library of Congress, (2008). Advanced biofuels are not made from corn starch.

gallon of cellulosic fuel. Since a gallon of ethanol has only about two-thirds the energy content of a gallon of gasoline, the remaining one-third of the extra cost would be borne by the consumer. Also, there was no inflation adjustment in these figures. At a 2–3% annual inflation rate, a $2.75/gallon cost of gasoline for the final target year of 2022 for reaching 16 billion gallons/year of cellulosic fuel translates to a maximum of $2.08 and a minimum of $1.82/gallon for gasoline prices a year in terms of year 2008 purchasing power. Unless gasoline prices were lower than this, the subsidy for cellulosic fuel would be limited to $0.25 per gallon, corresponding to between $0.19 and $0.17 per gallon in terms of 2008 purchasing power. Without any future adjustment in these numbers, the rest of the additional cost would be borne by the consumer.

The 2007 US energy bill also called for raising corporate fleet average fuel efficiency standards to 35 mpg (15 km/liter) by 2020 for passenger automobiles, excluding trucks weighing more than 8500 pounds (3.856 metric tons). Studies of possible fuel efficiency standards for heavier vehicles were also called for in the bill. The subsidies authorized to facilitate industry conversions to meet these standards were "such sums as may be necessary" — in effect a blank but unsigned check.

There were no specific enforcement provisions in the 2007 US energy bill either for the biofuels mandate or the CAFE mandate, but the Environmental Protection Agency Director was tasked to get the mandates not. The CAFE mandate did envision revenue from fines to be applied to research, in effect recycling such fines back into the transportation sector. The new CAFE mandate did appear to make a serious attempt to plug the large loophole in the previous standards, which had not inhibited a major consumer move to light trucks and sport utility vehicles. Both mandates allowed for considerable administrative flexibility in their implementation. So it remained to be seen how durable the mandates in the 2007 energy bill would be if inflation-adjusted international oil market prices fell appreciably before 2022.

Petroleum Stocks

The underlying philosophy of the IEA and the recent operational policy of the United States for petroleum stocks together provide a good example of the phenomenon of generational lag. The net oil importers in the IEA and the member states of the European Union are committed to maintaining ninety days worth of oil stocks, i.e. just under a quarter of annual use. How close various countries were to that target at the end of 2006 is shown in Table 28.5.[13] The idea is that there would be coordinated releases from these stocks in event of an emergency like the 1973 embargo oil shipments from the Middle East to the United States and the Netherlands. However, the decision about what constitutes an emergency has been so constrained that the run-up of oil prices toward record levels from 2003 through 2007 did

Table 28.5. OECD petroleum stocks (million barrels, and total in EJ).

Location/ Year End	2003	2004	2005	2006	2007
US Strategic	638	676	685	689	697
US Commercial	930	969	1013	1031	965
US Territories	17	16	19	19	17
Canada	170	160	178	180	205
Mexico	39	41	44	42	45
Australia, N. Zeal.	40	41	41	42	44
Japan	636	635	612	631	621
South Korea	155	149	135	152	143
France	179	177	185	182	180
Germany	273	267	283	283	275
Italy	135	136	132	133	133
United Kingdom	100	101	95	109	98
Other OECD Europe	603	611	646	670	675
Total	3914	2980	4068	4165	4097
Total (EJ)	23	23	24	24	24

Source: USEIA (2008a, 2008d); N. Zeal. = New Zealand.

not result in release of any of the largest government-held reserve stocks, which are those of the United States. Indeed, through this period the US government continued to buy oil to build up its reserve stocks, as evident from the first row of numbers in Table 28.5.

The increase in OECD petroleum stocks from the end of 2003 to the end of 2005 averaged just over twice the estimated 0.1 million barrels per day that China would need to continue purchasing to build up its reserves to a target value of about 102 million barrels by late 2009. Based on estimates on an analysis of the long-term response of oil prices to changes in consumption by Noureddine Krichene, Christopher Neely estimated that China's stock build-up should raise global oil prices by about one percent.[14] The OCED stock build-ups in 2004 and 2005 thus likely pushed prices up by more than two percent. For holders of US commercial stocks these purchases provided a cushion against even higher prices in 2007. However, even during the large price run-up in 2007, the US government, continued to build up stocks albeit more slowly, not selling them off even when the price touched $100/barrel.

US policy on managing government petroleum reserves during the period covered in Table 28.5 reflected a deeply engrained idea that oil is a strategic commodity, so these reserves are to be drawn upon only in response to actions initiated by another country during a military emergency. With no prospect that these stocks would be released to limit price increases and the increased price volatility that accompanied them,[15] US policy may have acted to aggravate rather than alleviate price pressure. As noted at the beginning of this book, there was no plausible prospect that US government oil reserves would be essential to sustain military operations. Moreover, there were five supply-side perturbations that came together to create a nearly "perfect storm" wave of oil price increases from 2003 to 2007. These included the occupation of Iraq, continuing political struggles over control of the oil industry in Venezuela[16], turmoil the Niger Delta,[17] unusual hurricane damage to production from the Gulf of Mexico, and concern about a possible US military attack on Iran. All that was missing was a revolution in Saudi Arabia. However, by 2007 it became apparent that the Bush administration was very unlikely to launch an attack on Iran, and a major disruption in Saudi Arabia before market forces reduced peak oil prices seemed implausible.

Indeed, if there is to be a major upset in Saudi Arabia leading to a serious disruption of oil exports, this is most likely to come *after* a period of declining per capita incomes resulting from a combination of declining oil prices and continuing rapid population growth. Thus, there was every reason to believe that US government oil stocks would have a chance to follow every stockbroker's wish, "buy low; sell high." Instead, the policy in practice appeared to be "buy low and high." In 2008, under pressure from the US Congress the US administration finally suspended purchases for the petroleum reserve. If the United States resumes buying and in practice never selling government petroleum reserves and carries through with a plan to double the size of that reserve[18] from its previously finally achieved target,[19] it will accomplish little but putting upward pressure on oil prices, and with considerable additional cost to the government.

Aside from China, the petroleum stocking plans of other oil importers were not on a track likely to have much impact compared to those of OECD countries. Some of these stocking plans are summarized in Table 28.6.[20] Together, all of these non-OECD countries' stocks and

Table 28.6. Various non-OECD petroleum stocks and possible storage capacity.

Where	Million barrels	Type	Source
China	102	2009 target	Neely (2007)
China	400	IEA standard	Neely (2007)
Taiwan	13	2006	Sakhuja (2006)
Singapore	96	All types, 2006	Sakhuja (2006)
Thailand	65	2006	Sakhuja (2006)
India	37	plan	Alexander's (2004)
South Africa	40	possible	Crowther Campbell (2007)
Total goal	651		
Total goal (EJ)	4		

Source: See references in the last column.

firmly or tentatively planned storage add to 651 million barrels, which is between one seventh and one sixth of the total for the OECD for 2007 shown in Table 28.5. This does not include stocks of most exporters. It also does not several other net oil importers, although together these are not likely to make a major increase in the total stocks held by importers. Notable among these latter is Israel, which reportedly also obtained an agreement in 1975 that the United States would make oil available for purchase for up to five years in an emergency.[21]

Prices Drive Technology Choices: Israel

Gasoline prices in Israel in early 2008 were about $6.28 per gallon ($1.80 per liter). This was about twice the level in the United States, where the incentives in the 2007 energy bill looked unlikely to induce electric cars to capture a very large share of the market. On the other hand, gasoline prices in Israel were sufficient to induce Israel Corporation Ltd. Chairman Idan Ofer to make available $100 million for a joint project with Nissan Motor Company and Renault to develop and market electric cars.[22] These would be paid for using a mileage-based fee arrangement, with the leasing company working with the Israeli government to provide electrical connections in places like city streets, and service areas where exhausted batteries can be replaced. The cars, to be provided by Renault and Nissan, were expected to have lithium-ion batteries capable of supporting a 124-mile drive on a single charge (about 200 km). There appears to be a good match for such a car to the Israeli market, where long distance driving of personal cars is not so common in the United States, and the round trip distance between Jerusalem and Tel Aviv is only 120 km.

When it comes to use of electricity for automobile propulsion, the contrast between the United States and Israel could not be more striking. In the United States, taxes on gasoline and diesel are a small fraction of the total cost of those products. Unlike other sales taxes computed on a percentage basis, special taxes on gasoline in the United States are fixed face value amounts per gallon and politically difficult to adjust for inflation. So the ratio of total gasoline

Table 28.7. Fuel prices for 2004, in $US2008.

Country	Diesel $/liter	Diesel $/gal	Gasoline $/liter	Gasoline $/gal
USA	0.62	2.35	0.59	2.23
Japan	1.04	3.92	1.37	5.20
China	0.47	1.78	0.52	1.98
South Korea	1.04	3.92	1.47	5.57
India	0.68	2.56	0.95	3.59
Singapore	0.60	2.27	0.97	3.67
Thailand	0.40	1.53	0.59	2.23
Australia	0.91	3.43	0.93	3.51
Philippines	0.37	1.40	0.57	2.15
South Africa	0.87	3.30	0.88	3.34
Pakistan	0.45	1.69	0.68	2.56
Switzerland	1.49	5.66	1.41	5.33
Ukraine	0.48	1.82	0.60	2.27
Chile	0.70	2.64	0.93	3.51
Israel	0.87	3.30	1.15	4.34

Source: International Fuel Prices 2005 (Metchies 2005); for 95 octane gasoline except 92 octane for South Korea and an average for 92 and 98 octane for Japan.

prices between the United States and other countries that levy higher taxes remained low even as the cost of refinery feedstock rose. This is evident from the numbers in Table 28.7, which also show Israeli gasoline prices being twice as high as in the United States in 2004.[23] The result is that a combination of demographic geography and government policy has created market conditions that may be ripe for building up an infrastructure for electric vehicles in Israel long before the appropriate market forces are suitable for this in the United States.

Biofuels in the European Union and the United States

In 2003, the European Union adopted a directive that set a target of a 5.75 percent market share for biofuels in the European Union by

Table 28.8.   Petroleum product prices and taxes and prices as of January 7, 2008.

Region	Netherlands	Germany	Belgium	Italy	France	UK	USA
Costs in $ per Gallon:							
Gasoline tax	4.94	4.87	4.66	4.48	4.69	4.89	0.36
Gasoline before taxes	3.52	2.92	3.08	3.25	3.02	2.80	2.94
Gasoline with taxes	8.47	7.79	7.74	7.72	7.71	7.69	3.30
Diesel fuel tax	3.19	3.76	2.84	3.55	3.48	4.96	0.46
Diesel fuel before taxes	3.54	3.40	3.34	3.65	3.32	3.12	2.91
Diesel fuel with taxes	6.74	7.16	6.18	7.21	6.80	8.07	3.38
Heating oil tax	2.29	1.23	1.06	3.48	1.20	0.95	0.43
Heating oil before taxes	3.29	2.98	2.92	3.33	3.17	2.83	2.97
Heating oil with taxes	5.59	4.21	3.97	6.81	4.37	3.77	3.40
Tax in $ per Liter:							
Gasoline	1.31	1.29	1.23	1.18	1.24	1.29	0.10
Diesel fuel	0.84	0.99	0.75	0.94	0.92	1.31	0.12
Heating oil	0.61	0.33	0.28	0.92	0.32	0.25	0.11

Source: (USEIA, 2008b).

2010. Environmental benefits and improvements in energy security were cited as motivations for this directive.[24] Also, tax policies in Europe had created what looked to be a favorable market for biofuels. As evident from the examples in Table 28.8, taxes on gasoline and diesel fuel were much higher in European Union countries than in the United States.[25] However, it gradually became evident that both the environmental impacts and the global economic effects of a rapid growth in biofuels use could be problematic. By January 2008, projections suggested that the biofuels fraction of the EU market would be closer to 4.2 percent by 2010. Moreover, European Union officials were ready to propose a ban on imports of some biofuels. These were likely to include palm oil and possibly some other biofuels from Latin America. The primary reason cited for this was concern about the environmental effects of growing some types of biofuels, particularly palm oil. Increasing emissions of carbon dioxide into the atmosphere from clearing peatlands in Southeast Asia for palm plantations was a particular concern.[26]

There was, of course, an implicit protectionist appeal to limiting imports of competing agricultural products. This especially when the proposal on limiting imports was combined with a one for a binding trading rights scheme aimed at reaching a ten percent portion of bio-fuels in the EU transport mix by 2020.

The 2007 US energy act took cognizance of the same concerns that were rising in the European Union, at least when it came to the idea of ensuring that the hoped for benefits of reducing greenhouse gas emissions by replacing oil products with biofuels.[27] However, what neither the European Union nor the United States approaches of the time had fully come to grips with was the impact of increased global biofuels production on staple food prices. Grain price increases ricocheted through global markets as the future prices for turn of year corn delivery doubled for the beginning of 2007 as compared to three of the four previous years. As a result, US farmers switched from acreage from soybeans to corn,[28] driving up the cost of soy as well. As consumers in developing countries tried to switch to palm oil for consumption, they found that biofuels markets had helped drive up the costs of edible oils as well. With the global fraction of vegetable oil used for biofuels increasing from 0.03 to 0.07 from 2005 to 2007, the price of edible oils and fats doubled over the same time period.[29] For the low-income people not in the agriculture sector and already spending a high proportion of disposable income just to maintain minimum or lower healthy calorie consumption, these developments were more than just an inconvenience.

The impact of increased biofuels production on agricultural commodities markets was compounded by a growing consumption of meat in emerging markets, particularly in China. Raising livestock by grain feeding reduces the amount of calories available for human consumption from a given level of grain production several fold. So when meat consumption exceeds the level that can be sustained with waste food and otherwise uncultivated grasslands, it puts additional pressure on the prices of staple agricultural commodities.

At the early stages of the European Union and US plans to raise the biofuels fraction of transportation fuels well above the ten percent level appropriate to use of ethanol as an anti-knock agent, it was not yet clear if the future of oil prices and feedback from price pressure on agricultural commodities would indeed allow the stated targets to be achieved by 2020–2022.

Automobile Fuel Efficiency in India and China

Increasing consumption of oil by China and India has fueled speculation that oil prices could even rise well over $100 per barrel as these and other developing countries' economies continue to grow. Between 1996 and 2004, the growth in the combined petroleum imports of India and China was slightly larger than that together for the United States and the countries that were in the EU as of 2007. From 2004 to 2006, the combined growth of such imports to India and China was only three quarters of that for the United States and EU together. How large a fraction of global oil imports these emerging economies will capture in the future depends in part on how sustainable their large GDP growth rates are and whether they continue to subsidize domestic transportation fuel sales. Their oil imports will also depend on the extent to which they "leapfrog" over the oil-intensity path pursued in the OECD by opting higher fuel efficiency earlier on their rise on the per capita GDP curve.

In 2008, India's Tata Motors was working on plans to mass produce a low performance car with a target price of about $2500. This was, as the author of a New York Times article wryly put it, "about the price of the optional DVD player on the Lexus LX 480 sport utility vehicle."[30] The car is designed for full maintenance life only when driven at or below 45 miles per hour (72 km/hr), and it has a low-acceleration continuous variable transmission. For the consumer preferences and typical driving speeds on the United States or European four-lane highways, such a car would not be an attractive option. It remained to be revealed whether this car would live up to its touted fuel efficiency of 50 miles per gallon (21 km/liter) and sell at the hoped for rate of a million per year in India alone.[31] In any case, the attempt illustrates the possibilities both of rapidly increasing the use of oil-based transportation in developing countries and of doing so with considerably higher fuel efficiency than even the most ambitious goals adopted by the United States.

In 2004, China issued mandatory vehicle fuel efficiency standards that were to take full effect for new vehicle sales at the beginning of 2009. As for the earlier US CAFE standards, the Chinese requirements allowed for lower fuel efficiency per vehicle for heavier cars and trucks. However, the required vehicle weight moved a given distance per liter of fuel increased with vehicle weight, thus providing some financial incentive toward lighter vehicles. Also, the Chinese requirements for 2009 were substantially more stringent than what the US CAFE standards would require in the same year. The Chinese standards are summarized in Table 28.9.[32] The standards are promulgated in terms of liters of fuel per hundred kilometers, which decrease with

Table 28.9.   China's fuel efficiency standards.

Vehicle weight up to		liter/100-km	US CAFE mpg	Tonne × mpg
Pounds	Tonnes			
1667	0.76	6.2	38.1	28.8
1922	0.87	6.5	36.4	31.7
2178	0.99	7.0	33.8	33.3
2422	1.10	7.5	31.5	34.6
2678	1.21	8.1	29.2	35.4
2933	1.33	8.6	27.5	36.6
3178	1.44	9.2	25.7	37.0
3422	1.55	9.8	24.2	37.5
3689	1.67	10.2	23.2	38.8
3933	1.78	10.7	22.1	39.4
4178	1.90	11.1	21.3	40.3
4444	2.02	11.5	20.5	41.4
4689	2.13	11.9	19.9	42.2
5066	2.30	12.3	19.2	44.1
5578	2.53	13.1	18.0	45.6
More	More	21.2	11.1	

Source: An and Sauer (2004); tonne = 2205 pounds. US CAFE miles per gallon are estimated differently from liter/100-km limits and do not exacty correspond to the inverse of those limits times (3.7854 gal/liter)/(1.602 km/mile). These standards are for manual transmission passenger cars. Limits for automatic transmission cars and all utility vehicles are about 6 percent less stringent.

increasing vehicle weight. The standards are also converted in Table 28.9 into equivalent US CAFE standards.

Energy Price Controls in China

Beset by a rising inflation rate, which reached an annual rate of 6.9 percent in November 2007, China resorted to a measure familiar to a country still emerging from having its heavy industry function as a command economy: price controls. In doing so, it ran into complications, as had the US economy with the price controls of the 1970s. "Refiners had cut back on the production of diesel because price controls were forcing them to sell the diesel for slightly less than the cost of the crude oil needed to make it".[33] The resulting nationwide fuel shortages kept trucks from delivering enough coal to electric power plants in northern China. Also, oil was still used to fire around a seventh of the electric power generation in southeastern China. There, many electric power plants scheduled maintenance and repairs to evade a government mandate to continue production at a loss in face of revenues not matching rising fuel costs.

The problems China had with price controls provide one of the most obvious examples of the difficulty of trying to mold energy markets with mandates. The most straightforward way to influence market behavior is with price signals. Price controls, production goals, emissions permits, and other types of mandates are more administratively complex and ever prone to exploitation of any number of ways to maximize profits while undermining the desired effect.

Prospects for More Coordinated Action by Oil Importers

As the first decade of the new millennium approached an end, the major oil importing countries were communicating informally and formally with each other about energy policy. They were working in parallel on common challenges, sometimes coming up with similar responses and sometimes with quite different ones.

Similarities were that both the United States and China were making their CAFE standards more stringent. So also were the European Union, Japan, and Australia, as was the oil exporter Canada.[34] The United States and European Union were also taking similar approaches and facing similar problems with biofuels targets. Attempts were being made to develop plug-in hybrid electric cars for significant penetration of the Japanese and United States markets, but development of suitable batteries remained a challenge.[35]

Petroleum stocks in most of the major importers were headed in the direction of the IEA target of ninety days worth of consumption. The early IEA procedures for availability of these stocks in an emergency remained in place, and additional agreements between smaller sets of countries had also emerged.

Still, the types of oil importer action needed to dampen recurrent oil price volatility remained illusive. Based on historical data from various time ranges between 1970 and 2005, estimates of short-term elasticity of demand for oil had very small magnitude. These estimates ranged from 0.01 to 0.09. A short-term price elasticity estimate of 0.025, for example, would imply an increase in oil prices by a about 40 percent from if a sudden loss of supply from storm damage or political upheaval were to reduce global supply by only one percent. Short-lived events of this type can be countered by release of commercial stocks built up to either to anticipate such events or prepare for seasonal variations or imbalances between shipments and immediate needs. However, if producers are unable or unwilling to adjust production elsewhere to compensate, more serious supply disruptions can lead to very large short-term price spikes unless governments have a policy of releasing their stocks under such circumstances.

Stocks releases do have their limitations as a means of reducing price volatility, under circumstances where enough potential production capacity is deliberately being kept off line in order to keep prices high. Importers relying solely on their stock releases under such circumstances could temp producers to force those importers to drain their stocks to near depletion and thus run out of leverage over prices. In order to combat the type of collusion amongst producers that would produce this result, consumers that do not themselves have spare production capacity need greater intermediate-term elasticity of demand. Many of the research and development initiatives like those in the 2007 US energy bill are aimed at enhancing longer-term elasticity of demand by bringing alternatives to oil-intensive transportation systems closer to marketability. However, such initiatives generally have much impact primarily only over the longer term, if at all.

An alternative, mentioned above, is for enough of the major oil importers to cooperate on using rising import tariffs to force producer cartel members to either increase their elasticity of supply or face continually declining revenues as the import tariffs continue to rise. This is one of the mechanisms available to consumers in the context of the World Trade Organization structure when faced with trade restraints by exporters. The WTO mechanism has become so effective in dealing with trade disputes in other heavy industries that in 2003 the United States took the domestically politically risky step of lifting tariffs on imported steel in order to avoid economic retaliation from Europe.[36] However, oil is not dealt with through the WTO, and coordinated action of this type on oil is not an easy thing to arrange. For just as a producer cartel like OPEC is unstable to the risk of individual members exceeding production quotas, so would a consumers union be vulnerable to defections with one or more members striking deals with producers to gain preferential access to oil supplies at favorable prices.

In practice, international oil markets are likely not to be much affected by formally coordinated consumer country action during the period of effective OPEC cartel action that started in 1998. A more likely outcome is that high oil prices will again stimulate higher production from conventional and unconventional resources outside of OPEC and also greater fuel use efficiency amongst importers. The resulting downward pressure on oil prices will be countered in part by growing consumption in rapidly developing countries. The net effect could keep inflation adjusted oil prices considerably higher than they were during the post-peak price years of 1980–1986 during the first period of effective OPEC cartel action. Whether OPEC will choose a sustainable longer-term price range target and manage to make it stick or face a less drastic version of the price collapse that happened after 1986 remained to be revealed. Much will depend on political and security situation in the producing countries. This will depend in part on the interplay between those security situations, and other parts of the world, a topic taken up in Chapter 29.

Endnotes

1 Smith (1988, p. 17).
2 USEIA (2007g, 2007h, and 2008b).
3 USEIA (2007g, 2007h, and 2008a).
4 Hakim (2002).
5 IEA (2008).
6 IEA (2007).
7 IRS (2007); ACEEE (2006).
8 Service (2007).
9 Mouawad (2008).
10 Friedman (2007).
11 USEIA (2008); USBLS (2007); IRS (2008).
12 Library of Congress (2007).
13 USEIA (2008a).
14 Krichene (2006); Christopher Neely (2007).
15 c.f. Krichene (2006).
16 Romero and Krauss (2007); Romero (2008).
17 Mouawad (2007).
18 AP (2007).
19 Romero (2004).
20 Neely (2007); Sakhuja (2006); Alexander's (2004); Crowther Campbell (2007).
21 Phillips (1979).
22 Erlanger (2008).
23 Metchies (2005).
24 European Parliament (2003).
25 USEIA (2008b).
26 Kanter (2008).
27 Kanter and Castle (2008).
28 Martin (2007).

29 Bradsher (2008a).
30 Giridharadas (2008a and 2008b).
31 New York Times (2008).
32 An and Sauer (2004).
33 Bradsher (2008).
34 An and Sauer (2004).
35 Ohnsman (2008).
36 Sanger (2003); Stevenson and Becker (2003).

Chapter 29

Spoilers

The dual roles of economics and ideology in violent conflict involve a complex feedback. At least since 1914, Anglo-American involvement in the Middle East and consequent opposition to it has been clearly connected to oil. The primary question for this and the next chapter is how long this involvement will persist as expenditures on oil dwindle as a fraction of the economic activity of its current major importers. A principle problem here is that particularly the United States has gotten enmeshed in a set of entanglements connected to Middle East that may not be easily unraveled. The entanglements of primary interest are the roles the United States played in interacting with the royal family in Saudi Arabia and the continued presence of Israel in the territories it occupies.

For Saudi Arabia, the United States has primarily played the role of oil customer and arms supplier. An important exception was the stationing of US troops in Saudi Arabia not only during but also well after operations Desert Shield and Desert Storm in 1990–1991. During the cold war, Israel was increasingly seen as a counterweight to Soviet influence with other countries in the Middle East. US support of Israel was particularly attractive during the Vietnam War, when the US military had more than enough on its hands elsewhere to simultaneously get directly involved in any conflict in the Middle East. Egypt was brought more in line with US foreign policy after the 1978 Camp David accords, but the 1979 Iranian revolution turned a former ally in the region into an antagonist. That the 1973 war and the Camp David accords left Israel in control of the West Bank and Gaza produced a particularly serious entanglement for the United States.

Israel's occupation of the West Bank proved to be an increasingly burdensome problem for both itself and the United States after the end of the cold war. That this would likely be the case had actually been understood by the Israeli security establishment just before the Six-Day War

> ...Leading Israeli policy planners had determined six months before the Six-Day War that capturing the West Bank would be bad for the country. Recently declassified Israeli government documents show that according to these policy planners, taking over the West Bank would weaken the relative strength of Israel's Jewish majority, encourage Palestinian nationalism and ultimately lead to violent resistance. These comprehensive political and strategic discussions began in November 1966 and concluded in January 1967. The participants were representatives of the Mossad, the Israeli Defense Forces' intelligence branch and the Foreign Ministry. The documents they prepared were approved by Prime Minister Levi Eshkol and the army's chief of staff Yitzhak Rabin, and therefore reflect Israel's strategic thinking six months before the war.[1]

According to Israeli newspaper columnist Tom Segev, "when Jordan attacked the Israeli part of Jerusalem on the first day" of the Six Day War, flush with a victory over Egypt a few hours earlier Israeli cabinet "ministers decided with their hearts, not their heads, to take East Jerusalem" and thus got stuck in the occupation of the West Bank with still no end in sight.[2]

From a military perspective, an initial compensating benefit accompanying the burden of the Israel's occupation of the West Bank was that this made it impossible for hostile military forces to be positioned a very short distance from the heart of the country. Israeli settlements deep in the West Bank also originally had the military function of providing a tripwire and impediment to another Arab armored attack from beyond the West Bank. Gradually the occupation evolved from a security asset to being a major part of Israel's security problem. For it became widely understood that Israel had developed a formidable nuclear arsenal, so that no conventional attack on it could ultimately prevail in any case. Then Iraq, Israel's most formidable antagonist nearby to the east, became seriously weakened. First came Desert Storm in 1991, then the subsequent sanctions, effective independence of Kurds in the north, no fly zones in the north and south, and then the occupation of Iraq in 2003.

Having taken over control of territory to reduce the hazards from attack by Arabs from outside, Israel found itself harassed by people from inside those territories. Its erstwhile primary enemy, the Palestine Liberation Organization, had been chased to Jordan and then Lebanon. In 1978 Israel struck deep into Lebanon to drive out the PLO leadership and then repeated another incursion into southern Lebanon in 2006. The latter operation accomplished little but demonstrating how strong a resistance the Shia Hezbollah could put up, and further frustrating Israelis over support for Hezbollah from predominantly Shiite Iran.

Hamas, Hezbollah, and al Qaeda

Three groups that the US State department lists as terrorist organizations came to be particularly problematic for the US government having its way in the Middle East: Hamas, Hezbollah, and al Qaeda. Hamas was less receptive to compromise than the al Fatah Palestinian leaders Israel had been trying to negotiate a settlement with. In February 2008, Hamas' military wing reportedly "signaled a possible end to its self-imposed moratorium" of three years on attacks like a lethal suicide strike in Dimona in southern Israel that month.[3] Concentrating their attacks on Israelis rather than US assets, Hamas was most directly problematic for Israel and the least so for the United States.

Hezbollah's principal military importance was its power within southern Lebanon, particularly after expected attacks organized under the leadership of Imad Mugniyah failed to materialize outside Lebanon, following an earlier campaign of violence against US targets connected with the US presence in Lebanon in 1982. Reportedly, Mugniyah was a leader of the Islamist Jihad Organization wing of Hezbollah and the United States considered him "so fearsome that a $25 million bounty was placed on his head".[4] According to a report by Robert Worth and Nada Bakri, at the time of his death in a car bomb explosion in 2008, "Mr. Mugniyah, 45, was suspected of planning the 1983 bombings of the American Embassy and a Marine barracks in Beirut; the hijacking of a T.W.A. jetliner in 1985; and a series of high-profile kidnappings in the 1980s, among other crimes".[5] However, the United States also identified Hezbollah as responsible for the first major attack on US personnel in Saudi Arabia, the Khobal Towers bombing in 1996. The primary direct significance of Hezbollah to the United States since 1996 has been support for that organization coming out of Iran has helped make influential parties within the US government very resistant to the idea of any possible thaw in United States–Iranian relations. An indirect irritant to the United States was that Hezbollah remained a thorn in the side for Israel.

By far the most directly problematic "spoiler" for the United States is al Qaeda. During the ultimately successful 1979–1986 campaign to induce the Soviets to withdraw from Afghanistan, the United States, and Pakistan's Inter-Services Intelligence (ISI) had worked in parallel with the domestic Afghani resistance and the group of expatriates that eventually came to be known as al Qaeda. During the massive 1991 conventional military operation of Desert Storm into Kuwait the United States had no need to work with its erstwhile de facto allies from the time of the struggle to oust the Soviets from Afghanistan.

The 1990–1991 war against Iraq had two additional side effects that would be fateful for the United States and al Qaeda. One of these was that it involved stationing of US troops in Saudi Arabia, and some of these stayed long after operation Desert Storm was over. The second was that the Palestinian Liberation Organization (PLO) had sided with Iraq and thus undermined the PLO's support from Saudi Arabia and other Arab states that had opposed Iraq's takeover of Kuwait. The resulting more tenuous position of the PLO induced its leader Yassar Arafat to enter into serious negotiations over a peace settlement with Israel, but not enough to convince him to accept to offer on the table at the Camp David summit in July 2000. This failure helped precipitate a September 2000 Palestinian uprising known variously as the Second Intifada or al-Aqsa Intifada.

These various events provided the backdrop for reasons reportedly given in October 2001 by al Qaeda Saudi expatriate leader Osama bin Laden for the year 2001 attacks on the United States. The grievances cited included the US presence on the Arabian Peninsula, the plight of the Palestinians, and the consequences of US actions for Lebanon and Iraq.[6] Ironically, the US invasion of Iraq facilitated a decision to "withdraw about 7,000 US military personnel from Saudi Arabia and terminate a significant military presence there that lasted more than a decade".[7] However, the occupation of Iraq added another grievance that brought transnational forces directly in conflict with US troops and was thus not immediately a direct step toward disengagement between such forces and the United States.

A Life of Its Own

The Israeli settlements deep in the West Bank and what the US administration labeled the "War on Terror" are prime examples of how conflict originally grounded on a competition of military and economic interests can help spawn an ideological commitment that takes on a life of its own. The Second Intifada evidently reinforced a growing conviction within the Israeli security establishment that Israeli settlements deep in the West Bank had become a security burden instead of being the military asset that was envisioned during the era of tank warfare against neighboring Arab states. After a suicide bombing in Tel Aviv in June 2001, there was increasing popular support for the idea of fencing off the West Bank. In February 2004, Israeli Prime Minister Sharon surprised even his own skeptical foreign minister by kicking off a "disengagement" from a proposed future Palestinian state that would start with removing 17 of 20 Jewish settlements from Gaza.[8] Initially, it was also skeptical because Sharon's plan "would in effect abandon the idea of negotiating with the Palestinians to achieve final statehood," but the US administration soon expected to get behind Sharon's plan.[9] The Israeli government's embrace of this idea created a dilemma. Which of the settlements in the West Bank would be included on the western side of the new barrier, and which would end up being surrounded by Palestinians on

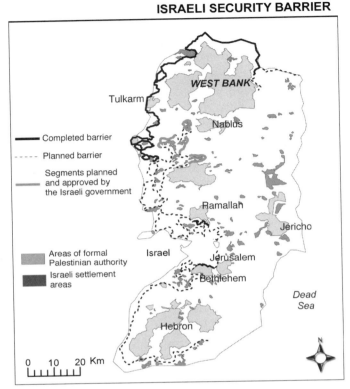

Fig. 29.1. Israeli security barrier 2002 plan.

the other side of it? The tentative decision on this made in 2002 is illustrated in Fig. 29.1.[10]

Later, several fateful decisions were made. First, the idea of extending the barrier down the Jordan River valley in the eastern portion of the West Bank appears to have been abandoned. Second, the extension of the barrier into the areas southwest of Nablus was still being pursued as of 2007, to encompass Kedukmin within the northeastern spur and the large settlement at Ari'el within the eastern spur. Third, the enclosed area around Jerusalem was to be extended farther into the West Bank than that indicated in Fig. 29.1. Finally, to the south the fence was to more closely follow the original Israel and West Banks separation line shown in Fig. 29.1.

If the entire area west of the security fence comes to define the Irsaeli position on what must be excluded the boundaries of a Palestinian state, then the convoluted path of the north central section of the fence could be a particular sticking point in negotiations with the Palestinians. However, on the other hand, from the viewpoint of domestic Israeli politics, any attempts to remove the Israeli settlements near Hebron is likely to pose a particular problem.

The settlers who moved into locations near and within the West Bank and Gaza had a mix of economic and ideological motivations. Near Jerusalem, simply acquiring suburban land for housing close to the city could be a factor. For recent immigrants, government support for living in more exposed areas was an economic motivation. For other settlers, particularly those attempting to throw up small settlements in the West Bank not officially approved by the Israeli government, ideological motivations appear to play a significant role.

When Israel took action to remove all of its settlements from Gaza in 2005, it encountered brief but nonviolent resistance from some who refused to vacate voluntarily. However, after Prime Minister Arial Sharon fell into a coma at the beginning of 2006, the government shrank back from continuing such removals in the West Bank. The underlying difficulty is that the domestic balance of power in Israel's politics is sufficiently delicate that only an unusually forceful leader like Sharon can even seriously contemplate weathering the political storm that would follow from an attempt to remove enough of the settlements east of the fence so that a commitment to their security would no longer provide such a drain on Israeli resources.

Settlements in the Occupied Territories

It was not just domestic politics in Israel that stood in the way of following up on Arial Sharon's plans for the future of Israeli settlements east of its security fence. For all the attention focused on a Palestine peace settlement starting in 2007, the US government did not appear to have a viable plan for breaking the logjam over the settlements question. For ever since the 1978 Camp David accords, the substantial flow of aid to Israel has essentially been a blank check. In 1991 US Secretary of State James Baker did follow through with threat not to give the Israelis a "$10 billion five-year loan guarantee for housing Soviet immigrants without an Israeli agreement to halt future settlements in the occupied West Bank, Golan Heights, and Gaza strip".[11] In the end, the United States did reduce previously anticipated loan guarantees by the estimated amount Israel spent on settlements in the occupied territories.[12] However, what was more important was that direct financial and military aid to Israel continued over the following sixteen years, as did settlement construction. Baker's statements on the settlement issue indicated that his administration had concluded either that additions to settlements had at least temporarily become more of a liability than an asset. Alternatively the conclusion may have been that trying to reduce the appearance that the United States was directly under such settlement activity was politically expedient.

The estimated number of people in Israeli settlements in the West Bank and Gaza Strip combined grew from about 11,000 in 1977, to about 80,000 in 1984, to over 150,000 in 1994.[13] By 2006, there were reportedly 406,000–415,000 Israelis living east of Israel's 1967 boundaries. Of these, 184,000–200,000 were in the eastern part of Jerusalem, an additional 171,000–175,000 in locations expected to end up on the Israeli side of the security fence, and another 52,000–70,000 in areas expected to end up on the West Bank side of the fence.[14]

"An Israeli advocacy group, using maps and figures leaked from the government, says that 39 percent of the land held by Israeli settlements is privately owned by Palestinians," according to a 2006 New York Times article.[15] A spokesman for the Israeli Civil Administration responded that a committee had been working on this question for three years but had not "finished checking everything." However, he "noted that sometimes Palestinians would sell land to Israelis but be unwilling to admit to the sale publicly because they feared retribution as a collaborator." This apparently muddled legal situation that is likely to further complicate an already difficult disengagement between Israel and a Palestinian state that is, even if unhappily,[16] eventually to be recognized on both sides as a *fait accompli*.

It was one thing for the Israeli military to conclude that settlements deep in the West Bank had become a strategic liability, but quite another thing for Israel's political leaders to pick through the domestic political minefield of removing them. Removal of settlers from Gaza was accomplished with minimal resistance in August 2005, and some isolated actions were taken against unauthorized settlements in the West Bank over the following year. However, the three thorniest problems were expected stiff resistance to removal of settlers in the south near Hebron, the retention of settlements in West Samaria, and the question of what to do about settlements out east in the Jordan valley. As noted above, the West Samaria settlements cut fairly deep into the West Bank, east to the university town of Ariel and north to Kedumim, about 10 km west of Nablus. At one point, an estimated 42,000 settlers lived in West Samaria, the largest concentration outside the Jerusalem area.[17] The total settler population in the Jordan valley is much lower, but the settlements there are spread out all the way from the northern border to the south of Jericho.

The relocation of 52,000–70,000 people would likely involve up-front expenses several times larger than the total annual US aid to Israel. Accounting not only for housing but also for the total public and private capital investment, it could require as much as $300,000 per capita to make resettlement of 52,000–70,000 people over the Israeli side of the fence both economically and politically attractive. This is the same amount of money as in a reference to press reports in a US Congressional Research Report of the costs for resettling Israelis out of Gaza,[18] and it is consistent with Israel's per capita GDP and a typical overall capital depreciation rate of around ten percent per annum. Assuming a range of half-to-all of this amount the overall cost spread over ten years for 52,000–70,000 people would be in the range of 1.1–1.5 billion dollars per year. Roughly speaking, this

364 Energy and International War

Table 29.1.   Partial list of US aid to Israel (G$US2008).

Fiscal Year	Loans All Types	Grants	
		Military	Other
1977	2.57	1.69	1.72
1978	2.42	1.55	1.71
1979	8.32	3.56	1.52
1980	2.60	1.22	1.35
1981	2.50	1.12	1.78
1982	1.84	1.18	1.78
1983	1.97	1.56	1.67
1984	1.70	1.70	1.86
1985		2.69	3.80
1986	0.03	3.27	3.66
1987		3.28	2.26
1988		3.14	2.17
1989		3.00	2.07
1990		2.81	1.95
1991		2.74	2.91
1992		2.66	1.92
1993		2.59	1.88
1994		2.53	1.82
1995		2.46	1.78
1996		2.38	1.78
1997		2.34	1.73
1998		2.31	1.64
1999		2.32	1.44
2000		3.77	1.22
2001		2.35	1.07
2002		2.37	0.94
2003		3.52	0.75
2004		2.37	0.60
2005		2.35	0.44
2006		2.35	0.29

Source: Congressional Research Service (Sharp, 2007). Adjusted to $US2008 using end of previous calendar year US consumer price index.

could be accomplished in principle by offering Israel a "double or nothing" deal on continuing the levels of non-military economic assistance listed[19] in Table 29.1 for the 1993–2000 Clinton Administration years. That is, economic aid would increase by something like $1.3 billion per year if accompanied by such resettlement but would otherwise not be given at all. However, US domestic politics made such a policy politically infeasible both during Bill Clinton's presidency and those of the presidents Bush that preceded and followed it.

Israel, Palestine, and US Politics

There is no question that political support within the United States for continuing aid to Israel has been widespread both in the US Congress and various US administrations, particularly since 1979. The inflation-adjusted average of the total of all of foreign aid figures in Table 29.1 is $5 billion per year. This includes the loan column, given that payments on the loans have often been waived.[20] The inflation-adjusted average from 1987, after the loan programs accounted for in Table 29.1 ended, is $4.2 billion per year. The totals for the Iraq occupation years of 2004–2006 were lower. However, in July 2007 the US administration pushed just over $30 billion of military aid for Israel over 10 years. The context of this proposal was that it followed one to include a variety of advanced weapons in sale of $20 billion worth of arms to Saudi Arabia and its neighbors.

> The proposed package of advanced weaponry for Saudi Arabia, which includes advanced satellite-guided bombs, upgrades to its fighters and new naval vessels, has made Israel and some of its supporters in Congress nervous. Senior officials who described the package on Friday said they believed that the administration had resolved those concerns, in part by promising Israel $30.4 billion in military aid over the next decade, a significant increase over what Israel has received in the past 10 years.[21]

A question of particular interest in this chapter is whether that a controversial article by professors John Mearsheimer and Steve Walt (2006) referred to as the "Israel lobby" in the United States has taken on a durable life of its own, capable of guiding US foreign policy even after it becomes clear that oil is too economically and militarily marginal to make the Middle East especially strategically important.[22] Mearsheimer and Walt seem to view the Israel lobby as a primal cause of US foreign policy in the region. A critique by Stephen Zunes makes the opposite claim.[23] Namely, the apparent influence of US political forces pushing to support Israeli government policy is rather a product of situation where those policies have been seen as useful to the United States in pursuit of US foreign policy goals. Zunes also points out that much of the US aid to Israel is provided in the form of military equipment, the manufacture and field testing of which serve special interests much more broadly based, globally focused, and financially powerful than what Mearsheimer and Walt identify as the Israel lobby.

Taking a more balanced view with a broader historical perspective, it is useful to keep in mind that all special and ideological interests that happen to align with wider perceived economic and military interests do to some extent have the capability to take on a life of their own. This does create a certain amount of momentum and tendency toward continuation of policies on conflict situations that outlive their practical usefulness. This can be particularly problematic in common situations where generational lag is getting in the way of rethinking old patterns of behavior. The earlier role of Israeli settlements in the West Bank as a tripwire and sacrificial frontline in the way of Arab-armored division attacks is a case in point. However, when political allies outlive their usefulness, they can be expected to sooner or later be cast aside. Sometimes this can happen quite quickly, and sometimes this can take a long time. The case of Israeli settlements deep in the West Bank is a particularly thorny one. This may continue for a decade or more to create friction that stirs up spoiler actions that impede a realignment of US perceptions about the strategic importance of oil-producing countries. On the other hand, there is some smaller chance that weariness with the conflict on the part of both the Israelis and the Palestinians might allow a tolerably stable resolution of the problem considerably more quickly.

Durability of the Long War

An underlying feature that is much more generic than the specifics of interactions of Israelis with their neighbors concerns the staying power of ideological constructs that spring up during international conflict. The idea, on both sides, that there is an irreconcilable conflict between "the West" and an intrinsically implacable and violent "Islamic jihad" is one example. The differences on either side are whether "the West" is seen as civilized or decadent and whether violence used against it is justified or terrorist. The historical roots in the oil politics of this contraposition have been amply illustrated here already. From them arose al Qaeda, the unprecedented attacks on the United States of 2001, and the response of the invasions of Afghanistan and Iraq.

Again, the question of interest in this chapter is to what extent these ideological concepts have taken on such a life of their own that they can maintain the momentum behind conflict long after the underlying economic motivation has largely evaporated. The likely answer is, quite a while. The reason is that there is a mutual reinforcement between the idea that oil is strategically significant, the idea that opposing sides of the conflicts this spawned are intrinsically implacable foes, and continual jockeying for domestic political advantage. On each side of the conflict, political factions are repeatedly tempted to point to the need to struggle against an external enemy as a foil for distracting attention from domestic political issues. This is as evident in political struggles within Palestine and Iran as it is in places like the United States and Israel.

It is an oft repeated pattern that dominant concentrations of wealth and power point to external threats as the key problem, justifying a continuation of a *status quo* where they retain domestic political dominance. However, raising concerns about external threats is a tactic also used by politicians who precipitate changes in the distribution of wealth and power. An example is when presidential candidate John Kennedy pointed to a putative strategic nuclear missile gap between the United States and the Soviet Union, bringing with him to the White House a vice president who went on to embrace the civil rights movement and the so-called war on poverty.

One way or another, the focal point of the external enemy invoked in domestic political struggles in the United States will wander away from the Middle East and land elsewhere. Shortly after the cold war, attention was focused on Japan as a commercial rival. After Japanese economic growth stalled in the late 1990s, the compass needle wandered for a while towards China. As the cost of energy imports from the Middle East eventually becomes a much smaller fraction of importers' GDP, by virtual of new events or just random walk, the focus will move elsewhere. This is, however, likely to take a long time, for the reasons examined in Chapter 30 of this book. The most interesting question is not so much the eventual outcome, but whether conflicts involving the world's strongest economies will continue to lead to war or tend in the direction of negotiated solutions. The future of energy and international war is an important part of this puzzle.

Endnotes

[1]   Segev (2007).
[2]   Segev (2007).
[3]   Kershner (2008).
[4]   Risen (2008).
[5]   Worth and Bakri (2008).
[6]   CNN (2002).
[7]   Hedges (2003).
[8]   Bennet (2004).
[9]   Weisman (2004).
[10] Jewish Virtual Library (2008); c.f. Economist (2003).
[11] Friedman (1991).

Spoilers 369

Mark (2004).
Kimmerling and Migdal (2002, pp. 287, 436, 442).
Wilson (2006); Rutenberg and Erlanger (2006).
Erlanger (2006).
Palestinian Center PSR (2003).
Mideast Web (2002).
Mark (2004).
Sharp (2007).
Mark (2004).
Cloud (2007).
Mearsheimer and Walt (2006).
Zunes (2006).

Chapter 30

Transition to Sustainability

The inevitable transition away from industrial economies' energy supply being dominated by fossil fuels will have profound implications for the future of energy and international war. Renewable energy sources are by their nature geographically distributed. Uranium ore accounts for only a few percent of the cost of nuclear electricity and results to be referenced here suggest that this will remain the case through much or all of the current century. Even in the very long run, widely geographically distributed lower grade ores and even seawater should be able to provide uranium at costs low enough to raise the price of nuclear electricity by less than about fifteen percent.

The order in which comparatively inexpensively extracted fossil fuel resources will be depleted enough to reduce their economic importance is: oil, natural gas, coal. The fluid fossil fuels, oil and natural gas, will become marginally economically important primarily as a result of depletion of resources that can be extracted cheaply enough to be competitive with other energy sources. Inexpensively mined coal is much more plentiful, and its use is more likely to be limited by costs of transporting it to distant markets and restrictions on emissions of carbon dioxide into the atmosphere. Since there are no signs of a renewal of international conflict over control of coal resources, the primary focus in this chapter is on fluid fossil fuels.

One possibility is that the outcome from the occupation of Iraq convinces the United States to act consistently with a realization that oil is no longer strategically important, and other major oil importers follow suit. If so, natural gas is likely to "go along for the ride" with oil. Another possibility is that one more round of intense US involvement in a war in the Middle East will first come and go. A third possibility is that international wars over who has control of fluid fossil resources will persist until the rate of use of such fuels in the global economy is substantially reduced.

This chapter delves into these three types of outcome in order to try to get some insight into which is the most likely. It then reiterates that there are no other natural resources regionally concentrated and economically important enough for the control over them to be an enduring focus of international war. So the end of an era of war over who has control over fluid fossil fuel resources is likely to be the end of a greater era of such conflicts over natural resources, reaching back even before the Spanish conquistadors, quest for gold and silver. Major international wars, if they continue at all, should then much more transparently be products of internal political conflicts disconnected from concerns about the supposed strategic importance of natural resources extracted from the earth.

Recurring Middle East Wars

Table 30.1 summarized some of the conflicts in the Middle East that the United States or Britain have had some kind of involvement with, starting with the defeat of the Ottoman Empire in WWI. Not counting the shorter duration conflict in cases where two conflicts overlapped, the average time between the end of one of the conflicts[1] listed in Table 30.1 and the end of the next is 12 years. If this pattern persists, then another war could be expected to start and end within 12 years of the end of the conflict that started with the 2003 US-led invasion of Iraq. As long as the predominant opinion that the Middle East is strategically important continues to survive the experience of the occupation of Iraq, some sort of US involvement in such a conflict is reasonably likely to recur.

"It's tough to make predictions, especially about the future," a quote attributed to Yogi Berra, applies much more strongly to particular events than to the extrapolation of general trends. The nature and outcome of a conflict that may end more than 12 years in the future is a good example. What can be done is that some problem areas that could lead to future conflict can be identified. A future

Table 30.1. Anglo-American roles in Middle East conflicts.

Name	Other Countries	Start	Stop	
World War I	Central Powers; Allies	1914	1918	Involvement of USA and UK
Iraqi Revolt	Iraq	1920	1922	Suppresed by UK
WWII in Mideast	Iraq, Axis; Allies	1940	1943	UK overcame Iraqi Fascists
Palestine	Israel; Arabs	1939	1948	Ended UK mandate
Suez	Israel, France; Egypt	1956	1956	USA opposed UK
Six Day	Israel; Its Neigbors	1967	1967	US arms replace French
Yom Kippur	Israel; Its Neigbors	1973	1973	US emergency airlift
Lebanon	Israel; Lebanon	1982	1985	US withdrew in 1984
Iran-Iraq	Iraq; Iran	1980	1986	USA helped Iraq
Kuwait	Iraq; UN	1980	1980	USA/UK led Iraqi ouster
Iraq	Miscellaneous; Iraq	2003		UK helped US occupation

Source: Dictionary of Wars (Kohn, 1999) for dates for wars up to 1999.
After the six-day War, the United States replaced France as a primary supplier of advanced weaponry to Israel.

Kurdish push for independence or autonomous control of oil resources in or near Kurdish-majority areas is one possibility. The United States and especially Israel have strongly opposed other countries in the Middle East acquiring the capability to make nuclear weapons. As advanced nuclear technology capabilities spread in the region, a calculated or miscalculated attempt to suppress the spread of such technology could also precipitate warfare. If a US withdrawal from Iraq leads to a redirection of attacks on US assets to the US homeland, the reaction could also lead to another war. The situations in the West Bank, Gaza, and Lebanon are often fluid, and internal conflict there could still over to embroil neighbors. There are other possibilities that involve possible conflicts between countries adjacent to the Persian Gulf, which might again attract intervention by the United States and possibly some of its allies.

A particularly difficult situation could arise in the Middle East if Saudi Arabia does not manage to guide OPEC through a gradual evolution of oil prices. If the price stays high enough and long enough, it will stimulate non-OPEC oil production and oil use efficiency measures that could subsequently put enough downward pressure on prices to precipitate another collapse of effective OPEC cartel action. In countries so dependent on oil revenues that per capita incomes fall far and fast enough, this could produce domestic turmoil that substantially perturbs oil production and perhaps also stimulates international conflict.

Looking Deeper into the Crystal Ball

The likely outcome for the United States of the 2003 occupation of Iraq was apparently five years into the war. The chances for the originally envisioned stable, fully democratic, unified, and durably pro-American government in Iraq were slim. Even if a new president took office in 2009 or 2013 with the intention of making an all-out effort to achieve the original goal, it was unlikely that the required domestic support and conditions in Iraq would be sufficient to achieve such an outcome. If Iraq's Defense Minister was correct in January 2008 in forecasting that US security help would be needed for another decade,[2] then judging by the available opinion poll measures of how US public support for wars has declined with their duration he was likely to be disappointed.[3] On the other hand, the US military and political establishments were also determined to eventually execute an orderly troop draw-down that would avoid a repetition of the traumatically chaotic way the Vietnam War ended. For the United States, the part of its combat battalions in the fight against Iraqi insurgents appeared destined to end "not with a bang, but with a whimper." For this reason, the occupation of Iraq appeared unlikely to traumatic enough to trigger the kind of epiphany about oil and war that the combined experience of WWI, the Great Depression, and WWII did about the strategic roles of coal and steel.

What impact would yet another future Middle East war have on attitudes about the strategic role of oil is very hard to say. Such a war

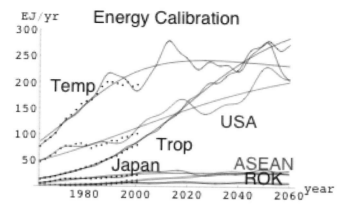

Fig. 30.1. Biennially averaged energy use rates (points) and fits with periodic variations (curves with multiple maxima) and background trends (other curves).

could have but a transient impact on international oil markets, like the 1990 Kuwait war, or it could trigger fundamental changes if it is much more traumatic. The best that can be done with looking deeper into the crystal ball is to examine how long-term global trends in population growth, overall economic production, and the use of various energy sources are likely to extrapolate farther into the future. Figures 30.1 and 30.2 give one example of such extrapolations, respectively, for total energy and for fluid fossil fuels.[4,a]

Figure 30.1 shows extrapolations of fits to the full temporal variation and background trends for total energy use in six different regions. These are divided on a geographical basis into two groups. The curve labeled "Trop" includes all countries lying wholly between 40° north and south latitude, except for the Republic of Korea (ROK) and the countries in the Association of Southeast Asian Nations

---

[a] These results based on a data-calibrated of economic development and energy use that smoothly extrapolate past background trends into the future without allowing for any fundamental changes in modes of economic development. Major departures from past behavior are not accounted for. For example, there could a substantially larger growth in tropical region energy use if the world successfully met the "millennium challenge" of lifting the poorest billion people out of a recurring poverty trap, as suggested by Sachs (2005).

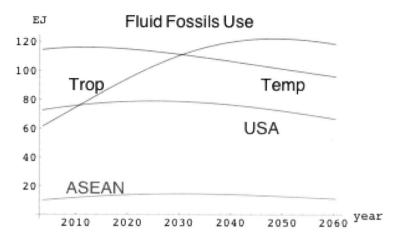

Fig. 30.2.   Extrapolated annual use trend for fluid fossil fuels (oil and natural gas).

(ASEAN). Except for China, most countries normally labeled as "developing" are included in the "Trop" group. Other than Japan and the United States, results for the rest of the world are included in the curve labeled "Temp." The curves in Fig. 30.1 include both background trends, which may sensibly extrapolate into the more distant future, and periodic oscillations of energy use around those trends. The longer-period oscillations of overall energy use in the past were heavily influenced by long-term variations in oil prices. For the reasons discussed above, such oscillations in oil prices are reasonably likely to recur. This could result from the overshoot of oil prices in the decade following 1998 compared to what the market can sustain, a subsequent correction, and quite possibly another overcorrection followed by a return back towards the underlying background trend reflecting the depletion of cheaply extracted resources. Coordinate with these trends in oil prices are variations in the overall economy and use of other energy resources as well.

Historical data give some hints on the timing and to some extent the size of the next oscillation in energy use. It is much harder to project whether subsequent such oscillations will occur, and if so what their timing and size will be. This expectation has been confirmed by a systematic study of probability distributions for energy use futures for models that produce the kind of results shown in Fig. 30.1.[5] So to break down total energy use into its constituent energy sources extrapolated farther into the future, it suffices just to take account of the background trends around which such oscillations occur. Examples are shown for total energy use rates as the smoother curves in Fig. 30.1, and for the use of fluid fossil fuels and nuclear energy in Figs. 30.2–30.4.[6] The projected drop-off in the use of fluid fossil fuels by the United States and other temperate region countries in Fig. 30.2 for the first half of the 20th century is very gradual. This is counterbalanced by a rise in use in developing countries through mid-century, notably including India.

An alternative viewpoint on energy futures is that global oil and natural gas use rates will each evolve along a symmetric bell-shaped curve. This would imply a much steeper decline after the peak use rates for fluid fossil fuels than shown in Fig. 30.2. The success that M. King Hubbert had back in 1956 in using a symmetric bell-shaped curve to forecast the subsequent timing of peak oil production in the contiguous forty-eight United States[7] spawned many sweeping conclusions about how such a behavior would apply to global oil production more generally. However, the addition of new oil reserves as prices rise and induce changes in technology and types of usable oil resources are mechanisms that tend to produce a temporally asymmetric use pattern, with a long tail-off after a steep rise. The same is likely to apply to natural gas.

The conclusion drawn here is that the transition to a sustainable energy future with much smaller rates of use of fluid fossil fuels is likely to be a very gradual one. While the ratio of fluid fossil use to total GDP is likely to decline substantially during the current century, a rapid decline in total rate of use of fluid fossil fuels is unlikely unless there are dramatic advances in competing energy sources, e.g. through the use of much more advanced technology than currently being developed for the production of liquid biofuels. This in turn implies that the process of understanding that oil and natural gas are not strategically significant in the WWII sense is likely to be predominantly driven by political and sociological rather than by technological processes.

It is possible that a period of reflection after the end of US combat operations in Iraq will lead to a fundamental reassessment of the idea that oil is so strategically important as to require being continually prepared for massive military intervention in the Middle East or other oil-exporting regions.[8] It is more likely that another round of such intervention will have to go sour before the impact of such a reassessment sinks in. Given particular combinations of domestic US internal politics and continuing tension over US policy on Palestine and elsewhere, it is also possible that reaction to attacks on the assets of the United States or its allies might perpetuate well into the present century the myth that oil, natural gas, or both are strategically important enough to require preparing for and executing interventions in internally troubled producing nations. It is also possible, though less likely, that other major fluid fossil fuel importers will undertake such interventions even if the United States evolves to a position where it is not willing to take the lead on accomplishing them.

Nuclear Energy and Nuclear Deterrence

One likely consequence of a shift away from fossil fuel energy sources sometime in the 21st century is a substantial growth in the rate of use of nuclear energy (c.f. Fig. 30.3). One reason for this is that use of wind and solar energy to produce electricity gives time-varying outputs that are very expensive to smooth out using overnight or seasonal energy storage. Also, other renewable electricity resources, primarily dams, are economically competitive with nuclear power only in restricted amounts and locations. If nuclear electric power production spreads to new regions, then so too will at least the technological base for potential nuclear weapons programs. As shown for the ASEAN case in Fig. 30.4, this process could be well along the road by about 2030. Even if countries with new nuclear electric power programs avoid domestic uranium enrichment and spent nuclear fuel reprocessing, their experience with and operation of nuclear reactors will put them substantially closer to the technical ability to construct nuclear weapons. Some countries may insist on developing domestic

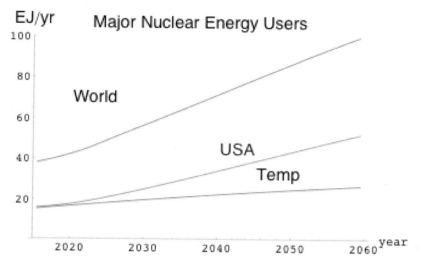

Fig. 30.3. Extrapolated nuclear energy use rates for the United States, other temperate region countries except for Japan, and for the entire world. Energy use rates plotted are the thermal energy released in nuclear power plants before conversion to electricity.

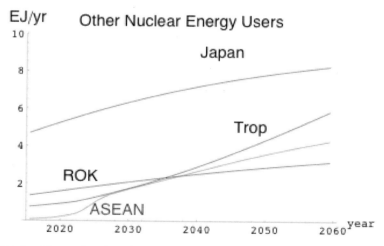

Fig. 30.4. Extrapolated nuclear energy use rates for Japan, the Republic of Korea (ROK), countries in the Association of Southeast Asian Nations (ASEAN), and other countries lying wholly between 40° north and south latitude (Trop). Energy use rates plotted are the thermal energy released in nuclear power plants before conversion to electricity.

capabilities to enrich uranium or recover plutonium from spent nuclear fuel without actually constructing nuclear weapons. Brazil and Japan belong to this category. This brings these countries closer to a state of recessed deterrence, making them effectively impervious to any build-up of conventional forces to invade them where that build-up proceeds faster than they could construct an active nuclear deterrent.

Iran has stated its intention of following Brazil and Japan in what amounts to developing a recessed deterrence posture. Other major oil exporters have announced intentions to acquired nuclear electric production reactors, and could follow the Iranian lead if domestic and international political developments lead them in that direction.

Unfolding developments in the nuclear energy and technology area have two consequences for the future of energy and international war. First, if conventional wars that seriously affect major oil producers persist, then the situation has evolved to the point where recessed or overt nuclear deterrence in such countries will likely not lag many decades behind. Second, the transition to a situation where such countries have acquired recessed or overt nuclear deterrence contains the potential for a confrontation with countries that already have nuclear weapons. Thus, while the nuclear dimension may make wars where energy resources play a major role less likely in the long run, in the transition to this state of affairs the opposite could be the case.

Natural Resources and International War

There is nothing historically inevitable about continuing international war over control of natural resources. A demographic transition is well on the way to nearly stabilizing or even peaking global population in the 21st century.[9] On a global scale, this is a state of affairs unprecedented in human history. The global population is finally becoming limited by fertility control rather than primarily by early mortality from disease, famine, or war. Periodic violent conflict as an inevitable consequence of struggle to survive is being replaced by international war as an option, to be chosen or rejected based on balances of domestic political forces in countries that launch attacks.

Gold, silver, diamonds, fertilizer, virgin timber, and nonprecious metals have all been relegated to minor importance as sources of international conflict over natural resources. Water resources remain important in domestic conflicts with consequences that sometimes spill over borders in Africa. Resolution of potential disputes over transboundary river flows by military means appears to be either impractical for aggrieved parties or more likely to be resolved through ongoing international negotiations over several major watersheds.

It is thus quite possible that the inevitable end to international wars where control of fossil fuels plays a major role could also signal the end of most or all international wars where control over natural resources more generally play a major role. Will international wars based on ideological or boundary disputes left over from an earlier era then persist? Or will international war follow the historical path of slavery, persisting at most in the shadows rather than on the center of the international political stage? Ultimately the answer to this question will not depend on what resources lie in the ground but on what ideas lie in the minds of political leaders and their bodies politic. The following excerpt from the constitution of the United Nations Educational, Cultural, and Scientific Organization inscribed on a monument in front of the US Veterans of Foreign Wars Memorial Building in Washington, DC puts it starkly:

> Since wars begin in the minds of men, it is in the minds of men that the defenses of peace must be constructed.

The conceptions in human minds that lead to war over natural resources or other matters are heavily influenced by the historical circumstances that led them to the point of making decisions between war and peace.

This book was written to shed light on the interactions between war and natural resources in the past, in the present, and in alternative possible futures. The histories of silver, coal, iron, and uranium that have been presented here illustrate how reliance on international trading markets can trump long-standing beliefs that national control over resources is essential for security. Other nonfossil natural mineral resources have played only transient roles in international wars. The same state of affairs for oil and natural gas may take many decades to develop, or the outcome of the war in Iraq could conceivably trigger a realization that the time for this has already come. Which will be the case will depend on how well the implications of the events described herein are understood.

Endnotes

1   Kohn (1999).
2   Shanker (2008).
3   Althaus (2007).
4   Singer and Taylor (2007).
5   Singer *et al.* (2008).
6   Singer and Taylor (2007).
7   Hubbert (1956).
8   ACDIS (2004).
9   UN Secretariat (1998); Cohen (1995, p. 138).

Bibliography

Abrams, E, R Armitage, W Bennett, J Bergner, J Bolton, P Dobriansky, F Fukuyama, R Kagan, Z Khalizad, W Kristol, R Perle, P Rodman, D Rumsfeld, W Schneider Jr, V Weber, P Wolfowitz, R James Woolsey and R Zoellick (1998). Letter to President William J. Clinton. January 26. http://www.newamericancentury.org/iraqclintonletter.htm (accessed 13 February 2008).

ABC News (2008). Transcript: ABC News/Facebook/WMUR Republicans Debate. January 5. http://abcnews.go.com/story?id=4091645 (accessed 11 February 2008).

About Geology (2006). The scandal of coltan: A destructive black gold rush. http://geology.about.com/od/conflictminerals/a/coltan.htm (accessed 11 February 2008).

Addario, L (2008). Congo death rate unchanged since war ended. *New York Times.* January 23.

ACDIS (Arms Control, Disarmament, and International Security Program) and Institute of Government and Public Affairs (IGPA) (2004). *Reinventing Multilateralism.* University of Illinois at Urbana-Champaign, rapporteured by Clifford Singer, James Walsh, and Dean Wilkening. http://www.acdis.uiuc.edu/Reinventing/ (accessed 11 February 2008).

Africa Week (2006). Mhz Network broadcast, June 12.

ACEEE (American Council for an Energy Efficient Economy) (2006). ACEEE estimates of light-duty vehicle tax credits. February. Reproduced at http://www.whybuyhybrid.com/hybrid-buying-incentives.htm (accessed 24 January 2008).

Albright, D and M Hibbs (1992). Iraq's bomb: Blueprints and artifacts. *Bulletin of the Atomic Scientists,* 48 (January/February), 30–40.

Alexander's Gas & Oil Connections (2004). India to build up storage of crude oil. September 21. http://www.gasandoil.com/goc/news/nts43834.htm (accessed 25 January 2008).

Althaus, S (2007). Democracies and war: Popular support for war in the modern U.S. http://www.clinecenter.uiuc.edu/research/fellows/ (accessed 17 February 2008).

An, F and A Sauer (2004). Comparison of passenger vehicle fuel economy and GHG emission standards around the world. December. http://www.pewclimate.org/global-warming-in-depth/all_reports/fuel_economy (accessed 25 January 2008).

Andrews, E (2003). Iraqi looters tearing up archaeological sites. *New York Times*. May 23.

AP (Associated Press) (1990a). Iraqis accused of smuggling nuclear detonating devices. *Champaign–Urbana News-Gazette*. March 28.

———— (1990b). 3 charged with smuggling nuke parts to Iraq. *Champaign–Urbana News-Gazette*. March 29.

———— (2003). Nigerian troops move into delta to put down ethnic riots. *New York Times*. March 20.

———— (2007). Spike in price of oil ignites rally: U.S. plan to double petroleum reserves. *New York Times*. January 24.

———— (2008). U.N. faults Congo army for violence. January 6. http://www.nytimes.com/2008/01/06/world/africa/06congo.html (accessed 5 February 2008).

Arvelund, E and H Timmons (2004). Conoco wins Lukoil bid, a window on Iraq. *New York Times*. September 30.

Asteris, M (1986). The rise and decline of South Wales coal exports, 1870–1930. *Welsh History Review*, 13, 24–43.

Asthana, V (2004). Personal communication.

Baker III, J and L Hamilton (2006). *The Iraq Study Group report*. December. New York: Vintage Books.

Barbosa, D and A Sorkin (2005). Chinese oil giant in takeover bid for U.S. company: Offer exceeds Chevron's; fight over Unocal likely to intensify debate on trade policies. *New York Times*. June 23.

Barraclough, G (ed.) (1978). *The Times atlas of world history*. London: Times Books.

Barringer, F (2003). Moving past scripts, envoys bring emotion to Iraq debate. *New York Times*. February 15.

Barrionuevo, A (2008). Hot prospect for oil's big league: A huge offshore discovery has the potential to make Brazil a major petroleum exporter. *New York Times*. January 11.

Barsky, R and L Kilian (2001). Do we really know that oil caused the great stagflation? A monetary alternative. *NBER Macroeconmics Annual*, 16, 137–183. Chicago: University of Chicago Press.

Bash, D (2003). White House pressed on 'mission accomplished' sign: Navy suggested it, White House made it, both sides agreed. CNN.com./Inside Politics. October 23. http://www.cnn.com/2003/ALLPOLITICS/10/28/mission.accomplished/ (accessed 10 February 2008).

Batteries News (2006). After cellular phones, will hybrid vehicle be the next mass market for batteries? March.

BBC (British Broadcasting Company) (2006). On this day, 13 September 1993: Rabin and Arafat shake on peace deal.

BBC News (British Broadcasting Company News) (2006a). Regions and territories: Western Sahara. April 27. http://news.bbc.co.uk/1/hi/world/africa/country_profiles/3466917.stm (accessed 27 May 2006).

——— (2006b). Russia signs gas deal with China. January 15. http://news.bbc.co.uk/1/hi/world/asia-pacific/4828244.stm (accessed 6 February 2008).

——— (2007a). Country profiles: Timeline Angola. August 28. http://news.bbc.co.uk/1/hi/world/africa/country_profiles/1839740.stm (accessed 21 January 2008).

——— (2007b). Country profiles: Timeline Algeria. December 12. http://news.bbc.co.uk/1/hi/world/middle_east/811140.stm (accessed 21 January 2008).

——— (2007c). Country profiles: Timeline Venezuela. December 4. http://news.bbc.co.uk/1/hi/world/americas/1229348.stm (accessed 21 January 2008).

——— 2008a. Country profiles: Timeline Saudi Arabia. January 15. http://news.bbc.co.uk/2/low/middle_east/820515.stm (accessed 21 January 2008).

Beaubouef, B (2007). International pipeline growth continues, September 1, http://www.pipelineandgastechnology.com/story.php?storyfile=bdc9b731-d452-4354-820b-5bf06bfe2e55.html (accessed 18 January 2008).

Becker, G (1901). *Report on the Geology of the Philippine Islands.* Washington: Government Printing Office.

Bellis, M (2003). Lester Allan Pelton — Water turbines and the beginnings of hydroelectric power. http://inventors.about.com/library/inventors/bl_lester_pelton.htm#How%20are%20Turbines%20Used%20to%20Generate%20Electricity (accessed 10 February 2008).

Bennet, J (2003). Mideast next for Bush: After Iraq, a strong hand. *New York Times.* April 25.

——— (2004). Angering settlers, Sharon says most may have to leave Gaza: Plan set it talks fail, but no date is given — Arafat scoffs. *New York Times.* February 3.

Bernstein, R (2003). With its nuances, Iraq report can't resolve U.N. stalemate. *New York Times.* February 15.

Berry, W (2003). A citizen's response to the National Security Strategy of the United States of America. *New York Times.* February 9.

Bichelonne, J and P Angot (1939). *Le basin ferrifère de Lorraine.* Nancy–Strasbourg: Imprimerie Berger–Levrault.

Blagov, S (2006). Russia's new China-bound gas pipeline plan sparks controversy. *Eurasia Daily Monitor.* March 31. http://www.jamestown. org/edm//article.php?article_id=2370940 (accessed 6 February 2008).

Bloy, M (2002). The Crimean War: Immediate causes. http://www.victorian web.org/history/crimea/immcauses.html (accessed 4 February 2008).

Bradsher, K (2008). A new, global oil quandary: costly fuel means costly calories. *New York Times.* January 19.

Broad, W (1991). U.N. says Iraq was building H-bomb and bigger A-bomb. *New York Times.* October 15.

Browne, M (1990). Atomic agency invited by Iraqis for inspections: Iraq invites atomic agency to inspect stock of uranium. *New York Times.* November 16.

———— (1991). Army reported ready for Iraqi germ warfare. *New York Times.* January 6.

Browning, R (1993). *The War of the Austrian Succession.* New York: St. Martin's Press.

Bumiller, Elisabeth. 2003. Baker is named to restructure Iraq's huge debt: A Bush troubleshooter; White House move is seen as admission of urgent rebuilding program. *New York Times.* December 6.

Bunch, W (2003). The invasion force. Knight Ridder Newspapers, *Champaign–Urbana News-Gazette.* February 2.

Burns, J (2003a). In Iraqi capital, sirens precede two direct hits. *New York Times.* March 21.

———— (2003b). A staggering blow strikes at the heart of the Iraqi capital. *New York Times.* March 22.

———— (2003c). As allied troops race north, Iraq warns of a fierce fight. *New York Times.* March 24.

———— (2003d). Hussein rallies Iraqi defenders to hold Baghdad: Leader says the allies will be dragged into a 'quagmire' by guerilla warfare. *New York Times.* March 25.

—————— (2003e). Blasts in Baghdad: Two explosions are said to kill 17 civilians — Cause is unclear. *New York Times*. March 25.

—————— (2003f). Iraqi defense chief vows fight, predicting Baghdad clash in days. *New York Times*. March 28.

—————— (2003g). Iraq says blast in Baghdad kills dozens of civilians; U.S. blamed. *New York Times*. March 29.

—————— (2003h). Iraqi general says 4,000 volunteered for suicide attacks. *New York Times*. March 31.

—————— (2003i). Warning of doom, edgy Iraqi leaders put on brave front. *New York Times*. April 1.

—————— (2003j). As U.S. moves in, Iraqi TV presents a relaxed Hussein: Film images of Baghdad stroll seek to dispel theory that the country's chief is dead. *New York Times*. April 5.

—————— (2003k). Dissonance of guns heralds ground war in Iraq's capital. *New York Times*. April 7.

—————— (2003l). Capital has look of a battlefield: Defenders face Americans on streets and bridges of city. *New York Times*. April 8.

—————— (2003m). Key section of city is taken in a street-by-steet fight. *New York Times*. April 9.

—————— (2003n). Cheers, tears, and looting in capital's streets. *New York Times*. April 10.

—————— (2003o). Looting and a suicide attack as chaos grows in Baghdad. *New York Times*. April 11.

—————— (2003p). G.I. who pulled the trigger shares anguish of 2 deaths. *New York Times*. April 12.

—————— (2003q). Baghdad residents begin a long climb to an ordered city. *New York Times*. April 14.

—————— (2003r). In the streets, a shadow lifts. *New York Times*. December 15.

—————— (2004a). 7 U.S. soldiers die in Iraq as Shiite militia rises up. *New York Times*. April 5.

—————— (2004b). Leading Shiites and rebel meet on Iraqi standoff: New hopes for solution; influential clerics begin negotiations to resolve conflicts with G.I.'s. *New York Times*. April 13.

—————— (2006). Military considers sending as many as 35,000 more U.S. troops to Iraq, McCain says. *New York Times*. December 15.

Butler, D (2003). 5-year hunt fails to net al Qaeda suspect in Africa: Sighting led to Kenya alert; Somalia is seen as sanctuary. *New York Times*. June 14.

Butler, R (2000). *The Greatest Threat: Iraq, Weapons of Mass Destruction, and the Crisis of Global Security.* New York: Public Affairs.

Calantone, C (1994). The dynamic impact of technological advance on gas reserves: A paradigm shift in North American natural gas supply research. In *Proceedings of the Global Gas Resources Workshop,* 19–21 September 1994, C Ruthven (ed.), pp. 82–95. Bureau of Economic Geology of the University of Texas at Austin.

Carey-Webb, A (2002). Colonial and postcolonial literary dialogues — Involuntary servitude: The variations of slavery, http://www.wmich.edu/dialogues/themes/involuntaryservitude.htm (accessed 11 February 2008).

Carter, J (1980). President Jimmy Carter's address to a joint session of Congress on the state of the union. January 28. http://www.c-span.org/executive/transcript.asp?cat=current_event&code=bush_admin&year=1980 (accessed 13 February 2008).

Cave, D (2007). Iraqi factions' self-interest blocks political progress. *New York Times.* August 25.

CEA (Commissariat à l'énergie atomique) (2002). *Elecnuc: Les centrales nucléaires dans le monde (Nuclear power plants in the world), édition 2002.* Paris: CEA.

——— (2006a). *Elecnuc: Les centrales nucléaires dans le monde (Nuclear Power Plants in the World), édition 2006.* Paris: CEA.

——— (2006b). *Mémento sur l'énergie (Energy Data Book), édition 2002.* Paris: CEA.

Chivers, CJ (2003a). Kirkuk's swift collapse leaves a city in chaos. *New York Times.* April 11.

——— (2003b). Groups of Kurds are driving Arabs from northern villages. *New York Times.* April 11.

CIA (Central Intelligence Agency) (2007a). The world factbook: Western Sahara. December 13. https://www.cia.gov/library/publications/the-world-factbook/geos/wi.html (accessed 21 January 2008).

——— (2007b). The world factbook: Iraq. December 13. https://www.cia.gov/library/publications/the-world-factbook/geos/iz.html#Econ (accessed 21 January 2008).

——— (2007c). The world factbook: Azerbaijan. December 13. https://www.cia.gov/library/publications/the-world-factbook/geos/aj.html#Issues (accessed 21 January 2008).

CIEP (Clingendael International Energy Programme) (2003). The role of liquefied natural gas (LNG) in the European gas market, from CIEP Gas

Market Seminar 'The future role of LNG in European natural gas markets,' 21 October 2003, The Hague: The Clingendael Institute, http://www.clingendael.nl/publications/?id=5700&&type=summary (accessed 11 February 2008).

Clarke, R (2004). *Against all enemies: Inside America's war on terror.* New York: Free Press.

Classic Encyclopedia (2008). Based on the 11th Edition of the Encyclopedia Britannica (published 1911). s.v. "Suez Canal," http://www.1911encyclopedia.org/Suez_Canal.

Clayton, L and M Coniff (1999). *A History of Modern Latin America.* Fort Worth: Harcourt Brace.

Cloud, D (2006). U.S. considers large, temporary troop increase in Iraq. *New York Times.* November 21.

—— (2007). U.S. set to offer huge arms deal to Saudi Arabia. 2007. *New York Times.* July 28.

CNN (2001). Khobar towers indictment returned. CNN.com/LawCenter. June 22. http://archives.cnn.com/2001/LAW/06/21/khobar.indictments/ (accessed 21 January 2008).

—— (2002). Transcript of Bin Laden's October interview, http://archives.cnn.com/2002/WORLD/asiapcf/south/02/05/binladen.transcript/ (accessed 26 January 2008).

—— (2003). The changing face of Europe: European Union embarks on expansion. http://www.cnn.com/SPECIALS/2000/eurounion/story/enlarge/ (accessed 11 February 2008).

Cohen, J (1995). *How Many People can the Earth Support?* New York: W. W. Norton.

Cohn, S (1997). *Too Cheap to Meter: An Economic and Philosophical Analysis of the Nuclear Dream.* Albany: State University of New York Press.

Collier, R (2005). China on global hunt to quench its thirst for oil. *San Francisco Chronicle* June 26. http://www.sfgate.com/cgi-bin/article.cgi?file=/c/a/2005/06/26/MNG27DF8HQ1.DTL (accessed 11 February 2008).

Columbia Encyclopedia (2001a). Bessemer process. http://www.bartleby.com/65/be/Bessemr-pro.html (accessed 11 February 2008).

—— (2001b). Ems dispatch. http://www.bartleby.com/65/em/Emsdispa.html (accessed 11 February 2008).

—— (2001c). Haber process. http://www.bartleby.com/65/ha/Haberpro.html (accessed 11 February 2008).

———— (2004). s.v. "Suez Canal," http://www.credoreference.com/entry/4301604 (accessed 04 January 2008).

Conry, B (1994). America's misguided policy of dual containment in the Persian Gulf. Cato Foreign Policy Briefing Vol. 33, November 10. http://www.cato.org/pubs/fpbriefs/fpb-033.html (accessed 4 January 2008).

Consulate General of Brazil, San Francisco (2003). History http://www.brazil.org.nz/main.php?page=brazil_content&article=25 (accessed 11 February 2008).

Cordell, D (2003). Niger. http://www.discoverfrance.net/Colonies/Niger.shtml (accessed 11 February 2008).

Cowell, A (2003a). British dissent over an Iraq war imperil's Blair's political future. *New York Times*. March 12.

———— (2003b). Blari did not knowingly use false report, inquiry is told. *New York Times*. August 12.

CQ Transcripts (2007). Ranking House committee members grill Crocker and Petraeus on U.S. progress in Iraq. *Washingtonpost.com*. http://media.washingtonpost.com/wp-srv/politics/documents/ranking_committee_members_grill_petraeus_crocker_10.html (accessed 9 January 2008).

Crawford, J (2005). *The Last True Story I'll Ever Tell: An Accidental Soldier's Account of the War in Iraq*. New York: Riverhead.

Crossette, B (1995a). U.N. report tells of "heinous" abuses in Iraq. *New York Times*. February 28.

———— (1995b). Iraq hides biological warfare effort, report says. *New York Times*. April 12.

———— (1995c). Iraq admits it produced germ arsenal. *New York Times*. July 6.

Crowther Campbell Associates (2007). Environmental impact assessment concerning storage of oil at Saldhanha Bay South Africa. http://fred.csir.co.za/www/sff/toc.htm (accessed 25 January 2008).

Cunningham, L (2004). Mineral resource of the month: Tantalum. *Geotimes–August*. http://www.agiweb.org/geotimes/aug04/resources.html#mineral (accessed 11 February 2008).

Dao, J (2003). Navy Seals easily seize two oil sites. *New York Times*. March 22.

Darbandi, K (2007). Putin the Great, NATO Ottomans & the pipeline labyrinth. http://www.payvand.com/news/07/oct/1231.html (accessed 21 January 2008).

Dargin, J (2007). Qatar's natural gas: the foreign-policy driver. *Middle East Policy*, 14.3 (Fall), 136.

Davidon, B (1998). *West Africa Before the Colonial Era*. London: Longman.

DDP Secretariat (Dams and Development Projects Secretariat of the United Nations Environment Program) (2006). Mahakali River. http://hqweb. unep.org/dams/documents/ell.asp?story_id=123 (accessed 17 February 2008).

Deffeyes, K (2001). *Beyond Oil: The Impending World Oil Shortage.* Princeton: Princeton University Press.

de Vries, J (1974). *The Dutch Rural Economy in the Golden Age: 1500–1700.* New Haven: Yale University Press.

de Vries, J and AM van der Woude (1997). *The First Modern Economy: Success, Failure, and Perseverance of the Dutch Economy 1500–1815.* Cambridge: Cambridge University Press.

de Vylder, S (1996). The rise and fall of the "Swedish model." Occasional Paper 26. New York: United Nations Human Development Programme.

Dole, R (1990). U.S. Senate debate on the Fiscal Year 1991 budget, broadcast on CSPAN in October, 1990

Diamond, J (1997). *Guns, Germs, and Steel: The Fates of Human Societies.* New York: W. W. Norton.

Diamond, L (2005). *Squandered Victory: The American Occupation and Bungled Effort to Bring Democracy to Iraq.* New York: Henry Holt.

Dimotakis, P, R Grober and N Lewis, study leaders (2006). *Reducing DoD fossil-fuel dependence.* JASON, The Mitre Corporation. September. http://fas.org/irp/agency/dod/jason/ (accessed 4 February 2008).

DoD Fuel Cell ERDC/CERL Programs (2003). Fuel cell information guide. http://www.dodfuelcell.com/proton.html (accessed 11 February 2008).

Duffy, M (2001). Feature articles: The minor powers during World War One — Romania, December 4. http://www.firstworldwar.com/features/minorpowers_romania.htm (accessed 11 February 2008).

EC (European Commission) (2006). "The EU & the Kimberley Process (conflict diamonds): Overview." http://ec.europa.eu/comm/ external_relations/kimb/intro/index.htm, March 2006 (accessed 16 May 2006; subsequently updated at http://ec.europa.eu/ external_relations/kimb/intro/index.htm#kpcs, accessed 11 February 2008).

Eckel, E (1920). *Coal, Iron, and War.* London: George Harrap.

Economides, M and R Oligney (2000). *The Color of Oil.* Katy, TX: Round Oak Publishing.

Economist (2003). Israel's security barrier: A safety measure or land grab? *The Economist,* October 11, 26–28.

Economist Intelligence Unit (2007). Democracy index 2007. http://www.intute.ac.uk/socialsciences/cgi-bin/fullrecord.pl?handle=20070423-091817 (accessed 21 January 2008).

Edgerton, R (2002). *The Troubled Heart of Africa: A History of the Congo*. New York: St. Martin's Press.

El-Fadel, M, Y El-Sayegh, K El-Fadl and D Khorbotly (2003). The Nile river basin: A case study in surface water conflict resolution. *Journal of Natural Resources and Life Sciences Education*, 32, 107–117.

Encyclopedia Britannica (2006). Online: Donets basin. http://www.britannica.com/ebc/article-9362969 (accessed 11 February 2008).

Erlanger, S (2006). Israeli map says West Bank posts sit on Arab land: A new obstacle to peace; one-third of Jewish area is on private property, organization says. *New York Times*. January 21.

——— (2008). Oil-free Israel is set to embrace broad project to promote the use of electric cars. *New York Times*. January 21.

Europa (2008). Treaty of Lisbon: In your country. http://europa.eu/lisbon_treaty/countries/index_en.htm (accessed 8 January 2008).

European Commission Delegation to Australia and New Zealand (2002a). Fifty years at the service of peace and prosperity: The European Coal and Steel Community (ECSC) Treaty expires. June 19. http://europa.eu.int/rapid/pressReleasesAction.do?reference=IP/02/898&format=HTML&aged=0&language=EN&guiLanguage=en (accessed 11 February 2008).

——— (2002b). Expiry of the European Coal and Steel Community (ECSC) Treaty: An overview. June 19. http://europa.eu/rapid/pressReleasesAction.do?reference=MEMO/02/145&format=HTML&aged=0&language=EN&guiLanguage=en (accessed 11 February 2008).

European Parliament and the Council of the European Union (2003). Directive 2003/30/EC on the promotion of the use of biofuels and other renewable fuels for transport. May 8. http://ec.europa.eu/energy/res/legislation/biofuels_en.htm (accessed 25 January 2008).

Everest, L (2004). *Oil, Power, and Empire*. Monroe ME: Common Courage.

FAO (Food and Agricultural Organization) (1999). *FAO/GIEWS Food Outlook* no. 1, February. http://www.fao.org/docrep/004/x1116e/x1116e00.htm (accessed 11 February 2008).

Fattah, H (2007). Putin visits Qatar for talks on natural gas and trade. *New York Times*. February 13.

FERC (Federal Energy Regulatory Commission) (2006). Alaska natural gas transportation projects: Open season regulations. February 1. http://www.ferc.gov/industries/gas/indus-act/angtp.asp (accessed 19 May 2006; subsequent update accessed 11 February 2008).

Filkins, D (2003a). Threats and responses: The Turks; Turkey will seek a second decision on a G.I. presence. *New York Times*. March 3.

———— (2003b). Muted joy as troops capture and Iraqi town. *New York Times*. March 22.

———— (2003c). Eyes on capital, U.S. troops flow past the south. *New York Times*. March 24.

———— (2003d). Iraqi soldiers say it was fight or die. *New York Times*. March 27.

———— (2003e). Endless supply convoy is frustrated endlessly: Iraqis attack ammunition and fuel trucks. *New York Times*. March 27.

———— (2003f). A pause in the advance, and some time to reflect: Either take a shot or take a chance. *New York Times*. March 27.

———— (2003g). U.S. troops meet Iraqis peacefully: Both work to find a common ground. *New York Times*. March 31.

———— (2003h). Under blizzard of bullets, a battle inches on: Marines move into 'bad guy' land. *New York Times*. April 1.

———— (2003i). Onward toward the Tigris, with Iraq's capital in mind. *New York Times*. April 2.

———— (2003j). U.S. force crosses Tigris, wondering where Republican Guard went. *New York Times*. April 3.

———— (2003k). Marines cursing to Baghdad: Many fleeing Iraqis jam the highway. *New York Times*. April 4.

———— (2003l). Little resistance encountered as troops reach Baghdad. *New York Times*. April 5.

———— (2003m). Bad roads frustrate plan for noose around Baghdad as prelude to final push. *New York Times*. April 5.

———— (2003n). Some Iraqis grateful to US but wary of any changes: Concern that help may come with strings attached. *New York Times*. April 9.

———— (2003o). People rise as icons of nation fall down. *New York Times*. April 10.

———— (2003p). Marines attack Baghdad mosque said to have been visited by Hussein, but prey slips away. *New York Times*. April 11.

———— (2003q). In Baghdad, free of Hussein, a day of mayhem: Mobs ransack homes and set fire to government sites. *New York Times*. April 12.

—————— (2003r). U.S. troops poised to oust loyalists in northern city: Marines meet resistance as the move into the edges of Tikrit. *New York Times*. April 14.

—————— (2003s). In hometown, Hussein's glory is quickly gone. *New York Times*. April 15.

—————— (2003t). Iraqis confront memories in a place of torture. *New York Times*. April 21.

—————— (2003u). Bank aide says a Hussein son took $1 billion: Seizure occurred just before war started. *New York Times*. May 6.

—————— (2003v). As U.S. fans out in Iraq, violence and death on the rise: Attacks and retaliation; 7 more Iraqis killed, military officials say, including 5 in a murky encounter. *New York Times*. May 6.

Filkins, D and CJ Chivers (2003). Threats and responses: Northern Iraq; U.S. in talks on allowing Turkey to occupy a Kurdish area. *New York Times*. February 7.

Filkins, D and J Glanz (2004a). U.S. begins main assault in Falluja, setting off street fighting: 6,500 G.I.'s and 2,000 Iraqis on attack. *New York Times*. November 9.

—————— (2004b). Rebels routed in Falluja; fighting spreads elsewhere: 38 G.I.'s killed in weeklong assault — New violence in Mosul and Ramadi. *New York Times*. November 15.

Firestone, D (2003a). Conferees bargain over $80 billion plan to finance war and its aftermath. *New York Times*. April 12.

—————— (2003b). Lawmakers back request by Bush on funds for Iraq: An $87 billion package, Afghan money is included — Senators want Baghdad to repay some of the aid. *New York Times*. October 18.

Fisher, I (2003a). Looting at a border post: All that's left is regret. *New York Times*. April 11.

—————— (2003b). U.S. forces said to kill 15 Iraqis during an anti-American rally. *New York Times*. April 30.

Fisher, I and J Kifner (2003). G.I.'s and Iraqis patrol together to bring order. *New York Times*. April 15.

Fleischer, L (2003). Economic and political troubles plague Venezuela. *AmericanDiplomacy.org*. April 18. http://www.unc.edu/depts/diplomat/archives_roll/2003_04-06/fleischer_venezuela/fleischer_venezuela.html (accessed 11 February 2008).

Freedom House (2007). Freedom in the world 2007: Subscores. http://www.freedomhouse.org/template.cfm?page=372&year=2007 (accessed 21 January 2008).

Friedman, TL (1990). Selling sacrifice: Gulf rationale still eludes Bush. *New York Times.* November 16.

———— (1991). U.S. ties Israeli aid request to freeze on settlements after talks end in impasse. *New York Times.* September 18.

———— (2007). Coulda, woulda, shoulda. *New York Times.* November 14.

Fromkin, D (1989). *The Peace to End All Peace: Creating the Modern Middle East 1914–1922.* New York: Henry Holt.

Gasunie (2002). The history of natural gas in the Netherlands. http:// 212.83.207.146/tradesupply/en/organization/history.html (accessed 7 July 2006; not available on 11 February 2008).

Gettleman, J (2004). 4 from U.S. killed in ambush in Iraq; mob drags bodies: Assault in Falluja — 5 G.I.'s die in bombing 15 miles away. *New York Times.* April 1.

———— (2007). Cracks in the peace in oil-rich Sudan as old tensions fester. *New York Times.* September 22.

Gettleman, J and D Jehl (2004). Up to 12 marines die in raid on their base as fierce fighting spreads to 6 Iraqi cities: Militia of rebel cleric keeps up attacks. *New York Times.* April 7.

Gillingham, J (1991). *Coal, Steel, and the Rebirth of Europe, 1945–1955.* Cambridge: Cambridge University Press.

Giridharadas, A (2008a). Four wheels for the masses: The $2,500 car. *New York Times.* January 8.

———— (2008b). How to build a $2,500 car: To design a 'people's car,' Tata's engineers went back to basics. *New York Times.* January 8.

Glantz, A (2005). *How America lost Iraq.* New York: Jeremy P. Tarcher/ Penguin.

Glanz, J (2007a). Iraqi Sunni lands show new oil and gas promise: Political impact is seen in revised estimates of deposits. *New York Times.* February 19.

———— (2007b). Draft law on oil money moves to Iraqi cabinet. *New York Times.* February 19.

———— (2007c). Billions in oil missing in Iraq, U.S. study finds: Output is short of goals; suspicions include theft or an overstatement of production. *New York Times.* May 12.

———— (2007d). Iraq compromise on oil law seems to be collapsing: New political setback: Baghdad at odds with Kurds — Talks seek to save deal. *New York Times.* September 13.

Global Policy Forum (2003). New list of Kimberley Process member countries. July 31. http://www.globalpolicy.org/security/issues/diamond/ 2003/0731member.htm (accessed 11 February 2008).

——— (2007). Western Sahara. http://www.globalpolicy.org/security/issues/wsahara/wsindex.htm (accessed 8 January 2008).

Gordon, M (1990a). U.S. aides press Iraqi nuclear threat. *New York Times.* November 26,

——— (1990b). 2 ex-military chiefs urge Bush to delay Gulf War. *New York Times.* November 29.

——— (2003a). A swift, and risky, attack by land, with surprise in mind. *New York Times.* March 21.

——— (2003b). Aerial pounding intended to push Iraq's government toward brink. *New York Times.* March 22.

——— (2003c). U.S. starts push on Iraqi forces near Baghdad. *New York Times.* March 22.

——— (2003d). The goal is Baghdad, but at what cost? *New York Times.* March 25.

——— (2003e). U.S. shifting focus of land campaign to fight in south: Resistance by militia is delaying Baghdad battle, officers say. *New York Times.* March 26.

——— (2003f). Allies adapt to setbacks. *New York Times.* March 27.

——— (2003g). New tactics, hard choices. *New York Times.* March 28.

——— (2003h). Slower pace, not a pause. *New York Times.* March 31.

——— (2003i). A new doctrine's test. *New York Times.* April 1.

——— (2003j). U.S. forces enter zone to confront Republican guard: Battle for Baghdad begins in area surrounding Iraqi capital. *New York Times.* April 2.

——— (2003k). Goal of U.S.: Avoid a siege. *New York Times.* April 3.

——— (2003l). A tightening of the noose. *New York Times.* April 4.

——— (2003m). New dangers in final push; developing strategies for a different battle. *New York Times.* April 5.

——— (2003n). Push to finish the job. *New York Times.* April 9.

——— (2003o). For many Iraqis, an American patrol is a welcome sight. *New York Times.* April 15.

——— (2003p). Allies to retain larger Iraq force as strife persists: Some U.S. units will stay; resistance leads to a shift — G.I.'s may move to trouble spots outside of Baghdad. *New York Times.* May 29.

——— (2007). A fuller picture: U.S. looks to Iraqi data. *New York Times.* December 1.

——— (2008). New weight in Army manual on stabilizing war-torn areas. *New York Times.* February 8.

Gordon, M and B Trainor (2007). *Cobra II: The Inside Story of the Invasion and Occupation of Iraq*. New York: Vintage Books.

Gottlieb, A, H Gottlieb, B Bowers and B Bowers (1998). *1,000 Years, 1,000 People: Ranking the Men and Women Who Shaped the Millennium*. New York: Kondasha International.

Grabosky, P (1989). A toxic legacy: British nuclear weapons testing in Australia. In *Wayward Governance: Illegality and its Control in the Public Sector*. Canberra: Australian Institute of Criminology. http://www.aic.gov.au/publications/lcj/wayward/ch16.html (accessed 11 February 2008).

Graffis, M (1997). Secessionists in Papua New Guinea say British, South African mercenaries in action. March 4. Agence France-Press. http://www.hartford-hwp.com/archives/24/146.html (accessed 11 February 2008).

Griffin, K (2006). World LNG imports by origin, 2004 (billion cubic feet). U.S. Energy Information Agency. December 21. http://www.eia.doe.gov/international/LNGimp2004.html (accessed 17 June 2006; subsequently updated on 20 November 2007 and accessed 11 February 2008).

Grimmett, R (1989). *Trends in Conventional Arms Transfers to the Third World by Major Suppliers, 1981–1988*. CRS Report 9-434. May 9. Washington: Congressional Research, Library of Congress.

Grynbaum, M (2007). Can a plucky U.S. economy surmount $80/barrel oil? *New York Times*. October 5.

Häfele, W, J Anderer, A McDonald and N Nakicenovic (1981). *Energy in a Finite World: Paths to a Sustainable Future*. Cambridge, MA: Ballinger.

Hakim, D (2003). Fuel economy hit 22-year low in 2002. *New York Times*. May 3.

Hanley, C (2003). Powell's case for war not holding up: AP examines validity of early U.S. assertions. *Champaign–Urbana News-Gazette*. August 10.

Harper, R (ed.) 1904. *The Code of Hammurabi King of Babylon About 2250 B.C.* Chicago: University of Chicago Press. http://www.wsu.edu/~dee/MESO/CODE.HTM (accessed 4 February 2008).

Hauser, C (2004). Iraqi uprising spreads; Rumsfeld sees it as 'test of will': U.S. may delay return home of 25,000. *New York Times*. April 8.

———— (2006). Bolivia nationalizes natural gas. *New York Times*. May 1.

Havini, M and R Havini (2003). Bougainville — The long struggle for freedom. http://www.eco-action.org/dt/bvstory.html (accessed 12 February 2008).

Hedges, S (2003). Military to leave Saudi Arabia: U.S. moving amid strained relations. *Chicago Tribune.* April 30.

Historical Foreign Exchange. (2003) http://www.oanda.com/convert/fxhistory (accessed 9 July 2007).

History Learning Site (2003). Abyssinia 1935 to 1936. Association of Teachers' Websites. http://historylearningsite.co.uk/abyssinia.htm (accessed 12 February 2008).

Hoge, W (2003). Blair survives a mutiny over joining U.S. in war. *New York Times.* March 19.

Homer-Dixon, T (1999). *Environment, Scarcity, and Violence.* Princeton: Princeton University Press.

House of Commons Library (1999). Inflation: The value of the pound 1750–1998, Paper 99/20, February 23. Referenced in the link "research paper" in "British coinage," Wikipedia, http://www.parliament.uk/commons/lib/research/rp99/rp99-020.pdf (accessed 9 uly 2007). For conversion to current prices, the British pound was adjusted to 1998 values (using table 1 of House of Commons Library 1999). The 1998 British pound was then converted to 1.6483 $US for 1 anuary 1998 (Historical Foreign Exchange, 2003), and the U.S. dollar was then inflation adjusted by a factor of 1.24 to 2003 (USBLS 2006).

Hubbert, MK (1956). Nuclear energy and the fossil fuels, Presented before the Spring Meeting of the Southern District, American Petroleum Institute, Plaza Hotel, San Antonio, TX, March 7-8-9. http://www.energybulletin.net/13630.html (accessed 9 February 2008).

IAEA (International Atomic Energy Agency) (1991). *Uranium 1991: Resources, Production and Demand.* Paris: Organization for Economic Cooperation and Development.

——— (1999). *Uranium 1999: Resources, Production and Demand.* Paris: Organization for Economic Cooperation and Development.

——— (2001). *Uranium 2001: Resources, Production and Demand.* Paris: Organization for Economic Cooperation and Development.

——— (2005). *Uranium 2005: Resources, Production and Demand.* Paris: Organization for Economic Cooperation and Development.

IEA (International Energy Agency) (2007). A new phase in IEA work with China and India. December 7. http://www.iea.org/textbase/press/pressdetail.asp?PRESS_REL_ID=245 (accessed 23 January 2008).

——— (2008). Member countries and countries beyond the OECD. http://www.iea.org/Textbase/country/index.asp (accessed 23 January 2008).

IguassuFallsTour.com (2003). History. http://www.iguassufallstour.com/main.php?run=articles&key=18#art44 (accessed 12 February 2008).

IMF (International Monetary Fund) (2002). Republic of Niger poverty reduction strategy paper. January. http://www.imf.org/External/NP/prsp/2002/ner/01/ (accessed 12 April 2003).

———— (2007). World economic outlook and financial surveys: World economic outlook database. April. http://www.imf.org/external/pubs/ft/weo/2007/01/data/index. (accessed 6 February 2008).

Infoplease (2003). Western Sahara, proposed state. http://infoplease.com/ipa/A0759052.html (accessed 12 February 2008).

———— (2006). Casualties in World War I. http://www.infoplease.com/ipa/A0004617.html (accessed 31 May 2006).

International Herald Tribune (2006). Russia cuts off gas supplies to Ukraine. January 1.

IRS (Internal Revenue Service) 2007. Summary of the credit for qualified hybrid vehicles. November 8. http://www.irs.gov/newsroom/article/0,,id=157557,00.html (accessed 24 January 2008).

———— (2008). Publication 15 (Circular E), Employer's Tax Guide http://www.irs.gov/pub/irs-pdf/p15.pdf (accessed 12 February 2008).

Isaac, J (1999). The Palestinian water crisis. Information Brief No. 4, August 18, Jerusalem: Applied Research Institute. http://www.thejerusalemfund.org/carryover/pubs/19990818ib.html (accessed 12 February 2008). Isaac notes that Israeli settlers in the West Bank used four times as much water per capita as Palestinians.

Jehl, D (2003). As order breaks down, allied forces pledge to rebuild Iraqi police. *New York Times.* April 12.

———— (2004). Wary Powell said to have warned Bush on war: Book describes clashes with Cheney over plan for invading Iraq. *New York Times.* April 17.

Jensen, W (1968). The importance of energy in the first and second world wars. *The Historical Journal,* 11, 538–554.

Jewish Virtual Library (2008). Israel's proposed security fence. http://www.jewishvirtuallibrary.org/jsource/History/fencemap.html (accessed 9 February 2008).

Johnson, DG (2002). The declining importance of natural resources: Lessons from agricultural land. *Resource Economics,* 24, 157–171.

Johnson, D and A Tegera (2005). *Digging Deeper: How the DR Congo's Mining Policy is Failing the Country.* Goma: Pole Institute.

Johnson, P (1991). *The Birth of the Modern*. New York: HarperCollins.

Johnston, D (2003). Top U.S. officials tell lawmakers of Iraq-Qaeda ties. *New York Times*. February 12.

Joshi, M (2008). Iran wants to sign a pipeline deal with an elected Pakistani government. January 23. http://www.topnews.in/iran-wants-sign-ipi-pipeline-deal-elected-pakistani-government-216086 (accessed 6 February 2008).

Kamal, R (2005). The petroleum industry in the Middle East (1869–1950). *The Leading Edge*, 24, 81822.

Kamp, N, M O'Hanlon and A Unikewicz (2006). The state of Iraq: An update. *New York Times*. June 16.

Kanter, J (2008). Amid doubts, Europe may ban some biofuels. *New York Times*. January 15.

Kanter, J and S Castel (2008). Stricter system to trim carbon emissions is considered in Europe. *New York Times*. January 22.

Kaufman, D A Kraay and M Mastruzzi (2007). Governance matters VI: Aggregate and individual governance indicators 1996–2006. World Bank Policy Research Working Paper 4280, July. Washington: World Bank. http://papers.ssrn.com/sol3/papers.cfm?abstract_id=999979 (accessed 21 January 2008).

Keegan, J (1998). *The First World War*. London: Hutchinson.

Kershner, I (2008). Hamas says military wing is responsible for bombing: Attack signals end of 3-year moratorium. *New York Times*. February 6.

Kimberley Process (2007). http://www.kimberleyprocess.com/ (accessed 9 January 2008).

Kimmerling, B and J Migdal (2002). *The Palestinian People: A History*. London: Harvard University Press.

Klare, M (1991). Fueling the fire: How we armed the Middle East. *Bulletin of the Atomic Scientists*, 47 (January/February), 19–26.

———— (2001). *Resource Wars*. New York: Metropolitan.

Kohn, G (1999). *Dictionary of Wars* (revised edition). New York: Checkmark Books.

Kolodziej, E (2000). The great powers and genocide: Lessons from Rwanda. Program in Arms Control, Disarmament, and International Security Occasional Paper, ACDIS KOL:24.2000. http://www.acdis.uiuc.edu/Research/OPs/Kolodziej/EAKGen/html/cover.html (accessed 9 July 2006).

Knight, R (2005). Western Sahara Resource Watch press release. February 28. http://richardknight.homestead.com/files/WS-Kerr-McGee-release2-27-05.htm (accessed 12 February 2008).

Kramer, A (2008). Ru.

Krauss, C (2008). Stocks plummet as oil soars and manufacturing appears to falter: Oil tops $100 a barrel, then settles at $99.62; jump of $3.64 for day. *New York Times.* January 3.

Krempel, L and T Pluemper (1999). International division of labor and global economic processes: An analysis of the international trade of cars with world trade data. January 14. http://www.mpi-fgkoeln.mgp.de/~lk/netvis/globale/ (accessed 19 May 2003).

Krichene, N (2006). World crude oil markets: Monetary policy and the recent oil shock. International Monetary Fund working paper WP/06/62. March. http://papers.ssrn.com/sol3/papers.cfm?abstract_id=898723 (accessed 6 February 2008).

Krüger, P and P Schroeder (2004). *"The Transformation of European Politics, 1763–1848": Episode or Model in Modern History?* New York: LIT Verlag/Palgrave Macmillan.

Kube, C (2007). Troop level in Iraq reaches highest mark. *msnbc.* August 27. http://firstread.msnbc.msn.com/archive/2007/08/07/306743.aspx (accessed 9 January 2008).

Labor Law Center (2007). 11/08/2007 Federal Minimum Wage Increase for 2007. November 8. http://www.laborlawcenter.com/federal-minimum-wage.asp (accessed 11 February 2008).

Lacey, M (2003). Hope glimmering as war retreats from Congo. *New York Times,* October 21.

Lambsdorf, JG (2006). Transparency International corruption perception index. http://www.transparency.org/policy_research/surveys_indices/cpi/2006 (accessed 21 January 2008).

League of Nations Photo Archive (2002). Chronology 1946. http://www.indiana.edu/~league/1946.htm (accessed 12 February 2008).

Learsy, R (2005). Live webcast/book launch — *Over a Barrel: Breaking the Middle East Oil Cartel.* October 17. Woodrow Wilson Center for Scholars. http://www.wilsoncenter.org/index.cfm?fuseaction=events.event_summary&event_id=146101 (accessed 23 May 2006).

Legro, J and A Moravscik (1999). Is anybody still a realist? *International Security,* 24 (Fall, No. 2), 5–55; http://www.princeton.edu/~amoravcs/library/anybody.pdf (accessed 9 July 2006). This reference provides a succinct if critical description how the idea of "unitary rational actors" fits in to an influential theory of international relations and conflict.

Lewis, J and X Litai (1988). *China builds the bomb.* Palo Alto: Stanford University Press.

Lewis, P (1991a). Iraq appears ready to yield over U.N. inspectors. *New York Times.* October 9.

——— (1991b). Baghdad is said to have hidden records. *New York Times.* October 14.

Lewis, P (1987). 'New thinking' in a nuclear society. *New York Times.* June 21.

Library of Congress. 2007. H.R.6.ENR: Energy Independence and Security Act of 2007.

Lichtblau, E (2004). President asked aide to explore Iraq link to 9/11: Acknowledgment by Rice; Adviser says Bush wasn't trying to intimidate — A 'logical question.' *New York Times.* March 29.

Lieber, K and D Press (2006). The rise of U.S. nuclear primacy. *Foreign Affairs*, 85, March/April, 42–55.

Lowry, J (2003). Postwar Iraq will face big water problems. Scripps Howard News Service. *Champaign–Urbana News-Gazette.* April 20.

Lynn, J (2003). *Battle: A history of Combat and Culture.* Boulder: Westview Press.

MacAvoy, PW (2000). *The natural gas market.* New Haven: Yale University Press.

MacFarquhar, N (2003). Hussein's 2 sons dead in shootout, U.S. says: Troops act on tip; house surrounded, then fierce gun battle — 2 others killed too. *New York Times.* July 23.

MacFarquhar, N and R Oppel Jr (2003). Car bomb in Iraq kills 95 at Shiite mosque: Moderate cleric is among dead. *New York Times.* July 23.

Maddison, A (2001). *The World Economy: A Millennial Perspective.* Paris: Organization for Economic Cooperation and Development.

Manchester, W (1968). *The Arms of Krupp: 1587–1968.* New York: Bantam.

Manne, A, R Mendelsohn and R Richels (1995). MERGE, a model for evaluating regional and global effects of GHG reduction policies. *Energy Policy*, 23, 17–34.

Marichal, C (2006). The Spanish-American silver peso: Export commodity and global money of the ancien regime, 1550–1800. In *From Silver to Cocaine: Latin American Commodity Chains and the Building of the World Economy, 1500–2000*, S Topik, C Marichal and Zephyr (eds.), Durham: Duke University Press.

Marquis, C (2006). Bush officials met with Venezuelans who ousted leader. *New York Times*, April 16.

Marquis, C and T Shanker (2003). Pentagon leaders warn of dangers for U.S. in Liberia. *New York Times.* July 25.

Martin, A (2007). Farmers head to fields to plant corn, lots of it. *New York Times.* March 31.

Masters, CD, DH Root and RM Turner (2002). World conventional crude oil and natural gas: identified reserves, undiscovered resources and futures, US Geological Survey Open-File Report 98–468. http://pubs.usgs.gov/of/1998/of98-468/text.htm#MAPS (accessed 12 February 2008).

Matthews, J (2002). Coercive inspections. In *Iraq, A New Approach.* Washington, DC: Carnegie Endowment for International Peace. August. http://www.carnegieendowment.org/npp/publications/index.cfm?fa=view&id=1064 (accessed 12 February 2008).

McCormick, T (1963). Insular imperialism and the open door: The China market and the Spanish–American War. *Pacific Historical Review,* 32, 155–169.

McDonald, J (2005). Personal communication.

McSherry, P (2003). Voyage of the USS Oregon. http://www.fortlangley.ca/pepin/USSOregon.html (accessed 4 February 2008).

Mearsheimer, J and S Walt (2006). The Israel Lobby. *London Review of Books.* March 23. http://www.lrb.co.uk/v28/n06/mear01_.html (accessed 27 January 2008).

Meltzer, M (1971). *Slavery: From the Rise of Western Civilization to Today.* New York: Dell.

Merritt, R (1986). Chronicle of Alaska Coal-mining history. http://www.dggs.dnr.state.ak.us/webpubs/dggs/pdf/text/pdf1986_066.PDF (accessed 4 February 2008).

Metchies, G (2005). *International Fuel Prices 2005.* German Technical Cooperation. http://www.zietlow.com/docs/engdocs.htm (accessed 25 January 2008).

Michel, L (2002). Deputy Prime Minister and Minister for Foreign Affairs Louis Michel over the Kimberley process. Foreign Affairs, Foreign Trade and Development Cooperation, 22 October 2002. http://www.diplomatie.be/en/press/homedetails.asp?TEXTID=3381 (accessed 12 February 2008).

MidEast W (2002). Mid East maps — Israeli West Bank settlements. http://www.mideastweb.org/map_israel_settlements.htm (accessed 12 February 2008).

Migdalovitz, C (2003). Armenia–Azerbaihan conflict, Congressional issue brief for congress IB92109. August 8. http://www.au.af.mil/au/awc/awcgate/crs/ib92109.pdf (accessed 12 February 2008).

Mouawad, J (2005). Oil's lessor role in U.S. economy limits damage from high prices. *New York Times.* April 23.

——— (2007). Growing unrest posing a threat to Nigerian oil. *New York Times.* April 21.

——— (2008). Wider troubles trickle down to oil sector. *New York Times.* January 24.

Mulder, M (2002. Liberalising the European natural gas market. CPB Report 2002/3. http://www.cpb.nl/eng/pub/cpbreeksen/cpbreport/2002_3/s2_2.pdf (accessed 12 February 2008).

National Academy of Engineering (2006). Greatest engineering achievements of the 20th century: Petroleum technologies timeline. http://www.greatachievements.org/?id=3675 (accessed 11 June 2006).

Neely, C (2007). China's strategic petroleum reserve: A drop in the bucket. *National Economic Trends.* Federal Reserve Bank of St. Louis. http://research.stlouisfed.org/publications/net/20070101/cover.pdf (accessed 12 February 2008).

News-Gazette Wire Services (1991). Iraqi meeting "Useful Step" — President. January 5.

New York Times (1903). New naval coaling station: Will be established immediately at Dutch Harbor, Alaska. May 26.

——— (1995). U.N. arms monitor says Iraq still withholds data. October 14.

——— (2003). Out of Africa? — Not the French. January 12.

——— (2008). Editorial: The other Nano. January 16.

Nile Basin Initiative (2003). Features. http://www.nilebasin.org/ (accessed 8 December 2003; not available 12 February 2008).

——— (2006). New release. May 1, http://www.nilebasin.org/pressReleases.htm#Release%20No:%2006/05/01 (accessed 19 May 2006; not available 12 February 2008).

Nile Basin Initiative Shared Vision Program (2001. Nile Basin Regional Power Trade Agreement Project Document. http://www.nilebasin.org/Documents/Documents/svp_power.pdf (accessed 8 December 2003; not available 12 February 2008).

NTI (Nuclear Threat Initiative) (2005). Nuclear overview. December. http://nuclearthreatinitiative.com/e_research/profiles/Iraq/Nuclear/print/index_2115.prt (accessed 18 January 2008).

Ohnsman, A (2008). Toyota Plans Plug-In Hybrids for 2010, Matching GM (Update4). *Bloomberg.com*. January 14. http://www.bloomberg.com/apps/news?pid=20601101&sid=aCHIecOjRDRs&refer=japan (accessed 28 January 2008).

Oppel Jr, R and R Worth (2003). Riots continue over fuel crisis in Iraq's south: Officials say shortages may grow in winter. *New York Times*. August 11.

ORNL (Oak Ridge National Laboratory) (2003). Carbon Dioxide Information Analysis Center's factors and units for calculating CO_2 emissions from fuel production and trade data. http://cdiac.esd.ornl.gov/trends/emis/factors.htm (accessed 9 February 2008).

Overlack, P (1998). German war plans in the Pacific, 1910–1914. *Historian*, 60, 578–593.

Packer, G (2005. *The Assassin's Gate: America in Iraq*. New York: Farrar, Strauss, and Giroux.

Palestinian Center PSR (Policy and Survey Research) (2003). Results of PSR refugees' polls in the West Bank/Gaza Strip, Jordan and Lebanon on Refugees' preferences and behavior in a Palestinian–Israeli permanent refugee agreement. http://www.pcpsr.org/survey/polls/2003/refugees june03.html (accessed 12 February 2008).

Parker, G (ed.) (1995). *The Cambridge Illustrated History of Warfare: The Triumph of the West*. New York: Cambridge University Press.

Pederson, N (2000). The French desire for uranium. Master's thesis, University of Illinois at Urbana–Champaign. Program in Arms Control, Disarmament, and International Security Occasional Paper, ACDIS PED:1.2000. http://www.acdis.uiuc.edu/Research/ResReports.shtml (accessed 12 February 2008).

Pelletiere, S (2003). A war crime or an act of war. *New York Times*. January 31.

People's Daily Online (2004). Oil firms clinch large overseas deals. December 16. http://english.people.com.cn/200412/16/eng200412 16_167609.html (accessed 1 June 2006).

Peterson, JE (2002). Historical pattern of Gulf security. In *Security in the Persian Gulf*, L Potter and G Sick (eds.), New York: Palgrave.

Petraeus, D (2007). Multi-national force-Iraq: Charts to accompany the testimony of Gen. David H. Petraeus. 10–11 September.

Phillips, J (1979). The Iranian oil crisis. Heritage Foundation Backgrounder #76. February 28. http://www.heritage.org/Research/MiddleEast/bg76. cfm (accessed 25 January 2008).

Pike, J (2005a). Liberia — Second civil war — 1997–2003. April 27. http://www.globalsecurity.org/military/world/war/liberia-1997.htm (accessed 10 February 2008).

——— (2005b). 1999 Kargil conflict. April 27. http://www.globalsecurity.org/military/world/war/kargil-99.htm (accessed 10 February 2008).

——— (2005c). WMD:World:France:Nuclear weapons. April 28. http://www.globalsecurity.org/wmd/world/france/nuke.htm (accessed 10 February 2008). This contains a summary of the events leading to France signing and ratifying the CTBT.

——— (2005d). W70. April 28. http://www.globalsecurity.org/wmd/systems/w70.htm (accessed 17 February 2008).

——— (2007). Military: US forces order of battle. October 10. http://www.globalsecurity.org/military/ops/iraq_orbat.htm (accessed 10 February 2008).

Pipes, D (1982). The curse of oil. *The Atlantic*, July. http://www.danielpipes.org/article/163 (accessed 6 January 2008).

Pirog, R (2004). Foreign trade effects of an Alaskan gas pipeline. RS21787 Report for Congress, March 30. Washington: U.S. Congressional Research Office.

Polgreen, L (2007). Fear of new war as clashes erupt over Congo's edge: Government struggles; hundreds of thousands flee — International concern grows. *New York Times*. December 13.

——— (2008a). Violence in Chad intensifies, and foreigners evacuate. *New York Times*. February 4.

——— (2008b). Thousands flee fighting in Chad's capital. *New York Times*. February 5.

Poole, W (2007). Energy prices and the U.S. business cycle. Global Interdependence Center (GIC) Abroad in Chile Conference, American Chamber of Commerce in Chile Breakfast, March 2. http://stlouisfed.org/news/speeches/2007/03_02_07.html#fig1 (accessed 4 January 2008).

Preston, J (2003). Powell calls for U.N. to act on Iraq and meets deep resistance. *New York Times*. February 23.

Priest, D and B Gellman (2002). U.S. decries abuse but defends interrogations. *Washington Post*, 26 December 2002.

Purdum, T and J Elder (2003). Poll shows drop in confidence on Bush skill in handling crises: Solid majority say the U.S. is seriously on the wrong track. *New York Times* October 3.

Rankin, K (1998). Tariffs, Deflation and the Depression of 1930. August 7. http://pl.net/~keithr/rf98_GreatDepression.html (accessed 12 February 2008).

Regan, T (2005). Prewar report cast doubt on Iraq-al Qaeda connection. *Christian Science Monitor csmonitor.com.* November 7. http://www.csmonitor.com/2005/1107/dailyUpdate.html (accessed 10 February 2008).

Reid, R and R Burns (2007). US starts Iraq troop pull-out. *The Scotsman.* November 14. http://thescotsman.scotsman.com/ViewArticle.aspx?articleid=3498274 (accessed 9 January 2008).

Reid, T (2007). Iran halted its nuclear weapons programme in 2003 US agencies say. *The Times* Dec. 4. http://www.timesonline.co.uk/tol/news/world/us_and_americas/article2995111.ece (accessed 6 February 2008).

Rethinaraj, TSG (2005). Modeling global and regional energy futures, PhD thesis, University of Illinois at Urbana-Champaign, Program in arms control, disarmament, and international security report ADCIS RET:1.2005. http://www.acdis.uiuc.edu/Research/ResReports.shtml (accessed 23 May 2006).

Reuters (1995). Questions on germ warfare. *New York Times.* February 28.

Reynolds, P (2004). Consultant digs into Romania's rich oil history. July. http://www.signaengineering.com/news/2004/romania.htm (accessed 16 May 2006).

Rhodes, R (1990). Bush's atomic red herring. *New York Times.* November 27.

Riedlmayer, A (2003). [Iraqcrisis] An "embedded" reporter, the well-guarded oil ministry, looted museums and libraries. May 7. https://listhost.uchicago.edu/pipermail/iraqcrisis/2003-May/000052.html (accessed 10 February 2008).

Risen, J (2003). Iraq said to have tried to reach last-minute deal to avert war: Way C.I.A. rebuffed back-channel proposal. *New York Times.* November 6.

———— (2004a). C.I.A. lacked Iraq arms data, ex-inspector says: Recent search indicates weapons programs were in disarray. *New York Times.* January 26.

———— (2004b). C.I.A. held back Iraq arms data, U.S. officials say: President not informed; scientist's relatives told agency of end to illicit weapons programs. *New York Times.* July 6.

———— (2008). Before bin Laden, one of the world's most feared men. *New York Times.* February 14.

Ritter, S (1999). *Endgame: Solving the Iraq problem — once and For All*. New York: Simon and Schuster.

(RIVM) Rijskinstituut voor Volksgezondheid en Milieu (2002). General oil production estimates for period 1800–1900. http://arch.rivm.nl/ env/int/hyde/eisp_oil2.html (accessed 13 August 2003); more recently accessed through http://www.mnp.nl/hyde/new/ (accessed 7 July 2006).

Roesler, M (1921). The iron-ore resources of Europe. U. S. Geological Survey Bulletin 706. Washington: Government Printing Office.

Rogner, H-H (1997). An assessment of world hydrocarbon resources. *Annual Review of Energy and the Environment*, 22, 217–262.

Romero, S (2003a). OPEC holds steady on output, at least for now. *New York Times*. December 5.

——— (2004). Topping off the biggest gas tank: After 30 years, the U.S. strategic petroleum reserve will finally be full. *New York Times*. December 7.

——— (2003b). Natural gas prices surge and fingers are pointing. *New York Times*. December 13.

——— (2008). Chávez threatens to end oil exports to U.S. in Exxon fued. *New York Times*. February 11.

Romero, S and A Barrionuevo (2005). The troubled oil company: Venezuela's president shakes Citgo to its core. *New York Times*. April 20.

Romero, S and C Krauss (2007). High stakes: Chávez plays the oil card. *New York Times*. April 10.

Rosenbaum, D and D Firestone (2003). $318 billion deal is set in Congress for cutting taxes. *New York Times*. May 22.

Roy, R (1997). WOW case studies: India-Bangladesh water dispute. http:// www.american.edu/ted/ice/indobang.htm (accessed 6 February 2008).

Rubin, A (2007). Iraqi cabinet moves forward on oil measure. *New York Times*. July 4.

——— (2008). Ending impasse, Iraq Parliament backs measure *New York Times*. February 16.

Rutenberg, J and S Erlanger (2006). West Bank pullout gets a nod from Bush. *New York Times*. May 23.

Sachs, J (2005). *The End of Poverty: Economic Possibilities for Our Time*. New York: Penguin.

Sachs, S (2003). Hussein caught in makeshift hide-out; Bush says 'dark era' for Iraqis is over: Arrest by U.S. soldiers — President still cautious. *New York Times*. December 15.

Safire, W (1990a). The Saddam bomb (3). *New York Times*. November 29.

———— (1990b). Iraq's bomb thought to be much closer. *Milwaukee Journal*. December 29.

Sakhuja, V (2006). A regional approach to strategic oil reserves? *Opinion Asia*. December 25. http://www.opinionasia.org/Aregionalapproachto strategicoilreserves (accessed 25 January 2008).

Sanger, D (2003a). Plans for postwar Iraq are re-evaluated as fast military exit looks less likely. *New York Times*. April 2.

———— (2003b). A blink form the Bush administration: Backing down on tariffs, U.S. strengthens trade organization. *New York Times*. March 17.

Sanger, D and D Filkins (2003). U.S. is pessimistic Turks will accept aid deal on Iraq. *New York Times*. February 20.

Sanger, D and W Hogue (2003a). U.S. may abandon U.N. vote on Iraq, Powell testifies. *New York Times*. March 14.

———— (2003b). Bush and 2 allies seem set for war to depose Hussein. *New York Times*. March 17.

San Joaquin Geological Society (2002). The history of the oil industry. http://www.sjgs.com/history.html (accessed 12 February 2008).

Santora, M (2003a). Abuse, distrust, and fear leave scars on children in battered Iraqi town. *New York Times*. April 7.

———— (2003b). Lacking necessities, many Iraqi's can't focus on the future. *New York Times*. April 14.

Schmitt, E (1991). U.S. says it misses 2 A-plants in Iraq. *New York Times*. October 10.

———— (2003a). Turkey seems set to let 60,000 G.I.'s use bases for war. *New York Times*. February 26.

———— (2003b). President order troop deployment to Liberian coast: Mission is not specific; 3 ships with 2,300 marines are expected in a week. *New York Times*. July 26.

Schorske. C (1955). *German Social Democracy, 1905–1917: The Development of the Great Schism*. Cambridge: Harvard University Press.

Schroeder, P (1994a). *The Transformation of European Politics, 1763–1848*. Oxford: Clarendon.

———— (1994b). *New World Order: A Historical Perspective*. University of Illinois at Urbana-Champaign Program in Arms Control, Disarmament, and International Security Report ACDIS SCH:3.1994. http://www. acdis.uiuc.edu/Research/OPs_N-Z.shtml#S (accessed 12 February 2008).

Sciolino, E (2004a). 10 bombs shatter trains in Madrid, killing 192: 1,400 are hurt — Top suspects are Basques and Al Qaeda. *New York Times.* March 12.

——— (2004b). Following attacks, Spain's governing party is beaten: Socialists gain upset victory in election. *New York Times.* March 14.

Secretary-General of the Commion of the European Communities (2001). Memorandum to the members of the commission: Summary of the Treaty of Nice. January 18. ec.europa.eu/comm/nice_treaty/summary_en.pdf (accessed 8 January 2008).

Segev, T (2007). What if Israel had turned back? *New York Times.* June 5.

Sengupta, S (2003a). The child soldiers of Ivory Coast are hired guns. *New York Times.* March 27.

——— (2003b). Ethnic dispute stills Nigeria's mighty oil wells. *New York Times.* April 1.

Sengupta, S and N Banerjee (2003). Nigerian strife, little noticed, is latest threat to flow of oil. *New York Times.* March 22.

Service, R (2007). Biofuels researchers prepare to reap a new harvest. *Science,* 315, 1488–1491.

Shanker, T (2003a). Cost of U.S. troops in Iraq put at $3.9 billion per month: New figure is double estimate in April — General says big force will remain. *New York Times.* July 10.

——— (2003b). Huge suicide blast demolishes U.N. headquarters in Baghdad; top aid officials among 17 dead: Chaos as an anti-U.S. strategy. *New York Times.* August 20.

——— (2004). Regime thought war unlikely, Iraqis tell U.S. *New York Times.* February 12.

——— (2008). Iraq defense minister sees need for U.S. security help until 2008. *New York Times.* February 12.

Sharp, J (2007). U.S. foreign aid to Israel. Congressional Research Service Report FL33222, April 25. http:// ftp.fas.org/sgp/crs/mideast/RL33222.pdf (accessed 27 January 2008).

Shaxson, N (2004). Profile: Equatorial Guinea's great survivor. *BBC News.* March 17. http://news.bbc.co.uk/1/hi/world/africa/3516588.stm (accessed 21 January 2008).

Shillington, K (1995). *History of Africa.* New York: St. Martin's Press.

Shiva, V (2002). *Water Wars: Privatization, Pollution, and Profit.* Cambridge, MA: South End Press.

Simons, M (2004). Spanish premier orders soldiers home from Iraq: A setback for U.S. effort; socialist sites U.N.'s role as seeming limited — 1,400 troops to exit. *New York Times.* April 19.

Singer, C (1998). An analytical uranium sources model, Proc. Technical Committee Meeting on Recent Developments in Uranium Resources, Production and Demand (Vienna, 10–13 June, 1997), IAEA-TEC-DOC-1258, International Atomic Energy Agency, pp. 27–38.

——— (2008a). Time after burial vs. temperature. http://acdisweb.acdis.uiuc.edu/NPRE201/coursematerial/oil_coal_gas/lecture14figures/Figure14.1d.html (accessed 12 February 2008).

——— (2008b). Petroleum traps. http://acdisweb.acdis.uiuc.edu/NPRE201/coursematerial/oil_coal_gas/lecture14figures/Figure14.1e.html (accessed 12 February 2008).

——— (2008c). World crude oil and natural gas reserves. http://acdisweb.acdis.uiuc.edu/NPRE201/coursematerial/resource_availability/lecture01tables/Table1.2.2a.html (accessed 12 February 2008).

——— (2008d). U.S. energy usage by source since 1850. http://acdisweb.acdis.uiuc.edu/NPRE201/coursematerial/resource_usage/lecture02tables/Table2.2a.html (accessed 12 February 2008).

——— (2008e). Advanced Energy Systems. NPRE/GLBL 480 link under ACDIS Courses at http://www.acdis.uiuc.edu (accessed 5 February 2008).

Singer, C, TS Gopi Rethinaraj, S Addy, D Durham, M Isik, M Khana, B Kuehl, J Luo, W Quimio, K Rajendran, D Ramirez, J Qiang, J Scheffran, T Nedjla Tiouririne and J Zhang (2007). Probability distributions for carbon emissions and atmospheric response: Results and methods. University of Illinois at Urbana-Champaign Program in Arms Control, Disarmament, and International Security Report ACDIS SIN:2.2007 (September). http://www.acdis.uiuc.edu/Research/ResReports.shtml (accessed 30 January, 2008); also accepted to appear in shorter form in *Climatic Change* (2008).

Singer, C and J Taylor (2007). Nuclear's role in 21st century Pacific rim energy use: Results and methods. University of Illinois at Urbana-Champaign Program in Arms Control, Disarmament, and International Security Report ACDIS SIN:1.2007 (September). http://www.acdis.uiuc.edu/Research/ResReports.shtml (accessed 30 January 2008); also in shorter form in Proceedings of American Nuclear Society Topical Meeting on Advanced Nuclear Fuel Cycles and Systems, Boise ID, September 9–13.

Smith, C (2003a). U.S.-backed Shiite cleric killed at shrine in Najaf. *New York Times*. April 11.

——— (2003b). Politics and religion join the fray in Shiite slum. *New York Times*. December 16.

———— (2003c). France says it is willing to make deal on Iraq's foreign debt. *New York Times.* December 16.

Smith, R (1988). International energy cooperation: The mismatch between IAEA policy actions and policy goals. In *Responding to International Oil Crises,* G Horwich and D Weimer (eds.), Washington: American Enterprise Institute for Public Policy Research.

Smith, RT (1981). In search of the 'just' U.S. oil policy: A review of Arrow and Kalt and More. *Journal of Business,* 54, 87–116.

Smitha, F (1998). *The Twentieth Century: Conflict Attitude, and Changing Religions.* Chap. 45, The Iranian revolution. http://www.fsmitha.com/h2/ch29ir.html (accessed 12 February 2008).

Snam Rete Gas (2003). Industrial experience stretching back more than 60 years. http://www.snamretegas.it/English/chi_siamo/storia.html (accessed 12 December 2003; website subsequently updated).

Spufford, P (1989). *Money and Its Use in Medieval Europe.* Cambridge: Cambridge University Press.

Stephenson, J (2007). *Losing the Golden Hour: An Insider's View of Iraq's Reconstruction.* Washington: Potomac Books.

Srivastava, S (2006). India fast losing energy. *Asia Times.* May 5, http://www.atimes.com/atimes/South_Asia/HE05Df06.html (accessed 12 February 2008).

Staff Reporter (2007). India, Myanmar trade project in final stage. *The Hindu.* March 14. http://www.hindu.com/2007/03/14/stories/2007031417220600.htm (accessed 12 February 2008).

Stein, S and B Stein, *Silver, Trade, and War: Spain and America in the Making of Early Modern Europe.* Baltimore: Johns Hopkins University Press.

Stevenson, R and E Becker (2003). After 21 months, Bush lifts tariff on steel imports: A trade war is averted; president risks backlash in '04 election in some industrial states. *New York Times.* December 5.

Stockton, E (1999). On making matters worse in the Balkans. June 15. http://www.orknet.co.uk/godiva/1999may/130-3.htm (accessed 11 August 2003; not available 12 February 2008).

Stolberg, S and J Rutenberg (2006). Rumsfeld resigns, and Bush pledges to work with a Democratic majority. *New York Times.* November 9.

Sudetic, C (2005). Chapter 1 — Historical Setting. In *A Country Study: Romania.* November 9. http://lcweb2.loc.gov/frd/cs/rotoc.html (accessed 12 February 2008).

Szczesniak, PA (2002). The mineral industries of Morocco and Western Sahara. http://www.mafhoum.com/press4/momyb01.pdf (accessed 12 February 2008).

Tagliabue. J (2003). France and Russia ready to use veto against Iraq war. *New York Times.* March 6.

Tarbell, I (1904). *History of the Standard Oil Company,* also available as *The history of the Standard Oil Company: Illustrated With Portraits, Pictures and Diagrams* (1937). New York: MacMillan.

Tavernise, S (2003a). Merger creates Russian oil giant with big dreams. *New York Times.* April 23.

———— (2003b). Iraqis anxiously await decisions about the operation and control of the oil industry. *New York Times.* April 28.

———— (2006). District by district, Shiites make Baghdad their own: While U.S. weighs options, militias push Sunni families from neighborhoods. *New York Times.* December 23.

———— (2007). Iraqi death toll exceeded 34,000 in 2006, U.N. says: Sign of war's trajectory; civilian casualty count is seen as thorough tally of official sources. *New York Times.* December 23.

Tavernise, S and R Worth (2007). As Iraqis flee, few are gaining sanctuary in U.S.: Calls to change policies; 'nothing to offer,' those who are in peril after helping in the war. *New York Times.* January 2.

Taylor, J and P Van Doren (2006). Economic Amnesia: The case against oil price controls and windfall profit taxes. *Policy Analysis* No. 561. January 12. http://www.cato.org/pub_display.php?pub_id=5352 (accessed 9 January 2008).

TED (Trade and Environment Database) (1997). Abu Musa: Island dispute between Iran and the UAE. http://www.american.edu/ted/abu-musa.htm#r0 (accessed 17 February 2008).

Thomas, S (2003). The seven brothers. *Energy Policy,* 31, 393–403.

Tierney, J (2003). A popular idea: Give oil money to the people rather than the despots; politicians debate sharing the riches. *New York Times.* September 10.

Torchia, C (2008). Turkey bombs Kurdish rebels in Iraq. http://news.yahoo.com/s/ap/20080204/ap_on_re_mi_ea/turkey_kurds_5;_ylt=As6ilEC50wASFVLYDMVZu4_tfLkA (accessed 6 February 2008).

Tussing, AR and CC Barlow (1984). *The Natural Gas Industry: Evolution, Structure, and Economics.* Cambridge, MA: Ballinger.

Tyler, P (1991). Study says Iraq's child mortality rate has doubled. *New York Times.* October 22.

———— (2002). Officers say U.S. aided Iraq in war despite use of gas. *New York Times*. August 18.

———— (2003a). A deepening fissure. *New York Times*. March 6.

———— (2003b). Last preparations: Soldiers and equipment head for Iraq border in vast formation. *New York Times*. March 19.

———— (2003c). U.S. and British troops push into Iraq as missiles strike Baghdad compound: 16 die on copter; U.S. and British forces suffer first losses in crash in Kuwait. *New York Times*. March 21.

———— (2003d). U.S. bombs ravage targets in Baghdad; waves of troops sweeping south Iraq: Surrenders by Iraqi forces — 2 marines die in fighting. *New York Times*. March 22.

———— (2003e). Allies and Iraqis battle on 2 fronts; 20 Americans dead or missing, 50 hurt: Convoy ambushed; Iraq broadcasts images of captured G.I.'s—U.S. assails ruses: G.I.'s regroup after setback — 2 prisoners on Iraq TV. *New York Times*. March 24.

———— (2003f). Allies confront Baghdad defenders; U.S. copters repelled; one is downed. *New York Times*. March 25.

———— (2003g). Heavy Iraqi losses seen in big battle: U.A. soldiers meet irregulars 100 miles south of capital. *New York Times*. March 24.

———— (2000h). 1,000 U.S. paratroopers open northern front: A nighttime drop; Iraqi forces head south toward allied units near the capital. *New York Times*. March 27.

———— (2003i). Baghdad bombed; desert skirmishes stretch 350 miles: Heavy strikes on Iraqi capital — No 'timetable,' says Bush. *New York Times*. March 28.

———— (2003j). Airstrikes continue as allies consider timing of a thrust. *New York Times*. March 29.

———— (2003k). Infantry attacks Baghdad defense with first probes: Armor moves out; Army and Marines take on Republican guard to shape big fight. *New York Times*. March 31.

———— (2003l). 2 U.S. columns are advancing on Baghdad defenses: Clashes persist in South with irregulars. *New York Times*. April 1.

———— (2003m). Iraq is planning protracted war. *New York Times*. April 2.

———— (2003n). U.S. ground forces sweep toward Baghdad: Defending Iraqis routed, but some fall back into city. *New York Times*. April 3.

———— (2003o). U.S. forces at edge of a blacked-out Baghdad: Allies at airport; Iraq's forces weakened but still dangerous, Rumsfeld warns. *New York Times*. April 4.

———— (2003p). U.S. squeezes Baghdad and readies next step: Little resistance; signs of hasty flight by Republican guard — 2nd suicide attack. *New York Times.* April 5.

———— (2003q). Allies press Baghdad and thrust into Basra: G.I.'s block roads; plane lands at capital airport as battles go on in the outskirts. *New York Times.* April 7.

———— (2003r). U.S. forces take control in Baghdad; Bush elated; some resistance remains: Hussein statue is toppled — Rumsfeld urges caution. *New York Times.* April 10.

———— (2003s). Allies widen hold on Iraq; civil strife on rise: Kurds take northern city — grim episodes in capital. *New York Times.* April 11.

UNCDF (United Nations Capital Development Fund) (2004). Niger: Fact sheet. http://www.uncdf.org/english/countries/niger/fact_sheet.php (accessed 9 February 2008).

USD (University of San Diego) (2002). The rise of Benito Mussolini. In the University of San Diego History Department World War II Timeline. September 20. http://history.acusd.edu/gen/WW2Timeline/Prelude05. html (accessed 11 August 2003; not available 12 February 2008).

USAID (U.S. Agency for International Development) (1998). The USAID FY 1998 Congressional presentation: Niger. http://www.usaid.gov/ pubs/cp98/afr/countries/ne.htm (accessed 12 February 2008).

USBLS (U.S. Bureau of Labor Statistics) (2007). Table 1. Employment by major industry sector, 1996, 2006, and projected 2016. December 4 http://www.bls.gov/news.release/ecopro.t01.htm (accessed 11 February 2008).

———— (2008). "Consumer Price Index" inflation converter link at http:// www.bls.gov (accessed 6 February 2008).

USDA (U.S. Department of Agriculture) (2003). Strategic and Critical Materials Stockpiling Act: Public Law 96–41 (93 Stat. 319; 50 U.S.C. 98).

USDOD (U.S. Department of Defense) (2002). Secretary Rumsfeld live interview with Infinity CBS Radio, Nov. 14 http://www.defenselink.mil/ transcripts/transcript.aspx?transcriptid=3283 (accessed 9 February 2008).

———— (2008). Personnel and procurement statistics: Military casualty information. January 5. http://siadapp.dmdc.osd.mil/personnel/ CASUALTY/castop.htm (accessed 8 January 2008).

USEIA (U.S. Energy Information Administration) (2001). Table F1a. Energy consumption in the United States, selected years, 1635–1945. *Annual Energy Review 2001.* DOE/EIA-0384.

———— (2003a). Crude oil prices by selected type, 1970–2002. http://www.eia.doe.gov/emeu/aer/txt/ptb1107.html (accessed 20 May 2003; subsequently updated at http://www.eia.doe.gov/emeu/international/oilprice.html, accessed 12 February, 2008).

———— (2003b). Crude oil prices, selected crudes and world average (U.S. dollars per barrel). http://www.eia.doe.gov/emeu/international/petroleu.html#IntPrices (accessed 20 May 2003; subsequently updated at http://www.eia.doe.gov/emeu/international/oilprice.html, accessed 12 February 2008).

———— (2003c). World LNG imports by origin, 1993 (billion cubic feet). http://www.eia.doe.gov/emeu/international/LNGimp93.html (accessed 12 February 2008).

———— (2006a). Saudi Arabia Saudi light spot price FOB (dollars per barrel). http://tonto.eia.doe.gov/dnav/pet/hist/wepcsaltw.htm (accessed 12 February 2008).

———— (2006b). U.S. natural gas imports by country. http://tonto.eia.doe.gov/dnav/ng/ng_move_impc_s1_a.htm (accessed 12 February 2008).

———— (2006c). International petroleum (oil) reserves and resources: January 1, 1980–January 1, 2006 estimates. http://www.eia.doe.gov/emeu/international/oilreserves.html (accessed 28 May 2006 subsequently updated through 1 January 2008, accessed 12 February 2008).

———— (2007a). Bolivia: Natural gas. December http://www.eia.doe.gov/cabs/Bolivia/NaturalGas.html (accessed 12 February 2008).

———— (2007b). Price of U.S. natural gas pipeline imports from Canada. December 21. http://tonto.eia.doe.gov/dnav/ng/hist/n9102cn3a.htm (accessed 19 January 2008; not available 12 February 2008).

———— (2007c). Price of U.S. natural gas pipeline imports from Canada. December 21. http://tonto.eia.doe.gov/dnav/ng/hist/n9102cn3.htm (accessed 19 January 2008; not available 12 February 2008).

———— (2007d). Natural Gas, in *International Energy Outlook 2007*. May. http://www.eia.doe.gov/oiaf/ieo/nat_gas.htmlhttp://tonto.eia.doe.gov/dnav/ng/hist/n9102cn3.htm (accessed 19 January 2008; not available 12 February 2008).

———— (2007e). International Petroleum (Oil) Imports and Exports, World Petroleum Trade, All Countries, 2004 (Thousand Barrels per Day): Crude Oil Imports and Exports. August 6. http://www.eia.doe.gov/emeu/international/oiltrade.html (accessed 20 January 2008).

—— (2007f). Top World Oil Producers and Consumers. http://www.eia.doe.gov/emeu/international/oiltrade.html (accessed 20 January 2008).

—— (2007g). http://www.eia.doe.gov/emeu/international/oilproduction.html. http://www.eia.doe.gov/basics/conversion_basics.html (accessed 20 January 2008).

—— (2007h). International petroleum (oil) production. August 24. http://www.eia.doe.gov/emeu/international/oilproduction.html (accessed 23 January 2008).

—— (2008a). International petroleum (oil) consumption: All Countries, Total OECD, and World Total, Most Recent Annual Estimates, 1980–2006: All Countries, Total OECD, and World Total, Most Recent Annual Estimates, 1980–2006. August 24. http://www.eia.doe.gov/emeu/international/oilproduction.html (accessed 23 January 2008).

—— (2008b). International energy price information. January. http://www.eia.doe.gov/emeu/international/prices.html (accessed 25 January 2008).

—— (2008c). Gross Petroleum Imports into Selected OECD Countries and Total OECD by Origin (From OPEC and Persian Gulf Countries, Total Persian Gulf, Total OPEC, and Total World): Most recent year. January 11. http://www.eia.doe.gov/emeu/international/prices.html (accessed 11 February 2008).

USGS (U.S. Geological Survey) (2006). Platinum-group metals statistics and information. May 26, http://minerals.er.usgs.gov/minerals/pubs/commodity/platinum/ (accessed 12 February 2008).

—— (2007). Mineral Commodity Surveys. http://minerals.usgs.gov/minerals/pubs/mcs/ (accessed 9 January 2008).

USMA (U.S. Military Academy) (1986). *History Department Maps: World War I*, sourced to *Atlas for the Great War*. Wayne, NJ: SquareOne Publishing Group, Inc. http://www.dean.usma.edu/history/web03/atlases/great%20war/great%20war%20index.htm (accessed 12 February 2008).

Van Natta Jr, D and D Broder (1998). Testing of a president: The overview; prosecutors seek testing for DNA in Lewinsky dress. *New York Times*, July 31 late edition.

Vick, K (2003). Oil money supercharges Sudanese Civil War. *International Herald Tribune*. June 13.

Viviano, F (2005). China's great armada. *National Geographic*. July.

Wall, JM (1990). Nuclear threat looks bogus. *Christian Century*, December 19–26, 1190.

Wallach, J (2005). *Desert Queen*. New York: Anchor Books.

Waltham, C (2001). Birkeland and Norsk Hydro. http://www.physics.ubc. ca/~waltham/d2o98/paper/node3.html (accessed 12 February 2008).

Warinner, E (1963). The ordeal of the Kanrin Maru. *American Heritage Magazine* (August). http://www.americanheritage.com/articles/ magazine/ah/1963/5/1963_5_95.shtml (accessed 4 February 2008).

Watkins, K (2006). *Human Development Report 2006, Beyond Scarcity: Power, Poverty, and the Global Water Crisis*. New York: UN Development Programme.

Weinberg, G (1994). *A World at Arms: A Global History of World War II*. New York: Cambridge University Press.

Weisman, S (2003). A long, winding road to a diplomatic dead end. *New York Times*. March 17.

——— (2004). Oil producers see the world and buy it up. *New York Times*. November 27.

——— (2007). U.S. may support Israeli approach on leaving Gaza: Signal of shift in policy; Sharon plan for unilateral actions turns aside idea of joint concessions. *New York Times*. November 27.

Weisman, S and F Barringer (2003). Urgent diplomacy fails to gain U.S. 9 votes in the U.N. *New York Times*. March 10.

WGBH (2003). Blair's War. http://www.pbs.org/wgbh/pages/frontline/ shows/blair/etc/script.html (accessed 12 February 2008).

Wickens, J (2004). Developments in the tantalum market, http://www. tanb.org/minor_metals_2004.html (accessed 12 February 2008).

Wicker, T (1990). Gambling on the bomb. *New York Times*. December 5.

Williams, D (2004). Despite agreement, insurgents rule Fallujah. *Washington Post*. June 7.

Williams, J (2007). Oil price history and analysis. http://www.wtrg.com/ prices.htm (accessed 9 January 2007).

Wilson, S (2006). In the village of nowhere, a fate soon sealed: Wall to enclose Palestinians inside Jewish state. *New York Times*. May 30.

Wines, M (1991). U.S. is building up a picture of vast Iraqi atom program. *New York Times*. September 27.

——— (2004). U.N. reports a possible push into Congo by Rwandans. *New York Times*. December 3.

WISE (2008). Uranium mine ownership — Europe. January 18. http://www. wise-uranium.org/uoeur.html (accessed 19 January 2008).

Wong, E and S Stolberg (2007). A draft oil bill stirs opposition from Iraqi blocs: Sunnis and Kurds balk; benchmark in danger — U.S. vote to override spending veto fails. *New York Times*. May 2.

World Diamond Council (2003). Kimberley Process. http://www.diamonds.net/selectednews.asp?list=4 (accessed May 19, 2003; not available 12 February 2008).

Worth, R and N Bakri (2008). Bomb in Syria kills militant sought as terrorist. February 14.

Yager, T (2006). Mineral industries of Djibouti, Eritrea, Ethiopia, and Somalia. *U.S. Geological Survey Minerals Yearbook — 2003*. http://minerals.usgs.gov/minerals/pubs/country/2003/djeretsomyb03.pdf (accessed 10 February 2008).

Yanity, B (2006). Alaska's other black gold. August 4. http://www.insurgent49.com/yanity_black_gold.html (accessed 4 February 2008).

Yergin, D (1991). *The Prize: The Epic Quest for Oil, Money and Power*. New York: Simon and Schuster.

Youssef, N (2006). Post-World War I diplomat to Iraq described obstacles similar to today's. Knigt Ridder. Feburary 8. http://www.realcities.com/mld/krwashington/news/columnists/nancy_youssef/13823870.htm (accessed 17 March 2006; not available 12 February 2008).

Zahoor, A (ed.) (1997). Muslims and the oil industries: Seventh to nineteenth century. http://cyberistan.org/islamic/islmoil1.html (accessed 12 February 2008).

Index

Aden, 52, 156
Adwa (Adua), battle of, 149–140
Africa, West. *See* West Africa
Air Force, British Royal, 130, 142
Air Force, US, 4–5
Afghanistan
    natural gas pipeline route,
        263–264, 267
    Soviet troops, 162
    US overthrow of Taliban, 195
Agadir incident, 129
agriculture, 16–17, 146, 291
Aïr Massif, 234
Alamein. *See* El Alaamein
al Qaeda, 36, 192, 215, 358–359; 24,
    25, 64, 136, 149, 254, 255, 261
al-Sadr, Muqtada, 207–208
Alaska, 78, 157, 272
Algeria
    France and, 242, 268, 280
    natural gas, 260, 271
    Polisario and, 94
    political stability, 280, 319, 321,
        324–325
Allende, Salvadore, 95
Alsace, 29, 62
Amoco, 124–126, 153–154
Andenauer, Konrad, 84
Anglo-Iranian Oil Company. *See* BP
Anglo-Persian Oil Company. *See* BP
Angola

Cabinda secessionist movement,
    315
Civil War, 99
diamonds, 99
oil production, 317
political stability, 319, 321,
    323, 325
War of Independence, 99
Antogasta province, 90–91
Arafat, Yassar, 188, 358
Arica city, 90–91
Aramco, 125–126, 153–154
Arab-Israeli War (1948), 154, 273
Arco, 85. *See also* Sun Oil Company
Argentina, 90, 265
Armitage, Richard, 193
Aswan Dam, 155
Atacama desert, 90
Atlantic Oil Company. *See* Sun Oil
    Company
Aurangzeb Bahadur Almagir I, 30
Australia
    concerns over nulcear testing,
        228, 238, 246
    vehicle fuel efficiency standards,
        351
    Labor Party, 239
    mining company RTZ-CRA,
        95
    natural gas, 263, 275
    occupation of Iraq, 203

tantalum production, 104–105
uranium mining, 238–239, 247
Austria
before 20th century, 30, 33,
41, 60, 68
World War I, 11–12, 45, 68–69,
132
World War II and later, 86,
132, 142
Azerbaijan, 146, 315, 319, 321,
323–324
"axis of evil," 195

Ba'th party members. *See under* Iraq
Baker, James, 94, 172, 362
Balkan Wars (1912 and 1913), 69
Barsky, Robert, 7–8
Baku, 131, 144–146, 323
Baku–Tblisis-Ceyhan pipeline, 324
Bathurst (former slave), 51
Battle of Britain, 143
Bergius process, 136
Belgium
diamond certification system,
101–102
European integration, 85–86
natural gas, 261
World War I, 65, 70–71, 73–74,
80
Bell, Gertrude, 160
Berry, Wendell, 221
Bessarabia, 132
Bessemer, Henry 62–63
Bechtel Corporation, 204
Biafra secession attempt, 156
bin Laden, Osama, 194, 222, 359
biofuels, 306–307, 329, 336,
338–340, 345–348
Bismark, Otton von, 38, 42, 60–62,
68, 79
Blair, Anthony, 195–196
Blitzkrieg, 142–144

Blix, Hans, 196
Bodine, Barbara, 205
Boer War,16
Bolivia, 90–91, 265–266, 280–281
Bosnia and Herzegovina, 68–69
Bougainville 95
Brazil
abolition of slavery, 51
diamonds, 102–104
ethanol, 306–307, 331
hydroelectricity, 287
natural gas, 265, 281,
nuclear technology, 169, 380
tantalum, 104
Bremer, L. Paul III, 206, 210
British Petroleum. *See* BP
BP, 124–126, 129, 135, 154, 324
Büchsel, Wilhelm, 78
Burmah-Castrol, 124
Bush, George H. W. (father), 176,
181
Bush, George W. (son), 173, 195,
215
Bush, Jeb, 193
Butler, Richard, 184
Byzantine empire, 15

Cabinda, 316
CAFE standards, 330–331, 340, 349
California, 259
calutron, 174–175, 180
Camp David, 355, 358
Canada
acquisition from Britain, 30
hydroelectricy, 285
nuclear reactors, 232, 237
natural gas, 256, 260, 270,
273–274
oil, 316, 322, 333–334
tantalum mine, 104
uranium, 232, 237–238,
246–247

vehicle fuel efficiency standards, 351
Cardiff, 54, 56
Carter Doctrine, 162, 168
Carter, James Earl, 162
casualties in World War I, 132–133
Cave, Damien, 216
cellulosic fuel, 312, 337–340
Central Powers, 70–73, 75, 80, 131–132
Chad, 242–243, 315, 318–319, 321–324
Chalabi, Salem, 205
Charles (Romanian King Carol I), 132
Chechnya, 146, 267, 324
chemical weapons, 164, 167, 185–186, 196–200
Cheney, Richard, 172, 191–193
ChevronTexaco, 124–126
Chile, 90–92, 97, 280
China
    ancient, 20
    Ching dynasty, 30, 52, 77
    cooperation with IEA, 333
    disease and war limiting population, 40
    Great Leap, 39
    nuclear energy, 264
    petroleum reserve stocks, 342–343
    price controls, 350
    standards for fuel efficiency, 349
    tantalum, 104
    wars with Japan, 81
Chinese National Offshore Oil Company (CNOOC), 126–127
Chinese National Petroluem Company, 126
Chirac, M. Jacqes, 58
chromium, 96, 98
Church of the Nativity, 59

Churchill, Winston, 129, 155
Clarke, Richard, 195
Clermont steamship, 18, 50
Clinton, William, 184, 188
coal. *See also* European Coal and Steel Union
    Alaskan, 78
    French, 62, 72
    Manchuria, 80, 146
    Philippine, 78
    Russian, 72
    Scottish serf miners, 21
    steamships, 49–54, 77–79
    synthetic fuels, 136, 143–144
    Welsh, 54–57
    World War I, 71–73, 80–81
Coalition Provisional Authority. *See under* Iraq
Cogema, 234
Cohn, Steve, 278
coltan, 102–107
Comprehensive Test Ban Treaty. *See* CTBT
COMUF, 243
Concert of Europe, 11, 33, 38, 42
Congress of Berlin, 68, 132
Congo, Democratic Republic of the
    coltan, 105–106
    diamonds and conflict, 107
    death rate, 245–246
Congress of Berlin. *See* Berlin Congress (1878)
Conoco. *See* ConocoPhillips
ConocoPhillips, 124–126
Continental. *See* ConocoPhillips
cooperate average fuel efficiency. *See* CAFE
copper, 22, 95, 98–99, 107
Corruption Perception Index, 321–322
Côte d'Ivoire, 102–103, 114, 245
Crimea, 30

Crimean War, 33, 38, 59–60
Crocker, Ryan, 214–215
Crowe, Willliam, 173
crusaders, 15
CTBT, 226, 228, 233, 241, 245
Cuban missile crisis, 150

Dawood, Qasim, 216
de Gaulle, Charles, 85, 227, 235–236, 238, 243
Deffeyes, Kenneth, 299–300
Democracy Index, 321–322
depression, 9, 21, 66, 70, 84, 255, 285, 374
Dewey, George (Commodore) 78
Diamond, Larry, 207
diamonds, 10–11, 95, 98–104, 106–107, 114
dicke Bertha, Krupp cannon, 73–74
Dobruja, 132
Dole, Robert, 171–172
Donestk region, 71–72
Dutch. *See* Netherlands

East India Company, 52–53
Eckel, Edwin, 17–18, 21, 61–67, 69–71
Eighty Years' War, 23
Eisenhower, Dwight 151, 154–155, 157, 236
Ekeus, Rolf, 176
El Alamein, 145–146
electric vehicles, 344
Elf. *See* TotalElfFina
energy consumption extrapolations, 374–378
energy units conversions, 253
Energy Policy and Conservation Act, 5
ENI (Ente Nazionale Idocarburi), 124–125
Environmental Conflict, 293

epistemic viewpoint, 43
Equatorial Guinea, 322
Eshkol, Levi, 356
ethanol, 306–307, 311–312, 331, 338–340
Ethiopia, 139–141, 289, 292
Euphrates River, 284, 289–290
European Coal and Steel Community, 83–85, 87
European Economic Community, 85
European Community, 86–87
European Free Trade Association, 85
European Union, 86–87
exceptionalism, 43–44
Exxon, 124–126

Fao Peninsula, 164–165
Farakka Barrage, 288, 292–293
Fallon, William, 213
Fallujah. *See under* Iraq
Federal Power Commission, 256–257
Ferdinand, Franz, 68
Fina. *See* TotalElfFina
financial panic (1873), 67
Fischer-Tropsch process, 136
force de frappe, 228, 236
foreclosures of mortgages, 8
France. *See also* Franco-Prussian War; Gabon; Niger; World War I; World War II
　　abolition of slade trade, 51
　　Algeria annexation, 241
　　alliance with Russia and UK (1894), 33
　　Cameroon intervention, 242
　　Chad intervention, 242
　　Comprehensive Test Ban Treaty, 234, 241
　　Congo intervention, 242
　　Crimean War, 59

defeat at Trafalgar, 52
demographic revolution, 42
Mauritania intervention, 242
mission civilatrice, 43, 241
neocolonialism, 241–248
nuclear electric power,
    229–232, 247
nuclear weapons, 236
post-WWII security, 226–229,
    235–236
Rwanda Hutu, support for,
    245
territories gained in Peace of
    Westphalia, 29
uranium supplies, 232–235,
    237–239
War of the Spanish Succession,
    30
Franco-Prussian War
mineral resources, 11
precipitants of, 38, 45, 59–61
results, 63, 223
Franks, Tommy, 206
Franz-Josef, Emperor, 45, 60
Fredrick "the Great", 30
French and Indian War. *See* Seven
    Years War
Frieman, Thomas, 171–172, 337
Friedman, Milton, 9
Fuel Use Act of 1979, 258
Fulani states, 32, 242
Fulton, Robert, 18, 50

Gabon, 228, 234, 242–243
Galicia,121–122
Garner, Jay, 205–206
gasoline. *See under* oil
Gaza, 355, 359, 361–363
Gazprom, 281
GDP. *See* gross domestic product
generational lag, 4, 32, 44, 185, 340,
    366

Genscher, Hans, 261
Geneva Convention, 72, 204
Germany. *See also* Franco-
    Prussian War
    coal, 56
    fertility rates, 42
    natural gas from USSR, 261–262
    nuclear reactors, 277
    Pacific naval stragey before
        WWI, 78–80
    World War I, 33, 70–75, 80–81,
        130–133
    World War II, 12, 137, 141–146
    WWII aftermath, 84–85, 227,
        236, 249
Ghana, 101–103
Gini index, 321–322
Giscard d'Estaining, Valéry, 244
gold
    conflict, 15–16, 23, 31, 92, 167,
        196
    money, 21–22, 98
Göring, Heramnn, 137
Great Anatolia Project, 289–290,
    292
Greece, 19–20, 25, 86
Greenspan, Alan, 259, 272
Groningen energy resources, 25,
    261
guano, 90
Gulbenkian, Calouste, 134
Gulf Oil Company 154.
    See also Chevron-Texaco
Gulf War I, 167–175

Haber process, 91
Hamani, Diori, 243–243
Hamas, 357
Hammurabi, 16, 54
Hausa states, 31, 244
heavy water nuclear reactors, 237
Hebron, 361, 363

Herbesthal tunnel, 74–75
Hezbollah, 357–358
Hitler, Adolf, 146–147
Holland. *See* Netherlands
Homer-Dixon, Thomas, 289–290,
    292–293, 305–306
Hubbert, M. King, 377
Huckabee, Michael, 36–37, 44
Hussein, Qusay, 201
Hussein, Saddam
    hunt for, 200–201
    Khomeini and, 161, 163, 165
    portrayal of, 37, 191, 204–205
    motivation for actions, 167–168,
        185, 187
    rise to power, 160
hybrid vehicles, 108–110, 336–337,
    351
hydroelectric power and irrigation
    before WWII, 285–285
    Nile Basin, 289
    South American, 286–287
    South Asian dams, 287–288
    Turkey, 289–290
hydrogen bomb, 148–149

IAEA, 168–169, 171, 173, 175, 180,
    310–311
IEA, 327, 333–335, 340, 351
India,
    natural gas, 251, 263–264,
        277–278
    nuclear, 309–310
    oil, 154, 330, 332, 333–334,
        348, 377
    water, 283, 287–288, 292–293
instabiliity index, 323–325
institutionalist view, 43
International Atomic Energy Agency.
    See IAEA
International Energy Agency. *See* IEA
Intifada, 358–359

Iran
    Airbus destrucition, 165
    instability indicators, 319, 321,
        324
    Mossadegh, 125, 154–155,
        161
    natural gas, 263–264, 267,
        274
    nuclear program, 309–310,
        380
    oil, 149, 153, 158, 183, 316,
        343
    relations with US, 162, 182,
        192, 355, 358
    Soviet incursion, 148–149, 154
Iran-Iraq War, 8, 163–165, 170, 220,
    317
Iraq
    Abu Ghraib prison, 209
    Ba'th party members, 204, 207
    bioweapons research, 178
    bioweapons purported 183–187,
        196–198
    British role before World War II,
        160
    Coalitions Provisional Authority,
        206–208
    Dir al-Qayyara oil pits, 12
    Fallujah, 201, 207
    Governing Council, 206
    inspections, 180
    Iraq Petroleum Company, 154
    National Assembly, 208
    no-fly zones, 184
    Northern and Southern Watch,
        175, 182
    occupation of, 200–216
    Republican Guard, 168
    sanctions, 8, 173, 181, 183–186,
        194, 204
    Shiite revolt (1991), 192
    Spanish withdrawal, 206

Sunnis, 160, 181–182, 203, 208, 212–215
unconventional weapons, 168–175, 185–187
UN Security Council Resolution 171, 176
US troop levels, 212
violence levels curing occupation, 211, 214
war over Kuwait, 167–170
Italy, 139–141
Irish referendum, 87
iron, 63–67, 70–72, 81
Israel, 162. *See also* Arab-Israeli War; Suez Canal; Six-Day War; Yom Kippur War
aid from United States, 364–365
decision to occupy West Bank, 356
effect on US politics, 366
settlements, 359–363, 366
Israel Corporation Ltd., 344
Itaipu dam, 287
Italo-Turkish War (1911–1912), 69
Ivory Coast. *See* Côte d'Ivoire

Japan
conflicts with China, 81
economic growth, 368, 375
expansionism, 5
famine, 40
fuel efficiency standards, 351
natural gas, 249, 265, 267, 270–271, 274
nuclear energy, 231–232, 277, 378, 380
oil, 149, 327–328, 332
Pearl Harbor attack, 3, 139, 146–148
JASON, 4
Jerusalem, 19, 59, 156, 188, 344, 356, 360–363

jet fuel, 5
Johnson, E. Gale, 16
Joliot-Curie, Frédéric, 237
Jordan River valley, 360
Jutland, battle of, 131

Kay, David, 186–187
Kazakhstan, 319, 321, 323–324
Kedumim, 363
Kennedy, John Fitzgerald, 368
Khadafi, Muammar, 157
Khalizad, Zalmay, 193
Khobar Towers, 325, 358
Khuzistan, Iranian, 164
Khomeini, Ruhollah, 161, 163, 165
Killian, Lutz, 7–8
Kimberley Process, 99 101–104
Kissinger, Henry, 157, 162
Klare, Michael, 293–294
Korea,
North, 195, 264, 309
peninsula, 81, 150, 249, 265, 274
South, 270–271, 333, 375
Krasnodar, 145–146
Krichene, Noureddine, 342
Krupp, Bertha, 73
Kurds
in Iraq, 191–192, 292
Iranian support for in Iraq, 163
Turkish, 87, 182, 290–291
Kuwait
Iraqi occupation, 167–170
Iranian attacks on, 164
oil production of, 8
sale of oil by Gulf Oil Company, 154
tanker re-flagging, 164

Lagash, 284
League of Nations, 141
Lebanon, 134, 154, 223, 357

Lebensraum, 77, 114, 139, 141, 144, 304
Lend-Lease, 143
Leopold of Hohenzollern-Sigmaringen, 61
Lepanto, battle of, 19
Legro, Jeffrey, 42–43
Libby, I. Lewis, 193
liberal view of international relations, 43
Liberia, 51, 101, 103, 114, 202
Libya, 69, 140, 156–158, 260, 325
Lieberman, Joseph, 213
Liège, 73–74
Lisbon Treaty, 87
Livingston, Robert, 50
Lorraine, 11, 28, 59, 62–63, 70–71, 130, 228
Louis XIV, 235
Louis XV, 235
Lucarno treaties, 141
Ludendorff, Eric, 73
Lukoil, 124
Luxembourg, 70–71, 85–86

Madrid, attacks on civilians of, 206
Mahakali Treaty, 288
Manchuria, 77, 81, 146–147
Manila, 77–78
Marshall Plan, 84
Matthews, Jessica, 176
Mauritania, 93, 242–243, 293–294
Mba, Leon, 242
McCain, John, 213
Mearsheimer, John, 366
Menelek II (King of Ethiopia) 139
Mexico
    conquest of, 19, 23
    natural gas, 266, 270–271
    oil, 135, 155, 323–324, 333–334
Meyers, Richard, 202

Middle East conflict recurrence, 372–374
mineral stockpiles, 95–100
mission civilatrice, 43
Mobil, 124–126
Mobutu, Joseph, 245
Moldova, 60
Mongol conquests, 18
monopoly, 52, 120, 123, 254–255, 281
Montenegro, 68–69
Moravscik, Andrew, 42–43
Morgenthau plan, 83–84, 221, 224
Morocco
    Agadir, 129
    gold trade, 15, 31
    Western Sahara, 92–94
Mossadegh, Mohammed, 154–155
Mosul, 121, 134
Mughal empire, 30
Myers, Richard, 202

Nagornao–Karabakh, 323–324
Namibia, 102–103, 238–239
Napoleon Bonaparte
    naval power, 50–51
    war, 32–33, 35
Napoleon, Louis, 38, 45, 61
Napoleonic Wars, 26, 33, 41, 49, 51
Nasser, Gamal Abdel, 155–156
NATO, 334
natural gas
    Canadian, 273
    competition with nuclear energy, 276–279
    consumption, 275–276
    deposits, 250–252, 265
    deregulation, European, 262
    deregulation, US, 258–269
    liquefied, and conflict, 279–282, 311
    liquefied, trade, 269–272

pipelines, 260–261, 263–267
prices, 273–277
production costs, 301–302
regulation, US, 254–257
Natural Gas Act, 256
Neely, Chrisopher, 342
Nepal, 287
Netherlands
European integration, 85–86
industrial revolution, 24–27,
30, 66
natural gas, 260–262
oil embargo, 342
slave trade suppression, 51
neutron bomb, 261
Newcommen, Thomas, 65
Newsom, David, 162
New Spain (Mexico), 22
Niger, 228, 234, 242–244
Niger delta, 31–32
Nigeria, 88, 105, 156, 275, 315–316
Nile Basin Initiative, 289
Nisson Motor Company, 344
nitrates, 90–92
Nixon, Richard, 5, 157
North German Federation, 60
North Sea, 158, 261
Norway, 316–317, 320–322, 333
nuclear weapons, 150, 378–380
Nuclear Nonproliferation Treaty,
168, 310

OECD, 327, 333–335, 342
Ofer, Idan, 345
Office of Reconstruction and
Humanitarian Assistance, 205
oil
consumption by U.S. military,
4
diesel prices and taxes, 345–346
gasoline prices and taxes,
345–346

gasoline rationing, 3, 5
embargo, 5, 157
exporters' economic indicators,
319–322
exporters' political indicators,
320–325
exporters' revenues, 320–321
German production and imports,
137
import tariffs, 332–333
imports, 328, 330
Iran's, 163
Iraqi, 121, 134, 202–203
Japans's supply, 136
legislation in Iraq, 203
naval use of, 57, 80
North Sea, 158
pits and shafts, 121
price controls, 5–6
prices 5, 159
production costs, 301–302
production levels, 122, 136,
143, 316, 318
reserves vs. resources, 299–301
Romanian, 132, 142
Saudi, 135
stocks, 340–344, 351
West Qurana concession in
Iraq, 124
World War I, 130–133
Oman, 319, 321–322
OPEC, 88, 119, 156–157, 164,
168, 179, 257, 300, 326, 329,
332–333, 335, 352
Opium War, Second, 77
Organization for Economic
Cooperation and Development.
See OECD
Osirak reactor, 169, 171
Ottoman Empire, 59, 60, 69, 129,
134, 160
Owen, Edward, 53–54

Pacific, War of. *See* War of the Pacific
Pahlevi, Mohammed Reza, 155, 158
Pakistan
    natural gas, 263–264
    nuclear, 169, 174, 288
    water, 287–288, 293
Palestine
    peace process, 188, 222, 361
    partition, 304
    settlements, 362–365
    World War I, 133–134
Palestinian Liberation Organization,
    188, 358
palladium, 109
palm oil, 346–247
Papua New Guinea, 90
Paris taxi fleet, 129
Passchendale, 70–71
Paul, Ronald, 36–37
Peace to End All Peace, The, 223
Pearl Harbor, 3, 139, 146–148
peat, 25–26
Pennsylvania oil boom, 121, 123
Peru, 19, 22, 90–92
Petreus, David, 213–215
PetroChina, 126
petrodollars, 7
petroleum. *See* oil
Philippines, 78
phosphates, 93–95
Pig War, 69
platinum, 108–110
Ploiesti oil fields, 132, 142
plutonium, 180, 232, 238, 246–247,
    285, 380
Polisario, 93–94
Pompidou, George, 244
Poole, William, 7
population growth
    conflict 12, 32–33, 114, 305,
        317, 319–321

food and water, 40–41,
    290–291, 307, 312
Port Said, 56
Powell, Colin, 197–200
prestige, imperial, 12, 45
price controls, 5, 7–8, 257–258, 350
Prius, 337
Process Theory, 147–148
Project for the New American
    Century, 193
property rights index, 322
Prussia, 60
psychology, of war leaders, 35

Qatar, 322–323
Qaeda, al. *See* al Qaeda

Rabin, Yitzhak, 188, 356
Raffles, Thomas Stanford, 53
railroads, 66, 90, 123
Reagan, Ronald, 5, 43; 2, 30, 116,
    183
realist school, 43
recession, 7–8, 164, 172
Red Line Agreement, 135, 154
Red Sea, 3
Renault, 344
renewable energy and security,
    297–304
Renouvier, Charles Benard, 241
Republican Guard, 168, 185
Resource Wars, 293
revolution in military affairs, 202
Rhineland, 142
Rhodes, Richard, 173–175; 47, 121,
    122, 123, 288
Ribbentrob, Joachim von, 142
Ritter, Scott, 184
Rockefeller, David, 162
Rockefeller, John D., 123–124
Rogner, Hans-Holger, 300–301

Romania
Berlin Congress, 68
Crimean War, 60
European Union, 86
World War I, 132–133
World War II, 142–144
Rommel, Erwin, 145
Romney, Willard Mitt, 37
Roosevelt, Theodore, 78
Roosevelt, Franklin Delano, 139–140
Royal Dutch. *See* Shell
Ruhr Valley, 56, 73, 84, 145, 227
Rumsfeld, Donald, 193–195, 201, 204–205, 212
Russia. *See also* Soviet Union
Crimean War, 33, 38, 59–60
czarist, 30, 41, 69–70, 77, 79, 81, 132
Iraq's debt, 184, 194
natural gas, 249–250, 260–262, 264–266, 274, 280–281
nuclear reactors and uranium, 231–232, 238
oil, 121, 124–125, 131, 136, 315–316, 323–324, 333, 335
World War I, 72–73, 133–134
Russo-Turkish War (1877–1878), 68
Rwanda, 105–106, 245–246

Sadr, Muqtada al-. *See* al-Sadr, Muqtada
Safire, Wiliam, 173–174
Saidi, Seyyid bin Sultan Ali Bu, 52
Saudi Arabia, 319–321, 323, 325, 365
Sault St. Marie, 67
Savak, 161
Savery, Thomas, 65
Scotland, 21
Schlieffan plan, 80

Schmidt, Helmut, 261
Schröder, Gerehard, 86
Schuman, Robert, 85
Scowcroft, Brent, 172
Segev, Tom, 356
Senegal, 293–294
Serbia, 68–69
Servile Wars, 20
Seven Sisters, 125
Seven Weeks War (of 1866), 33, 60
Seven Years War, 30
Shah Mohammed Reza Pahlevi, 108
Sharon, Ariel, 188, 359, 361
Shatt-al-Arab, 163
Shell, 124–126, 129
Shia, 160, 164, 207, 212, 215, 358
Shiva, Vandana, 293–294
Siachen glacier, 305
Sibnet, 124
Sierra Leonean Civil War, 99
Silesia, 30, 73
Siljeholm, Jorn, 197
silver, 15, 22–23, 92, 107
Singapore, 53, 114
Sino-Japanese War (1894–1895), 81
Sinopec, 126
Six-Day War, 156–157
slavery
abolition 12, 15–16, 31, 49–54, 381
Africa, 30–31, 33
ancient, 16, 19–21, 33, 113
galeases, 20
Smith, Rodney, 327
Smoot-Hawley tariff, 70
Social Democrats, German before WWI, 80
Socony (Socony-Vacuum). *See* Mobil
Sohio, 124–126
Songhay empire, 31, 242

South Africa, 32, 99–100, 109–110,
   169, 238
Soviet Union
   cold war, 97, 99, 149–150, 227,
      238, 368
   in Iran, 148–149, 154
   World War II, 141, 144–146,
      148
Spain, 22–24, 206
Spanish Saharan War, 93–94
Spanish-American War, 78
Spanish Succession, War of, 30
stagflation, 7, 164
Stalingrad, battle of, 142, 145–146
Standard Oil, 123–124
Standard Oil of California (Socal),
   153. *See also* ChevronTexaco
Standard Oil of Indiana. *See* Amocoa
Standard Oil of New Jersey, 154.
   See also Exxon
Standard Oil of New York.
   See Mobil
Standard Oil of Ohio. *See* Sohio
steel. *See* iron.
steam engine, 18, 65
steamships. *See under* coal
Stephenson, George, 66
Stephenson, Robert, 66
Stimson, Henry, 84
Strategic and Critical Materials
   Stockpiling Act, 95–97, 107
submarines, 50, 131, 256
Sudan, 202, 289, 315–316, 319, 321,
   323–324
Sudetenland, 142
Suez Canal, 3, 155–156
Sun Oil Company (Sunoco), 125
Sweden, 8, 15, 19, 20, 28, 29, 31, 58
   fertility transition, 40–42
   wars, 29–30, 41
Sykes-Picot agreement, 134

Syria, 134, 204
synthetic fuels. *See under* coal

Taiwan, 81
Talleyrand-Périgot, Maurice de, 50
tantalum, 98. *See also* Coltan
Tarbell, Ida, 123–124
tariffs, 29, 69–70, 257, 264, 332–338
Tata Motors, 348
Tenet, George, 196–197
Tennessee Valley Authority, 285
Texaco, 153. *See also* ChevronTexaco
Texas, 135, 257, 259,
Thirty Years War, 29, 45
Thomas-Gilchrist process, 62, 67
Three Mile Island nuclear plant,
   158–159
Tigris River, 283–284
timber, virgin, 304
TotalFinaElf, 124
Trafalgar, battle of, 52
trans-Pacific cable, 77–78
Transparency International, 331–332
Transylvania, 132
Treaty of Paris, 85
Treaty of Ucciali, 139
Turkey, 68, 87, 182, 191, 201,
   289–292, 323
Turkish Petroleum Company, 134
Turkmenistan, 263–264
Turner, Charles, 51
Tuwaitha nuclear facility, 180

Umma, 284
Ukraine, 72, 280–281
United Arab Emirates, 319, 321–322
UN Security Council, 95, 171, 176,
   196–197
United States
   aid to Israel, 364–367
   "city on a hill," 43

cold war, 148–150
energy policy, 329–332, 334–340
ethanol, 306–307, 331, 339–340
foreign petrodollar investments in, 7
future energy use, 375–379
gasoline rationing, 3, 158
industrial development, 66–67
Iran, 161–162, 165
Iraq, 167–168, 182–187, 191–216
Lebanon intervention, 223
materials stocks, 95–99, 340
Mideast policy, 8, 52, 154–159, 222
monetary policy, 7, 21–23
Morgenthau plan, 83–84
natural gas, 250, 252–260, 269–275
nuclear energy, 229–231, 233, 238, 278
oil imports, 5, 153, 327–329
oil production, 121–124, 136, 141
Pacific Ocean naval power, 77–709
pax Americana, 44
petroleum reserve stocks, 340–344
price controls and fuel taxes, 7, 346
Western Sahara, 94
World War I, 65, 72–73, 75, 130
World War II, 143–146
Unocal, 264
uranium
African, 200, 234, 242–244
Brazil, 380
enriched, 169–171, 173–175, 180, 195, 198
global market and India, 309–312, 371
France, 223, 226–229, 232–234, 237–239
Iran, 310, 325
Tennessee Valley Authority, 285
USSR. *See* Soviet Union

Venezuela, 88, 135, 168, 251, 265, 280, 315–316, 319, 325, 342
Verdun, 70–71
Versailles treaty, 141
Viera de Mello, Sergio, 206

Wallachia, 60, 132
Walt, Stephen, 366;104, 260, 262, 285
War of Austrian Succession, 30, 235
War of the Pacific, 90–92, 285
War of the Spanish Succession, 30
water
    conflict, 10, 284, 288–294, 381
    power, 26, 283–287, 303
    transport by, 18, 25, 50
Watergate, 158
Watt, James, 18, 65
welding, 235
Welsh coal. *See under* coal
West Africa
    early history, 15–16, 30–32, 242
    modern, 103–104, 241
West Bank, 156, 292, 355–356, 359–366
Western Front in WWI, 63, 70–71, 131
Western Sahara, 92–94

454 *Energy and International War*

Westphalia, Peace of, 29, 32, 45
Wicker, Thomas, 173–174
William I (German Kaiser Wilehm I), 61
Wilhelm II (German Kaiser), 74, 79
Wolf, Aaron, 284
Wolfowitz, Paul, 44, 192–193
World War I
    precursors, 68–69
World Trade Organization, 352

Yamamoto Isoroku, 147–148
Yom Kippur War
    oil embago and US gasoline rationing, 3, 5
    US support of Israel, 8, 157–158
Ypres, 70
Yukos, 124
Yushcehko, Vikton, 281

Zaire. *See* Congo, Democratic Republic of the Zunes, Stephen, 366